QUALITATIVE METHODS IN FAMILY RESEARCH

To our families

QUALITATIVE METHODS IN FAMILY RESEARCH

Jane F. Gilgun
Kerry Daly
Gerald Handel
editors

SAGE PUBLICATIONS
International Educational and Professional Publisher
Newbury Park   London   New Delhi

For information address:

SAGE Publications, Inc.
2455 Teller Road
Newbury Park, California 91320

SAGE Publications Ltd.
6 Bonhill Street
London EC2A 4PU
United Kingdom

SAGE Publications India Pvt. Ltd.
M-32 Market
Greater Kailash I
New Delhi 110 048 India

Printed in the United States of America

Library of Congress Cataloging-in-Publication Data

Qualitative methods in family research / Jane F. Gilgun, Kerry Daly, Gerald Handel, editors.
  p. cm.
 Includes bibliographical references and index.
 ISBN 0-8039-4462-4. — ISBN 0-8039-4463- 2(pbk.)
  1. Family—Research. 2. Family—Research—Methodology.
 I. Gilgun, Jane Frances. II. Daly, Kerry. III. Handel, Gerald.
 HQ503.Q36 1992
306.85'072—dc20   92-14934
                             CIP

92 93 94 95 10 9 8 7 6 5 4 3 2 1

Sage Production Editor: Judith L. Hunter

Contents

Preface

Interest in qualitative methods in family research is on the rise. Membership in the Qualitative Family Research Network of the National Council on Family Relations numbers more than 400. Qualitative methods interest groups are thriving in many major academic disciplines, such as psychology, sociology, gerontology, education, social work, family therapy, family studies, and nursing. Interdisciplinary groups of academics interested in qualitative methods have proliferated on the local, national, and international levels. Journal editors and editorial boards are beginning to ask for manuscripts based on qualitative methods. Graduate students in all parts of the country are pressuring faculty not only to teach courses on qualitative methods but also to allow them to conduct their own qualitative studies.

The interest is much higher than the ability to teach and to do qualitative research, however. Most academic researchers are trained almost exclusively in quantitative and positivistic methods. They want training in how to do qualitative research. The formation of qualitative methods interest groups represents attempts of academic researchers to learn more about qualitative methods. In response to this search for information on qualitative methods, many texts have been written and published. Sage Publications has taken leadership in providing the academic community with texts on qualitative research, but to date no text focuses exclusively on qualitative methods in family research.

This book is a response to the need for training in qualitative family research. The family is a specialized area of study. Family phenomena are complex, subjective, and private. The study of families requires methods and perspectives tailored to this complexity and subjectivity. Until the present, however, the survey has been the primary research method in family studies. Many family researchers recognize the inadequacy of one research method to be responsive to the complexity of family phenomena. They want to learn other methods of conducting family research.

AUDIENCES FOR WHOM THIS TEXT WAS WRITTEN

The intended audiences are researchers already doing qualitative research, researchers trained in quantitative and positivistic traditions who want to learn more about qualitative approaches, professors who teach methods courses and want to include content on qualitative family research, students who are exploring ways of answering their own research questions, and members of editorial boards of journals that primarily have published quantitative research but are open to other approaches.

This book is intended to reflect the diversity of qualitative approaches to the study of families as well as the diversity of families' experiences. The authors of the individual chapters represent several different disciplines: family studies, sociology, nursing, and social work. They write for an audience equally varied.

In edited volumes, unity is an issue. We worked closely with the authors to ensure comparability across chapters. We instructed the authors to include which family members were interviewed or observed, which type of qualitative research they conducted (e.g., grounded theory, ethnography, life history, analytic induction, or other), and how these related to their theoretical and methodological perspectives (e.g.,symbolic interactionism, feminism, life course, naturalistic inquiry, phenomenology, or other). We asked the authors the following questions, which are specific to research on families:

- How did the qualitative method you used facilitate dealing with difficult or sensitive areas of family studies?
- What issues of access to the families did your experience raise?
- Did you encounter ethical dilemmas in your research? What are the special issues related to your research on families?
- What effects did the research experience have on you? What roles did you take on in the lives of family members? Did involvement with family members weaken or strengthen your findings?
- How intrusive was your method?
- Why did you choose the method you did? What did you gain by using this method? What did you lose? What were the trade-offs?
- What guided your decisions about who in the family to include in your research? Did you interview couples? Together? Separately? One member of a family only? Why? Why not the whole family?
- How did time, access, and money shape your methodological choices?

- How do you think the method you used can be used in other types of research on families? In other words, can other researchers apply your methods to other areas of family research?

Not every author discussed all of these questions, but each of these questions is discussed within this book. As a whole, then, the volume addresses some of the most significant contemporary questions about the conduct of qualitative family research.

BRINGING RESEARCH PROCESSES TO LIFE

Because this book is intended to help researchers learn how to do several different types of qualitative family research—as well as to sharpen the skills of those familiar with these methods—the individual authors discuss method in more detail than is usual. To help readers understand what types of findings the methods can produce, each author includes substantive results from each study. This approach accomplishes three important tasks: (a) readers are able to make an informed judgment about whether qualitative methods will aid them in pursuing their own research questions, (b) readers will learn through example as well as through discussion of method how to do qualitative research, and (c) readers will be exposed to recent innovations in the use of qualitative methods. We adopted this approach to bring the research process to life. This book is not an "armchair" approach to research on families, but intended to invite readers into the research experience.

ORIGINS AND AFFILIATIONS OF THIS TEXT

This book began at the 1989 Preconference Workshop on Theory Construction and Research Methodology held in New Orleans as part of the annual meeting of the National Council on Family Relations. At the workshop, we asked and grappled with the question: "What is qualitative family research?" We thought developing a book might help answer the question. The next day, we brought the idea for a book to the annual meeting of the Qualitative Family Research Network, a focus group of the Research and Theory Section, National Council on Family Relations. Network members enthusiastically endorsed the idea for the book, and the book became a project of the Network. We sent out a call for papers to members of the Network and to other groups and individuals we knew were involved in qualitative research. We sought and received a variety of papers, although ultimately we were not able to include the full breadth of qualitative family research, the scope of which still might not be fully explicated. Almost all the authors, including we three editors, are members of the Qualitative Family Research Network. Our version of the answer to our original question—What is qualitative family research?—therefore is rooted in the work of qualitative family researchers and is reflected in the pages that follow.

The text is organized by methods of data collection in qualitative research: interviews, observation, and document analysis. Each of these methods and their combinations are represented in this volume, including a section on combined qualitative and quantitative designs. Although we considered other approaches to organization, we chose these methods of data collection for the sake of organizational clarity and teaching effectiveness. Each method can be used with a variety of conceptual frameworks and philosophies of science. Ethnographers, grounded theorists, analytic inductionists, conversation analysts, event analysts, phenomenologists, existentialists, personal narrative specialists, participant interactionists, field-workers, and psychobiographers may have differing worldviews, but they all use the same methods of data collection. Using method as an organizing principle allows us to confront the "how to" of qualitative research while leaving the interesting and important debates on philosophy of science to other texts.

SPECIFIC, CONCRETE LANGUAGE

The language of the volume is specific and concrete. We asked the authors to avoid jargon and abstract discussion except where necessary to help readers understand more about families or more about how the authors used the methods they did. We also asked the authors to reread their drafts and ask themselves whether someone not well versed in their special vocabulary will understand what they are saying. By this means, we hoped to make the book more useful to persons from many different disciplines.

With this dual focus on method and findings, this book should provide readers with opportunities to make informed decisions about whether and how qualitative methods fit their research, teaching, and editorial agendas.

JANE F. GILGUN
KERRY DALY
GERALD HANDEL

Part 1

Introduction

Although the exemplars of qualitative research represented in this volume give definition to qualitative family research, we as editors introduce the book with a set of papers designed to provide historical and methodological contexts for qualitative studies of families. In the first chapter, Kerry Daly discusses the appropriateness of qualitative research for the study of families with attentiveness to some of the issues that arise in attempting to study this unique social group. In Chapter 2, Gerald Handel presents an overview of the qualitative tradition in family research, a tradition that originated in the middle of the 19th century, gained influence after World War I, and was developed and elaborated in the decades after World War II. In the third chapter, Jane Gilgun presents an extended definition of qualitative family research and shows how this definition encompasses the diversities characteristic of families and how families are researched. Practical in its purpose, the chapter attempts to orient readers to ways of thinking about and doing qualitative family research.

The Fit Between Qualitative Research and Characteristics of Families

KERRY DALY
University of Guelph, Ontario

The historical contributions of qualitative methodologies to our understanding of families have been well documented (Handel, Chapter 2 this volume; LaRossa & Wolf, 1985). The long-standing relationship between qualitative research and families attests to their fundamental compatibility. The purpose of this chapter is to examine the nature of the fit between the assumptions and methods of qualitative research and the characteristics of families as unique social groups. To this end, I will discuss some of the distinctive challenges encountered in doing qualitative research with families.

Families are a distinctive focus of study. Several characteristics reflect the unique nature of families as social groups: privacy; a collective consciousness that is not readily available to nonfamily members; relationships rooted in blood ties, adoption contract, or marriage and intended to be permanent; shared traditions; intense involvement, ranging from the most violent to the most intimate; and a collage of individual interests, experiences and qualities.

Qualitative methods are particularly amenable to the study of this unique social group. In keeping with Weber's (1947) *verstehen* tradition, qualitative methods are suited to understanding the meanings, interpretations, and subjective experiences of family members. Consistent with the movement in family sociology challenging monolithic presentations of family structure and reality (Eichler, 1988), the versatility of qualitative methods is a good match for examining the diversity of family forms and experiences. With qualitative methods, the focus is not on identifying structural or demographic trends in families, but rather on the processes by which families create, sustain, and discuss their own family realities. What are the individual and collective phenomenological experiences of family members? Families are groups that construct individual and shared meanings. There is a concordance between families as a primary locus for the construction of meaning and the assumptions of qualitative research that focus on capturing that meaning. What we seek to do with qualitative research on families is not to count the number of families exhibiting some set of characteristics, but to understand how some families give insight into the meanings of their experience.

Qualitative methods facilitate holistic studies of families. This means looking at interactions, dynamics, contexts, rather than variables that isolate particular fragments of family experience like an attitude or a behavior. Qualitative methods give us windows on family processes through which we can observe patterns of interaction and the ongoing negotiations of family roles and relationships.

Getting at these family realities poses some unique challenges and opportunities for qualitative researchers. These include gaining access to the private activities of family members; studying parts and wholes in families; negotiating the research roles in families; managing bias; and giving consideration to ethics in the research bargain.

GAINING ACCESS TO PRIVATE SPHERES

Social groups are defined by boundaries that demarcate insiders from outsiders (Hess & Handel, 1959). Although families vary with respect to the permeability of their boundaries, they typically are thought of as being one of the most closed and private of all social groups. Family members coalesce in the processes of preserving and protecting their traditions, secrets, and habits. Keeping sexual, conflictual, or dysfunctional behaviors from the scrutiny of outsiders is a key mechanism by which families construct and maintain their unique self-definitions.

A challenge for qualitative researchers is to enter the relatively closed and highly protected boundaries of families' experiences. Qualitative research, in comparison with more remote methods of data collection, allows for the construction of relationships with participants that gradually can build trust and rapport, and in turn, result in increasing accessibility to "backstage" family meanings. For example, unstructured interviews, observations, and diaries and letters allow participants to discuss their experiences in their own language, in their own natural setting, and according to their own comfort in disclosing. By offering to enter participants' life worlds, rather than imposing the formality of a survey or an experiment, qualitative researchers are in a good position to access the private meanings of families. The chapters in this volume demonstrate how this can be done.

Regardless of how researchers attempt to enter the private spheres of families, there will be secrets and loyalties that remain inaccessible. Few researchers acknowledge their limitations in accessing these, but making these limitations obvious in the research can provide insight into the ways boundaries are defined and maintained in families. These limitations become apparent when participants avoid sensitive topics or request that the tape recorder be shut off so they can reveal something "off the record." Rather than seeing these instances as barriers to accessibility, researchers can use them as rich data in themselves. Although researchers have ethical obligations to honor participants' requests that some statements not be included as data, these moments can provide the researcher with insight into disclosure limits and the norms of social acceptability. Moreover, the face-to-face intimacy of interviews or observation allows the researcher to observe these processes firsthand, gaining opportunities to understand private-public boundaries as well as the processes by which these boundaries are presented and maintained.

Although some aspects of family experience are deliberately hidden from researchers, other aspects of family reality are hidden simply because of their apparent mundaneness. Routine, repetitive aspects of family roles and relationships can be so much a part of taken-for-granted reality that they are not considered important by participants. Qualitative research with families is one way to take the obvious (and therefore the hidden), and through comparative analysis, put it in a new light and make it comprehensible. What participants think of as habitual, takes on new meaning when compared and contrasted with the habits of others.

Of course, the taken-for-granted family meanings become even more understandable when we study the problematics, the disruptions or the nonnormative transitions, in family experience. For example, a study of infertility can provide insight into the taken-for-granted meaning of parenthood, or a study of divorce can offer insight into the everyday meaning of marriage. These family crisis points, or "epiphanies" (Denzin, 1989), make taken-for-granted family meanings manifest and apparent to researchers.

STUDYING FAMILY PARTS AND WHOLES

Families also present a challenge as to the unit of analysis. Most survey research takes the individual as the unit and focuses on that individual's characteristics, attitudes, and behaviors. By contrast, qualitative research can accommodate multiple perspectives and can better deal with families, marriages, or sibling relationships as units and enable richer accounts and closer approximations of lived family experiences (Handel, 1989). Although the practical limitations of an observation or interview segment or the nature of some research questions may lead researchers to focus on one family member at a time, the focus on the composite family picture, with all its inherent corroborations and contradictions, is a strength of qualitative research.

As part of working with family boundaries, researchers need to be attentive to the fact that families may have spokespersons who present the family to the outside world. As Saffilios-Rothschild (1969) warned some years ago, women often are sources for explaining families' realities. Although these spokespersons can serve as key informants, they also can act as a kind of gatekeeper in the presentation of family images. Research questions will determine with whom we speak in the family, but in many types of family research, the value of multiple-member perspectives is paramount. For example, when the focus of investigation is parent-child relationships, data minimally would be gathered from mothers, fathers, and children. A particular challenge in this regard is to access men's perspectives of family experience, because men typically have been difficult to recruit in qualitative family research (Daly, in press). Several chapters in this volume are reports of studies in which the informants include entire families or multiple family members.

RESEARCHERS' ROLES

Qualitative work with families raises questions about how to present and maintain researcher roles. Researchers must decide how to present their motives, how much to participate, how structured their interviews will be, and how intensively they will become involved in participant families' lives.

In doing qualitative family research, there is a high potential to confuse the researcher role with the "expert helper" or therapist role. Qualitative researchers ask questions about the intimate sphere, observe family struggles, and provide openings for family members to discuss their "personal troubles" as a way of gaining insight into families' day-to-day reality. When family members are having difficult or discordant experiences, they may come to expect the opinion of the expert as part of the research exchange. In this regard, participants may be less concerned with the research process as a scientific endeavor than they are with researchers as professionals with answers and resources. Quite often, this emerges in the form of a question of normality: Are other families like us?

How do qualitative family researchers deal with these role demands? How do we stick with the research agenda? Should we give advice, information or counseling? What are the implications for switching into therapist roles during the data collection phase? There is no clear formula for dealing with these expectations, but there are a variety of issues to consider. First, it is important to acknowledge that the researcher and participant(s) establish a relationship that is based on a fair exchange. Once researchers could rationalize the unilateral extraction of data from a "subject" under the guise of "scientific objectivity," but this is no longer reasonable or appropriate. Power relations may never be fully abolished in research settings, but clearly interviewers should strive to establish non-hierarchical relationships with interviewees (Oakley, 1981).

Second, requests for information, advice, or reactions in response to intimate disclosures are expectable parts of research relationships. (See Matocha, Chapter 5, this volume.) The degree to which we are able to respond to requests for advice or information is contingent on our training and ability. Identifying our limitations for participants is far preferable to overstepping our professional boundaries. Nevertheless,

it is appropriate to anticipate requests and be prepared to give participants information about the subject matter of the study and to direct
them to other resources, such as reading material or referrals to quali-
fied therapists. When participants ask questions about how others in the
study have responded, timing is a consideration. For example, researchers may obtain more realistic accounts of family experiences if they
leave the discussion of what other families are like until the end.

In some ways, reactions are more difficult to control. As participants
in a relationship, we may naturally convey some uneasiness when we
listen to the expression of intimate emotions, embarrassing disclosures,
or conflict. In such instances, we may wish to acknowledge the pain,
difficulty, or embarrassment that emerge in the research situation, and
we may be tempted to impose our own values on the experiences of
family members. A guideline for such situations is to focus on the
research goal, which is to understand how participants assign meaning
to their realities, rather than to evaluate their realities through our
responses or opinions.

Third, if researchers choose to provide advice or therapy as part of
the research process, it is important that this be negotiated clearly and
separately from the research relationship. As in any other therapeutic
relationship, goals, boundaries, and limitations need to be addressed
explicitly. Carrying the dual roles of researcher and therapist, however,
will have implications for how questions are phrased and how data are
collected, analyzed, and interpreted. Qualitative research is expanding
in clinical settings, and the ramifications for role ambiguity and conflict
are now being addressed. At a minimum, it is important to recognize
that informants in qualitative research may seek and experience therapeutic effects, even though researchers state clearly that their purpose
is to conduct research. (In Chapter 13, this volume, on family incest
treatment, Gilgun elaborates on this point.)

Finally, researchers who study families for extended periods risk
becoming immersed in the family system. This can result in alliances
being formed and things said in confidence that require the careful
management of researchers' positions in the family system. How do
researchers move in and out of the system? Although such intense
involvement can signify that the private sphere has been accessed, it
does pose challenges to researchers for maintaining balanced relationships with all family members. Careful monitoring of our own position
in the family system is an important requisite for maintaining a focus
on the research agenda.

PERSONAL EXPERIENCES AND
QUALITATIVE FAMILY RESEARCHERS

In contrast to an arm's length methodology like a mailed question-naire, qualitative family research closely involves the researcher with participants and data. Given the stronger presence of researchers in all aspects of the research, questions about how personal experiences, perceptions, and interpretations enter into the data are of particular interest. Specifically, how do our own family experiences affect the choices we make about what to study, who to ask, and how to ask it? For example, in my current research on the social construction of fatherhood, my experience as a father and my relationship with my own father had an important bearing on my interest in the topic and what I thought was important to ask. In light of this, I engaged in a process of self-reflection before jumping into the field. Before I formally started any interviews, I went to an intensive workshop on father-son relationships and subsequently interviewed my own father. It was important for me to identify and separate my personal agenda from the research agenda.

Researchers' own family experiences also will play a role in the collection and analysis of data. Listening to participants' stories may stir personal responses. These, in turn, may affect the direction of questioning or the extent to which we are willing to probe deeper into issues at hand. Furthermore, in the process of generating substantive theory, researchers add layers of meaning to the participants' meanings. This corresponds with Schutz's (1971) distinction between first- and second-order constructs; whereas first-order constructs are rooted in the everyday language of families, second-order constructs arise from the process of analytic induction. The challenge for qualitative family researchers when inducing these constructs is to preserve the participants' family meanings while at the same time monitoring the infusion of their own family and professional meanings. This may be especially challenging when researchers have some prior acquaintance with the family issue. Although a case can be made that this circum-stance increases theoretical sensitivity to the issue, it may also blind researchers to significant aspects of informants' experiences. Douglas (1985) calls such potential blind spots "black holes."

In considering bias in qualitative family research, the role of gender is salient. Researchers' own gender may affect their perceptions of how family members carry out roles. Reflection on personal gender issues— our own gender socialization, expectations we have of our own family

members, and our comfort with persons of the same or other gender—
may enhance the quality of our research. Reflection on gender issues
also may raise issues of who we think is credible as informants. Do we
consider same-sex or other-sex informants more or less credible? How
is the interview discourse different when it is man to man versus woman
to woman or woman to man? How do gender and power hierarchies
shape our perceptions of what is appropriate or inappropriate in the
families we study? Clearly, self-reflection on gender issues in research
is warranted.

ETHICAL CONSIDERATIONS

Several ethical issues already have arisen in this chapter: respecting
families' boundaries of privacy; being clear about research and therapy
role boundaries; and the need for researchers to constrain their judgments about participants' experiences. In addition, there are at least two
other ethical dilemmas faced by qualitative family researchers: informed consent and unanticipated self-exposure (LaRossa, Bennett, &
Gelles, 1985).

Because of the emergent design, informed consent is problematic in
qualitative research and particularly acute in research on families.
Discussions of family life might range widely and include comments
about friends, work associates, or neighbors. It may be impossible for
qualitative family researchers to inform participants fully of the precise
scope of the research at the outset. In light of these problems, qualitative
family researchers could encourage participants to draw their own
boundaries of privacy and emphasize participants' prerogative to withdraw materials from the study at any time.

Unanticipated disclosures may result from the inherent power imbalance between researchers and participants. This imbalance may result
in some participants feeling obligated to respond to questions they
might otherwise not answer. For others, the informal atmosphere of an
unstructured interview in the home may lead them to disclose more than
they had originally planned. The problem may be further compounded
by interviewing more than one family member, eliciting disclosures by
one that might violate the privacy of others. Sometimes the nature and
timing of these disclosures may be beyond the control of researchers.
Nevertheless, a respectful stance to a informants' privacy is a useful
ethical guideline. Among other things, this involves checking out peri-

odically with participants their comfort levels, and if necessary, with-drawing segments of data from the record. Researchers may actively encourage informants not to talk about topics that make them appear anxious or under stress.

CONCLUSION

The complex and dynamic interplay of family meanings, coupled with a phenomenological and structural diversity in families, requires a method that is malleable, sensitive, and practical. Qualitative meth-ods, designed to capture emergent meanings, are well suited to the study of a wide range of family experiences. This brief chapter provides an overview of some of the distinctive issues encountered in doing quali-tative research on families. In the chapters that follow, readers are invited to explore the many issues that have arisen for the other quali-tative family researchers represented in this volume.

REFERENCES

Daly, K. (in press). Uncertain terms: The social construction of fatherhood. In M.L. Dietz, W. Shaffir, & R. Prus. (Eds.), *Doing everyday life: Ethnography as human lived experience.* Reynolds Series in Sociology. New York: General Hall.

Denzin, N. K. (1989). *Interpretive interactionism.* Newbury Park, CA: Sage.

Douglas, J. D. (1985). *Creative interviewing.* Beverly Hills, CA: Sage.

Eichler, M. (1988). *Families in Canada today.* Toronto: Gage.

Handel, G. (1989, November). *Qualitative study of whole families in a time of great change.* Paper presented at the preconference workshop on Theory Construction and Research Methodology, National Council on Family Relations, New Orleans, Novem-ber 3-5.

Hess, R. D., & Handel, G. (1959). *Family worlds.* Chicago: University of Chicago Press.

LaRossa, R., Bennett, L. A., & Gelles, R. (1985). Ethical dilemmas in qualitative family research. In G. Handel (Ed.), *The psychosocial interior of the family* (pp. 95-111). New York: Aldine.

LaRossa, R., & Wolf, J. H. (1985). On qualitative family research. *Journal of Marriage and the Family, 47,* 531-541.

Oakley, A. (1981). Interviewing women: A contradiction in terms. In H. Roberts (Ed.), *Doing feminist research* (pp. 30-61). London: Routledge & Kegan Paul.

Saffilios-Rothschild, C. (1969). Family sociology or wives' family sociology? A cross-cul-tural examination of decision making. *Journal of Marriage and the Family, 31,* 290-301.

Schutz, A. (1971). *Collected papers I: The problem of social reality.* The Hague: Martinus Nijhoff.

Weber, M. (1947). *The theory of social and economic organization* (T. Parsons, Ed.; A. M. Henderson and Talcott Parsons, Trans.). New York: The Free Press.

The Qualitative Tradition in Family Research

GERALD HANDEL
The City College and Graduate School,
City University of New York

This volume is a novel undertaking, bringing together for the first time an array of different methods for qualitative family study. Yet it builds upon a research tradition that is as old as social science itself. In this introductory chapter, I want to give a brief overview of that tradition. I can do no more than touch on some of its highlights, but I want to communicate in a somewhat more comprehensive way than has been done before the strengths and continuities of the research approach that this volume seeks to advance.

Admittedly, where one chooses to locate the beginning of social science is a matter of definition. The Old Testament prophets, forecasters of serious social problems, and the philosophers of Periclean Athens, analysts of the good society and much else, are plausible candidates for this recognition, and there are perhaps other ancients whose astute observations or searching analyses merit similar consideration. For a more modern definition, we must turn to more recent figures. According to Catherine Bodard Silver (1982), "Frederic LePlay (1806-82) was the first social scientist to undertake field research of the 'monographic' type, to collect his own data specifically to test hypotheses, and to undertake systematic, comparative cross-national research" (p. 3).

This many-talented Frenchman, an eminent mining and industrial engineer, for many years spent 6 months each year in field research on

12

mining in several European countries. His interest extended not only to the mine workers and their families, but to workers in many occupations as workers and as family members. His massive study of working-class families, *Les Ouvriers Europeens* (European Workers), covering 36 types of workers, was published in 1855. As Silver (1982) observed:

> This work represents the first instance of large-scale empirical research based on a standardized method that combined both qualitative field observation and quantification. LePlay's method of family monographs, which used data collected directly from persons through what, today, would be called participant observation and interviews, provided a comparative framework for the study of family structure and work relations in different types of societies. (p. 5)

What LePlay (1982) called a monograph would later come to be called a case study: "Each monograph is a collection of questions answered by observation. It is a living picture of a family, in which we see in action the principles leading toward progress or decadence" (p. 163). LePlay developed a standardized three-section format for his monographs: the first and third sections were based on qualitative data, with the second providing a quantitative analysis of the family's budget.

LePlay's study of families was part of his larger effort to understand social stability, happiness, and social change, topics too vast to summarize here. Among students of the family, he is best known for presenting his results according to the following typology:

1. The patriarchal family, in which the father exercises continuing authority over married sons and their children, and in which family property remains undivided. . .

2. The unstable family, prevalent among factory workers but also found among wealthier classes, in which children leave home when grown, whether married or not, and have no further obligation to parents and relatives. . .

3. The stem family, which "develops spontaneously among those people who, having reaped the benefits of agricultural work and sedentary life, have the good sense to defend their private lives against the domination of lawyers, the inroads of bureaucracy, and the excesses of the modern manufacturing system. In this type of social organization, only one married child remains with the parents. All others receive a dowry and enjoy an independence which is impossible in the patriarchal family. This system perpetuates work habits, moral influences, and ancestral traditions in the

paternal home. The family is a permanent source of protection on which all the members can rely throughout life's trials. This system offers individuals a security they could never find in the unstable family." (pp. 259-261)

Despite his demonstrable inauguration of empirical social science, family research, and the qualitative methods of participant observation and qualitative interviewing, LePlay was not directly influential in the subsequent development of social science. His work is widely neglected in historical accounts, and except for brief excerpts, *Les Ouvriers Europeens* has never been translated into English (LaRossa & Wolf, 1985; Silver, 1982).

THE POLISH PEASANT IN EUROPE AND AMERICA

More universally recognized as a landmark is W. I. Thomas and Florian Znaniecki's five-volume work, *The Polish Peasant in Europe and America* (1918-1920, reissued in 2 volumes, 1927). As LaRossa and Wolf (1985) noted: "While LePlay may be the first qualitative researcher, it was not until Thomas and Znaniecki published their book that qualitative research was fully recognized" (p. 533). The study has a wider significance as well. According to Bulmer (1984):

> The significance of the publication of *The Polish Peasant* can hardly be exaggerated . . . it was a landmark because it attempted to integrate theory and data in a way no American study had done before. . . . *The Polish Peasant* marked a shift in sociology away from abstract theory and library research toward a more intimate acquaintance with the empirical world. (p. 45)

In their study of "the profound disintegration" of peasant family life due to industrialization in Poland and emigration to the United States, Thomas and Znaniecki emphasized what Thomas called "documentary materials." These included newspapers, pamphlets, court records, and records of peasant agricultural societies and Polish-American societies (Bulmer, 1984; LaRossa & Wolf, 1985). Most notably, they included personal documents—letters among family members, diaries, and auto-biographical life histories. The great virtue of these materials is that they reveal the meanings of social situations for the participants, how they define situations, and how they adapt to them (Volkart, 1951). The first two volumes presented letters published in family series from 50 families. The third volume was devoted to the life history of one man.

A contemporary use of data provided by diaries is the work of Rosenblatt, who (1983) studied expressions of grief over family separations and deaths in 19th-century diaries and related his findings both to the theory of grief work and family systems theory. An example in this volume of document analysis is Harbert, Vinick, and Ekerdt (Chapter 14), who studied popular media to understand the nature of advice about retirement given to older couples. Rank used social service case records as one of many sources of data for his study of the fertility of low-income women (Chapter 15, this volume).

Although letters have not since been much used in family research (Plummer, 1983), life histories have, after a period of decline, come to be much appreciated in a variety of research endeavors, although not yet extensively in family studies. Among the few later family researchers to use them was the anthropologist Oscar Lewis, whose book *The Children of Sanchez* presented a single poor Mexican family through the medium of multiple autobiographies obtained from a widowed father and his four young adult children (Lewis, 1961).

STUDIES OF FAMILIES DURING THE GREAT DEPRESSION

The Great Depression, which began in 1929, stimulated several qualitative studies of its impact on families. Robert Cooley Angell (1936) studied 50 families who had suffered "a sudden and apparently lasting decrease of at least 25 percent in real income from accustomed sources" (p. 9). These were families of University of Michigan students, to whom he gave a 15-page Family Analysis Form, with open-ended questions and instructions to add extra pages if necessary. Each family case yielded an average of 30 closely written pages. His results were presented according to a typology based on two dimensions: integration and adaptability. The typology consisted of eight types, ranging from "Highly Integrated, Highly Adaptable" to "Unintegrated, Unadaptable," with six intermediate types.

Ruth Cavan and Katherine Ranck (1938), a sociologist and a psychiatric social worker respectively, collaborated on a study of 100 Chicago families in which from one to five family members contributed to "the interview"; i.e., according to circumstance, more than one family member was sometimes present for the interview (p. 15). The families all were known to the Institute for Juvenile Research (a child study organization) in the two years preceding the onset of the Depression, and the case files were used to develop a picture of each family's pre-Depression organization. The authors regarded their study as partially overlapping and confirming Angell's (1936), but as also providing detailed individual member reactions, whereas Angell's was confined to the unit of the family as a social group.

The sociologist Mirra Komarovsky's (1940) *The Unemployed Man and His Family* focused on the relationship between the man's role as economic provider of the family and his authority in the family. The study's research question was: "What happens to the authority of the male head of the family when he fails as a provider?" (p. 1). Family names and addresses were obtained from the Emergency Relief Administration. Sample selection criteria were:

1. Parents native-born Protestants
2. Family head a skilled laborer or white-collar worker
3. Families consisting of father, mother, and children living together
4. At least one child over age 10
5. Father had been sole provider
6. Father has been unemployed for at least one year

The interview was constructed of open-ended questions followed by more structured probes.

Two methodological procedures are of interest in this study. One was the attempt to ascertain the reliability of interviews by having another researcher reinterview 5 of the 59 families 4 months after the initial interviews, with the comparison conducted by an analyst specifically hired for the purpose. The second was formulation of a "procedure of discerning" for judging whether unemployment was the cause of changes occurring within each of the families. A three-step analytic procedure is described in an appendix.

Elizabeth Bott's (1957) study of 20 London families was one of the first to study "ordinary families" rather than troubled ones. It also was one of the first to consider each family as a social system, although she interviewed only the husbands and wives and not the children. Within its domain, the study achieved unusual depth, with an average of 13 interviews conducted with each couple. The chapter on methodology is unusually rich in its candid discussion of a range of research problems.

STUDIES OF WHOLE FAMILIES

None of the studies discussed so far, nor any other known to me, attempted to study whole families by including the perspective of each member, although Komarovsky took a step in that direction by recognizing the importance of interviewing at least one child in addition to both parents. Ernest Burgess (1926) formulated the concept of "the family as a unity of interacting personalities," but the concept was revered and reiterated for a quarter century without being implemented in research. George Herbert Mead (1934) argued more generally that although the self is developed in a social process and reflects the group, each member of a group has an individual perspective. Burgess's concept can be regarded as a charter for the study of whole families (Handel, 1965). Although the concept of whole families is intrinsically inexact and even more ambiguous today, until about 1970 the most prevalent type of family in the United States and other Western countries was the nuclear family, a two-parent family with children living in a shared household for an extended period of time. The term "whole family," for that historic context, refers to such units.

Hess and Handel's *Family Worlds* (1959) was the first study of families with the explicitly formulated goal of understanding how families function, based on taking account of every member's perspective. They selected families with two or three children between the ages of 6 and 18, so that all members could be interviewed. In subsequent papers, Handel (1965, 1967, 1986, 1989, 1991) has continued to argue the necessity of building on Cooley's (1909) conceptualization of families as primary groups. The approach can even, and should, be applied to families with newborns who, though they cannot be interviewed, can be observed in interaction with parents and, where present, older siblings. (See Murphy, Chapter 9, and Sandelowski, Holditch-Davis, and Harris, Chapter 16, this volume.) As Caplow (1968) argued, and Ehrensaft (1985) demonstrated, even newborn infants can become members of family coalitions of two against one. Bell (1968) analyzed infants' contributions to interaction. Of course, in today's context, the concept of whole families takes many more forms, including single-parent, binuclear, blended, two-parent lesbian, two-parent gay. This increased variety of forms constitutes a continuing rationale for studying whole families, whatever their form. Families are groups, and the adult marriage or cohabitation relationship, the parent-child relationships, and the sibling relationships need to be understood concurrently in their group context as mutually influencing and as resulting in individual family cultures and group structures.

FAMILIES IN RACIAL AND CLASS CONTEXT

One of the few studies to address this task on a large scale is Rainwater's (1970) study of poor black families, *Behind Ghetto Walls,* which included an analysis of the families' interactions in the larger social context of racism and poverty. Over a 3-year period, a team of eight field-workers engaged in participant observation and intensive, repetitive open-ended interviewing in a public housing project of 2,760 apartments, 74% occupied, with almost 10,000 inhabitants. Each field-worker developed rapport with a small number of families and individuals and followed them for a considerable time, in a few cases for the entire 3 years. These data were supplemented by two 10% sample surveys in the project, and by a survey of 69 private rental slum households in the adjacent neighborhood. The study presents what is probably the most richly documented and most theoretically sophisticated analysis in the literature of poor black family life.

Rainwater's (1970) study is an example of studies whose point of departure is the families' social standing in the community. Some earlier examples that should be cited are Allison Davis, Burleigh Gardner, and Mary Gardner's (1941) *Deep South,* which presented clearly delineated portraits of upper-class, middle-class, and lower-class white family relationships from an anthropological perspective, and Seeley, Sim, and Loosely's (1956) *Crestwood Heights,* subtitled *A Study of the Culture of Suburban Life,* which presented an analytic description of the upper-middle-class suburban family, based on anthropological and sociological fieldwork methods focused at the community level. Here the interest was not in particular families, but in the family as an organization in patterned interaction with other organizations, such as the school, and as influenced by the community structure.

Three studies of working-class families, though carried out differently, provide a kind of replication and thereby suggest how the accumulation of studies can strengthen confidence in findings. Rainwater, Coleman, and Handel's (1959) *Workingman's Wife* was based on lengthy qualitative interviews with 480 working-class and 120 middle-class housewives in four different cities. This procedure was possible because the study was conducted by a research firm with interviewing facilities in several locations.

Komarovsky's (1962) *Blue-Collar Marriage* was based on qualitative interviews with 58 wife and husband couples in a single town of about 50,000 people, apparently in the eastern United States. Rubin's (1976) *Worlds of Pain* was based on qualitative interviews with husbands and wives in 50 working-class couples in the San Francisco Bay area. Despite the different methodologies, locations, and times of study, there is considerable similarity in the overall picture of working-class family life in these three studies. Komarovsky's study includes a refinement in analysis that the other two lack in that it distinguishes differences in marriages of high school graduates from marriages of those with less education. Both Komarovsky and Rubin included marital sexuality within their domain, but Rainwater et al. (1959) did not. Rainwater's (1960) *And the Poor Get Children,* sponsored by the Planned Parenthood Federation of America, was an early qualitative study of this aspect of working-class marriage, however.

THE ROLES OF HOUSEWIVES IN THE SUBURBS

The years following World War II were characterized in the United States by the growth of suburbs. Women who had entered the labor force during wartime to replace absent men returned in great numbers to full-time domestic roles, many in new suburban homes. In a sequence of studies of the housewife role, Lopata (1971) began by conducting 299 depth interviews with full-time homemakers in 12 Chicago suburbs of various prestige and income levels. She then guided a team that conducted similar interviews with 192 full-time Chicago housewives and 1000 Chicago-area married women who also worked in the labor market. Lopata concluded, "The content of the open-ended responses gave insight into the ways in which different groups of women approach their various roles—insights which precoded schedules cannot convey" (p. 10). Specific hypotheses formulated on the basis of this material were tested in precoded interviews with 205 women. The work that resulted, *Occupation: Housewife,* surely is unique in being based on far more qualitative interviews than survey interviews. Oakley's (1974) study of the housewife role in London is based on 40 interviews, a more typical number of informants in qualitative interview studies.

Innovations in qualitative study of families were introduced by Piotrkowski (1979) and Speedling (1982). Piotrkowski studied the impact of work setting and experience on family interaction in 13 working-class and lower-middle-class families. Most of her data were gathered in qualitative interviews, but she was also able to do participant observation for brief periods, both in the home and at the workplace, in two cases. Her study includes a 33-page methodological appendix that is exceptionally detailed and thoughtful.

Speedling studied eight families in which the husband-father suffered a heart attack. He participated with and interviewed family members at the hospital bedside, began participant observation in the homes while the men were hospitalized, and continued after they came home, so he was able to observe the processes of family restructuring in response to both the absence and the return of the hospitalized husband-father. Although participant observation has proved possible in lower-class and working-class families (see also Howell, 1973), it has been more difficult and rarer to gain observational access to middle- and upper-middle-class families. This is one of the new frontiers of qualitative family research.

The studies discussed scarcely exhaust those worthy of discussion; I did not intend a comprehensive review, but rather focused on studies that introduced innovations into qualitative methodology, regardless of the substantive topics studied. Most of these studies have had a significant impact on family studies because of their methodological innovations, their expositions of methodological struggles, and their theoretical and empirical results. Space limitations required abbreviating discussion, but I hope I have conveyed enough to indicate why these studies constitute landmarks in the development and diversification of qualitative family research. We hope as well that the current volume will lead to notable additions.

REFERENCES

Angell, R. C. (1936). *The family encounters the depression.* New York: Scribner.
Bell, R. Q. (1968). A reinterpretation of the direction of effects in studies of socialization. *Psychological Review, 75,* 81-95.
Bott, E. (1957). *Family and social network.* New York: Free Press.
Bulmer, M. (1984). *The Chicago school of sociology.* Chicago: University of Chicago Press.
Burgess, E. W. (1926). The family as a unity of interacting personalities. *Family, 7,* 3-9.
Caplow, T. (1968). *Two against one.* Englewood Cliffs, NJ: Prentice-Hall.

Cavan, R. S., & Ranck, K. H. (1938). *The family and the depression*. Chicago: University of Chicago Press.

Cooley, C. H. (1909). *Social organization*. New York: Scribner.

Davis, A., Gardner, B., & Gardner, M. (1941). *Deep south*. Chicago: University of Chicago Press.

Ehrensaft, D. (1985). Dual parenting and the duel of intimacy. In G. Handel (Ed.), *The psychosocial interior of the family* (3rd ed., pp. 323-337). New York: Aldine.

Handel, G. (1965). Psychological study of whole families. *Psychological Bulletin, 63,* 19-41.

Handel, G. (1967). Introduction. In G. Handel (Ed.), *The psychosocial interior of the family* (pp. 1-8). Chicago: Aldine.

Handel, G. (1986). Beyond sibling rivalry: An empirically grounded theory of sibling relationships. In P. A. Adler & P. Adler (Eds.), *Sociological studies of child development* (Vol. 1, pp. 105-122). Greenwich, CT: JAI.

Handel, G. (1989, November). *Qualitative study of whole families in a time of great change.* Paper presented at the preconference workshop on Theory Construction and Research Methodology, National Council on Family Relations, New Orleans, November 3-5.

Handel, G. (1991). Case study in family research. In J. R. Feagin, A. M. Orum, & G. Sjoberg (Eds.), *A case for the case study* (pp. 244-268). Chapel Hill: University of North Carolina Press.

Hess, R. D., & Handel, G. (1959). *Family worlds*. Chicago: University of Chicago Press.

Howell, J. T. (1973). *Hard living on Clay Street: Portraits of blue collar families*. Garden City, NY: Anchor.

Komarovsky, M. (1940). *The unemployed man and his family*. New York: Dryden.

Komarovsky, M. (1962). *Blue-collar marriage*. New York: Random House.

LaRossa, R., & Wolf, J. (1985). On qualitative family research. *Journal of Marriage and the Family, 47,* 531-541.

LePlay, F. (1982). *On family, work, and social change*. (C. B. Silver, Ed. and Trans.). Chicago: University of Chicago Press.

Lewis, O. (1961). *The children of Sanchez*. New York: Random House.

Lopata, H. (1971). *Occupation: Housewife*. New York: Oxford University Press.

Mead, G. H. (1934). *Mind, self, and society*. Chicago: University of Chicago Press.

Oakley, A. (1974). *The sociology of housework*. London: Martin Robinson.

Piotrkowski, C. (1979). *Work and the family system*. New York: Free Press.

Plummer, K. (1983). *Documents of life*. London: George Allen & Unwin.

Rainwater, L. (1960). *And the poor get children*. Chicago: Quadrangle.

Rainwater, L. (1970). *Behind ghetto walls*. Chicago: Aldine.

Rainwater, L., Coleman, R., & Handel, G. (1959). *Workingman's wife*. New York: Oceana.

Rosenblatt, P. (1983). *Bitter, bitter tears*. Minneapolis: University of Minnesota Press.

Rubin, L. (1976). *Worlds of pain: Life in the working-class family*. New York: Basic Books.

Seeley, J., Sim, R., & Loosely, E. (1956). *Crestwood Heights*. New York: Basic Books.

Silver, C. B. (1982). Introduction. In F. LePlay, *On family, work, and social change* (pp. 3-134). Chicago: University of Chicago Press.

Speedling, E. (1982). *Heart attack: The family response at home and in the hospital*. New York: Tavistock.

Thomas, W. I., Znaniecki, F. (1927). *The Polish peasant in Europe and America*. New York: Knopf.

Volkart, E. (1951). *Social behavior and personality: Contributions of W. I. Thomas to theory and social research*. New York: Social Science Research Council.

Definitions, Methodologies, and Methods in Qualitative Family Research

JANE F. GILGUN
University of Minnesota, Twin Cities

Defining either families or qualitative family research is not for the faint of heart. Families appear in diverse forms, and there are many types of qualitative research. The political, theoretical, and practical implications of our definitions are enormous, for definitions circumscribe who and what are included within or excluded from domains of interest, and therefore who are accorded the benefits, rights, and responsibilities of family membership. The authors of the individual chapters of this volume have simplified our definitional tasks: The chapters themselves are definitions of qualitative family research. The authors show that families appear in diverse forms: parents and their adoptive, foster, or biological minor and adult children; extended families in which many forms of families are embedded; families centering around committed homosexual relationships; elder mothers and their middle-aged daughters; elders and the generations born after them; and premarital couples who define themselves as in love. Topics covered range from heterosexual love to birth and adoption of children to child rearing, sibling relationships, family incest treatment, African-American families,

Southeast Asian refugee families, retirement, caring for elder parents, and caring for disabled and dying family members. Families represented in this volume are rich, poor, and in-between. Diversity, then, is a key word for defining families in qualitative research.

The definitions listed above are concrete. Abstract definitions of families also can be drawn from the chapters of this volume. Although legal and biological factors are parts of general definitions of families, three other themes related to definitions emerge: (a) persons mutually define themselves and each other as members of families, (b) members make enduring commitments to each other, and (c) members have a sense of a shared personal history. Through thick and through thin, as the cliche goes, the informants in these chapters are deeply engaged in committed—and often difficult—relationships with persons they define and who define them as family and with whom they share personal histories. The introductory chapters by Daly and Handel (chapters 1 and 2, this volume) contain complementary definitions of families.

The chapters add depth to the meaning of Burgess's (1926) description of families as units of interaction. Although the focus overall is on family interactions, some chapters also examine interactions between family members and systems outside of the family. We encourage researchers to consider questions involving more than one family member in research processes, although we recognize that some questions and circumstances result in a single informant. (Again, see chapters 1 and 2, this volume.) The research remains family research as long as it centers around experiences within families or between families and other systems. Detzner's (Chapter 6, this volume) investigation of the experience of Southeast Asian elders is an example of qualitative family research using one informant per family.

The diversity of qualitative family research also comes through clearly in the individual chapters. The research methods the authors use, their methodologies, their theoretical frameworks, the substantive areas of their research, the theory and research they use to interpret their findings, and their purposes in doing their research evidence the diversity of qualitative family research. A common thread in their work may be a focus on the construction of meaning. As Daly (Chapter 1, this volume) pointed out, qualitative research is strongly associated with Weber's *verstehen* tradition, or "the meanings, interpretations, and subjective experiences of family members" (pp. 3-4).

A DEFINITION OF QUALITATIVE
FAMILY RESEARCH

To avoid issues related to who really is doing qualitative research and who is not and to avoid "paradigm" debates, we have chosen a definition based on a set of unadorned core ideas. In this volume, qualitative research is defined as processes used to make sense of data that are represented by words or pictures and not by numbers. The processes of qualitative research include ways of conceptualizing, collecting, analyzing, and interpreting data. Most forms of qualitative research are qualitative in all four of these processes. We recognize a mixed type of research, in which aspects of these four processes might be quantified, although we include no mixed-type studies in this volume. Two examples are LaRossa, Gordon, Wilson, Bairan, and Jaret (1991), who studied depictions of fatherhood in cartoons, and Rosenblatt et al. (1991), who interviewed family members about bereavement. Each study involved one qualitative data set, which was analyzed both qualitatively and quantitatively. In addition, Rosenblatt et al. used random sampling, which is based on probability theory and does not use qualitative thinking for sample selection. Examples of sampling using qualitative thinking include "snowball sampling," negative case analysis, and theoretical sampling. (See Bogdan & Biklen, 1982; and other chapters in this volume for more on qualitative sampling strategies.) Some computer programs also analyze qualitative data sets quantitatively (Tesch, 1990). Finally, our definition of qualitative research also includes research using open-ended questions appended to questionnaires and survey interviews.

Qualitative family research, then, is research with a focus on experiences within families as well as between families and outside systems; data are words or pictures and not numbers; the data are conceptualized, collected, analyzed, and interpreted qualitatively; the subjects or informants of the research are persons who mutually define themselves as family, are in committed relationships, have a shared sense of personal history, and who usually but not always have legal and biological ties. This is a lean definition. Its sparseness provides a basis for including many types of research under the rubric *qualitative family research*.

Rationale for a Lean Definition

Dissatisfaction with positivistic philosophies of science has produced an explosion of interest in other methodologies (Guba, 1990). By methodology, I mean the principles, procedures, and values that guide research processes (Blumer, 1969; Schwandt, 1990). Because I am not an expert on all of the methodologies, it seemed wise to construct a definition of qualitative family research intended to be compatible with them. Methodologies currently under discussion and relevant to qualitative approaches include interpretive interactionism and interpretive biographies and narratives (Denzin, 1989; Polkinghorne, 1988), naturalistic inquiry (Lincoln & Guba, 1985), radical-critical theories (Osmond, 1987), constructivism, critical theory (Schwandt, 1990), Heideggerian hermeneutics (Packer, 1985; Wilson & Hutchinson, 1991), emancipatory research (Lather, 1986), postmodernism and deconstructionism, feminist deconstructionism, and feminist postmodernism (Baber & Allen, 1991; Flax, 1987, 1990; Harding, 1987; Hare-Mustin & Marecek, 1990; Nuccio & Sands, in press).

These methodologies—which have many overlapping principles, procedures, and values—have had or are likely to have a major impact on the conduct of qualitative family research. Each of these methodologies potentially can add new dimensions to qualitative family research and thus increase its diversity yet again. Each of these methodologies fits well with Blumer's (1969) approach to research. He urged researchers to develop "a firsthand acquaintance with the sphere of life under study" (p. 32) by basing their work on "exploration and flexible pursuit of intimate contact with what is going on," "a conscientious and continuous effort to revise" concepts and hypotheses, and the goal of understanding the meanings and interpretations of informants (p. 29). As Blumer noted, this approach is much different from approaches in which researchers are remote from social settings and persons of interest, start with a model and formulate hypotheses on the basis of the model, do not modify the model in the course of conducting research, and use standardized instruments. Getting close and "digging deep" through "careful study," and "respecting the nature" of the phenomena of interest, for Blumer and for qualitative researchers in general "lifts the veils" that obscure the group life we wish to understand so we can "know what is going on" (p. 32). Many of the currently discussed methodologies, such as feminist theory, interpretivism, and hermeneutics, share these goals. In this volume, Daly (Chapter 7), Lightburn (Chapter 12), and Matocha (Chapter 5) demonstrate many of the issues that may arise when researchers become close to family worlds; Gilgun (Chapter 13) shows how therapists and other gatekeepers may block direct access to families.

METHODOLOGIES IN SEARCH OF METHODS

Methodological perspectives infuse all aspects of research processes: the choice of questions, purposes of the research, theories, methods, sampling strategies, data collection, data analysis and interpretation, and writing up the results. Many methodologists, among them Blumer (1969), Hill (1970), Merton (1957), and somewhat more recently, Bailey (1984), have decried the tendency to treat methodology, substantive theory, and methods as if they were separate enterprises. Yet, contemporary discussions of methodology generally do not extend to the implications for methods and findings and often fail to make links with substantive theories. They stop short of delineating methods that might carry forth the methodological principles so ardently espoused. Osmond's (1987) masterful discussion of radical-critical theories is an example of a methodological discussion that fails to indicate how researchers can apply the principles. Conversely, research reports and discussions of substantive theory and method frequently are less than explicit about relevant methodological underpinnings. Many of the chapters in this volume, representing a number of the methodologies discussed earlier, attempt to show connections among methodologies, substantive theories, methods, and findings.

Making these connections is important for qualitative researchers. Much of the research world—as represented by authors of textbooks and articles, by journal and proposal reviewers, and by our colleagues—does not understand qualitative approaches. Making our methodological and theoretical perspectives clear may be a means of helping others understand what we are doing and why. In addition, it is a form of the "thick description" Geertz (1973) described so well and which I discuss later in this chapter.

USING COMBINATIONS OF METHODS
TO APPROACH THESE DIVERSITIES

A methodological underpinning of qualitative family research as represented in this volume is diversity. Qualitative researchers are part of a growing movement of people who understand that families appear in diverse forms in diverse settings, have diverse experiences, and appear differently in different times in history. Because we recognize families as diverse groups, we can ask rhetorically, does one method or one perspective—even one qualitative perspective—fit these diversities? Of course not. When we reflect upon the serious issues with which families contend—poverty, violence, divorce, war, and illness—and the cultural diversity of families, it becomes clear that families are best served by researchers who tailor their research methods to the diversities in which families are embedded.

Along with interviews, participant observation, and document analysis, doing qualitative research with families may involve using questionnaires and standardized instruments. The researchers of the Chicago school of sociology and their contemporary counterparts within the tradition of symbolic interactionism used any method they thought would enlighten them about phenomena of interest (Bulmer, 1984; Denzin, 1970). The studies in most of the chapters in this volume each used at least two methods of qualitative data collection. Two studies combined qualitative and quantitative approaches (Rank, Chapter 15; Sandelowski, Holditch-Davis, & Harris, Chapter 16).

AM I DOING IT RIGHT?

The downside of moving toward diversity of research methods, methodologies, and theories is insecurity. Qualitative researchers are prone to asking: Am I doing it right? Data collection and data analysis in qualitative research, for example, are much more open-ended than in quantitatively oriented procedures. Such open-endedness understandably leads to the question of doing it "right." This is an important question for us because it can spur us on and give us energy for learning how to do it better. Yet, wondering if we are doing it right also can restrict our inner processes and our creativity and therefore our abilities to develop both our research methods and knowledge about families. As increasing numbers of qualitative researchers grapple with the question of whether they are doing it right, my hope is that we will conclude there is no one way to do qualitative family research. The more central questions may be: Am I doing it my way? Am I doing it in ways that fit me in all my diversities? Am I doing it in ways that help me achieve my own research goals? Do my methods fit the diversities of the families with whom I am doing research?

An essential bottom line—and perhaps a guideline for the conduct of qualitative research—is whether we are successful at communicating our processes and our findings. Am I communicating with my audiences? Am

I communicating what my informants are telling me? Are my interpretations faithful to what my informants are telling me? Is my approach getting in the way of what my informants are telling me? We also need to grapple with whether someone else will interpret our data differently. Sometimes others will. Will others see something I cannot see? Are there multiple perspectives in my data? Chances are there are multiple perspectives in our data. We are not necessarily going to be able to see all of them by ourselves as lone researchers.

CLARITY AND THE GATEKEEPERS OF OUR DISCIPLINES

Being clear will help us to communicate with others. A significant group with whom to communicate are the gatekeepers of our disciplines: journal reviewers, reviewers of research proposals, and members of dissertation committees. Gatekeepers are beginning to state they welcome submissions based on qualitative methods. As we clarify our understandings of qualitative research, we will improve our abilities to demonstrate what qualitative research is and what it can do. Qualitative research has characteristics that set it apart from work based on statistics and probability theory and approaches that distance researchers from the social life of interest. As the chapters of this volume show, how qualitative research is done and how findings are presented can be much different from the way most social science research currently is being done. Gatekeepers have a responsibility to learn about qualitative approaches to family research and to judge our work by principles that fit what we are doing (cf. Gilgun, 1991a). As we communicate more clearly and as gatekeepers become educated about qualitative approaches, we will increase opportunities to have our articles accepted for publications, our research proposals funded, and our dissertation proposals supported. Morse (1991) and Sandelowski, Holditch-Davis, & Harris (1989) include excellent discussions of proposal writing and qualitative methods.

THE CENTRALITY OF THEORY

Theory is central in qualitative family research. Not only is development of theory a major goal, but data analysis and interpretation are organized by theory.

Theory as a Purpose of Qualitative Family Research

One of the major tasks of family researchers is the development of family theory. At present, family research is dominated by statistical, hypothesis-testing approaches. A perusal of mainstream family journals supports this observation. Qualitative methods can propel studies of families into new eras of theory development.

Where does theory come from? When I was a graduate student, I sometimes wondered if the origins of theory were supposed to be secret, or at least mysterious. Qualitative methods offer ways to demystify theory development. The procedures of qualitative research make public the processes of developing theory. This is an advantage because it invites others to scrutinize the processes as well as the products. Scrutiny improves the quality of our knowledge.

I take theory development seriously because, given my applied background as a social worker, I know theory has implications for family policy, programs, and practice. In short, theory has implications for personal well-being and the quality of life. During the years in which I worked at using grounded theory approaches (Charmaz, 1990; Corbin & Strauss, 1990; Gilgun, in press; Glaser & Strauss, 1967; Strauss & Corbin, 1989) in my own research, I became persuaded that theory can be developed from grounded theory approaches. When doing grounded theory, researchers systematically develop theory through interweaving observations of phenomena of interest, abstractions from these observations, and previous research and theory. Researchers continually modify their theory to find new findings. Within this tradition, theory is forever tentative, and it forever challenges itself because the next situation to which it may be applied could be different from the situations in which it was developed.

Grounded theory approaches are more likely to generate pattern theory—sometimes called factor theory or concatenated theory—rather than hierarchical theory (Gilgun, in press; see Kaplan, 1964, for a detailed discussion of pattern and hierarchical theory). Most family researchers have been trained to recognize hierarchical theory as theory, and they generally have not been exposed to pattern theory. Briefly, the hypotheses of pattern theory are arranged in horizontal relationship, and the factors composing the theory are assumed to interact. Variations in combinations of factors, their interactions, and situational factors lead to diversity in phenomena of interest. This type of theory is very different from hierarchical theory, where the goal is to produce general principles from which can be deduced hypotheses, which then are tested against the "facts." In hierarchical theory, the route from the empirical world to the conceptual world is conceptualized as a pyramid, with increasing parsimony as the developing theory moves to increasingly higher levels of abstraction. Persons who work in applied family studies may find pattern theory more compatible with their experience because we normatively work within and try to make sense of individual settings. The more "pure" family scientists, who usually are not oriented to individual situations, may find hierarchical theory more compatible with their experience. Both applied and "pure" family scholars, however, use theory in their work. Finally, pattern theory may be more compatible with ideas of diversity, as hierarchical theory can lead to "norming" families and overriding individuality and diversity.

Grounded Theory as a Challenge to Our Expectations

Patterned, grounded theory is the kind of theory that qualitative approaches can provide, but it might not be the kind of theory we have been trained to want to create. Grounded theory by definition is rooted in data, which in turn is rooted in place and time. Yet, much of our training assumes that high-quality theory is independent of persons, places, and time. Cronbach (1975) supported a grounded perspective in reminding us that "any generalization is a working hypothesis, not a conclusion" when applied to local settings (p. 125).

Grounded theory can be of two general types: substantive and formal (Glaser & Strauss, 1967). In substantive grounded theory, the concepts and hypotheses that researchers develop are based on data focusing on one area of study. Discovering similar concepts and hypotheses across areas of study, time, setting, and informants leads to formal theory. Formal grounded theory may have wider explanatory powers than grounded theory based on a single substantive area, setting, time, and sample. For example, the scope and depth of Boss's theory of ambiguous loss increased as she studied these concepts and hypotheses among families of men missing in war, families of Alzheimer's patients, and families with missing children. (See Fravel and Boss, Chapter 8, this volume.)

Grounded Theory as "Real" Theory and as "Thick Description"

Ideologies that view the findings of qualitative research as preludes to the really important and rigorous work of hypothesis testing may obscure the significance of the theory building grounded theory offers. These ideologies relegate theory development to second- or third-class status, dismissing theory generating efforts with such terms as "hypothesis generating" or "exploratory." Almost 30 years ago, Glaser and Strauss (1965) argued persuasively that the substantive theories generated by qualitative approaches are ends unto themselves.

Geertz's (1973) explication of Ryle's (1968) concept of "thick description" is not an argument for detail of description, but an elegant discussion of description as a process of elucidating a matrix of meaning. Geertz pointed out that ethnographers—he used this term because he was writing in the context of social and cultural anthropology—are "faced with . . . a multiplicity of complex conceptual structures, many of them superimposed upon or knotted into one another, which are at once strange, irregular, and inexplicit, and which he [sic] must contrive somehow first to grasp and then to render" (p. 10). In delineating the implications of thick description, Geertz used two of Ryle's examples. One is Ryle's penetrating analysis of the possible meanings of winking and the other is a description of actions and interpretations of three cultural groups—Jewish, Berber, and French—of an incident of robbery and murder in central Morocco in 1912. Just as ethnographers "pick their way" through "piled up structures of inference and meaning" (p. 7), so do researchers on families. The implications of thick description for our understanding of the major issues families face in our day are enormous. If qualitative family researchers could "grasp and render" such thick descriptions, we not only would leap into an era of rich theory building, but we also would have the kind of information we need on which to base enlightened family policy, programs, and practice. The findings would be multilayered, compelling, and hard to ignore.

Grounded Theory and Analytic Induction

The procedures of analytic induction (Bogdan & Biklen, 1982; Robinson, 1951; Znaniecki, 1934) and grounded theory lead to the construction of theory grounded empirically and conceptually. Although these approaches have some procedures in common, they differ in significant ways. Analytic induction, formulated by Znaniecki more than 30 years before Glaser and Strauss (1967) developed grounded theory procedures, seeks to develop theory that approaches universality and is causal in nature. Grounded theorists seek to construct substantive theory and the concepts that compose the theory without emphasis on causality or universality. Procedures in common include modifying hypotheses during the conduct of the analysis, actively seeking to disconfirm emerging hypotheses, and within- and across-case comparisons. A major procedural difference is in the use of prior constructions. Researchers using analytic induction begin the research with a set of hypotheses, sometimes roughly conceptualized and often quite focused. Grounded theorists enter the field in an open-ended way and seek to discover key issues. They do not use prior constructions. Once grounded theorists develop working hypotheses, the distinctiveness of procedures from analytic induction blurs. For the sake of clarity, some methodological discussions have used the term constant comparison in place of grounded theory (e.g., Bogdan & Biklen, 1982; Gilgun, 1991b). Yet, this term does not satisfactorily distinguish between analytic induction and grounded theory, because the former also is a comparative method. For now, we have two terms whose meanings overlap, but which in general stand for two styles of research.

Pattern matching as used in qualitative research has much in common with analytic induction. Like analytic induction, research using this approach begins with a conceptual model based on previous research and theory and, possibly, researchers' experience. Unlike analytic induction, data are collected in a standardized fashion and are not used to change the model until data analysis is complete. The model is like a grid, and its patterns are matched with the patterns discovered through data analysis. Such an approach has much to recommend it, but it rarely is used in family research. Campbell (1979) has been an advocate of both quantified and qualitative pattern-matching research. The study of Rettig & Dahl (1991), although not labeled as a qualitative pattern-matching approach, is an example. The authors used data from one open-ended question from a self-administered questionnaire. As in any other qualitative approach, they coded their data, matched their findings to their prior constructions, and suggested modifications of the prior construction. The use of pattern matching, analytic induction, and grounded theory can lead to compelling thick descriptions.

The Use of Theory to Organize Research Processes

Qualitative methods generate a great deal of data. Various uses of theory organize research processes, from the initial formulation of the research problem through data analysis and interpretation to the creation of the research report. Researchers often use theory to "sensitize" them in the initial stages of the research. As patterns emerge during data collection, at least two types of theory come into play: previous research and theory and hypotheses developed in situ through analysis and interpretation of data. Codes, which are categories around which researchers organize findings, are developed through knowledge of previous theory and the theory developed in situ. Observer comments and memos, written in field notes or recorded on audio- or videotapes, also are theory-generating processes. In addition, researchers often use previous research and theory as they develop their comments and memos. Extended discussions of coding and observer comments are contained in Bogdan and Biklen (1982), Gilgun (1991b), Strauss and Corbin (1990) and throughout the chapters in this volume.

AN APPROACH TO THE CONDUCT OF QUALITATIVE RESEARCH

As this discussion demonstrates and the other chapters in this volume attest, qualitative approaches offer choices of questions, sampling, data collection, analysis, and interpretation within various methodological perspectives. I am most familiar with the processes of grounded theory, which itself is laden with assumptions and values. Even persons with similar training may vary in how they do qualitative research, although there are fundamental commonalities across researchers. In general, however, qualitative researchers analyze and interpret their data during data collection. The following description of the conduct of qualitative research is based on my own experience and the work of Blumer (1969), Bogdan and Biklen (1982), Corbin and Strauss (1990), Glaser and Strauss (1967), and Murphy (1990; Chapter 9, this volume). Researchers generally engage in the following steps:

1. Develop a general area of inquiry based on previous knowledge, such as personal experiences as members of families, observations in clinical practice, or ideas generated through knowledge of research and theory, or a combination of these types of experience.

2. Brainstorm possible research questions.

3. Think about, write down, or discuss your own theoretical perspectives, ideologies, and biases.

4. Review the literature based on what you think is relevant to your area of inquiry.

5. Formulate a list of questions based on numbers 2-4. Symbolic interactionists call these questions "sensitizing." Allow them to change as you collect and analyze data.

6. Develop an idea of the parameters of your study, such as the time you will devote to it, range of informants, and settings. Some people set few parameters and others set more. Many of these decisions are guided by emerging findings.

7. Enter the field as open-mindedly as possible, attempting to be aware of your personal styles, ideologies, and theoretical perspectives and how they may influence how you ask questions, how you present yourself to informants, and how you interpret data.

8. Observe the first case, literally through observation or through combinations of observations and interview questions.

9. Write field notes. Include observer comments in the field notes. (Observer comments are subjective reactions researchers record in field notes, but label as observer comments and set off from the descriptive portions of the notes.)

10. Write memos in the field notes. (Memos are speculative and wide-ranging comments, including comparisons of findings with and across cases, speculations about the theoretical sense of the data, and ideas about the relevance of emerging findings to existing bodies of research and theories.)

11. Develop initial definitions of emerging concepts and speculate on the connections among concepts. These processes are steps toward developing hypotheses.

12. Observe the second case, and as you do, many of your questions will be based on emerging findings.

13. Write field notes, including observer comments and memos as with the first case. Continue to develop definitions of concepts and the connections among them.

14. Compare patterns (hypotheses) within the second case and with patterns in the first case.

15. Change hypotheses to fit both cases.

16. Continue these processes, choosing cases through theoretical sampling—meaning you have a rationale for the selection of the next case—to explore themes further either with similar cases or with cases that vary slightly from the cases you have observed so far.

17. When you have some confidence that you have developed some hypotheses, even if they are tentative, review the literature you think might be relevant to your emerging findings.

18. Link relevant literature to the empirically grounded hypotheses. You could guide your efforts with the question: How do these findings fit with other theories and research in this or related areas? What you develop in this process can be considered theoretical formulations.

19. Test the theoretical formulations on a subsequent case or cases.

20. Change the theoretical formulation to fit the empirical patterns of this subsequent case.

21. Continue this process until you have developed findings that are linked both to phenomena of interest and to theoretical formulations.

Many researchers use computer programs to help them manage their data. Tesch's (1990) work on computer-assisted qualitative analysis provides a helpful overview of current programs.

An enduring question is: When do I stop data collection? Glaser and Strauss (1967) discussed theoretical saturation as the stopping point. This is the point at which researchers no longer are discovering new information. I am not sure I have ever reached an "absolute" theoretical saturation. I consider my findings forever tentative, open to modification through the findings of other researchers or my own subsequent research. At the same time, I have confidence in my findings. They are grounded in data, the concepts and hypotheses I extract from the data have been tested many times within and across cases, and they have been linked to previous research and theory.

DEVELOPING GROUNDED INSTRUMENTS

The development of instruments based on data gathered and analyzed through qualitative methods is an emerging development in family research. Taynor, Nelson, and Daugherty (1990) used procedures similar to grounded theory to construct The Family Intervention Scale, a clinical rating scale. Using data from a study reported in Chapter 13, this volume, I developed clinical rating scales for incest treatment. Imle and Atwood (1988) described procedures for estimating the reliability and validity of The Parenthood Concerns Scale, an instrument they developed through grounded theory methods. They also provided a useful review of how to use qualitatively generated concepts for instrument development.

Grounded theory methods lead to the development of instruments that are grounded in data and thoroughly cover categories of interest. Clinical rating scales developed in this manner fit the treatment setting for which they were constructed, and they are sensitive to change, major advantages over standardized instruments developed through traditional procedures (Gilgun, 1991c).

PRESENTING THE RESULTS

The following chapters of this volume provide examples of how to write up the results of qualitative research. The general principles are (a) to present the general findings, which can be considered hypotheses; (b) to present supporting data under each general finding; (c) to include dominant patterns as well as exceptions to them; and (d) to discuss the linkages of the findings to previous research and theory. These linkages could enhance cross-validation when it exists, or the discussion could point out how the findings enhance previous knowledge, as correctives, as new knowledge, or both. In grounded theory studies, the findings are so extensive that journal-length articles rarely can represent them in their fullness. The chapters in this volume illustrate several styles of writing journal-length articles, including (a) presenting an overview of findings and then elaborating on one or more themes and (b) presenting the range of findings in a cogent and condensed manner. The chapter by Daly, among others in this volume, is an exemplary representative of this second style. Because the general findings of qualitative research can be lost in the wealth of detail, it is helpful to summarize findings at the beginnings of the Results sections and then to repeat the general findings in the Discussion section. Several chapters demonstrate this.

Though not yet appearing in research on families, some approaches present "findings" only; that is, only the words of the informant are presented. Discussions of method and related literature are placed in an appendix or may be absent. Taylor and Bogdan (1984) include several examples of life histories presented in this style.

Performance Science

Performance science eschews written words and presents findings as stage performances. Paget (1990) argued for this mode in terms reminiscent of Ryle's argument for thick description, discussed earlier. She said through a performance an audience could react to complexly textured characters. The layers, the dimensions of live actors performing, would signal so much more than I could communicate in writing. There is something odd about privileging an analysis of discourse in its least robust form, a written text, exploring it in great detail while ignoring the speakers' miens and intentions. (p. 142)

McCall, Becker, and Morris (1987), cited in McCall and Becker (1990), originated performance science. McCall and Becker proposed it as a way of presenting the "multivocality" of texts, as opposed to the "privileged monotone of 'scientific' representations" (p. 118), the former being an analogue of Ryle's thin description, discussed earlier. Another style of performance science is singing the text, a form Helen Kivnick (personal communication, May 1991) sometimes uses to present findings from her fieldwork with elders. As far as I know, performance science has not yet appeared in family research, but its methodological principles could enhance some forms of qualitative family research.

Though not exhaustive, this discussion of presenting results should be helpful to beginning and experienced researchers. Writing up the results has been challenging to me, and I continue to look for more effective ways to present my work. This brief excursion into performance science suggests that others, too, are engaged in similar efforts.

THIS VOLUME AS LIGHTING THE WAY

Most of us still are learning how to think about and do qualitative family research. What is particularly stimulating for me about qualitative approaches is that I continually am learning about how to do my research. The chapters in this volume are intended to light the way for advances both in our approaches to qualitative family research and in our development of solid theory on which to base policy, programs, and practice.

REFERENCES

Baber, K. M., & Allen, K. R. (1991, November). *Toward a postmodern feminist construction of women's sexualities*. Paper presented at the preconference workshop on Theory Construction and Research Methodology, National Council on Family Relations, Denver, CO, November 15-16.

Bailey, K. D. (1984). On integrating theory and method. *Current Perspectives in Social Theory, 6*, 21-44.

Bogdan, R. C., & Biklen, S. K. (1982). *Qualitative research for education.* Boston: Allyn & Bacon.

Blumer, H. (1969). *Symbolic interactionism: Perspective and method.* Englewood Cliffs, NJ: Prentice-Hall.

Bulmer, M. (1984). *The Chicago school of sociology.* Chicago: University of Chicago Press.

Burgess, E. W. (1926). The family as a unit of interacting personalities. *Family, 7,* 3-9.

Campbell, D. T. (1979). "Degrees of freedom" and the case study. In T. D. Cook & C. S. Reichardt (Eds.), *Qualitative and quantitative methods in evaluation research* (pp. 49-67). Beverly Hills, CA: Sage.

Charmaz, K. (1990). "Discovering" chronic illness: Using grounded theory. *Social Science in Medicine, 30,* 1161-1172.

Corbin, J., & Strauss, A. (1990). Grounded theory research: Procedures, canons, and evaluative criteria. *Qualitative Sociology, 13,* 3-21.

Cronbach, L. (1975). Beyond the two disciplines of scientific psychology. *American Psychologist, 39,* 116-127.

Denzin, N. K. (1970). Introduction: The naturalistic perspective. In N. K. Denzin (Ed.), *Sociological methods: A sourcebook* (pp. 7-11). Chicago: Aldine.

Denzin, N. K. (1989). *Interpretive interactionism.* Newbury Park, CA: Sage.

Flax, J. (1987). Postmodernism and gender relations in feminist theory. *Signs, 12,* 621-643.

Flax, J. (1990). *Thinking fragments: Psychoanalysis, feminism, and postmodernism in the contemporary west.* Berkeley: University of California Press.

Geertz, C. (1973). *The interpretation of culture.* New York: Basic Books.

Gilgun, J. F. (1991a). *A case for case studies in social work research.* Manuscript submitted for publication.

Gilgun, J. F. (1991b). Discovery-oriented qualitative methods relevant to longitudinal studies of child abuse and neglect. In R. H. Starr, Jr., & D. A. Wolfe (Eds.), *The effects of child abuse and neglect* (pp. 144-163). New York: Guilford.

Gilgun, J. F. (1991c, August). *Hand into glove: The grounded theory approach and social work practice research.* Paper presented at a conference on Qualitative Methods in Social Work Practice Research, Nelson A. Rockefeller Institute of Government, School of Social Welfare, State University of New York at Albany, Albany, August 23-25.

Gilgun, J. F. (in press). Hypothesis generation in social work research. *Journal of Social Service Research.*

Glaser, B. G., & Strauss, A. L. (1965). Discovery of substantive theory: A basic strategy underlying qualitative research. *American Behavioral Scientist, 8,* 5-11.

Glaser, B. G., & Strauss, A. (1967). *The discovery of grounded theory.* Chicago: Aldine.

Guba, E. G. (Ed.). (1990). *The paradigm dialog.* Newbury Park, CA: Sage.

Harding, S. (1987). *Feminism and methodology.* Bloomington: Indiana University Press.

Hare-Mustin, R. T., & Marecek, J. (Eds.). (1990). *Making a difference: Psychology and the construction of gender.* New Haven, CT: Yale University Press.

Hill, R. J. (1970). *On the relevance of methodology.* In N. K. Denzin (Ed.), *Sociological methods* (pp. 12-19). Chicago: Aldine.

Imle, M. A., & Atwood, J. R. (1988). Retaining qualitative validity while gaining quantitative reliability and validity: Development of the Transition to Parenthood Concerns Scale. *Advances in Nursing Science, 11,* 61-75.

Kaplan, A. (1964). *The conduct of inquiry.* San Francisco: Chandler.

LaRossa, R., Gordon, B. A., Wilson, R. J., Bairan, A., & Jaret, C. (1991). The fluctuating image of the 20th century American father. *Journal of Marriage and the Family, 53,* 987-997.

Lather, P. (1986). Research as praxis. *Harvard Educational Review, 56,* 257-277.

Lincoln, Y., & Guba, E. (1985). *Naturalistic inquiry.* Beverly Hills, CA: Sage.

McCall, M. M., & Becker, H. S. (1990). Performance science. *Social Problems, 37,* 117-132.

Merton, R. K. (1957). *Social theory and social structure* (rev. ed.). Glencoe, IL: Free Press.

Morse, J. M. (1991). On the evaluation of qualitative proposals. *Qualitative Health Nursing, 1,* 147-151.

Murphy, S. (1990). Thoughts about patterns of qualitative research. *Qualitative Family Research, 4*(2), 9-10, 12, 21.

Nuccio, K. E., & Sands, R. G. (in press). Back to the future: Using postmodern feminist theory to deconstruct "phallacies" of poverty. *Social Work.*

Osmond, M. W. (1987). Radical-critical theory. In M. B. Sussman & S. K. Steinmentz (Eds.), *Handbook of marriage and the family* (pp. 103-124). New York: Plenum.

Packer, M. (1985). Hermeneutic inquiry in the study of human conduct. *American Psychologist, 40,* 1081-1093.

Paget, M. A. (1990). Performing the text. *Journal of Contemporary Ethnography, 19,* 136-155.

Polkinghorne, D. (1988). *Narrative knowing and the human sciences.* Albany: State University of New York Press.

Rettig, K. D., & Dahl, C. M. (1991, November). *The unlikely possibility of justice in divorce settlements.* Paper presented at the preconference workshop on Theory Construction and Research Methodology, National Council on Family Relations, Denver, CO, November 15-16.

Robinson, W. S. (1951). The logical structure of analytic induction. *American Sociological Review, 16,* 812-818.

Rosenblatt, P. C., Spoentgen, P., Karis, T. A., Dahl, C., Kaiser, T., & Elde, C. (1991). Difficulties in supporting the bereaved. *Omega, 23,* 119-128.

Ryle, G. (1968). *The thinking of thoughts.* University *Lecutrues,* no. 18. Saskatoon: University of Saskatchewan.

Sandelowski, M., Holditch-Davis, D. H., & Harris, B. G. (1989). Artful design: Writing the proposal for research in the naturalistic paradigm. *Research in Nursing and Health, 12,* 77-84.

Schwandt, T. R. (1990). Paths to inquiry in the social disciplines: Scientific, constructivist, and critical theory methodologies. In E. G. Guba (Ed.), *The paradigm dialog* (pp. 268-276). Newbury Park, CA: Sage.

Strauss, A. L., & Corbin, J. (1990). *Basics of qualitative research.* Newbury Park, CA: Sage.

Taylor, S. J., & Bogdan, R. (1984). *Introduction to qualitative research methods* (2nd ed.). New York: John Wiley.

Taynor, S. J., Nelson, R. W., & Daugherty, W. K. (1990). The Family Intervention Scale: Assessing treatment outcome. *Families in Society, 71,* 202-210.

Tesch, R. (1990). *Qualitative research: Analysis types and software tools.* Philadelphia: Taylor & Francis.

Wilson, S. W., & Hutchinson, S. A. (1991). Triangulation of qualitative methods: Heideggerian hermeneutics and grounded theory. *Qualitative Health Research, 1,* 263-276.

Znaniecki, F. (1934). *The method of sociology.* New York: Farrar & Rinehart.

Part 2

Interviews

Establishing relationships with one or more participants through interviews is foundational in qualitative studies of family experience. The chapters in this section are organized according to the nature of this relationship: one to one, interviews with couples, or interviews involving the participation of several family members.

The first three studies described used interviews with individuals. Susan Snyder recruited couples and then conducted individual interviews with each member of the couple in order to develop a substantive theory of constructions of love. Her interviews were semistructured, meaning that her questioning style fell somewhere between the rigidity of an ordered, formal interview schedule and the looseness of an unstructured exploration of what appears to be meaningful to participants. She posed broad questions within a given area of inquiry, following with reflective comments, probes, and clarifications. Linda Matocha used in-depth case study interviews with persons who care for persons with AIDS. Of interest here is the design of the research: She purposively selected caregivers from a range of family backgrounds with each representing a particular phase in the progression of AIDS. As a result, the design is cross-sectional and the analysis focuses on caregiving experiences as they changed over phases. Dan Detzner used a two-step design, beginning with participant observation and moving to semistructured interviews. Observations and informal interviews helped him see the suitability of a life history approach to research with Southeast Asian elders. With the help of interpreters, he investigated the memories, perceptions, and meanings that elders from Southeast Asian refugee families have developed to explain the changes in their individual and family histories.

Kerry Daly and Deborah Fravel and Pauline Boss used conjoint interviews to get at shared constructions of meanings within marriage. Daly used a two-stage model of data collection. In the first phase, he identified themes through unstructured interviews with couples and participant observation at infertility support group meetings. In the second phase, he used these themes to construct a more structured interview schedule. The implications of being an insider for researcher roles and the validity of data gathered by insiders also are discussed in this paper. Rare insight into the experience of ambiguous loss is achieved in the case study interview by Fravel and Boss. After carefully working through a set of unusual ethical challenges with respect to the protection of anonymity, the two researchers jointly carried out an in-depth, unstructured interview with the parents of three missing children. They demonstrate how a single case study can contribute to formal theory, in this case, the theory of ambiguous loss.

Researchers can elicit multiple perspectives on family experiences through interviews with two or more family members. In an effort to understand sibling relationships within a family context, Susan Murphy interviewed both children and parents. Her purpose was to understand relationships between school-age siblings and newborns within the context of their families. In addition, she used videotapes and drawings as other sources of field data. This grounded theory study is rooted in clinical practice, previous research on sibling relationships, and life-span developmental theory. The longitudinal design of this work is unique in, as Murphy points out, providing an opportunity for both the genera-tion and verification of hypotheses.

Katherine Allen and Alexis Walker took a feminist perspective in their conceptualization, analysis, and interpretation of data from semistructured in-terviews with elderly mothers and their daughters. Responding to the emphasis placed on "burden" in the traditional caregiving literature, they found a feminist approach sensitized them to positive aspects of mother-daughter relationships. They discuss the implications of a feminist approach for their perspective, focus, role, and method of data analysis. Robin Jarrett responds to the quantitative emphasis in the underclass debate with an in-depth, case study look at one family. She used a two-step design that began with a series of focus groups with never-married African-American mothers and moved to family case studies of some of the participants in the focus groups. Jarrett presents a case study of the Moore family, a study she based on a set of naturalistic observations and intensive interviews with several family members. She shows how a single case study can be used as part of a comparative analysis and therefore can both contribute to the development of theory and challenge generalizations about phenomena—such as poor African-American families, who often emerge from aggregate data as stereotypes and not in their variability and diversity.

4

Interviewing College Students About Their Constructions of Love

SUSAN U. SNYDER
Onondaga Pastoral Counseling Center, Syracuse, New York

Recent sociological and philosophical writings have made a strong case for rethinking our conceptualizations about human emotions (Finkelstein, 1980; Jaggar, 1989; Stearns, 1987). Such writings describe the fundamentally social nature of emotion—the embeddedness of its interpretation and modes of expression within our familial, sociocultural, and historical contexts. The research I report on here was motivated by a desire to contribute to the development of theory in the area of love and the family. As a family scholar and family therapist, I am impressed on a daily basis with the significance and power of love in the construction and maintenance of both healthy and dysfunctional couple and family relationships. I am equally impressed with the diverse meanings that love holds for those who experience it and with the numerous behaviors within relationships that are explained with the words, "Because I love him/her/them."

The objectives of my inquiry, then, were twofold: (a) to gain insight into what love meant for individual persons who described themselves as being in love and (b) to arrive at some conceptualization about how dyadic love relationships were constructed. I used qualitative data-gathering and analytic techniques because of my personal interest and my conviction that a phenomenological approach would substantially add to the theoretical and substantive findings to date.

Love: A Theoretical and Methodological Critique

Numerous theories or perspectives on love have been advanced over time (Alberoni, 1983; Branden, 1980; Byrne, 1971; de Rougemont, 1940; Erikson, 1968; Fine, 1985; Freud, 1963; Fromm, 1956; Kenrick & Cialdini, 1977; 1984; Maslow, 1962; May, 1969; Ortega y Gasset, 1957; Peck, 1978; Peele, 1976; Reik, 1941; Schachter & Singer, 1962; Solomon, 1981; Sternberg, 1986; Tennov, 1979). With few exceptions such theorizing has been individualistic rather than structural in nature—explaining love by physiological and psychological forces rather than interpersonal, situational, and historical factors.

Psychoanalytic theory (for example, Freud, 1963; Reik, 1941) accounts for love by repressed drives and unconscious motivations. Misattribution theory (Kenrick & Cialdini, 1977; Schachter & Singer, 1962) contends that love results when an individual labels an unexplained source of physiological arousal (heart palpitations, rapid breathing, etc.) as "love" by relying on social cues. Reinforcement theory (Byrne, 1971) explains love as a fairly simple case of classical conditioning: We like individuals associated with pleasant affective states (i.e., those connected with frustration reduction) and dislike those associated with unpleasant affective states (i.e, those connected with frustration induction). In sum, individualistic theories are based on an implicit assumption that men and women are passive and largely controlled by internal forces.

Less individualistic theoretical perspectives consider the effects of social factors and personal action in the area of love (Alberoni, 1983; Erikson, 1968; Fromm, 1956; Peck, 1978; Solomon, 1981). Additionally, some of the sociological theories concerning love, the family, and mate selection (Bolton, 1961; Goode, 1959; Kerchoff & Davis, 1962; Murstein, 1971; Reiss, 1960; Winch, 1958) have provided important perspectives on the interactional aspects of love relationships. Theory generated by qualitative approaches (Bowker-Larsen, 1990; Kostere, 1990; McCready, 1981; Schwartz & Merten, 1980; Seawell, 1984; M. H. Snyder, 1984; S. U. Snyder, 1986) explores the role of interpretive processes in love relationships and the salience of human beings as symbolizing creatures who actively construct the meaning of their experiences within a specific sociocultural and historical context. Further, because these theories have been systematically induced from the actual experiences of individuals, they also constitute what Glaser and Strauss (1967) referred to as grounded theory.

Social scientists have given significantly more attention to the empirical study of love since the early 1970s. A number of researchers have formulated typologies of love or love scales that variously attempt to discriminate between liking and loving (Rubin, 1973), to discern how romantic an individual is (Knox & Sporakowski, 1968; Munro & Adams, 1978), or to define what form or style of love is characteristic of a particular person (Lasswell & Lobsenz, 1980; Lee, 1976; Tennov, 1979). Developmental trends in the experience of love have been noted (Bokor, 1988; Knox, 1970a, 1970b; Levinger, 1983; Munro & Adams, 1978), as have gender differences (e.g., Brehm, 1985). Females, more than males, generally report more romantic experiences, more intense romantic sensations, and behavior that is affected more by feelings. More romantic attitudes are found among younger individuals, individuals involved in long-term committed relationships (e.g., 20 years or more of marriage), and individuals involved in new romantic relationships.

The area of interpersonal attraction as it relates to love relationships has also been the focus of experimental studies (e.g., Huston, 1974; Levinger & Raush, 1977; Walster & Walster, 1978). Such research has addressed behavioral changes associated with the love experience, and the role of the partner's perceived beliefs, attitudes, and values in mate selection.

In conclusion, quantitative treatments of love have generated a body of significant findings that have both research and clinical applications. Qualitative approaches extend these findings and add a new dimension by emphasizing the role of interpretation and the social construction of reality.

The Case for a Qualitative Approach

Understandings about love are shaped both by the theoretical perspectives of researchers and by the methodologies they employ. Quantitative research designs are informed by logical positivism and are, by their very nature, structured, predetermined, formal, and specific (Bogdan & Biklen, 1982). In many of the foregoing studies, romantic love was assumed to mean the same thing to all those who talked about it (i.e., researchers and subjects). Further, love was often so tightly operationalized or so narrowly focused by the particular methodology that findings sometimes seemed one-dimensional or otherwise lacking in the richness and vitality that common sense understandings about love, or personal experience, might lead one to expect.

Qualitative research methods are specifically designed to explore questions about meaning. Researchers typically use participant observation, in-depth interviewing, or a combination of these data-gathering techniques as primary research instruments and analytic tools. The data generated are thus highly descriptive and expressive of the actual thoughts and feelings of the individuals studied. Hypotheses and generalizations are then derived inductively from the data themselves rather than established a priori at the outset of the study (Bogdan & Taylor, 1984).

The field of marriage and the family is broadening its focus to include a consideration of the process and evolution of close interpersonal relationships. Qualitative methodology is well suited to such a shift.

METHOD

Sample

The sample was one of convenience, selected from students taking an undergraduate class in human sexuality at Syracuse University for which the author was then the teaching assistant. All were young adults in their late teens or early twenties. All were involved in love relationships with only one partner ranging from 8 months to 3 years in duration (The average length of relationship was between 2 and 2-1/2 years).

That the sample was drawn from a human sexuality class had an impact on student interest in the research topic and on the ways in which participants talked about their love experiences. Although no specific inquiries about the interest were built into the study, I have the impression that the students who volunteered to participate were especially thoughtful about their relationships and enjoyed talking at length about them. They also discussed aspects of love and sexuality in terms of some of the ideas expressed by Sol Gordon, the primary instructor of the course (Gordon & Everly, 1983).

Students were eligible to participate in the study if they conformed to the following parameters: were unmarried and without children, were heterosexual, described themselves as being in love with their current partner for a period of at least 3 months, were exclusively involved in the relationship with their current partner for at least 6 months, and were not involved in a long-distance love relationship. Some of these parameters (such as those concerning sexual orientation) were arbitrary and were established solely for the purpose of limiting the scope of the research. Others served to define the author's specific interests: the desire to study unmarried and childfree couples who were involved in an ongoing, committed love relationship exclusively with each other. Learning how a love relationship is constructed required access to both members of a couple. The examination of long-distance relationships was impractical from the standpoint of being able to meet with individuals on a regular basis over time, and so these were excluded from study. To promote intensive analysis and corresponding development of a rich conceptual framework, a relatively small sample size was selected.

I recruited a total of 10 couples from the human sexuality class over two consecutive semesters, with several stages involved in the sampling process. First, I developed a list of potential participants. In the first semester of the academic year, I randomly selected two couples from this volunteer pool and interviewed them. The following semester, I chose eight additional couples from the same list, with selection informed by the concept of theoretical sampling (Glaser & Strauss, 1967). Theoretical sampling is an intentional approach to data collection based upon careful determination of theoretical purpose and relevance. Because my first two couples were both from the senior class, both Caucasian, both exemplifying relatively long-term relationships, and both sexually active, I decided to select additional couples with different characteristics in order to broaden my conceptual base.

Each member of a couple was interviewed individually. Participants took part in a series of three in-depth interviews, with the time commitment per individual totaling 3 to 5 hours over the course of 2 to 3 weeks. The decision not to conduct conjoint couple interviews in addition to the individual interviews was a difficult one, and was largely based upon the practical considerations of time, money, and the ability to complete comprehensive analysis of all of the data. Due to my own personal interests, I also placed slightly more research emphasis on obtaining as comprehensive an understanding as possible of individual constructions of love. The trade-off, therefore, was in the area of interactional data. Because I did not speak with couples together, the induction of shared constructions of love was based upon participant reports of how they acted and felt in relationship with their loved one.

The Nature of the Interviews

Symbolic interactionism (Blumer, 1969; Mead, 1934) places a premium on the personal and social construction of meaning and the essential importance of interpretation in human experience. Although such a perspective establishes no definite working hypotheses at the beginning of a study, it is common to begin with some general sensitizing questions to stimulate critical thinking. The meaning of sensitizing questions is here derived from Blumer's (1954) discussion of sensitizing concepts: points of reference that provide guidance for the researcher in approaching the empirical world. The following represent the kinds of questions raised at the outset of the research:

1. If love exists, how is it known by those who experience it?
2. How is love talked about and thought about?
3. What is the vocabulary of love, and how might it relate to individuals' implicit assumptions and theories of what love is all about?
4. When individuals say that they are in love, what do they mean?
5. What are the dimensions of the love experience?
6. How is love distinguished from not-love, or "real" love from facsimile?
7. What influences how individuals come to perceive and conceptualize the love experience for themselves?
8. How do individual understandings about love translate into a dyadic experience?
9. How is a love "relationship" constructed?

As Bogdan and Biklen (1982) noted, in-depth interviewing may best be considered along a continuum. Some researchers make use of a formal interview schedule in which the same questions are covered with all participants in roughly the same order. This very structured approach may be contrasted with the unstructured interview with very loosely defined queries posed by an interviewer who prefers instead to track and explore what seems meaningful to the particular person.

My own approach to interviewing fell somewhere in the middle of this continuum and may be thought of as semistructured. Ten general topical areas were probed to some degree with all participants, depending on the extent to which the topic(s) seemed meaningful to the individual and relevant to his or her love experience. These areas were: participants' relationships in their families of origin and influences on their ideas about love, sexuality, and male-female relationships; felt degree of commitment to partner; societal and cultural influences on the love experience; prototypical experiences (i.e., how the love relationship was unique); changes effected by the love experience (e.g., in self-concept); development and experience of the current love relationship; sexuality; past love relationships; perception of the partner's experience; and a miscellaneous category that addressed compatibility issues and questions of "real" love, ideal love, and the role of fantasy in the love relationship.

My interviewing style was to pose as broad a question or idea as possible within a given area of inquiry and then to track and clarify participants' responses through reflective comments and follow-up questions. I attempted to "match" participants' vocabulary preferences and manner of expression throughout the interviews. In this way, probes related to the broader content areas described above were uniquely tailored for each individual.

Special Issues and Ethical Concerns

Although all researchers face ethical dilemmas, the kinds of issues that qualitative family researchers face are unique in that they actively have chosen to enter into a personal relationship with the participants. Thus, qualitative researchers are more likely to become party to participants' intimate thoughts and feelings and may also become aware of conflicts and abuses. With regard to participants' discussions of their private experiences, I was sensitive to the importance of rapport and the need for anonymity and confidentiality. I met with participants at their own apartments or dorm rooms and dressed casually for the interviews. Emotionally charged issues such as race and ethnicity were discussed openly with participants for whom there was relevance (e.g., the interracial and interreligious couples in the study); no conflicts or overt discomfort about such discussions emerged. I assured all persons that names and identifying information would be altered during the write-up of the research, and I emphasized that I would not discuss any of what they told me with their partners. In addition, I explicitly stated that it was OK not to discuss any given issue if they found it too uncomfortable to do so.

Participants would occasionally express concern about my reactions to their responses. For example, it was not uncommon for some of them to preface their remarks with, "You're gonna think this is stupid," or "You're gonna think I'm a terrible person." Also, many asked what I thought about a particular issue or wondered aloud how other people in the study were responding. I assured them that I was not judging them on their remarks and that I was really most interested in whatever was meaningful to them. I also pointed out that for any given query a whole range of responses was typical and said that I would be happy to make the final results available to them so that they could get a sense about how others reported upon their experiences. In most instances these kinds of responses were reassuring to participants, and as rapport continued to develop, it was rare for people to report being uncomfortable with my questions or observations.

An ethical issue emerged concerning whether or how to respond to couples who were clearly experiencing serious conflicts. Some persons directly asked me for advice, but others seemed to be less conscious of their intense difficulties. In both cases, my roles as therapist and researcher were clearly at odds. To intervene in the couple relationship directly by identifying obvious conflicts or dysfunctional patterns or by offering corrective suggestions would be overstepping the bounds of our stated relationship with one another. Such interventions would jeopardize the validity of the research data, and in some cases, identifying a pattern of behavior or particular couple interaction as problematic would be placing *my* construction of reality on their experience. In addition, to suggest change in relationship dynamics would potentially change the way in which relationship meaning was constructed.

I decided to respond to couples in difficulty, but never gave direct advice during the course of the interviews. I privately noted throughout the study which couples might benefit from therapeutic intervention, and at the end of our time together I offered to help clarify the conflicts and make referrals for professional assistance. I also made it clear that it would not be possible for me simultaneously to be both researcher and therapist. One individual and one couple that broke up during the course of our interviews were referred for therapy. These participants followed up on the referrals, and I later learned that the couple reconciled and was engaged to be married. (See Daly's introduction, Chapter 1, and Matocha, Chapter 5, this volume, for additional perspectives on these dilemmas.)

Finally, I experienced a sense of ongoing responsibility to the participants in my study. Therefore, I kept them informed about the progress of the research and notified them when and in what form the results would be available. I also gave those persons who expressed interest a copy of their transcripts or audiotapes.

ANALYSIS

An ongoing dialogue between data collection, identification of significant themes, and subsequent coding and analysis is a hallmark of qualitative research (Bogdan & Biklen, 1982; Denzin, 1978; Glaser & Strauss, 1967; Schwartz & Jacobs, 1979). Ideally, these processes occur simultaneously—in a pulsating fashion—over the course of the research. As Bogdan and Biklen (1982) pointed out, however, the bulk of analysis actually often happens after researchers leave the field and have more time to sift carefully through their data. This was the case in my study. Some analysis did in fact take place during the interviews. For example, I continually made decisions regarding which themes to pursue with people, how to structure probes, when to diverge from the interview outline to pursue what emerged as meaningful in the context of the interviews. All of these kinds of decisions were based upon in-the-field analysis of participants' material. The additional detailed analyses necessary for conceptualization occurred primarily after interviewing was complete and interview transcripts were available to study and code. The actual data consisted of the complete transcripts from 12 individuals (six couples), partial transcripts from the remaining 8 individuals (four couples), and analytic memos I had written during both the course of the research and the process of writing up the study. In these memos, I attempted to document the analytic process and included such information as personal reactions to participants and how the study was proceeding, themes that emerged over the course of the interviews, and comments about the dynamics of couples' relationships.

The volume of interview data was substantial, amounting to between 900 and 1,000 pages of transcript. Analytic memos comprised approximately 100 additional pages. The decision to limit the transcription process occurred midstream during the research because of the large amount of accumulated data and time constraints. Although the possibility remained that new subcategories of interest might emerge from line-by-line analysis of the untranscribed data, I was confident that I already had identified the major categories involved in the construction of the individual and couple theoretical frameworks in previously transcribed data. Further, I thoroughly reviewed the audiotapes from the partially transcribed interviews with an eye toward gleaning all information relevant to the induction process. The method of analysis consisted of a combination of modified analytic induction (Becker,

1963; Bogdan & Biklen, 1982; Glaser & Strauss, 1967; Robinson, 1951; Turner, 1953) and the constant comparative method (Glaser, 1978; Glaser & Strauss, 1967). The former involves establishing an early definition (theory) from the data of what the participant's experience is about and then holding all subsequent data up to this theory to test for fit—i.e., Does the initial understanding of an individual's experience hold up under the pressure of subsequent data? If not, how might his/her experience be explained in a way that would account for new material? The goal of this process is both a comprehensive and refined conceptualization of participants' experiences.

The constant comparative method is designed for use in studies with multiple sources of data and was appropriate for my research because I considered each member of the 10 couples a separate data source. Multiple comparisons of individuals' experiences were therefore possible. The method supports the researcher's focusing in on key issues (themes) that emerge from the data and become categories of interest. Many incidents of these categories are subsequently collected, with emphasis placed upon seeing the diversity of the data within categories. That is, the researcher must attempt to work with the creative tension that exists between generalizing from (categorizing) data and awareness of the uniqueness of individual experiences. Relationships between categories are later identified, with analysis and discussion centered around those that are most significant. The combination of the two related approaches proved most useful because it enabled a comprehensive examination of multiple aspects of each individual's experience as well as a comprehensive examination of how each individual's experience was both similar to and different from every other individual's experience.

The mechanical tasks of the analysis were facilitated by the QUALOG series of mainframe computer programs designed to sort and code qualitative data and test for relationships among the categories established (Shelly & Sibert, 1985).

FINDINGS

Love is a metaphor, a kind of shorthand, for a complex system of attitudes, beliefs, feelings, and behaviors. It is actively constructed both by persons individually, and by couples involved in love relationships.

The Personal Construction of Love

Love Talk

People's "love talk" is the principal organizing concept from which all of the following individual and couple constructions of love are induced. An analysis of how participants spoke about love revealed that in many ways, each individual has his/her own unique definitions. I derived these definitions from the metaphors and idiosyncratic key words and phrases that participants used to describe their experiences:

Interviewer: I'm interested in learning how people think about love . . .

Jim: Love. It's a state of mind that two people are in. It's in varying degrees—there's love for your family, love for your friends, love for your partner. Love for pets. Love for a hobby, etcetera. There's all different kinds of love.

Jason: So—what do you mean? Define it? Oh gee—that's a tough one. Um . . . hmmm. How to define love. [long pause] I don't know, it's more a—I don't think it really is definable. It's just a feeling. Uh, emotional.

"Thinkers" and "Feelers"

One aspect of individuals' definitions of love concerns their orientation along a thinking-feeling continuum. Jim was more "cerebral" and had no difficulty responding to my probe, but it would have been more congruent with Jason's experience if I asked him how he *felt* about love. This interchange is illuminating from a number of standpoints. It illustrates first how people's love talk can be an analytic window through which beginning hypotheses and theory develop (i.e., there are "thinkers" and "feelers"). It illustrates, too, how qualitative research becomes a truly interactive process. I had learned something important about the nature of Jason's experience, and I would subsequently modify my probes and vocabulary to be more in line with it (i.e., more "feeling oriented").

Personal Theories

The foregoing transcript excerpts also show two very different conceptualizations about love: Jim's response indicates that love is a kind of typology; Jason's experience is more ineffable, mysterious. It was possible to begin to group the 20 participants' definitions of love into larger *personal theories*. For the purposes of the study, personal theory refers to a relatively broad conception of love that was not explicitly stated as such—i.e., no participant said, "This is my theory of love." Recurrent themes in the data warranted these generalized categorizations of people's experiences, however. An example of the kind of data from which the Love as Mystery personal theory was induced follows:

Suzanne: I think we happened to end up together because of the way we both are. You know, we just had something that clicked— like fate. And it's not something you can plan. It just sort of happened—you really don't know why.

Perry: It's a freak—I just found the right person. . . . It's beyond me. I guess somebody up there is playing the cards. I can't figure it out. It's all fate, I guess.

Betty: It was mostly fate, I think. If there had been somebody else better looking, if I had been in a different mood or had gotten to the party an hour later, I never would have met Bill. I was wearing my lucky hat that night, too . . .

The personal theories I identified through the induction process were: (a) Love "Types" (e.g., Jim's description of love for family, friends, partner, etc.); (b) Love as Learning (the more "love experience" you accrue, the better partner you are in a love relationship); (c) Love as Completion (love is the missing puzzle piece that somehow completes the part of the self that is missing); (d) Love as Anchor (love as the safe port in the storm, the haven in a heartless world); (e) Love as Mystery; (f) Love as Natural (love as inevitable, a kind of biological imperative); and (g) Love Is Here and Now (past relationships were once believed to be "true love," but *this* one is the real thing).

Participants often subscribed to more than one personal theory and sometimes to incompatible theories (e.g., love as both mysterious and rational). This finding highlights the need to appreciate the complexity of individuals' subjective experience. The data also indicated that members of couples frequently shared the same, or compatible, personal theories. For example, Jason and his partner, Suzanne, together formed a "mysterious" couple. Such similarity within couples will be noted in later sections. The existence of such convergence or divergence of meaning and interpretation is not the crucial issue, however. The process by which couples negotiate the similarities and differences is what is most essential in the shared construction of love—and ultimately in the maintenance of the love relationship.

Love Dimensions

Different dimensions of the love experience also became apparent through the analysis of people's love talk. The experience of self is transformed through a complicated process of affirming and differentiating love from all other experiences. People come to recognize changes in their subjective realities, which they subsequently label as "love." Substantial shifts in inner and outer awareness, of the sense of oneself and one's place in the world, accompany this process.

Participants associated love with an energizing and affirming state of being. They reported feeling happier, more secure, more understanding, and generally more worthwhile. The world itself sometimes looked better—or worse. Some participants noted, for example, that feelings of jealousy, pain, and fear of loss or separation from the loved one were particularly instrumental in helping them to label the experience as love:

> *Shannon:* Paul and I had never discussed our feelings for each other until a week before he was gonna come to my house. That weekend there was a party in the dorm and one of his old girlfriends came to the party. And she was clinging to Paul and was very attached to him. And I think that's when I realized how deeply I felt for him, because I was jealous.

Such subjective changes are but a part of the process of objectifying the new love reality. Love becomes real when people talk and behave in ways consistent with their understandings of the experience. Saying "I love you," for example, profoundly alters the personal experience of everyday life:

> *Interviewer:* Could you say more about your reactions to being told that someone loves you? You said that it was kind of scary.
>
> *Maria:* Yeah, it was. Because it meant seriousness with somebody. And I didn't want that seriousness. "I love you" is too high of a step—I didn't want my feelings involved with any guy.

Interviewer: Because if feelings got involved . . . it's almost as if you were
                 not wanting something to happen. Is that right?

      Maria: Yeah. Yeah, I didn't want to lose my freedom, that's one
                 thing. Because if somebody loves me and I get involved with
                 that person, it changes everything. It changes all, everything.

Past, present, and future are also redefined as the loved one becomes
a part of subjective reality. Society is perceived differently. How love
is portrayed in the larger sociocultural milieu is reevaluated in light of
individual experience and expectations:

      Chris: When I see a black and white couple, when I see people who
                 are different and who are together, I get excited because
                 they're different: They're making it, they're going through
                 what we're going through. Like when I see a black and white
                 couple with a baby, I want to run up to them and ask them
                 how it's working out—do both families approve of them, do
                 they see the baby?

Realizing love also involves a reexamination and reinterpretation of
personal history. The individual engages in a process of evaluating the
present love relationship in light of past loves, other kinds of relationships (e.g., friendships), and personal maturity. A common sentiment
expressed by participants was that the current love was better or truer
than previous love experiences for a variety of reasons—some of which
included the assessment that past relationships were actually "puppy"
loves, or "flings."

The Couple Construction of Love

Chronology and Choreography

The construction of a love relationship involves the ongoing negotiation of lovers' individual subjective realities. The couple identity, or
love system, is therefore appropriately conceived of as a dynamic
process characterized by attempts to synchronize individual feelings
and experiences. There are two fundamental dimensions of couple love:
chronology and choreography. *Chronology* refers to the time dimension

of the love relationship, *choreography* refers to the enactment dimension, i.e., how couples orchestrate their relationship with one another (private) and in the social sphere (public). Erving Goffman's (1959) concept of *performance team* is useful in thinking about couple choreography: A successful love performance is dependent upon lovers coming to behave, believe, and feel in a harmonious manner with each other.

The Love Story

The performance begins with the *love story,* which chronicles the couple's first meeting and initial reactions to one another. Particular marker events come to be associated with the development of the love system—occurrences that punctuate the couple chronology and define the relationship as real. These typically include memories of experiences of we-ness, a subjective awareness of being with and uniquely important to the loved one:

> ***Bill:*** The weekend that I went to visit Betty and we spent a lot of time in New York City really cemented the relationship. Things just seemed to fall into place. I think we dropped our expectations—and I think the relationship has been on the same level ever since. It was a major turning point in our relationship. It gave us a boost upward in intensity and level.

Enactment (choreography) of we-ness can vary with particular stage and typically manifests persons' experiences of mutuality—the deepening sense that one's partner feels and thinks the same way as oneself. People test for mutuality by objectifying their love in words, cards, songs, and other actions (e.g., suggesting a candlelight dinner). Such testing is simultaneously exciting and terrifying: Will the potential loved one respond and reciprocate?

> ***Shannon:*** I was afraid to tell Paul that I was becoming attached to him and thought that we could go somewhere in the relationship because I was afraid maybe he wasn't feeling that way and maybe I was reading him all wrong. You know, maybe I was just wanting him to show some feeling toward me, when in reality it wasn't even there. Maybe I was just imagining all this.

Mutuality and Enacting Roles of Loved One

Establishing the roles of loved one occurs in tandem with the realization of mutuality. The transition to these roles shakes up the previously shared understandings about the meaning of the relationship. The experience of self and other may radically change, along with expectations about how to behave in the relationship:

> **Ellen:** Valentine's Day is our anniversary, and that was the first time that Perry let me know he had feelings for me that were more than friendship. He gave me this card, and I was so surprised. It was like I started to see him through different eyes. I got shy, I didn't know what to do. And for a while after that—maybe a couple of weeks or so—we were in a transition. Neither of us knew what the other was thinking. There were times when I wanted to take his hand when we were walking together but I was afraid, kinda—I didn't know what I should be doing. It seemed like neither of us wanted to be pushy.

The meanings of loved one are constructed by the couple, and partners' individual definitions about the roles must be sufficiently similar for the love system to endure. As an illustration, note how Bob talked about why his relationship with a former girlfriend ended:

> **Bob:** Everyone has their own interpretation of what "girlfriend" means. It can range from a real casual kind of thing—you know, like just seeing someone. Or it can refer to someone you really truly love, like being preengaged. And I guess it was in my past relationship with Girl X that I first realized that everyone does have a different interpretation. I thought we were girlfriend and boyfriend. She thought we were just seeing each other. Her idea was a lot different—she felt she could see other people. Whereas I—I guess I liked her more than she liked me. I agreed to it, but I thought we were more girlfriend and boyfriend . . .

Couple Identity and Team Impression

The couple identity, then, is not a static entity but an evolving process. Like ballet dancers in a pas de deux, lovers must choreograph and synchronize their individual, separate rhythms in ways that create a united performance. This team impression is a publicly choreographed expression of the understandings that couples arrive at about how they will fit together. Love is a metaphor for these understandings.

One of the primary understandings that must be negotiated is who will take the lead in particular areas of the relationship: i.e., how will the energy of the love system be expressed, modulated? Frequently, one partner is the more "energetic" in a particular area of the relationship:

> *Maria:*   Byron will just make friends with anybody. Anybody. I get very embarrassed when he does that, because I'm not that way. It's very hard for me to make friends. I'm really very shy.

The flip side of the coin is that the "teammate" (Goffman, 1959) often provides a kind of direction or stability to the partner's activity or expressiveness in other areas of their relationship together: There is a reciprocal and mutually reinforcing aspect to couples' interactions. For example, Maria functions in ways that modulate Byron's expressiveness:

> *Maria:*   He really needs my stability, I think. He's too hyper about everything. Like spending money. I know I control him from going splurge, splurge—buying everything. I just tell him, "If you need it, go ahead. But if you don't need it, wait." He's really dependent on me for that.

Individual couples also channel energy in particular directions, resulting in the development of a *love theme:* a public enactment of what the couple "stands for." Love themes are best conceived as central tendencies in couples' interactions and are illustrative of some of the significant ways in which persons have negotiated fit in their relationships. Some of the couples in the current study embodied a particular theme more than others; not every couple could be readily described in terms of a theme. The themes I identified are:

- The Caretakers: Love as Nurturant, Protective. Love was the solution to partners' complementary needs to parent, be parented.
- The Entrepreneurs: Love as Pragmatic, Opportunistic. Love was the solution to partners' mutual desires to get ahead, be successful.
- The Individualists: Love as Liberating. Love was the solution to partners' mutual wishes to preserve individuality and autonomy.
- The Rebels: Love as Binding in the Face of Opposition. Love was the solution to partners' needs to rebel against outside (family) expectations and yet remain connected in a significant relationship.

Communication and the Continuation of "We"

The negotiation of team impression and enactment of love themes most often occurs out of couples' awareness. Communication emerged as the critical, mediating factor in maintaining shared definitions about such relationship dynamics, however. Partners who don't sustain the team impression may be experienced as "performance risks" (Goffman, 1959). This seemed to be the case for Maura and Ray, a "caretaking" couple who were having increasing difficulty with maintaining shared understandings about their roles. Maura and Ray's ultimate breakup may be understood in part as a failure to renegotiate a change in the their couple choreography:

Interviewer: What do you mean when you say you've changed, Maura?

Maura: Well, maybe I got a little too dependent on Ray for my happiness. I've learned now to be happy without him. I've kinda become more independent. . . . And now I'm thinking maybe what I say gives off the impression to him that I might take a job over him. That maybe he thinks I don't need him as much. . . . I guess it is hard for him because I do change.

The continuation of love systems, then, is dependent upon couples' ability to communicate about and cope effectively with change and the inherent tension in maintaining both shared and separate identities. The ways in which couples manage this can only be fully appreciated in context, by considering the day-to-day functioning of the love team. This includes examining how time is spent, how decisions are made, how conflict is addressed, the meaning and degree of intimacy in the relationship, the role of sexuality, and the place of outsiders (e.g., friends, family, larger sociocultural milieu). Love, then, may also be understood as a metaphor for couples' "rules" about the above: What are partners' beliefs about what is important in the private world of their relationship, and are these beliefs sufficiently similar to allow a "we" to continue?

Janie: To have a relationship you have to start out with a couple of basic building blocks. An example is trust, which is very, very important in our relationship. I first have to trust that we don't have to be together all day, that I don't have to worry that he's fooling around with someone. And caring for a person—knowing that if I do get hurt he'll be there. I would

> say these are basic things. Honesty is another one. . . . I don't
> have to worry: Is he really telling me the truth—or is he
> saying this to make me feel better? . . . Those things for me
> make everything.

The private world of couples in love is characterized by its own unique language. Pet names or other private couple talk help to establish the boundaries between the love system and the outside world and define the former as a secret society with its own unique inner workings. These inner workings include the celebration of special days and dates, the creation of couple traditions, and the acquisition of specific *love trappings* (e.g., "our songs," love letters, lockets). The meaning of these for couples is related to the experience of their uniqueness—the sense that no one else has ever before felt or expressed love in this way. This is why it is appropriate to think of love as being recreated anew by every couple that experiences it. The building and recalling of memories is an especially powerful form of couple communication because it objectifies and recreates love and functions as testimony to the couple's history together.

DISCUSSION AND IMPLICATIONS

One of the primary contributions of this research is the induction of grounded, substantive theory in the area of love. As such, the study represents an attempt to dereify love by considering it within the context of everyday life and as a creation of human action. Paradoxically, the elaboration of the social construction of love among 20 college students was itself also partially a study of reification, "the apprehension of human phenomena as if they were things, that is, in non-human or possibly suprahuman terms" (Berger & Luckmann, 1966, p. 89). This is not surprising: U.S. society presents few realistic images and role models for love. Consider one of our most popular symbols for the experience—Cupid's arrow plunging into the heart of the unsuspecting potential lover who subsequently succumbs to a kind of "love swoon." From this point of view, love simply happens to us. We are "struck" by it, perhaps even "blinded." Those who subscribe to the Love as Mystery, Love as Natural theories exemplify this kind of perspective.

My research suggests an alternative understanding of love—namely, that love's complexity and the unique meanings that it has for those who experience it can only be appreciated when it is understood as *negotiated reality*. Love is created through the interaction of persons and is a metaphor for the beliefs, feelings, attitudes, and behaviors associated with a uniquely human experience. Thus, love is conceptualized as simultaneously ordinary and extraordinary (exhilarating!) . . . *because* it is actively constructed by human beings within the context of their everyday lives.

Clinical Applications

The potential clinical applications of my findings are significant. Clinicians are in a powerful position to challenge the reified, external-locus-of-control theories that pervade our culture and to extend these with an appreciation of love as a belief system that orders personal and social worlds by defining roles and understandings. Specific recommendations for clinical practice follow:

- Identify in your role as clinician the personal theory(ies) you construct with respect to love and how these influence your work with clients.
- Consider how individual and couple love talk might help you to access clients' implicit belief systems about love and human relationships.
- Question clients closely about terminology. Ask them to define the meaning of terms (e.g., "boyfriend," "commitment," "intimacy," etc.). Keep in mind that the members of couples need to negotiate meanings within their relationship and that definitions must be sufficiently similar for their system to endure.
- Help persons to begin to identify their personal and couple mythologies about love—particularly those mythologies derived from a failure to perceive themselves as architects of their own experience or relationship.
- When working with love systems, defocus from couples' love talk per se and attend to how they negotiate shared reality: What is the choreography or team impression? Where are they in their chronology and the process of determining mutuality and establishing a "we"?
- Teach about love themes, and make explicit the implicit understandings couples construct about roles. What are the relationship rules? How successfully have they been able to respond to competing needs for shared and separate identities and to manage the conflict associated with such tension?
- Teach about the inevitability of change—including change of individuals' subjective feelings about themselves, their partner and their relationship. Renegotiating shared understandings about these is one key to relationship survival.

Recommendations for Future Research

My recommendations for future research have two different but related thrusts. The first is to continue development of substantive theory in the area of love by studying the experiences of other populations and age groups (e.g., married couples, the elderly, homosexuals) to gather important data about the ways in which personal meanings change over time, and how the chronology and choreography of different kinds of love relationships are similar and unique.

My second recommendation is for the construction of formal theory, "that developed for a formal, or conceptual, area of sociological inquiry, such as stigma, deviant behavior, formal organization, socialization . . . " (Glaser & Strauss, 1967, p. 32). Comparative study of the conceptual frameworks induced from the social construction of anger, fear, grief, etc. would provide additional rungs on the ladder toward development of formal grounded theory in the area of human emotions and the family. Concepts such as chronology and choreography, synchronization, performance team, relationship rules and roles might be useful in understanding the full range of affective experiences.

REFERENCES

Alberoni, F. (1983). *Falling in love.* New York: Random House.
Becker, H. S. (1963). *Outsiders: Studies in the sociology of deviance.* New York: Free Press.
Berger, P. L., & Luckmann, T. (1966). *The social construction of reality.* Garden City, NY: Anchor.
Blumer, H. (1954). What is wrong with social theory? *American Sociological Review, 19,* 3-10.
Blumer, H. (1969). *Symbolic interactionism: Perspective and method.* Englewood Cliffs, NJ: Prentice-Hall.
Bogdan, R., & Biklen, S. K. (1982). *Qualitative research for education: An introduction to theory and methods.* Boston: Allyn & Bacon.
Bogdan, R., & Taylor, S. (1984). *Introduction to qualitative research methods* (2nd ed.). New York: John Wiley.
Bokor, E. (1988). Love styles and relationship development. (Doctoral dissertation, University of Cincinnati, 1988). *Dissertation Abstracts International, 48*(12), 3673B.
Bolton, C. C. (1961). Mate selection as the development of a relationship. *Marriage and Family Living, 22,* 234-240.
Bowker-Larsen, J. K. (1990). Women's images of intimacy: Personal voices. (Doctoral dissertation, University of Oregon, 1990). *Dissertation Abstracts International, 50*(9), 2703-2704A.
Branden, N. (1980). *The psychology of romantic love.* New York: Bantam.

Brehm, S. S. (1985). *Intimate relationships*. New York: Random House.

Byrne, D. (1971). *The attraction paradigm*. New York: Academic Press.

Denzin, N. K. (1978). *The research act* (2nd ed.). New York: McGraw-Hill.

de Rougemont, D. (1940). *Love in the western world*. New York: Harcourt & Brace.

Erikson, E. (1968). *Identity: Youth and crisis*. New York: Norton.

Fine, R. (1985). *The meaning of love in human experience*. New York: John Wiley.

Finkelstein, J. (1980). Considerations for a sociology of the emotions. *Studies in Symbolic Interaction, 3,* 111-121.

Freud, S. (1963). *Sexuality and the psychology of love* (P. Rieff, Ed.). New York: Collier.

Fromm, E. (1956). *The art of loving*. New York: Bantam.

Glaser, B. (1978). *Theoretical sensitivity: Advances in the methodology of grounded theory*. Mill Valley, CA: Sociology Press.

Glaser, B., & Strauss, A. (1967). *The discovery of grounded theory: Strategies for qualitative research*. Chicago: Aldine.

Goffman, E. (1959). *The presentation of self in everyday life*. New York: Doubleday Anchor.

Goode, W. J. (1959). The theoretical importance of love. *American Sociological Review, 24,* 38-47.

Gordon, S., & Everly, K. (1983). *How can you tell if you're really in love?* (rev. ed.). Fayetteville, NY: Ed-U Press.

Huston, T. L. (1974). *Foundations of interpersonal attraction*. New York: Academic Press.

Jaggar, A. M. (1989). Love and knowledge: Emotion in feminist epistemology. *Inquiry, 32,* 151-176.

Kenrick, D. L., & Cialdini, R. B. (1977). Romantic attraction: Misattribution versus reinforcement explanations. *Journal of Personality and Social Psychology, 35,* 381-391.

Kerchoff, A. C., & Davis, K. E. (1962). Value consensus and need complementarity in mate selection. *American Sociological Review, 27,* 295-303.

Knox, D. (1970a). Conceptions of love at three developmental levels. *Family Coordinator, 19,* 151-157.

Knox, D. (1970b). Conceptions of love by married college students. *College Student Survey, 4,* 28-30.

Knox, D., & Sporakowski, M. J. (1968). Attitudes of college students toward love. *Journal of Marriage and Family, 30,* 638-642.

Kostere, D. M. (1990). What is the experience of romantic love? (Doctoral dissertation, Union Institute, 1990). *Dissertation Abstracts International, 50*(11), 5322B.

Lasswell, M., & Lobsenz, N. M. (1980). *Styles of loving*. New York: Ballantine.

Lee, J. A. (1976). *The colors of love*. Englewood Cliffs, NJ: Prentice-Hall.

Levinger, G. (1983). Development and change. In H. H. Kelley (Ed.), *Close relationships* (pp. 315-359). New York: Freeman.

Levinger, G., & Raush, H. L. (Eds.) (1977). *Close relationships: Perspectives on the meaning of intimacy*. Amherst: University of Massachusetts Press.

Maslow, A. H. (1962). *Toward a psychology of being*. Princeton, NJ: Van Nostrand.

May, R. (1969). *Love and will*. New York: Norton.

McCready, L. (1981). Experiences of being in love: An interview study describing peak times in reciprocal love relationships. (Doctoral dissertation, New York University,

1981). *Dissertation Abstracts International, 42*(7), 2994B-2995B. (University Microfilms No. DA8127933)

Mead, G. H. (1934). *Mind, self, and society.* Chicago: University of Chicago Press.

Munro, B. E., & Adams, G. R. (1978). Love American style: A test of role structure theory on changes in attitudes toward love. *Human Relations, 31,* 215-228.

Murstein, B. I. (1971). *Theories of attraction and love.* New York: Springer.

Ortega y Gasset, J. (1957). *On love: Aspects of a single theme* (T. Talbot, Trans.). New York: Meridian.

Peck, M. S. (1978). *The road less traveled.* New York: Simon & Schuster/Touchstone.

Peele, S., with A. Brodsky. (1976). *Love and addiction.* New York: Signet.

Reik, T. (1941). *Of love and lust.* New York: Farrar, Strauss & Rinehart.

Reiss, I. L. (1960). Toward a sociology of the heterosexual love relationship. *Marriage and Family Living, 22,* 139-145.

Robinson, W. S. (1951). The logical structure of analytic induction. *American Sociological Review 16,* 812-818.

Rubin, Z. (1973). *Liking and loving.* New York: Holt, Rinehart & Winston.

Schachter, S., & Singer, J. (1962). Cognitive, social, and physiological determinants of emotional state. *Psychological Review, 69,* 379-399.

Schwartz, G., & Merten, D., with F. Behan and A. Rosenthal. (1980). *Love and commitment.* Beverly Hills, CA: Sage.

Schwartz, H., & Jacobs, J. (1979). *Qualitative sociology. A method to the madness.* New York: Free Press.

Seawell, A.A.F. (1984). The caring relationship in violent marriages: A descriptive study of love and pair attraction. (Doctoral dissertation, United States International University, 1984). *Dissertation Abstracts International, 45*(3), 1063B. (University Microfilms No. DA8413722).

Shelly, A., & Sibert, E. (1985). *The QUALOG user's manual* (DEC-10 version). Syracuse, NY: Syracuse University.

Snyder, M. H. (1984). The essential meaning(s) of the dyadic love relationship (as manifested and experienced in the daily lives and characteristic interactions of functional, intimate, committed, primary heterosexual couples: A phenomenological study. (Doctoral dissertation, Fielding Institute, 1983). *Dissertation Abstracts International, 45*(2), 687B. (University Microfilms No. DA8410901)

Snyder, S. U. (1986). Love making: A symbolic interactionist approach to the experience of love among unmarried heterosexual young adult couples. (Doctoral dissertation, Syracuse University, 1986). *Dissertation Abstracts International, 47*(8), 3201-A. (University Microfilms No. DA8625854)

Solomon, R. C. (1981). *Love: Emotion, myth, and metaphor.* New York: Anchor.

Stearns, P. N. (1987). The problem of change in emotions research: New standards for anger in twentieth-century American childrearing. *Symbolic Interaction, 10,* 85-99.

Sternberg, R. J. (1986). A triangular theory of love. *Psychological Review, 93,* 119-135.

Tennov, D. (1979). *Love and limerence. The experience of being in love.* New York: Stein & Day.

Turner, R. H. (1953). The quest for universals in sociological research. *American Sociological Review, 1*(18), 604-611.

Walster, E., & Walster, G. W. (1978). *A new look at love.* Reading, MA: Addison-Wesley.

Winch, R. F. (1958). *Mate selection.* New York: Harper.

Case Study Interviews
Caring for Persons With AIDS

LINDA K. MATOCHA
University of Delaware

AIDS, a disease of epidemic proportions, threatens U.S. families with unique stresses and crisis situations. In its individual characteristics, AIDS can be compared to other diseases, but its processes and its multiplicity of associated societal taboos are unique. The disease process generally is considered to be terminal, has no cure, has few effective treatments, and has both acute, short-term and chronic, long-term phases. More important, the response to the virus is manifested differently in infected individuals and their families.

Family members responsible for care of persons with AIDS (PWAs) frequently do not have the necessary information to develop and use appropriate individual and family coping mechanisms and support systems (Matocha, 1989). This information is desperately needed as the numbers of PWAs drastically increase. Because persons with AIDS live in traditional and nontraditional families, I found a broad definition of family most useful for studying family caregivers of persons with AIDS. The definition by Settles (1987), "those who function for one in familistic ways" (p. 160), served as my basis for identifying family caregivers in this study. Those familistic ways included providing family members with nurturance, intimacy, support in times of need (economic, social, and psychological), health maintenance, companionship, and mediation with systems outside of family boundaries. (See

Lightburn, Chapter 12, this volume.) This definition of family embraced members who may or may not be related through blood ties and who may or may not have relationships recognized by legal systems. I included caregivers who were homosexual lovers (spouses), heterosexual lovers (spouses), birth-family members, and friends who were perceived as family because they functioned in ways mutually recognized as familistic.

The purpose of this qualitative study was to provide a timely and critical understanding of a contemporary, complex disease confronting U.S. family care providers. Following a grounded theory approach, I used in-depth interviewing to identify the adaptations made by U.S. caregivers to confront and manage the disease. Eight families were the subjects of the study. From the data, I developed findings that should assist other family caregivers who provide care for persons with AIDS and assist professionals to understand the process of that care so effective interventions can be made and constructive policies formulated. Finally, the findings of this study should further theory development and refinement in disciplines dealing with families.

My general research question was: How do caregivers confront the insult of AIDS to a family member in the attempt to control and neutralize its consequences over time? In answering this general question, I explored the characteristics of the caregivers, the effects on caregivers, the needs of caregivers, and the resources used by caregivers.

THE DOMAINS OF THE STUDY

In this study, I primarily used procedures of grounded theory (Glaser & Strauss, 1967), but I also developed four domains, which were the basic units of study. These domains were based on basic needs concepts and assumed that caregivers have basic human needs that must be fulfilled for them to have an acceptable quality of life (Burns, 1989). These needs are physical, psychological, social, and economic (Brody, Poulshock, & Masciocchi, 1978; George & Gwyther, 1986; Morley, 1981). My choice of these four domains was based on my 2 years' experience working with PWAs and their families and research and theory. I used these basic domains to generate a framework for data collection and analysis. Within the framework, I intended to generate concepts grounded in data. I attempted not to force data into these domains, but maintain an open mind to the possibility that one or all of the domains could be inappropriate and that I might discover a new domain. Indeed, one new domain did emerge. This was the spiritual domain.

I collected, coded, and analyzed data simultaneously. Data from one case provided guidance for data collection for the next case. I assumed theoretical saturation had occurred when the interviews revealed no new information. Data analysis, including constant comparison within and across cases, transformed the information to grounded theory (Glaser & Strauss, 1967; Miles & Huberman, 1984).

REVIEW OF LITERATURE

Needle, Leach, and Graham-Tomasi (1989) noted that little research specific to caregiving and AIDS was available. To develop as full an understanding as possible, I reviewed related literature on caregiving for other chronic and terminal illnesses as well as the AIDS literature.

The related literature identified some general characteristics for caregivers of other illnesses. Women generally have been care providers. Daughters most frequently assume primary responsibility for caregiving, followed by daughters-in-law, sons, other female relatives, and finally nonrelatives (Brody, 1974; Cantor, 1983; Kiecolt-Glaser et al., 1987). Caregivers generally have lower educational and income levels than noncaregivers (Haley, Levine, Brown, Berry, & Hughes, 1987).

Studies from other health care situations supported the assumption that caregiving affects the physical well-being of caregivers. For example, parents of chronically ill mentally retarded adults reported chronic fatigue (Lefley, 1987; Thobaben, 1988). Immunity against common infections has been affected among caregivers of persons with Alzheimer's disease (Kiecolt-Glaser et al., 1987). Studies of caregiving in non-AIDS families considered the psychological responses more pervasive than physical or economic responses (Cantor, 1983; George & Gwyther, 1986; Holing, 1986; Horowitz, 1985). Mood changes, fatigue, and lack of time affected caregivers' ability to relate to other people (Haley et al., 1987; Lefley, 1987; Ross-Alaolmoiki, 1985). The social lives, therefore, can be affected.

What literature there is on caregiving and AIDS suggests the effects of caring for PWAs have some elements in common with caregiving in other health situations, but there are some elements unique to AIDS. Kiecolt-Glaser and Glaser (1988) reviewed studies from other diagnosed diseases to draw conclusions about caring for PWAs. They stated that unpredictability of the disease process and the inordinate amount of time needed for direct care during the acute stages of AIDS would be expected to produce chronic stress and feelings of guilt, helplessness, and loss of control.

AIDS is different from other terminal diseases because of the social stigma and the consequences of the stigma (Frierson, Lippmann, & Johnson, 1987). Employers sometimes terminate PWAs because of unreasonable fears of possible contagion to other employees and health costs to the employer (Arbeiter, 1987). Family caregivers, too, are threatened with terminations for similar reasons. Ridicule is a common experience. Difficulties obtaining health care, including dental work, and funeral services may be experienced (Macklin, 1988, 1989). Family caregivers who try to keep the diagnosis of AIDS a secret from fear of becoming social outcasts find it more and more difficult to keep the secret as time passes (Tibler, Walker, & Rolland, 1989).

The economic losses of the individual and family with AIDS, therefore, can be severe (Sussman, 1989). PWAs able to keep their jobs eventually become debilitated and can no longer work (Kaplan, Wofsy, & Volberding, 1987). Family members frequently assume economic responsibility for persons with AIDS who no longer can provide for themselves. This financial burden can affect the family beyond the responsible member's capability to cope successfully with the stresses of the disease.

At the same time, the literature reveals some positive coping. Sussman found (1989) that caregivers displayed a potential for spirituality: "The giving of one's self that is required can lead to profound spiritual growth. It is necessary to tap one's deepest, most mature, humane self and in turn, to recognize the spiritual qualities and needs of the person with AIDS" (p. 244). This spirituality was not necessarily grounded in a religion, but caregivers frequently expressed the feelings as religious beliefs (Soeken & Carson, 1987). Researchers characterized spirituality as grace, heroism, love, strength, dignity, energy, creativity, faith, and hope that cannot be denied (Brommel, 1986; Gallagher, 1987; Norwood, 1987; Peabody, 1986; Veninga, 1985). Living with AIDS sometimes was experienced as a test of the human spirit (Watkins, 1988).

METHOD

I used a qualitative, in-depth, multiple case study approach to discover the effects of AIDS on family members responsible for care of persons with AIDS. I chose a qualitative approach because I wanted to capture complex, real-life events and processes and, following Yin's (1989) perspective on case studies, answer "how" questions, rather than "why" questions. My design incorporated a specific case study procedure and included two family cases in each anticipated time-oriented phase. The comparison of cases between and among phases, exploring similarities and differences, resulted in relevant theory building (Bromley, 1986).

Sampling

Qualitative researchers can elect to base selection of participants on similarities to study specific aspects of phenomena, or selection can attempt to reflect a "real-world" situation through the choice of participants on the basis of differences (Bromley, 1986). I selected my families to reflect a general model of the "real world." The selection of family cases incorporated families of different combinations of sex (both males and females were caregivers and PWAs), age (caregiver ages ranged from 26 to 69 years and PWA ages ranged from 23 to 57 years), ethnic group (including Caucasian, Hispanic, and African-American), modes of transmission (including blood transfusion, homosexual contact, heterosexual contact, and intravenous drug use); the participants' educational levels included 10th-grade level through master's degree college level. The study incorporated many different family relationships. Mothers, sons, sisters, daughters, homosexual lovers/spouses, heterosexual lovers/spouses, and a very close friend who was considered a brother were all represented.

Assignment of Families to Phases

I selected and assigned eight family cases to one of four different time-oriented phases, resulting in two family cases per phase and a cross-sectional design. I chose this approach instead of following the families longitudinally because I thought I would have time constraints. Sadly, I found that my time was not the constraint I had anticipated because death came quickly for each PWA. I identified phases based on my personal knowledge of the progression of AIDS and its impact on the responsible family caregivers. The phases included time from diagnosis through death of the PWA to at least one year after death:

Phase I: From 2 weeks after diagnosis of AIDS to 6 weeks after diagnosis.

Phase II: From at least 6 weeks after diagnosis for as long as the health of the PWA is stable.

Phase III: From at least 6 weeks after diagnosis after the health of the PWA is unstable.

Phase IV: After death of the PWA.

Case Study Protocol

I designed a case study protocol (Yin, 1989), which entailed identifying who was to be included in the phases of the study, procedures for data collection, and guidelines for participants' review of case study reports that I would write. In each case, the PWA was interviewed. The design called for the PWAs to identify family caregivers and ask if they, too, wanted to be included in the study. Persons with AIDS identified one caregiver for each family even though others helped in providing care. I, therefore, interviewed one PWA and one care provider per family.

The qualitative methodology protocol allowed design changes during data collection to be responsive to individual family members without jeopardizing results. Unlike quantitative designs, where the protocol must remain the same for data collection for each participant, qualitative designs allow for these changes and even encourage them to enable obtaining "truer" contextual data. For example, the health of the participants was safeguarded by the time spent with each participant being limited to that appropriate for each participant rather than mandated by the design.

Referrals and Initial Contact With Potential Subjects

The design protected the confidentiality of the persons with AIDS and their family caregivers. A third party (e.g. nurse, physician, social worker, friend, or family member) who had direct contact with the PWA recruited subjects. I used a third party so PWAs and family caregivers had the freedom to refuse to participate. I conducted all the interviews. At the initial contact with the PWA or family caregiver, I explained the purposes and procedures of the study, and when they had agreed to be part of the study, they signed a written consent form. Establishing trust with and showing acceptance of persons with AIDS was central to my study. Before family members agreed to participate in the study, they asked me to eat dinner with the PWA and with them. This was their initiative and not mine. In each case dinner was served by the PWA or the caregiver using their dishes. Trust developed from this simple act. This trust continued past the end of the research process, and in most family cases continues to this time.

Data Collection

I tape-recorded the interviews and made duplicate tapes. I replaced respondents' names with numbers and deleted other identifiers, such as places and other names. Locked cabinets secured the audio tapes of the interviews. Separate secure files protected the written data. Original tapes were destroyed. Two persons transcribed the data. I instructed each transcriber on the importance of maintaining confidentiality of the participants and the content of the data. The transcriptionists experienced powerful emotions and high stress. They grieved and became angry as the lives of the participants unfolded, and I spent hours listening to them and assisting them to resolve feelings.

Field Procedures

I designed specific field procedures to collect relevant data for each time phase and domain, including at least three in-depth, face-to-face interviews or conversations with the PWAs and their identified caregivers. I scheduled telephone contacts during the weeks of unscheduled face-to-face interviews. Each interview lasted 2 to 8 hours. Most of the participants were interviewed separately, as they felt more comfortable revealing their thoughts and feelings if they did not have to keep up a front before other family members. The data revealed powerful, honest revelations of feelings, but the downside was being unable to capture interactional data. I was careful to maintain confidentiality between and among family members. At times this was difficult, especially when I thought sharing of information would have helped in individual situations, but I held strictly to my promise of confidentiality.

Interview Processes

PWAs and family caregivers told their stories. I used no questionnaires or interview schedules. I asked only one formal question of each participant: "Tell me your story. Start wherever you would like." As interviews progressed, I asked open-ended questions to clarify and elicit data about needs, resources, and the interactions of family caregivers with others. I noted nonverbal as well as verbal communications and often based my responses partially on these cues. At the conclusion of data collection, I wrote a case study report (Spradley, 1979; Yin, 1989) for each person interviewed. The participants read these case studies and gave me written or verbal feedback on the accuracy of my portraits.

Becoming an Active Participant

I experienced strong emotions while conducting this research. I cried, laughed, and exhibited anger and confusion along with each participant. I did not remain untouched or removed from the participants. The sessions were full of sharing. I felt accepted by the families. For short periods of time, the family system seemed to open to include me. Family secrets were shared. This was important information, but frequently there was an accompanying burden of knowledge placed on me.

The PWAs frequently were very ill. Within 2 years, they all had died. I set interview times so that PWAs and caregivers would not be unduly taxed physically or psychologically. Yet, I found participants needed to talk. The interviews were frequently long. Many times I terminated the sessions because I became tired. Participants told me the sessions were not fatiguing, but rather spiritually uplifting and cathartic.

I participated in caregiving during the third phase of a case studied in a previous phase. I stayed with a dying PWA when the caregiver's health began to deteriorate. The caregiver went on a much-needed vacation. I also helped caregivers to network with health care professionals whom they did not know. When caregivers were not available, I provided transportation for PWAs needing health care. I attended the funeral of each PWA.

Family members began to depend on me to listen to them and to understand what they were going through. At the formal conclusion of the research, each family member and PWA thanked me for including them. Not only did the participants provide me with information, but they also continue to look to me as helper, family member, or therapist. These are roles I continue to cherish. Others doing this type of research may not wish to continue relationships after the research concludes, but terminating relationships made during research can be difficult. (See

Daly's introduction, Chapter 1, this volume, for a complementary discussion.)

Data Collection and Analysis

I developed four types of logs for recording data, procedures Spradley (1979) recommended: (a) a condensed report, (b) an expanded report with more detail and my thoughts as the researcher, (c) a running record of data analysis, and (d) problems encountered during the research. In addition to information included in logs, I kept data sheets of demographic information. I used a nine-stage data analysis scheme designed by Turner (1981): (a) develop categories; (b) saturate categories; (c) construct definitions; (d) use the definitions; (e) exploit categories fully; (f) note, develop, and follow up links between categories; (g) consider the conditions under which the links hold; (h) make connections to theory; and (i) use extremes to test relationships. Through these processes, I identified key findings. Gilgun's introduction (Chapter 3, this volume) contains another style of procedures of data analysis.

FINDINGS

The resulting findings were rich in subtleties and insights into the processes of giving care to persons with AIDS. Qualitative researchers frequently encounter space problems when reporting their findings. Journals and book chapters such as this one rarely can accommodate the full range of findings in qualitative studies. Some researchers report one aspect of their findings per report. I prefer to present a broader range of my findings, which for me provides a holistic view. In the following sections, therefore, I summarize the major findings of my study on the characteristics of caregivers and the effects of caregiving in the five domains of the study (physical, psychological, economic, social, and spiritual). I also outline how caregivers' needs changed over time.

Characteristics of Caregivers

Interesting caregiver characteristics emerged. Compassion for other human beings and a focus on others rather than on self were evident. One caregiver reported having a "peoplistic" attitude. Caregivers were compassionate, reached out to others, and tried to protect others, even when their own lives were burdened with caring. They shared their lives with others. They allowed others to touch their lives.

> I keep the house up the best way I can. I keep him clean. I cook for him. Most of the things that were needed to be done for him, I made sure they were done before I left to go to work in the evening. . . . I always have other people tell me about their problems, and I try to support them in any way I can. I keep trying. I love people in general. . . . I feel for others just like I feel for my husband. I share myself with everybody. My feelings, my joy, my sadness, whatever it takes. If you want to be friends with me, you have a friend. I love people.

Caregivers served as advocates for persons with AIDS. One example of this occurred when a caregiver made the decision to discontinue life-sustaining measures to prevent additional pain to the person with AIDS even though the caregiver did not want to lose the loved one. Numerous caregivers endured fear of being infected with the virus, but they continued to care for their loved ones.

Caregivers were often optimistic. They drew on their inner strength to maintain that optimism. They stated they were not always happy, but they met life on its terms. They lived one day at a time. Caregivers did not hide medical information from their loved ones. Most were blunt and related new information to PWAs as it became available. Caregivers allowed PWAs to remain in control of their lives whenever possible. Those who were parents tried not to put their children into child roles. They let the PWAs manage their own medical care whenever possible.

Caregivers felt, rather than used logical thinking. Logical thinking facilitated withdrawal from the caregiving role. Caregivers consistently demonstrated a commitment to life. Caregivers in each case did not become passive when the health of the person with AIDS became poor. They responded by actively seeking assistance from medical, psychological, and religious professionals.

Physical Effects

Caregiving was taxing physically. During the phases of the PWAs being newly diagnosed, each caregiver experienced a deterioration in physical health. Weight loss or gain, sleep disturbances, and reduced exercise were characteristic of this phase. After learning of the AIDS infection of her daughter, one mother said:

At night when I go to bed, I have this weird dream. I usually don't remember dreams, but this one I do. I don't sleep very well at night. I am up and down all night long. I don't sleep. I keep thinking about what's ahead. . . . When I first found out I gained about 15 pounds. I just didn't eat right. Now I'm trying to take it off. It's real hard.

During the second phase, caregivers returned to pre-AIDS health status as caregiving demands decreased. During the third phase, caregivers' health again declined as direct demands increased. After the death of the PWA, caregivers gradually returned to pre-AIDS physical health.

Psychological Effects

The psychological well-being of caregivers deteriorated during the first three phases. In Phase I, they experienced increased stress from attempting to cope with the diagnosis. They felt alone. During the second phase, they thought about the future demands of caring for the person, about the possible death of the PWA, and about life without the PWA. During the third phase, as the PWA came closer to death, there was a pileup of stressors, stemming from direct caregiving, from making significant decisions, from dealings with health care professionals, and from anticipatory grief. One caregiver, who considered himself to be the spouse of his homosexual lover during their 8-year relationship, expressed deep love for his partner and stated:

I can handle myself being sick, but I have a hard time taking care of someone I love and seeing them suffer. That's just, it turns me inside out. . . . I get mean, angry. I would like to be able to escape sometimes and be crazy and free. That's the word—free. But I'll never be free again. I don't live my life any more. I'm living his life. I can't make decisions any more. I can't seem to do anything right any more.

After the death of the PWA, caregivers' psychological status returned to a pre-AIDS level. Each of the interviewed caregivers reported higher levels of well-being. They reported learning coping mechanisms, which they used effectively in other situations as well.

Social Effects

During the newly diagnosed phase, caregivers often experienced social isolation. Isolation had more than one source. Sometimes friends and family members distanced themselves from the ill persons and their caregivers. Caregivers often spent a great deal of time at the bedside of the PWA. Not telling family and friends of the diagnosis also increased the isolation. A great secret was created. Contacts with others and the quality of relationships suffered because there was fear the secret would be inadvertently revealed.

> I have close family members that I want to tell about this, about my husband, but I'm scared if I do. . . . I'm scared they will shy away from us and never want to have anything else to do with us. I know he needs his family, but I lie to them about what is wrong. . . . It don't seem to make a difference, cause neither family have come forward. I hope now they don't come around. I really don't want nothing to do with them. They don't have enough sympathy in their hearts to call us and say they would help.

As the health of the PWAs improved during the second phase, so did the social lives of their care providers, who had more time for friends. They established new friendships with other persons experiencing the same problems, old friendships were strengthened through evident continued support, and some shallow friendships were lost. During the third phase, social contacts and relationships again diminished as direct caregiving demands controlled lives. Caregivers during the fourth phase reported a return to the pre-AIDS level of socializing. They had more time, and they once again sought relationships with others.

Economic Effects

Surprisingly, economic effects on caregivers in this study were minimal. There were some differences, however. Caregivers did not experience significant spending on behalf of the PWA during the first phase. The spending that occurred was the spending of money by the caregiver and the PWA to do things that had been planned for the future. The advent of AIDS changed their time lines. One person said:

You always wanted to go to Europe. You always wanted to go on a cruise. But you think of pensions and retirements and IRAs and all that crap. All that's of absolutely no concern. Right now my taxes and personal finances are just screwed up like you would not believe. I could care less. It doesn't bother me one bit. We're going on a cruise in January. Who cares what happens after that with money.

During the second phase, spending decreased. Caregivers and PWAs made wills and decided how they would dispose of belongings. The third phase was characterized by a decrease in income when PWAs could no longer work. Frequently caregivers, too, lost income because they spent more time with very ill persons with AIDS. Economic effects were minimal during the fourth phase if funeral plans had been made and prepaid during earlier phases. One caregiver received money from the estate of the PWA, but that improvement in financial status was minimal. In general, it was not the poorer participants who suffered economic effects the most. Instead I found that middle-class people, who did not know how to "work" the social assistance system, suffered the most.

Spiritual Effects

This domain of spiritual effects emerged during data collection and analysis. I found that spiritual effects were difficult for caregivers to identify. All of the caregivers attempted to describe them, but found their vocabulary did not adequately convey their experiences. During data analysis, I categorized as spiritual effects qualities such as hope and emotional strength. There was a decrease in spiritual strength during the first phase as caregivers began to accept the diagnosis and recognize the potential bleakness of the future. During the second phase, as the health of the PWA improved, spiritual strength and hope increased. Caregivers began to believe the PWAs had a chance to beat the expected outcome, death. One person said:

Every article that's in the paper, I mean I go through that paper, and I really read it. I guess what I'm looking for is hope. Maybe my daughter will make it.

During the third phase, death became probable. Caregivers realized the future would not include their beloved family member. Those caregivers who talked with the PWA about possible death reported a positive spiritual uplifting. Caregivers and persons with AIDS functioned as a team to prepare the PWA for death. Plans were made and wishes revealed. Those caregivers who participated in decisions about when to withdraw life support described an enrichment in inner strength and ability to meet the demands of the impending death. One participant reported:

> He was in a coma. The doctor had asked if we wanted our son put on life-support systems. We had already decided no. I didn't even hesitate. . . . I really felt that we basically gave him the last gift that we could give him—the gift of not letting him be in pain any more.

After the death of the PWA, spirits initially fluctuated day by day. Gradually, as time passed, spiritual strength increased; life improved and memories of the PWA remained.

Needs Changing Over Time

In each of the five domains, the needs of the caregivers changed over time. Some of the most pressing needs were for environmental changes to accommodate the necessary medical supplies and for respite from the stress and fatigue of caregiving.

Psychologically, caregivers needed to talk about their situations and to vent their anger, fears, and frustrations. They celebrated each success no matter how small. Caregivers said they took one day at a time. If they thought too much about the future, they felt overwhelmed. Time to be by themselves was valued. They learned what they could and could not control. Caregivers stated they wanted to make decisions with PWAs while they were still well. This decreased the stress at later times.

Socially, caregivers wanted continued contact with family and friends throughout the illness and after death of the PWA. The secret needed to be told. This was most difficult for the caregivers, but those who did not tell the secret of the diagnosis eventually became distanced from their family and friends. Those caregivers who revealed the secret often worked at understanding that family and friends might take time to adjust to the diagnosis. They learned not to give up on people just because knowledge of the diagnosis initially made them turn away from the PWA.

Although caregivers indicated that the economic impact of caring for a person with AIDS was minimal, economics played a key role in planning for the future. Good insurance was needed. The making of wills and the impact of resources on decisions for prolonging life, funerals, and body disposition were important. Financial advice from experts frequently assisted caregivers. That advice included not using all resources on the PWA. The caregiver sought protection from total depletion of resources. For example, an elderly couple could spend most of their savings on their child with AIDS. Spouses in homosexual and heterosexual relationships also need resources after the death of the PWA. Caregivers needed to learn about available financial assistance from government and private agencies and use those resources whenever necessary.

Caregivers benefited from being around people who helped them maintain hope. They wanted to learn to feel good about themselves as caregivers. Acceptance of the diagnosis led to increased strength. They did not always accept death as inevitable, and they found spiritual strength in fighting the disease. Both PWAs and caregivers needed to have fun without feeling guilty. Throughout all four phases, they sought laughter and humor. Finally, they wanted people to remember the PWAs and not deny their existence after death. It strengthened them to talk with others and have others remember the PWA.

Utilization of resources changed for caregivers over time, and there were individual variations. Some caregivers relied on individuals and some on groups for support. Caregivers used those resources that met their individual needs at each point in time. They often needed the help of professionals to find resources. Throughout all phases, family and friends were identified as the most important resources for caregivers. Caregivers also identified me as an important resource.

DISCUSSION

Qualitative, in-depth case studies were appropriate for answering my research question in this study. Caregiving for PWAs is not well understood. The flexible design allowed me to contribute new knowledge to this area of high social concern. I did not seek to manipulate variables as in experimental research, and for this study, I was not seeking information on prevalence, attempting to make predictions, or testing hypotheses. The domains I identified through my professional experience and through research and theory guided me in my research. Finally, I did not attempt to generate complete answers. I wanted to develop questions grounded in the complex experiences of persons whose lives were affected by AIDS. Such questions provide a basis for future research.

Limitations

There were some limitations in the design. Each time I read a transcript, I saw some data were missing. With participants allowed to tell their stories in their own ways, some questions were not answered. There were potential problems with reliability even though the design was explicit and the characteristics of the participants were included in the reporting. My personal thoughts and feelings affected the results. In this study, my biases grew to favor the persons giving care. It may be that they simply were doing what was expected of them, but in allowing me to enter their lives and look at their fears and expectations, I began to understand their fears and experience their expectations.

The research did what it was supposed to do: provide knowledge of caregiving for PWAs. Replication by other researchers may be problematic, however, for each researcher might elicit different responses from care providers and PWAs and might interpret experiences differently. In addition, researchers, informants, times, and settings differ across studies. I would, however, expect much of what I have found to be replicated by others.

There are several recommendations I would make for persons who want to do studies similar to mine. First, I suggest being prepared for intense emotional reactions. I continually reviewed my thoughts, feelings, and potential actions. I felt guilty about intruding on the time and energy of research participants whom I saw as already extremely stressed. Informal support from others was helpful to me, but in retrospect, I would have felt less guilty and felt better about communication with participants had I elicited formal support from a counselor or support groups.

On a more technical side, had I used a computer program to assist in data analysis (Tesch, 1990), I might have reduced the time it took to do this research, which was time and labor intensive. Furthermore, I sometimes worried I was not keeping up with the dramatic changes taking place within the families I was studying. I think a computer-assisted approach might have been helpful to me.

Another recommendation for the design would be to ask caregivers to keep daily journals. I felt it would be too burdensome. When I reviewed the case studies with the participants, however, two caregivers stated they believed a journal might have helped them relieve their tensions and solve problems more efficiently.

This study provided insight into the process of caregiving, but additional questions arose. More research identifying the characteristics of caregivers and PWAs is needed. Who assumes responsibility for caring for others? What are their idiosyncrasies, their qualities? Does the age, sex, or culture of the caregiver make a difference? This knowledge could result in effective programs for caregivers; interventions by professionals might become specific to caregivers. We need more information on role conflict, because care providers give up their normal daily lives to provide care. Research is needed to develop tools to measure the caregiving burden and factors affecting the burden. Those tools could assess caregivers and ascertain which caregivers are coping and which need help.

In conclusion, findings developed through a qualitative approach added to the body of knowledge about processes of giving care to persons with AIDS. The knowledge gained provided rich insights into the lives of caregivers, but more important, it facilitated the asking of more grounded questions in future research. Finally, I realized that my dedication and emotional commitment were powerful adjuncts to the flexible methods I used in this research.

REFERENCES

Arbeiter, J. S. (1987). Can a nurse be fired for having AIDS? *RN, 50*(2), 53-54.

Brody, E. M. (1974). Aging and family personality: A developmental view. *Family Process, 13,* 23-37.

Brody, S. J., Poulshock, S. W., & Masciocchi, C. F. (1978). The family caring unit: A major consideration in the long-term support system. *Gerontologist, 18,* 556-561.

Bromley, D. B. (1986). *The case-study method in psychology and related disciplines.* New York: John Wiley.

Brommel, H. van (1986). *Choices: For people who have a terminal illness, their families and their caregivers.* Toronto: NC Press.

Burns, D. J. (1989). Current approaches to the study of higher level human needs. *Home Economics Forum, 3*(2), 9-10.

Cantor, M. H. (1983). Strain among caregivers: A study of experience in the United States. *Gerontologist, 23*(6), 597-604.

Frierson, R. L., Lippmann, S. B., & Johnson, J. (1987). AIDS: Psychosocial stresses on the family. *Psychosomatics, 28*(2), 65-68.

Gallagher, J. (1987). *Voices of strength and hope for a friend with AIDS.* Kansas City, MO: Sheed & Ward.

George, L. K., & Gwyther, L. P. (1986). Caregiver well-being: A multidimensional examination of family caregivers of demented adults. *Gerontologist, 26,* 253-259.

Glaser, B. G., & Strauss, A. L. (1967). *The discovery of grounded theory: Strategies for qualitative research.* Chicago: Aldine.

Haley, W. E., Levine, E. G., Brown, S. L., Berry, J. W., & Hughes, G. H. (1987). Psychological, social, and health consequences of caring for a relative with senile dementia. *Journal of the American Geriatric Society, 35*(5), 405-411.

Holing, E. V. (1986). The primary caregiver's perception of the dying trajectory. *Cancer Nursing, 9*(1), 29-37.

Horowitz, A. (1985). Family caregiving to the frail elderly. *Annual Review of Gerontological Geriatrics, 5,* 194-246.

Kaplan, L. D., Wofsy, C. B., & Volberding, P. A. (1987). Treatment of patients with acquired immunodeficiency syndrome and associated manifestations. *Journal of the American Medical Association, 257,* 1367-1374.

Kiecolt-Glaser, J. K., & Glaser, R. (1988). Psychological influences on immunity. *American Psychologist, 43,* 892-898.

Kiecolt-Glaser, J. K., Glaser, R., Shuttleworth, E. C., Dyer, B. A., Ogrocki, B. S., & Speicher, C. E. (1987). Chronic stress and immunity in family caregivers of Alzheimer's disease victims. *Psychosomatic Medicine, 49,* 523-535.

Lefley, H. P. (1987). Aging parents as caregivers of mentally ill adult children: An emerging social problem. *Hospital and Community Psychiatry, 38,* 1063-1070.

Macklin, E. D. (1988). AIDS: Implications for families. *Family Relations, 37*(2), 141-149.

Macklin, E. D. (1989). Introduction. *Marriage and Family Review, 13*(1/2), 1-11.

Matocha, L. K. (1989). The effects of AIDS on family member(s) responsible for care: A qualitative study. *Dissertation Abstracts International, 51A*(2), 648. (University Microfilms No. 90-19, 300)

Miles, M. B., & Huberman, A. M. (1984). *Qualitative data analysis: A sourcebook of new methods.* Beverly Hills, CA: Sage.

Morley, P. (1981). Reflections on the biopolitics of human nature and altruism. In M. M. Leininger (Ed.), *Caring: An essential human need* (pp. 145-157). Thorofare, NJ: Slack.

Needle, R. H., Leach, S., & Graham-Tomasi, R. P. (1989). The human immunodeficiency virus (HIV) epidemic: Implications for families. *Marriage and Family Review, 13*(1/2), 13-37.

Norwood, C. (1987). *Advice for life: A woman's guide to AIDS risks and prevention.* New York: Pantheon.

Peabody, B. (1986). *The screaming room.* New York: Avon.

Ross-Alaolmoiki, K. (1985). Supportive care for families of dying children. *Nursing Clinics of North America, 20*(2), 457-466.

Settles, B. H. (1987). A perspective on tomorrow's families. In M. B. Sussman & S. K. Steinmetz (Eds.), *Handbook of marriage and the family* (pp. 157-180). New York: Plenum.

Soeken, K. L., & Carson, V. J. (1987). Responding to the spiritual needs of the chronically ill. *Nursing Clinics of North America, 22,* 603-611.

Spradley, J. P. (1979). *The ethnographic interview.* New York: Rinehart & Winston.

Sussman, M. B. (1989). AIDS: Opportunity for humanity. *Marriage and Family Review, 13*(1/2), 229-239.

Tesch, R. (1990). *Qualitative research: Analysis types and software tools.* Philadelphia: Taylor & Francis.

Thobaben, M. (1988). What you can do for the depressed caregiver. *RN, 51*(1), 73-75.

Tibler, K. B., Walker, G., & Rolland, J. S. (1989). Therapeutic issues when working with families of persons with AIDS. *Marriage and Family Review, 13,* 81-128.

Turner, B. A. (1981). Some practical aspects of qualitative data analysis: One way of organizing the cognitive processes associated with the generation of grounded theory. *Quality and Quantity, 15,* 225-247.

Veninga, R. L. (1985). *A gift of hope: How we survive our tragedies.* Boston: Little, Brown.

Watkins, J. D. (1988). Responding to the HIV epidemic. *American Psychologist, 43*(11), 849-851.

Yin, R. K. (1989). *Case study research design and methods* (2nd ed.). Newbury Park, CA: Sage.

Life Histories
Conflict in Southeast Asian Refugee Families

DANIEL F. DETZNER
University of Minnesota, Twin Cities

Many Southeast Asian families caught in the middle of the decades-long Indochinese conflict have streamed out of Vietnam, Cambodia, and Laos since the withdrawal of U.S. troops in 1975. More than 1.2 million refugees from that part of the world came to the United States seeking a safe place to live and reunification with lost family members. Little is known about the internal and external pressures affecting the multigenerational families who migrate under duress or the long-term impact of such a dramatic and rapid change in sociocultural environment (Liu, 1988). Are refugee families from each Southeast Asian cultural group distinct in their adjustment patterns? What are the characteristics of individuals and families who do not adjust well in their new environment? In what ways does forced relocation change family structure, dynamics, and rituals, and how do reconstructed families

AUTHOR'S NOTE: This report is part of a larger study entitled *Southeast Asian Families With Elders (SAFE)*, with the overall goal of investigating the long-term memories, perceptions, and constructed meanings that Southeast Asian elders have developed to explain the changes and current realities of their individual and family histories (Agricultural Experiment Station Project No. MIN. 52668). The multicultural research team in this project was composed of Carol Elde, Punnary Koy, Jennifer Inthisone, Peter Inthisone, Roger Light, Mai Ly, Mary Seabloom, Chantha Sok, Phuong Thai, Khiem Thai, and Doaunkgamol Vechbunyongratana.

85

manage the generational conflict that may arise out of these changes? Have family and gender roles changed, and if so, is the change for each generation and gender? These are a few of the research questions that might help us understand the fastest-growing and poorest ethnic minority group in the United States (Rottman & Merideth, 1982). I am investigating some of these questions with Southeast Asian elders in life history research on their long-term memories, perceptions, and the meanings they have constructed to explain changes and current realities in their individual and family lives. In this chapter, I report on patterns of conflict these elders have experienced within their families, findings that I developed with my research team through life history interviews and a grounded theory approach.

In traditional Asian cultures, individual lives are subsumed under the larger construct of a hierarchical extended family encompassing all generations (Rottman & Merideth, 1982). Asian refugees are members of diverse groups composed of Vietnamese, Cambodian, Lao, and Hmong peoples, and the groups have unique histories, traditions, family systems, and internal diversities. Yet, elderly refugees in all of these groups also share many common disruptive life events and similar adaptation problems in their reconstructed households. The older refugees in this study survived the horrors of war, dangerous escape attempts, crowded refugee camps, resettlement in a Western country, and the multiple pressures of readjustment (Nicassio, 1985). A study of their experiences and perceptions can shed light on aspects of family life not well understood by scholars, social service practitioners, or the majority culture (Gozdziak, 1989).

Fieldwork and the Development of Preliminary Insights

I developed some preliminary insights into the family lives of Southeast Asian refugees during a year of part-time fieldwork where I observed several educational, social, and cultural groups that involved participants in varying activities, such as field trips, language classes, sharing meals, and sewing and knitting together. I participated in a variety of religious events, educational field trips, language classes, and social activities sponsored by the Vietnamese Buddhist Association, the Cambodian Buddhist Association, the Hmong and Lao Family Association, and the American Refugee Committee. Insights from this fieldwork helped me to develop general areas of inquiry and appropriate research methods for the more formal study on which I am reporting here.

Issues

My preliminary fieldwork helped me to discover that members of the oldest living generation of refugees from these four groups often perceived themselves in conflict with members of younger generations on issues related to the preservation of family and cultural traditions. Many informants reported cross-generation disagreements over the elders' expectations for continuity in traditional Eastern family rules, beliefs, and practices. These were in direct conflict with adult children's and grandchildren's expectations for egalitarian family and gender relationships. I reviewed both continuity theory and conflict theory to obtain insight into these issues.

Continuity theory (Atchley, 1989) was useful for examining the strong needs elders reported for internal and external stability within the multiple contexts of their individual, family, and community lives. Internal continuity manifested itself in the recurring need for familiarity of language, food, and the practices of filial piety. Elders expressed their desires for external continuity in broader environmental, cultural, and spiritual contexts. Continuity theory suggests that individuals confronted with forced relocation late in life will attempt to restore traditions, practices, and mores of their homelands. They will do so in an effort to retain emotional comfort and a sense of familiarity, even when their efforts promote cross-generation conflicts.

Not previously used in cross-cultural studies with Asian families, family conflict theory (Sprey, 1979) also seemed appropriate for interpreting the life histories of Southeast Asian refugee elders. According to this theory, conflict within families results from competition among family members for goals and scarce resources. Conflict is normative and functional and has potential for positive outcomes if disputes are managed well. Conflict is considered inevitable when there is an inequality of relationships, and it is inherent in the process of social change.

Life History Methods

During informal conversations with elders and staff members in the organizations in which I did my fieldwork, I tested several research approaches and interview questions to check for cultural sensitivity with a population of non-English-speaking older refugees. A semi-structured life history interview approach emerged as least intrusive and most viable for gathering family life data from this cohort.

Scholars have used life history research methods for decades to provide an insider's long-term perspective on the events, sociohistorical context, and everyday life experiences of individuals and groups (Bertaux, 1981; Dollard, 1935; Erikson, 1975; Langness, 1965; Langness & Frank, 1981; Turner & Bruner, 1986; Watson & Watson-Franke, 1985). Life history research methods are appropriate to study Asian elders because oral traditions and storytelling in Asian cultures historically have positioned elders in the prestigious roles of wise person, teacher, adviser, and keeper of the past. In addition, elderly informants want their life stories to be told as a means of leaving family, cultural, and historical legacies to the younger generation (Lieberman & Falk, 1971), a desire of older people that apparently transcends cultural boundaries. Social gerontologists have noted the potential therapeutic value of life review processes for the elderly (Baum, 1981; Butler, 1963). In a review of studies on reminiscence, Merriam (1980) demonstrated the powerful urge of elders to review and contextualize their experiences.

In my many discussions with elders and ethnic staff working with them, it became clear to me that the opportunity to tell their stories for future generations was a powerful incentive for the elders to participate in the study. The potential for cultural sensitivity of life history inquiry helped me—a white, male, Western academic—approach this difficult-to-reach population with some confidence about their willingness to participate.

Life history research is rooted in symbolic interactionist perspectives. This perspective proposes that individuals act on the basis of the meanings they ascribe to words, events, persons, and things. Meanings develop from the language and behavioral interactions between individuals and the groups with which each person is associated. Meanings are interpreted and reinterpreted over time through the cultural and experiential lenses of each person. We can view the recounting of life histories in old age as current and cumulative constructions of reality that informants have created over the life course (Berger & Luckmann, 1966; Cohler, 1982).

Shared experiences and meanings across a number of life histories can illuminate the impact on individual and family development of historical macrosocial events such as war and the forced relocation of millions of people. Ways to create a detailed understanding of events and their meanings include (a) analyzing multiple life histories for recurring expressions, perceptions, constructions, and behaviors; (b) approaching topics from various perspectives within individual cases; (c) continuing this process over a series of interviews; and (d) performing multiple field observations (Kirk & Miller, 1986). The overall aims of research conducted within the symbolic interaction perspective are to identify the constructed meanings of human interactions to determine the underlying patterns of these interactions—aims consistent with the methods I used.

Grounded Theory Research

I combined ethnographic participant observation and in-depth interviewing with the grounded theory research, which, among other things, is characterized by comparative analysis during data gathering. I saw these combinations as well suited to study the family lives of culturally diverse populations because the approach allows meanings and explanations to emerge from the words and constructs of the informants rather than from the preconceived notions of investigators (Strauss & Corbin, 1990). An important step for the development of grounded theory in my research was to link my findings with major theoretical constructs in family and gerontological research.

Learning to Be Culturally Sensitive

When I field-tested specific questions on family conflict, I received an almost universal denial that any differences of opinion or disagreements existed. Because my earlier fieldwork discussions repeatedly had indicated a contrary finding, I consulted with the multicultural research team tat worked with me throughout data gathering. We developed a series of questions concerning family rules and rule breaking as alternative ways of accessing the nature and sources of family conflict. This indirect approach led to more than 200 distinct cases of conflict embedded in responses to the family rules questions and in the larger life history narratives.

METHOD

Life history data were collected from 40 elderly Southeast Asian refugees who were living in the Minneapolis-St. Paul metropolitan area in 1988 and 1989. Vietnamese, Cambodian, Lao Hmong, and lowland

Laotian elders were nominated from membership lists of social and recreational groups organized for elders by the ethnic leaders and staff of the Vietnamese Buddhist Association, the Cambodian Buddhist Association, the American Refugee Committee, and the downtown Minneapolis YMCA. A purposive sample was selected from these lists with the goal of balance in cultural groups, age, gender, and socioeconomic status in the countries of origin. Ten persons from each of the four Southeast Asian refugee groups were chosen, equally divided between men and women. Every participant had children living in the United States, although this was not used as a selection criterion,. The number of children ranged from 1 to 13, with an average of 6. The average age of the elders was 65, with a range of 48 to 83. They had lived in the United States an average of 6 years, with a range of from 1 to 13 years.

A little less than half said they currently were married, and an additional one-quarter were unsure of their marital status because their spouse was missing. They did not know if the spouse was living or had died in prison, refugee camps, or another country. All but three of the elders were living in family groups, such as with spouses and children, with adult children, with grandchildren, with more distant family and clan members, or with friends while awaiting reunification with family members. Variety in family configuration stemmed from family disruptions caused by war, hurried escapes, and the relocation process.

The Interviews

We collected data through a series of in-depth, semistructured interviews with informants who were members of the oldest generation of their families. The interviews consisted of a series of questions and follow-up probes designed to encourage respondents to reconstruct and reflect on early memories, significant life events, turning points, and family experiences during youth, middle age, and old age. We asked specific questions concerning family structure, gender and generational roles, and family rules. Each informant was asked the same general questions so that comparable data would be available across cases. The semistructured format allowed informants to take the interview into areas of individual and family life not anticipated by the research protocol, however.

Persons who were members of each of the four groups worked as interpreters in the project and participated in the development of interview schedules and in the interviews with the elders. They were part of a research team I formed with graduate students. By design, they sometimes acted as co-interviewers who probed interesting topics, ideas, and experiences. The interview schedule was developed in English. Interpreters translated it into appropriate languages. Second native-speaking interpreters then back-translated the schedule into English. We spent a lot of time in research team meetings discussing particular words and concepts so we could clarify meanings across languages and cultures.

Thirty-eight of the 40 informants used their native language in the interviews, and 2 used fluent English. Informants were interviewed in the households where they were living for approximately 2 hours on three separate occasions, for a total of 6 hours each and 240 total interview hours. The first interview concerned overall family structure, family history, and memories of childhood. The second covered important events, transitions, and turning points from early adulthood until about age 50, the approximate age when a person from these cultures may be considered an elder. The third interview concerned aspects of more recent history and what it means to be an elder in a refugee family.

Analysis

Several stages of analysis brought the patterns within interviews into increasingly clear focus. In the first stage, we did line-by-line coding of the transcripts. Through this process we identified the more than 200 episodes of conflict discovered through our questions on family rules, discussed earlier. We then coded these episodes. The computer program Ethnograph (Seidel, Kjolseth, & Seymour, 1988) helped us in our coding. After extensive in-depth discussion, we found that almost all of the episodes could be classified into two broad categories—family and gender roles. We defined family conflict as disagreements or perceptions of differences between members of an extended family about goals, resources, and roles. Gender conflict, which we saw as nested within the larger framework of family conflict, we defined as disagreements or perceptions of differences about roles and rules related to one's status as male or female. There are overlaps in these categories, and classifying narrative episodes as exclusively under one category sometimes was difficult.

After we identified and categorized conflict episodes, we reviewed the classifications through multiple close readings and continuing discussions. I separately recoded the episodes with the assistance of two family science graduate students, one a native of Thailand and fluent in

Laotian and English and the other from the United States, with experience living in Asia. As a group, we discussed each coded segment and its interpretation within the family and gender role change categories established in the first stage of analysis. I separately analyzed unresolved differences about the coding of some segments and classified them according to my understanding of the entire life history or placed them in an undefined miscellaneous category to be reviewed again during the explanation-building stage of the analytical process.

To understand family and gender role conflicts more fully, the second stage of analysis also included an examination of each informant's perceptions of current and past family and gender roles. We defined roles using Linton's classic (1936) definition, which links appropriate individual behaviors to a particular position or status in a family or social structure. Responses to interview questions about the roles, responsibilities, and behaviors of the elders as children, middle-aged adults, and at interview time were coded by role type and the gender and generational cohort performing the role. Space and the purposes of this chapter do not permit an analysis of the many variations in role performance revealed in these responses. A general discussion of our findings, however, should further the understanding of conflict.

During the third stage of analysis, the research team interpreted the findings in light of conflict and continuity theories—and social role theory, which I discuss later—in order to "thicken" our understanding of Southeast Asian refugee families.

FINDINGS

Conflict in the families of these elders often involved disagreements about who in the family was supposed to be fulfilling what role(s) and the expectations surrounding role performance. In many cases, conflict involved the elder's belief that the young should appropriately perform traditional practices of filial piety involving respect, deference, and absolute obedience (Seabloom, 1991). In other cases, there were disagreements between husbands and wives, children and parents, and in-laws about appropriate roles and responsibilities in the family and community for males and females.

Despite the reluctance of informants to discuss conflict directly, there is evidence of conflict in almost every life history case, across the four cultural groups, and at each major stage of the life course. We interpreted conflict as *normative* in these Southeast Asian refugee families, a tenet in family conflict theory that our research identified as relevant to these families. Although disagreements and differences were a regular part of family life, informants *avoided or denied* direct or overt conflicts among family members, consistent with our observations when fieldtesting interview questions. Because expectations for appropriate filial behaviors are well known through traditional Confucian and Buddhist teachings, direct discussions of family conflicts are painful or shameful, but these informants told stories about family conflict when asked about family rules, as discussed earlier.

The expectations of the older generation for the performance of traditional filial piety practices and the apparent difficulties of younger generations in performing in expected ways represented the primary family issue informants perceived as conflictual. Most of these older refugees believed that the members of the younger generations did not respect them in the same ways that members of older generations were respected in their homelands, nor did these elders see themselves being treated in the reverential manner they nostalgically remembered that their grandparents were. As filial piety traditions also influence male-female relationships, failure to perform traditional practices that demonstrate respect for husbands and males also suggested changes in gender roles and behavior rules for men and women as well.

A case example from the life history data illustrates these interrelated sources of family conflict.

Le Duc Tao

Le Duc Tao is a 67-year-old Vietnamese who arrived in the United States with his wife in 1986. They left Vietnam because of constant fear of the official Communist government. They have seven adult children who are now scattered on three continents. Currently they live with a daughter and her two children in a suburban community outside a major metropolitan area in the Midwest.

Le remembers from his early family life that his grandfather was a teacher who followed a rather strict, traditional approach to family life. When Le was a child, conflict was easily avoided in his family because:

> During dinner my father would review what we did. If we did something wrong, parents would show us the right way. We didn't get very serious

punishment . . . [however], if I played around too much or was too stub-
born, then my mother would beat me.

He can remember very little overt conflict in his family as a child, as
his father always seemed to be able to find ways to make everyone
happy. He reports that as a young boy:

Conflict between the child and parent never happens because the kids
listen, obey, and carry out what the parents said. Usually, [the kids] won't
dare to conflict with parent or between brothers and sisters since kids don't
talk back to parents.

Although Le remembers his father was very strict in controlling his
educational and career choices, he also believes his own children and
grandchildren should strictly follow his wishes for their educational and
career futures. He insists that maintaining strict traditional practices of
absolute obedience to elders is necessary to ensure the young continue
to respect the old. He is fearful of the impact of Western values, as he
has observed firsthand the lack of respect of the young for the old in
the United States. He continues to think that parental arrangement of
marriages for children is a good idea, although it is not often practiced
in Vietnam today and is rarely practiced in the refugee community.

Le feels that his family roles and authority are diminished in the
United States. His primary role in the family now is more honorary and
advisory, lacking real decision-making authority and traditional re-
spect. He points out that his children are more knowledgeable about
U.S. life than he as they have been living here longer and they speak
English. He is sad when he goes to his 45-year-old son's home because:

Sometimes when I go over to their place for a visit, they would tell me
some of their decisions. Of course, I have to agree. If not, they'll do it their
way anyhow.

Social role theory assumes that the family and community roles
performed by individuals symbolically are important indicators of place
and status within a social system. The loss of important work, family,
and social roles typically experienced by older persons in U.S. society
is cited as evidence of the declining age status often associated with
modern developed countries (Cowgill, 1986). An increase or decrease
in roles or a significant change in the nature of the roles performed

usually indicates a change in status. Le's efforts to maintain his traditional roles as head of the family and adviser to the young are central
to understanding the filial piety origins of the conflict that he and many
other informants experienced in their interactions with adult children,
grandchildren, and spouses. He believes it is important to maintain
continuity in traditional practices, thus enabling the old to use inherent
powers to make important family decisions and the young to show their
respect by unquestioning obedience.

Le continues to believe that marriage and career decisions should be
made by parents even though he resented that himself as a young man
and it is seldom the practice today in Vietnam. He believes that continuity in filial piety traditions is important because he sees them as the
foundation of the belief system that structures all relations in the
Vietnamese family. Le thinks that without filial piety, the Vietnamese
people will not prosper in the United States because the family will lose
its cohesion, and the economic survival of future generations will be in
peril. Living as he now does in the midst of a society that he experiences
as having no significant roles or functions for him, Le has difficulty
performing even the roles he considers most fundamental to male
household heads and teacher-advisers, roles that might give meaning
and purpose to life in old age. Although he does not directly confront
his children about his feelings of loss, Le expresses unhappiness to the
interviewers with his current position in the family and the loss of power
he has experienced. He metaphorically explains his losses in the United
States when he describes himself as disabled because he lacks mobility,
being unable to drive a car, and as being deaf and mute because he does
not speak or understand English. Like Le, several other men informants
were saddened by and resigned to the loss of traditional family and
community roles performed by their parents and ancestors.

Women Gain Roles; Men Lose Them

In their homelands, men almost always took the higher-status community roles of maintainer of traditions and performer of religious
rituals. Women almost always performed lower-status jobs such as food
preparation and child care. In this country, men, however, appeared to
perform a far narrower range of roles than women in all four cultural
groups. Men generally were more specialized in role performance and
constricted by traditional cultural boundaries than women. For example,

some males performed honorific and instrumental activities such as
family head, breadwinner, role model, teacher-adviser or external community roles. They rarely reported involvement with housework, food
preparation, shopping, or elder care. Of the three men in the study who
were living alone at the time of the interview, two had demonstrated
their abilities to perform nontraditional male roles such as food preparation. They both, however, expressed sadness at their plight.

Women performed traditional female roles in the household, including child care and food preparation, and many traditional male roles as
well, including shelter provider, protector of the family, breadwinner,
and teacher-adviser. As more than half of the female sample were not
living with a spouse at the time of the interviews, it was not surprising
to observe this crossover in traditional gender roles. Many of the male
informants complained of role loss, but the women complained of role
overload. For both genders together, we discovered 24 different roles
within the family and in the cultural community currently performed by
informants. This large number of roles indicates the continuing centrality of both family and community to the elder informants despite some
role and status changes, which some men experienced as loss.

Conflict and Changing Gender Roles

When we compared the accounts of the men and women informants
in this sample on a case-by-case basis, we found how changing gender
roles can become the source of conflict within families. In efforts to
retain a position of power in the family, a number of older men and
women household heads attempted to control their spouses and children
in authoritarian ways. These incidents often became sources of conflict
in the family, which they recounted in telling their life histories.

Informants reported conflict between themselves and their spouses
and between themselves and their children. We interpreted many of
these conflicts as *power and control* issues. The men informants viewed
women who worked outside the home as important contributors to the
financial well-being of the family. Yet several expressed deep-felt
concerns about the loss of control they experienced as their wives or
daughters learned English and earned their own money. Mothers and
fathers who attempted to assert their traditional decision-making power
often felt rebuffed by sons or daughters who had their own ideas about
clothing, schools, careers, and spouses. Although these clearly are

family-related issues, we classified them as gender issues, because it was almost always the males who sought to reestablish their control over wives, children, and grandchildren, and it was almost always the women who sought more balance in the power relationships within families.

In traditional Southeast Asian families, wives and children, especially female children, are expected to be unquestioning in their obedience to the wishes of husbands and older males. Information provided by our informants suggests that Asian women working outside the home observe the more egalitarian gender relationships experienced by U.S. women and sometimes challenge the authoritarian positions of husbands and fathers. Children socialized in U.S. schools observe the striving for independence and strong dose of individualism that characterizes childhood in the United States and sometimes bring home with them attitudes that challenge the authority of mothers, fathers, and grandparents who still remember how dutiful and respectful they had to be as children.

A third gender conflict theme involves gender-related dyadic disagreements and differences of opinion, especially recurring conflicts about rules, roles, and values between mothers and daughters in-law, husbands and wives, and grandparents and grandchildren. One example is the traditionally conflictual mother- and daughter-in-law relationship, in which the younger woman is strictly supervised by the older woman and becomes a virtual servant in the household of her husband's parents. The transference of that already strained relationship to the United States become especially problematic for many of our elder informants as younger women, especially those with education and English-language skills, challenged the authority of their mother-in-law.

War-Related Trauma and Conflicts Over Filial Piety

The account of Phousang Phouvanna shows the complexity of the struggle between a Cambodian elder and her only surviving son in their negotiations over his education. In this dyadic conflict, she insisted on obedience to her wishes, while at the same time she recognized his need for the best education he could obtain. She was a widow, and she blamed herself for the death of her other children in war. Mother-son conflict took place in the shadow of war-related trauma.

Phousang Phouvanna

Phousang Phouvanna is a 58-year-old Cambodian who fled to the United States in 1975 when Cambodia was overtaken by the Khmer Rouge forces. She originally came from a well-off family in the capital city of Phnom Penh. After her husband died in 1971, she opened a restaurant there to support her family. When the overthrow of the capital city seemed near in 1974, she left her Phnom Penh business in the hands of her son and moved to another part of the country where she would be safe. She blames herself for not gathering all of her dispersed children together with her in this safe place quickly enough. As a consequence of the Pol Pot terrors, only one of her six children is still living.

As a child, Phousang remembers her parents gave her almost no freedom to play with other children and that she was always very obedient to them.

> When I was 10 years old, I was put into a school. After school, I could not go anywhere. My parents were very strict. When I got home I had to stay home and study.

She can remember no overt conflict in her childhood family and cites the fear that she and her siblings felt towards the authority of their parents. In the rare cases in which one of the children broke a family rule, her father usually gave the punishment.

> Nobody dared to break the rules, because my parents were very strict. Whatever they told us we followed. I did not know what my brothers or sisters did outside the house, but inside the house we had to follow the house rules.

When her children were young, Phousang did not assert as much power over them. She especially wanted them to join their friends for play as this was denied to her in childhood because of strict parental rules concerning the importance of education and female children staying close to the home.

> I know when I was their age I did not like the way my parents treated me, so I didn't want to be hard on my children. When I was young I was not allowed to do any fun activities far away from home. . . . I wanted to go so

bad [to the festival]. I hid in my room and cried, but I did not dare to say anything to my father. So I wanted my children and younger people to have some freedom to go places.

Now living in the United States with her one remaining child, she reports that her son respects her a great deal and so far has not disappointed her. A lingering disagreement with her son, however, continues to be a source of conflict between them. Although he wanted to continue his education after completing his bachelor's degree, she did not want him to live far away from her to attend graduate school. He acceded to her wishes and did not go away to school after she reminded him that he was her only living child. Now she feels very unhappy because she wants her son to have as much education as possible, although she also wants the emotional and tangible support only he can provide to her. Even though he respects her wishes now, she is uncertain if he will do so in the future. This fear is based on her observations of many other Cambodian young people who disappoint their parents by not respecting them as they grow older. She thinks Cambodian children should respect parental authority by treating the parents like gods who have even greater power than those at the temple.

Phousang remembers sadly the conflict she experienced as a child having to obey her father's family rule concerning young girls staying close to home. As a mother herself, Phousang fostered in her children more independence than she had as a child. The conflict here concerns her only living son's desire for education and independence and her desire for security and continuity. Although this conflict can be understood as a normative parent-child generational conflict over values, it may also be analyzed as a larger dyadic conflict between a mother and her adult son concerning her control, his obedience to her wishes, and the filial piety responsibilities of a sole surviving son for his elderly mother. Although the context is very different, Phousang responds to her son's desire to leave home by asserting parental authority in the same way she remembers her own parents responding to her childhood requests for autonomy. The son's remaining at home is evidence of the power a Cambodian woman elder can still assert over her offspring and the continuing importance of filial piety to both the younger and the older generations. In this case, the conflict is complicated by the trauma of the death of most of the immediate family.

DISCUSSION

Although elders continue to play important roles in many refugee families, they have lost important positions of status because their knowledge and experiences are often viewed by the young as not relevant in U.S. contexts. Typically, elders' family roles are instrumental in nature, helpful to the family system, but not highly prestigious. Their capacity to enforce traditional roles and family values is diminished by the difficulties of adaptation in a modern, urban, Western environment. When all the family resources are expended on outside work, daily survival needs, and education for the children, there may be little time or energy left for the family to express traditional reverence for its elders. Although their adult children and grandchildren continue to respect them, the absence of many traditional rituals of respect is a recurring concern and a source of conflict for elders.

The conflicts within families and between genders can be interpreted as a clash between modern and traditional values, and between continuity and change, normative in the forced relocation confronting refugees. Seeing the young embracing individualism and materialism eagerly, elders consistently emphasize the retention of culture and the importance of family. Many traditional practices of deference, obedience, and self-denial are in opposition to the modern values of self-expression, freedom, and individualism that are expressed and practiced every day by the young generation's peers in U.S. schools. One Laotian elder expressed the dual cultural dilemma that all refugee families confront on a daily basis:

> In my family, the children must be respectful to the elders and polite to the guests. They must bow their heads, greet the elders, and they must serve tea to the guests in the proper way. The children must speak Laotian at home. When they are at home, they are Laotian, and when they leave home, they are Americans.

The desire for continuity with the past is a powerful and recurring theme that runs throughout virtually every life history interview. It is so important that it becomes a regular source of conflict between husbands and wives, parents and children, and grandparents and grandchildren in extended refugee families. In our analysis of the life histories, we found evidence that conflict is normative in Asian families. There also was evidence, however, that conflict is not brought into the open because of family rules concerning obedience and respect for elders.

Overtly, informants did not question the power and authority of elders when they were children. They did, however, resent power and authority privately and retrospectively as they reviewed their lives in this study. When elders extend and enforce this traditional authority in their families today, they report conflict, stress, disagreement, and tension. These types of generational conflicts may be inherent in refugee families and part of the adaptation process that families undergo as they struggle through change in virtually every important aspect of their lives.

The modern setting in which these elderly refugees find themselves at a late stage of life forces them to be pragmatic and adaptable. That they are alive with their families here in the United States is testimony to their survival skills and ability to adapt. The impact of modernization and the loss of continuity with the past are so great, however, that efforts to reestablish traditional family boundaries in this country may be seen as a functional adaptation strategy for them even if it is conflictual within the larger family group. Efforts to reestablish traditional family and gender norms are destined to promote further conflict within families and between genders and generations. Although there is a tendency to avoid conflict, it is perhaps through the processes of conflict that adaptation and adjustment to dramatic social change are negotiated and mediated. From these life histories, it is clear that strong vestiges of traditional family practice continue to be a part of everyday family life. Continuity is maintained, however, through a conflictual process that further diminishes the status of the aged, especially the male patriarchs who have exerted unquestioned power over family life in the past.

REFERENCES

Atchley, R. (1989) A continuity theory of normal aging. *Gerontologist, 29,* 183-190.

Baum, W. (1980-1981). The therapeutic value of oral history. *International Journal of Aging and Human Development, 12*(1), 49-53.

Berger, P., & Luckmann, T. (1966). *The social construction of reality.* New York: Doubleday Anchor.

Bertaux, D. (Ed.). (1981). *Biography and society.* Beverly Hills, CA: Sage.

Butler, R. (1963). The life review: An interpretation of reminiscence in the aged. *Psychiatry, 26,* 65-76.

Cohler, B. (1982). Personal narrative and the life course. *Life Span Development and Behavior, 4,* 205-241.

Cowgill, D. (1986). *Aging around the world.* Belmont, CA: Wadsworth.

Dollard, J. (1935). *Criteria for the life history.* New Haven, CT: Yale University Press.

Erikson, E. (1975). *Life history and the historical moment.* New York: Norton.

Gozdziak, E. (1989). New branches . . . distant roots: Older refugees in the United States. *Aging, 359,* 2-7.

Kirk, J., & Miller, M. (1986). *Reliability and validity in qualitative research.* Beverly Hills, CA: Sage.

Langness, L. (1965). *The life history in anthropological science.* New York: Holt, Rinehart & Winston.

Langness, L., & Frank, G. (1981). *Lives: An anthropological approach to biography.* Novato, CA: Chandler & Sharp.

Lieberman, M., & Falk, J. (1971). The remembered past as a source of data on the life cycle. *Human Development, 14,* 132-141.

Linton, R.(1936). *A study of man.* New York: Appleton-Century.

Liu, W. (Ed.). (1988). *The Pacific/Asian American mental health research center: A decade review.* Chicago: Pacific/Asian American Mental Health Research Center.

Merriam, S. (1980). The concept and function of reminiscence: a review of the research. *Gerontologist, 20,* 5, 604-609.

Nicassio, P. (1985). The psychosocial adjustment of the Southeast Asian refugee: An overview of empirical findings and theoretical models. *Journal of Cross Cultural Psychology, 16*(2), 153-173.

Rottman, L., & Merideth, W. (1982). Indochinese families: Their strengths and needs. In L. Stinnet, N. Stinnett, J. DeFrain, K. King, H. Lingren, G. Rowe, S. VanZandt, R. Williams (Eds.), *Family Strengths #4: Positive Support Systems* (pp. 579-587). Lincoln: University of Nebraska Press.

Seabloom, M. (1991). *Filial Piety Beliefs in the Life Histories of Vietnamese Elders.* Unpublished master's thesis. Family Social Science Department, University of Minnesota, St. Paul.

Seidel, J. V., Kjolseth, R., and Seymour, E. (1988). Ethnograph. Qualis Research Associates, PO Box 3129, Littleton, CO, 80161.

Sprey, J. (1979). Conflict theory and the study of marriage and the family. In W. R. Burr, R. Hill, F. I. Nye, & I. L. Reiss (Eds.), *Contemporary theories about the family* (Vol. 2, pp. 130-159). New York: Free Press.

Strauss, A.,

Parenthood as Problematic
Insider Interviews With Couples
Seeking to Adopt

KERRY DALY
University of Guelph, Ontario

Parenthood has taken on many new meanings in light of recent changes in the norms and structures of families. Where once we could more easily place the identity of parents as spouses living together to create and raise their own biological children, we now must take into account a much wider situational variation in the way that this role identity is taken on and carried out. Adoptive parents, unmarried single parents, divorced single parents, and parents in blended families are representative of the divergent ways that the parenthood role is carried out.

In light of the diversity of parenthood roles, a concept like the "transition to parenthood" (Rossi, 1968), because of its tendency to gloss over the different kinds of parenthood people take on, loses some of its ability to explain the process of taking on the role identity of parenthood. If the transition to parenthood is to be understood as the transition in its many forms, then the transition needs be examined in light of the unique features of each kind of parenthood. In this study, the focus is on the transition to adoptive parenthood by infertile couples.

Although processes of becoming adoptive parents involve different sets of experiences from those of becoming biological parents, each type of parenthood occurs against the backdrop of a common set of values and norms for what parenthood should be. As Blake (1974) has pointed out, pronatalist values underlie our beliefs about family. Pronatalist values are manifested through a set of expectations and pressures exerted on couples to have children soon after they are married. In our culture, one could argue that parenthood holds the central place in identifying a family as a family. "To become parents" is "to have a family," suggesting that taking on *real* family identity occurs when a couple begins to have children rather than at the time of marriage itself. From this perspective, parenthood, not marriage, may be seen as the critical transition into "family-hood."

Given the importance of parenthood for family identity within our culture, couples typically invest heavily in the role identity of parenthood. As one indication of this, 95% of newly married couples in the United States anticipate that they will have children at some point in their lives (Glick, 1977). Although this figure may since have dropped as a result of increasing rates of voluntary childlessness, the vast majority of married couples desire to have children. For many couples, becoming parents and in so doing becoming families is nonproblematic insofar as they are able to choose to have biological children and then simply proceed to do so without difficulty. For other couples, however, taking on this family identity is blocked by a fertility problem. Approximately 15% of all couples who desire to have children will have difficulty doing so (Matthews & Martin-Matthews, 1986). In light of this block to parenthood, couples are faced with the problems of defining and redefining what both parenthood and family mean to them.

Couples for whom infertility prevails over time choose between remaining childless, pursuing increasingly sophisticated reproductive technologies, or pursuing parenthood through some other means. For those for whom parenthood continues to be prominent in their identity hierarchy (Stryker, 1980), adoption becomes an alternative route for achieving this identity. Data from the National Survey of Family Growth suggest that among childless nonfecund women in the United States, about one-half will take some step toward adoption (Bachrach, London, & Maza, 1991).

In this chapter, I report on my research with infertile couples at various stages in their consideration of adoptive parenthood. The focus of the chapter is on the events they identified as important in reshaping the anticipated identity of parenthood to accommodate adoption in the face of infertility; I will discuss my theoretical assumptions, the design of the research, the implications of being an "insider," and the data themselves.

THEORETICAL AND METHODOLOGICAL ASSUMPTIONS

Purists in the grounded theory tradition have argued for the "tabula rasa" approach to fieldwork, in which preconceived notions are suspended in order to allow for the natural emergence of themes and categories. Recent work in the field argues for the importance of taking stock of one's assumptions, experiences, and knowledge as an important starting point in the qualitative endeavor. Lincoln and Guba (1985), for example, stressed making "tacit knowledge explicit" (p. 198) at the beginning of the research in order to shape insights and hypotheses. Similarly, Strauss and Corbin (1990) emphasized the use of theoretical and empirical literature as a way of enhancing "theoretical sensitivity" to the object of inquiry (p. 51). In my research, the symbolic interactionist concept of "transformation of identity" (Strauss, 1959) provided a set of sensitizing concepts for approaching the study of the process of becoming adoptive parents.

Change in adult life can be seen as a series of related "transformations of identity." Arguing against a view of human development that purports a movement along a continuum according to fixed norms or goals, Strauss (1959) suggested this interpretation is inadequate because it does not take into account "the open-ended, tentative, exploratory, hypothetical, problematical, devious, changeable and only partly-unified character of human courses of action" (p. 91). Within this context, changes in adult life can be seen as a series of related transformations that involve perceptual change and coming to new terms and evaluations of self and others. In this sense, subjective reality is "ongoingly maintained, modified and reconstructed" (Berger & Luckmann, 1966, p. 172) on the basis of conversations and interactions with significant others. This ongoing, and at times unpredictable, process of personal change occurs against the backdrop of a typified, taken-for-granted reality.

These changes are especially acute in light of "critical incidents" that constitute "turning points in the onward movement of personal careers" (Strauss, 1959, p. 93). These incidents result from changes in the expected roles or institutionalized paths of one's taken-for-granted reality and force the individual to take stock, reevaluate, revise, and rejudge the direction of one's personal career. In this regard, one must "gain, maintain and regain a sense of personal identity" in light of "unexpected places and novel experiences" (Becker & Strauss, 1956, p. 263). Thus, "old identities, beliefs, and values may have to be abandoned in the process of creating a new self-concept and world view" (Gecas, 1981, p. 168).

In the face of a fertility problem, there are many such "critical incidents" that precipitate a reevaluation and reshaping of the parenthood identity. Through these critical incidents, which reflect a couple's increasing realization that the two of them cannot have their own children, there is a transformation from an identification with biological parenthood to an identification with adoptive parenthood. In this sense, they begin to dismantle images of themselves as biological parents and slowly start to construct for themselves a new parenthood identity based on adoption.

RESEARCH DESIGN

The research design for understanding this process consisted of two phases. First, I carried out a preliminary study to sensitize myself to the predicaments of infertility and the ways in which adoption was being considered as an alternate route to parenthood. The preliminary study consisted of my attendance at five infertility support group meetings followed by open-ended, unstructured interviews with five couples. In the support group setting, I did not record data for use in the study, but rather used the situation as a way of coming to a cursory understanding of what some of the salient issues were for the couples who participated. This activity was useful for giving me some sense of direction in the five unstructured interviews that followed. I used these interviews to explore in greater detail what infertility meant to these people in their day-to-day lives and as a way of identifying some of the main issues in their consideration of adoption. These interviews were audiotaped and transcribed verbatim. In the preliminary activities, I followed the principles of grounded theory (Glaser & Strauss, 1967). These early interviews were an important mechanism for becoming "theoretically sensitized" (Strauss & Corbin, 1990) to the issues as well as a way of establishing categories for further collection of data.

Based on the information I collected during this preliminary stage of the research, I designed an open-ended interview schedule. I interviewed 74 couples selected from a fertility clinic at a large teaching hospital and from the adoption lists at two Children's Aid societies. To be included in the study, couples had to be experiencing a fertility problem and have no children (adopted or biological) living with them. Couples were recruited deliberately from these different sources in order to ensure that there were couples at various stages in the transformation of identity to adoptive parenthood. For example, many couples recruited from the fertility clinic had considered adoption as an option but had not taken concrete steps toward adoption, whereas all couples recruited from the agencies were actively pursuing adoption. Interviews lasted between 1 and 4 hours with the average being 2-1/2 hours.

The mean age of the sample was 31 for husbands and 30 for wives. The mean length of marriage was 6 years. The couples had experienced a fertility problem for a mean average of 5 years. The sample was predominantly white, with above-average levels of education and occupational status. For example, one-third of the men and one-fifth of the women held university degrees. Corresponding to this education attainment, one-third of husbands and one-quarter of wives held professional or managerial positions.

I interviewed couples rather than individual spouses. Unlike other kinds of identities, in which individuals can strive for an identity independent of others, parenthood is usually contingent on a *shared* construction of reality. As Berger and Kellner (1970) point out, taking on new roles in marriage involves an ongoing process whereby "each partner's definitions of reality must be continually correlated with the definitions of the other" in order that these definitions have a "common objectivated reality" (p. 58). Adoptive parenthood, as one such identity in marriage, involves a set of negotiations about being ready for adoption and can therefore be seen as representing a shared construction of reality. I believed interviewing couples was the best way of trying to capture this shared reality.

Drawbacks of interviewing couples involved the potential for conflictual and embarrassing issues not to emerge. In this regard, there may have been a more collusive tendency in the couple to protect their "backstage behavior" (Goffman, 1959) than might be the case when interviewing spouses alone. With these kinds of difficulties in mind, Lofland and Lofland (1984) suggested interviewing more than one person at a time may be most productive when the topics are public or nonembarrassing. In addition, conjoint interviews may result in some unanticipated disclosures by one spouse that violate the privacy or consent of the other spouse (LaRossa, Bennett, & Gelles, 1985).

Interviewing spouses together had other advantages, however. With two accounts, a more reliable picture can emerge in that the bias in one version may be balanced by that in the other; spouses can jog one another's memory; and most important for reliability and validity, spouses tend to keep each other honest (Allan, 1980). Bennett and McAvity (1985) similarly argued that interviewing the couple generates expanded information resulting in the validation of agreement between husbands and wives or in the clarification of differences. Furthermore, interviewing the couple on a private family topic such as this had the further advantage for the study of including men, who have typically been difficult to recruit for this kind of research (Miall, 1985). Indeed, in recruiting couples for this study, the men were more likely to resist, and I welcomed wives as allies in encouraging husbands to participate.

Role Considerations: Being an Insider

In carrying out the research, I made it a point to be open about my personal experience with infertility and adoption. Although couples appreciated knowing of our common experiences, my colleagues repeatedly questioned the effect this kind of personal involvement would have on the study. After all, being too close to the subject matter threatens the objectivity and detachment that typically are thought to be necessary to make research "good science." Although the history of qualitative research is filled with examples of researchers examining aspects of the empirical world with which they have personal experience (Becker, 1963; Davis, 1959; Gans, 1962; Polsky, 1967), little attention has been paid to the methodological implications of this research role.

Considerably more attention has been directed toward problems associated with researchers being outsiders who must maintain marginal positions with those under study. For example, Blum (1970) discussed the problem of getting individuals to give information to an outsider, Whyte (1955) discussed the importance of the outsider having sponsorship in order to get information from the individuals one is studying, Vidich (1955) emphasized the necessity of remaining marginal to the organization or group one studies, and Wax (1971) warned against the dangers of "going native." The implications of being native to begin with have been largely overlooked, however.

In a discussion of carrying out roles in fieldwork, Gold (1957) reminded us of the tension between "role demands" and "self demands": "Every fieldwork role is at once a social interaction device for securing information for scientific purposes and a set of behaviors in which an observer's self is involved" (p. 218). In light of the emphasis on "objectivity," the demands of the self or the subjective perceptions of researchers often are overlooked or perhaps more frequently consciously denied in favor of a detached or "objective" approach (see Douglas, 1985). For insiders, however, these demands are forces with which to reckon. Personal involvement predisposes researchers to enter the field with perspectives shaped by idiosyncratic thoughts, feelings, and experiences.

Insiders and Their Expectations

Although all researchers enter the field with predetermined assumptions and expectations, insiders perhaps are unique in the degree to which their taken-for-granted realities shape their expectations. Few researchers, however, have explored the effect that these subjective demands have on research processes. In reflecting on the subjective origins of his own research on urban crime, Friedrichs (1981) came to the disturbing conclusion that most academic papers, including his own, are presented as "products of a disembodied intellect" (p. 217).

How do we bring the self back into research processes? I would argue that for insiders these past-related experiences are essential parts of research processes, and they demand not just acknowledgment, but conscious and deliberate inclusion. Practically speaking, this means that the presentation of self in the research process includes statements and disclosures about one's experiences with the phenomena in question. In this regard, I argue that the "role demands" of inside researchers are best met by being adequate to the "self demands" as experiencing, thinking, feeling persons. Consistent with this, Oakley (1981) argues that the goal of finding out about people through interviewing is best achieved when "the relationship of the interviewer and the interviewee is non-hierarchical and when the interviewer is prepared to invest his or her own personal identity in the relationship" (p. 41).

To this end, my personal experience with infertility suggested the kinds of things to say, how to say them, and when to bring them up in the course of the interview. For example, having been exposed to a number of suggested infertility remedies from well-wishing friends or family such as "drink sherry before bed" or "you're just trying too hard—take a vacation," I was aware of the significance of these comments. In my own experience, these comments were significant because first, they were frequent, and second, they tended to trivialize the problem and contribute to a sense of isolation from my peers. By raising these experiences in the interview and asking couples about their own similar experiences, I was able, in a nonintimidating way, to get couples to reflect on the responses of others to their infertility and the impact that those responses had on their feelings about themselves. Thus, the deliberate use of the self in the research process helped to unravel the experience of the other. This is consistent with Berk and Adams (1970), who pointed out that the revelation of some intimate facts promotes acceptance and trust in the fieldwork relationship that can pay dividends in the depth and quality of the data collected. Of course, this only stands to reason, for a relationship within the research context is not unlike any other developing relationship, for which the reciprocity of disclosure is crucial for understanding.

Wax (1971) also emphasized the importance of establishing the "reciprocal social response" (p. 20) by showing respect and interest and by giving assistance to respondents. Insiders are positioned to do this because of the broad base of experiences and resources on which they can draw to enhance the reciprocity of interview interactions. In my research, it seemed appropriate to provide information as a way of "giving back" to the respondents. This took the form of giving them information about books, counselors, support groups, or "how the adoption system worked." Such responses helped maintain the exchange aspects of the interview relationship. (Snyder, Chapter 4, this volume, made similar decisions.)

Giving Assistance and Role Confusion

Giving assistance can lead to role confusion. Because of the familiarity of the researcher with the subject matter and the casual style with which this information is shared, there may be a greater likelihood that the researcher's role is confused with the role of therapist, problem solver, friend, or informed expert. (See Daly, Chapter 1, this volume.) Informants may perceive researchers as experts who not only ask questions but who can also provide answers. Lopata (1980) describes the difficulty she and her staff encountered in doing research with widows:

> Over and over, we found the respondents expecting some sort of direct help as a result of the interview, a solution of problems and even a complete change in life. They assumed that the interviewer . . . has the power to bring societal resources to them. . . . It is difficult to be faced by a respondent who is so obviously in pain or need and whom we are not trained to help. (p. 78)

In my interviews with infertile couples, similar expectations emerged that made it difficult to stay in the researcher role. For example, one husband and wife were having widely different experiences in the way that they were coping with infertility and were finding it difficult to understand each other's experience. As a result they turned to me:

> *Wife:*   He doesn't know exactly how I feel and I find that hard to understand, because he is my husband and this is his problem too. He wants a child too. He just seems to be able to accept it so much easier without asking questions.
>
> *Husband:*   Well, you just have to accept it, no?
>
> *Wife:*   Well, I agree with him, you have to accept it because I have no choice. Like what am I going to do? I can't go on crying all my life. But what I can't understand is: How can it be so much easier for him to accept than me? How? [turns to me inquisitively]

In this instance, I avoided being placed in the role of therapist or expert by simply reflecting the same question back at her. I asked her why she thought it was easier for him to accept it, and she responded with a long explanation about his family background. This technique was effective insofar as it served both the respondent's need to understand her husband's behavior and my need as researcher to get data. Further, by not offering advice or possible explanation, I avoided being triangulated or overstepping the bounds of my professional expertise as a researcher without professional therapy training.

Being "in the know" can also work against investigators. When researchers and the participants operate from shared realities, there may be a tendency to take too much for granted. This can serve to inhibit the flow of data in two ways. First, researchers may overlook certain aspects of participants' realities because of their presumed familiarity with those realities. Familiarity with the phenomenon under study, therefore, risks blindness to certain details that might be important. Infertility is personal and sensitive, and it touches on the highly private areas of self-esteem, sexuality, and life goals. I made a conscious effort, therefore, not to overemphasize shared realities. I thereby maintained some social distance between myself and the couples under study. Miller (1952) warned against the problems associated with "over-rapport" and recommended that a balance be struck between rapport and objectivity. McCracken (1988) emphasized the importance of "manufacturing distance" to "create a critical awareness" of matters with which we have "blinding familiarity" (p. 33). This advice takes on added importance when the issues are highly private and personal.

In addition, respondents may withhold information they see as too obvious in light of the shared reality with the researcher. In one instance, a woman began to talk about her experience of going to the gynecologist for infertility investigation and having to sit in a waiting room of pregnant women. She said: "It's not fun going to these things . . . but, well, you *know*." In this situation it was necessary to establish a "pretence awareness context" (Glaser & Strauss, 1967) that conveyed a message of my own ignorance. Therefore, regardless of whether or not I could anticipate what informants were going to say, I encouraged them to continue by saying something like, "No, I'm not really sure what you mean. Could you explain?" or "No, I've not had that kind of experience. Please go on."

Talking to Strangers

Ironically, it seems when it comes to highly personal issues, some people are more comfortable talking to someone who is somewhat of a stranger and with whom there is little possibility of future interaction. This became evident when the tape recorder was shut off at the end of the interview. Many respondents said they had never talked about some of these things either between themselves or with close friends or family members. This was also evident throughout the interview. For example, one couple's interaction was illustrative of things that could be told to me as stranger but had not yet been said to the spouse:

Husband: Everyone believes that "it [i.e., infertility] will not happen to us," and until it does, I don't think that they will ever understand. When I realized that the only way we were going to have our own children was through adoption—even to the day that we picked up our little girl, I was really very tentative. I really wanted to—but I think I went along with it because it meant a lot to her.

Wife: That's a terrible thing to say! [nervously laughs]

Husband: Well, . . . I was in agreement, but I was in all honesty very tentative about the whole thing. [uncomfortable silence]

Perhaps Simmel's (1950) discussion of the "stranger" comes closest to accounting for these intimate disclosures. For Simmel, the perceived "objectivity" of the stranger may give rise to "the most surprising openness—confidences that sometimes have the character of a confessional and which would be carefully withheld from a more closely related person" (p. 404). Furthermore, playing the role of the objective stranger incorporates a structured balance between "distance and nearness, indifference and involvement" (p. 404). The implications of this for insiders are clear: Use the nearness and involvement afforded by shared experiences to gain access and establish trust, but maintain whenever possible the distance and mystery of the stranger in order to encourage a full account of the participant's experience.

Validity and Insider Data

Important validity issues arise with insider data. All research is both valid and invalid to some degree because scientific reports of human action remove it from the actual reality. By putting data through sociological filters, researchers remove them from their original contexts, intentions, and meanings. Everyday occurrences are thereby encoded in "constructs of the second degree" (Schutz, 1971), which represent the difference between everyday and scientific conceptions of reality (Denzin, 1978). By the very presence of the interpretive process inherent in the research act, there will always be problems of validity. Validity, then, is not a question of presence or absence, but one of degree.

In field methods, as in all social research methods, it is impossible to avoid some level of subjectivism when recording and interpreting data (Bogdan, 1972). For insiders, dangers of subjectively distorting data are salient because acquaintance with the subject matter is perhaps more likely to color the way phenomena are seen. As a result, how researchers report their findings may reflect their own experiences more than the experiences of participants.

Objectivity and Insider Status

Lest we write off insiders as bobbing aimlessly in a mire of subjectivity, however, we would do well to consider what it means to be "objective" in this kind of research. There is some consensus that researchers achieve objectivity to the degree they get closer to phenomena under study. Wolff (1964), for example, suggested that the best method for achieving objectivity is not for researchers to distance themselves, but to "surrender" to phenomena they wish to understand. This involves "total involvement, suspension of received notions, pertinence of everything, identification and the risk of being hurt" (p. 236). Only when researchers are close enough can phenomena reveal themselves. Then researchers are "being adequate to the object" (p. 236). Likewise, Blumer (1969) emphasized the importance of the researcher "taking the role of the acting unit whose behaviour he [sic] is studying" to get accurate data. To try to collect data from a distance is to risk "the worst kind of subjectivism" (p. 86) or the "fallacy of objectivism" (Denzin, 1978, p. 10). From this perspective, the assessment of validity is contingent on the proximity of the researcher to the account and its context in terms of who produced it, for whom, and why (Hammersley & Atkinson, 1983).

The insider has a head start on this proximity because of prior acquaintance. As a result, "surrender," identification, and taking the role of the other are facilitated. Working from a base of shared reality, the insider can get closer to the "other's" domain of experience. In so doing, the insider is afforded an intimate glimpse of the other's reality, which, in the currency of objectivity and validity, is of considerable value.

CRITICAL INCIDENTS IN THE TRANSITION TO ADOPTIVE PARENTHOOD

What were the "turning points" or the "critical incidents" (Strauss, 1959) in the onward movement of the respondents' parenthood careers? What were the events that arose to disrupt their anticipated, taken-for-granted transition to biological parenthood? These events can be categorized as defining biological parenthood as problematic, letting go of biological parenthood, turning attention to adoptive parenthood, and dealing with obstacles in the transition to adoptive parenthood.

Defining Biological Parenthood as Problematic

On the basis of their taken-for-granted view of parenthood, the respondents usually assumed that they would simply become parents when they chose to do so. Fertility tended to be seen as something that they could simply "turn on" at the appropriate moment after a period of having "turned it off" with the aid of contraceptives. As one man put it, "You use birth control all the time, and you just think it's going to happen when you want it to." When couples were faced with the prospect of being unable to turn on their fertility as they had expected, they had to replace the "parent" identity with an "infertile" identity.

For many couples, infertility is the kind of life event that happens to other people. As a result, shock and surprise was the usual response. A woman described the way that the diagnosis of a fertility problem shook her taken-for-granted world:

> When the doctor phoned to tell me, I just don't remember coming off the phone. It was something I had never thought about. I thought I was as normal as everyone else. It was a shock.

There was considerable variation in the way that couples came to define their situations as problematic. The type and timing of a medical diagnosis played a key role in how situations came to be defined as problematic or nonproblematic. At one extreme were those couples who had received a definite diagnosis of absolute or near-absolute sterility. These couples clearly identified themselves as being infertile or having a fertility problem and realized that biological parenthood was problematic. At the other extreme were those couples who had been through a lengthy period of tests and treatments, but who were still without a diagnosis. For many of these couples, coming to an acceptance that biological parenthood was problematic was particularly difficult. One woman, who had gone through 4 years of testing without a diagnosis, explained:

> We don't have a problem. It's just taking longer. So it depends what you call a problem. Even now we aren't sure that there's a problem. I don't

allow myself to think that there is a problem so I believe that I will get pregnant.

Reference groups played an important role in the construction of biological parenthood as problematic. Changes in the taken-for-granted world of biological parenthood were reinforced by the responses of others to the problematic situation. For one woman, this occurred as a result of her friends pitying her:

> It has made me feel like you can't take anything for granted. You see people struggling or in pain and you thought that would never be me. Now I see them and I feel like them. I work with the handicapped, and they say: Don't pity me. I understood that intellectually, but now I understand it emotionally. Many of my friends are pregnant and they say: Poor you! They are pitying me!

Because couples were unable to make the expected transition to parenthood, they were in a position of having to explain or "account" (Scott & Lyman, 1981) for this normative violation. The need to account for the behavior usually arose innocently in the course of day-to-day interaction when significant others would ask about the presence of children. For those experiencing parenthood as a problematic, the question called out for an account of their childlessness. One woman described feeling compelled to explain:

> I wish there was a simple explanation of yes or no with this, but when people ask whether or not we have kids, there is no simple explanation. I wish there was. What really bothers me with all this is that you have to explain anyway.

Letting Go of Biological Parenthood

As couples increasingly defined their situations as problematic, they began to relinquish their identification with biological parenthood. No doubt one of the key aspects for initiating the process of letting go of biological parenthood was the sense of having lost control over their fertility, and ultimately their family plans:

> *Husband:* After month in and month out we began to feel it was beyond our control. The more things didn't work out, the more we began to feel that it was more out of control.

> *Wife:* Having infertility is like being an alcoholic, only worse. Being an alcoholic, at least if you are going to do something, you have control over it. If you are going to change it, it has to come from you. With infertility, though, you don't have control over it. That's what is so frustrating!

The loss of control that couples felt was in large part due to their dependence on the medical experts to identify the problem and come up with a solution. As couples typically spent several years in the course of these tests and treatments, their process of letting go of biological parenthood was often a choppy one. Respondents spoke about the infertility process as a series of stops and starts. They would hit a saturation point or a tolerance threshold and would need to withdraw from the infertility process. With energy renewed or the prospect of a new test or treatment, they would reinvest in the medical process. These tolerance thresholds gave the process of relinquishing biological parenthood a reverberating quality:

> *Husband:* It seems that it goes in cycles. You get so down and want to leave it. I am tired of all the problems and going ahead with it.
>
> *Wife:* I think he reached that point [the end] a long time ago. I've reached that point a number of times. I have said "enough" and need a break away from it. For me the end will come in a few months when I have to go on with Danazol [a medication for endometriosis]. I don't want to take it, so that may be the end. Although each time I reach those points I change and end up continuing on.

Turning Attention to Adoptive Parenthood

Ultimately, however, couples spoke of reaching a turning point that shifts attention from biological parenthood to adoptive parenthood:

> Once we had explored all the alternatives [for having a biological child], rationally we had to give up having our own. We had to wake up to the fact that we had to do something else. That's when we got very active in pursuing adoption.

It is during this time that couples engage in a critical reevaluation of the meaning of parenthood. In the same way that the man in the above quotation talked about having to "give up having our own," a woman talked about the implications for thinking about becoming an adoptive parent when you can't have "your own":

> I think that you have to be completely convinced that you couldn't have your own baby. Then, is it your own baby or a baby that you want? You have to come to a point where if your own baby is not possible or so dim that you then ask the question: Do we just want a baby? Or was it to have our own baby?

When couples began to think of "a baby" rather than "a baby of their own," they began to look to significant others for cues about what it would mean to become adoptive parents. In some cases, this meant being more attentive to media presentations of adoption or observing and discussing with friends or acquaintances who had some experience with adoption. For others, it meant telling others about their adoption plans to check out the reactions they might receive to the anticipated identity of adoptive parents:

> Sometimes I tell people about adoption to see what their reaction is. I want to see how they respond. I knew that there were some negative ideas. It's part of the preparation. If they have something crummy to say [about adoption], I want to hear it now before I have a child.

A significant turning point in the transition to adoptive parenthood is the active initiation of the formal adoption process. One couple provided some insight into why the call to the agency is such an important part of adoption readiness:

> *Husband:* It was a long time just psyching up to fill in the application forms. It took us 10 months, and in that time you go through so much emotional stuff to actually make the call.
>
> *Wife:* It was an admission to myself that I was out of control. We had testing done and the choice was either a laparoscopy or Danazol [a drug for endometriosis] and we didn't want either of those so we talked about adoption. It took 10 months from then to actually call the agency.

Coming to terms with the difference of adoptive parenthood was perceived to be an important part of getting ready for adoption:

> The signs that tell you that you are ready are that you can accept that you
> have a problem, accept taking help, and accept the child of someone else's
> making. It's an acceptance of what it would be like if the child were to
> search and how I would feel. I had to think about whether I was ready to
> accept all the things that an adopted child could throw at you.

Perhaps one of the most fundamental features of coming to terms with
adoptive parenthood was to "fantasize" themselves in the role of adoptive parents. Schutz (1971) emphasized the importance of fantasizing
as the foundation for any projects of action. For one man, fantasizing
was an important part of adoption readiness because it took adoption
from the abstract and made it more real when he placed himself in the
role of adoptive parent:

> You are ready when you stop saying it [adoption] as a word and start
> thinking about yourself as a parent. My response to being blocked from
> being a biological parent was to put it out of my head. With adoption, I've
> had to come back to that. We talked about adoption as an idea and really
> didn't visualize ourselves doing it. Once she sent away for the [adoption]
> forms and information, I really began to think about it more.

Spouses did not always move toward adoptive parenthood at the same
rate or with the same readiness. For one couple, the spouses' awareness
of differences emerged out of the process of negotiation involved in
coming to some consensus on adoption readiness:

> We are getting closer. We are merging. We've not got there yet. It is more
> urgent for me. We do have different feelings but we are getting closer all
> the time.

Consistent with Berger and Kellner's (1970) notion of socially constructing a marriage through conversation, the couples in this study
emphasized the importance of talking through their infertility and
adoption plans as a way of coming to a shared definition of the adoptive
parent identity.

A crucial aspect of preparing for the role identity of adoptive parenthood was the process of gaining formal support from the adoption agency.
As discussed more fully in other reports (Daly, 1988, 1989a, 1989b,
1990), couples expressed feelings of anger, dependency, resentment,

and powerlessness in seeking legitimation from the agency. Couples tended not to view this process as a way of preparing for adoptive parenthood, but rather as an obstacle to be overcome. In this sense, respondents did not perceive the agency as a source of support in helping them to prepare for adoptive parenthood, but rather as gatekeepers who would judge their worthiness to take on the role of adoptive parents. A strategy of impression management in which they presented themselves as the "perfect parents" was one way of overcoming this obstacle to get a child.

Nevertheless, the respondents perceived agencies as powerful socializing agents. For one couple, the formal adoption processes were positive socializing influences providing answers to questions and enabling confrontation of fears:

Husband: They talk about all your worries. The things you don't know about adoption until you get into it. For me it's been a process of understanding what's involved. You only understand what it means once you are in it.

Wife: It's made me feel good about adoption. They have been open about answering questions and they are doing good things for the birth mother and adoptees.

Others expressed similar sentiments when they stated that by "going to the agency we felt ready" or "they have helped out by showing that it is a big experience and what we have to do."

Obstacles in the Transition to Adoptive Parenthood

Understanding the way that couples came to a state of adoption readiness can be furthered by examining some of the obstacles that prevented couples from identifying fully with adoptive parenthood. The most commonly expressed concern about adoption was the uncertainty of the child's background. According to one couple:

Husband: You worry about the kind of person who gives up a baby.

Wife: My biggest concern is the heredity or the personality traits that are passed on. I believe a lot in heredity. The kids come with characteristics already established.

The absence of background information would create for one woman an ongoing sense of "wonder about whose child you have." For others, the child comes with its "own set of baggage" or a "set of characteristics that are in the genes." These unknown biological characteristics created concerns about the kind of child one might get. As one couple put it:

> I am afraid that the kid would be stupid or have birth defects. You are buying an unknown product. You are more familiar with the parameters when it's your own.

In addition to the genetic unknowns, the uncertainty of whether the biological mother would change her mind about adoption emerged as a significant concern. One woman explained her concern as "the insecurity of not knowing whether or not the parents show up on your doorstep." Another explained it this way:

> If the real parent tries to find the child, that would hurt me more than having your heart cut out. It would be like them taking your own flesh and blood.

Respondents frequently used such expressions as the "real" parents would come to take the child back, suggesting that they, as adoptive parents, would be once removed from "real" parenthood. In this regard, adoption was often considered second best.

Reservations about adoptive parenthood and corresponding restraints in identifying with it were also the result of anticipating having to tell the child about adoption, and related to this, the possibility of being rejected by a child who found out he or she was adopted. One woman described her concern about telling the child about adoption:

> I'm apprehensive about telling my child that they are adopted. How do you deal with that possible hurt?

Couples also described the potential of being "hurt and betrayed" if the child decided to search for his or her birth parents after being told about adoption. Although these concerns resulted in the careful evaluation of the adoptive parenthood identity, the persistent and intensifying need to become a parent continued to move the respondents toward their desired goal.

CONCLUSION

Becoming an adoptive parent has been conceptualized in this analysis as a process of identity transformation. At one level, this transformation involves the redefinition of the taken-for-granted meaning of parenthood as a result of the disruptive effect of infertility on the process of becoming biological parents. At another level, it involves the construction of a new and unanticipated identity, based on the unique contingencies of adoption. The transformation from biological to adoptive parenthood can therefore be viewed as a process by which infertile couples dismantle images of themselves as biological parents and replace the images with new ones of themselves as adoptive parents, both in their own eyes and in the eyes of others.

A number of critical incidents emerged in this analysis that mark the key transition points in the reevaluation of the parenthood identity. Acknowledging that their fertility was problematic was typically the first step in this process. This was followed by having to let go of the image of oneself as a biological parent. Of central importance in letting go was the admission that the spouses could no longer control their fertility in light of the repeated frustrations of unsuccessful tests and treatments. Turning attention to adoptive parenthood was marked by a shift in the meaning of parenthood from having "one of your own" to having a baby of someone else's making. Calling the adoption agency, telling significant others, coming to terms with the difference of adoption, fantasizing themselves in the role, and going through the adoption agency procedures were important turning points for the respondents in moving toward adoptive parenthood. Concerns about the kind of child they would get through adoption, the potential interference of the birth parents, and possible rejection by an adopted child introduced some trepidation in their movement toward adoptive parenthood.

As the findings of this study suggest, the transition to adoptive parenthood is marked by a set of unique contingencies that are quite different from the taken-for-granted transition to biological parenthood. In light of the increasing diversity in the kinds of parenthood that people take on, transformation of identity can serve as a useful conceptual tool for the analysis of these unique transitions.

Participant observation and interviews were the most appropriate methods for discovering the key events in the transition to adoptive parenthood. Whereas large survey studies can provide important insight into the proportion and circumstances of those who seek to adopt

(Bachrach et al., 1991) qualitative methodology is essential for elucidating the processes by which infertile couples come to embrace the
adoptive parenthood identity.

In this study, several methodological procedures proved to be of
particular value. First, taking stock of both scientific information and
personal experiences was an important first step. Being clear about the
nature of my prior acquaintance with the phenomenon at hand was
important for theoretical sensitivity as well as for sorting out my own
biases and expectations. For qualitative researchers, it makes sense to
take stock of who you are and what you already know in determining
what you need to know. Second, the two-step procedure of unstructured
observations and interviews followed by a more structured interview
allowed for both the undirected emergence of key themes and a more
directive, efficient, in-depth exploration of these themes. Finally, being
an insider presented some unique challenges with respect to managing
the self in the research process. On the one hand, being an insider
presents challenges with respect to manufacturing distance and resist-
ing the expectation to be the expert or therapist. On the other hand,
having an intersubjective experience with participants is highly advan-
tageous in establishing a reciprocal, nonhierarchical relationship with
them. In addition, it allows the researcher to achieve a high level of
validity by virtue of being able to get closer to the participant's subjective experience.

REFERENCES

Allan, G. (1980). A note on interviewing spouses together. *Journal of Marriage and the
    Family, 42,* 205-210.
Bachrach, C. A., London, K. A., and Maza, P. L. (1991). Adoption seeking in the United
    States, 1988. *Journal of Marriage and the Family, 53,* 705-718.
Becker, H. S. (1963). *Outsiders: Studies in the sociology of deviance.* London: Collier-
    Macmillan.
Becker, H. S., & Strauss, A. L. (1956). Careers, personality and adult socialization.
    American Journal of Sociology. 62, 253-63.
Bennett, L., & McAvity, K. (1985). Family research: A case for interviewing couples. In
    G. Handel (Ed.), *The psychosocial interior of the family* (pp. 75-94). New York:
    Aldine.
Berger, P. L., & Kellner, H. (1970). Marriage and the construction of reality. In H. P.
    Dreitzel (Ed.), *Recent sociology* (No. 2, pp. 49-72). New York: Macmillan.
Berger, P. L., & Luckmann, T. (1966). *The social construction of reality.* New York:
    Doubleday.

Berk, R. A., & Adams, J. (1970). Establishing rapport with deviant groups. *Social Problems, 18,* 102-117.

Blake, J. (1974). Coercive pronatalism and American population policy. In R. L. Coser (Ed.), *The family: Its structure and functions* (pp. 276-317). New York: St. Martin's.

Blum, F. H. (1970). Getting individuals to give information to the outsider. In W. J. Filstead (Ed.), *Qualitative sociology: Firsthand involvement with the social world* (pp. 83-90). Chicago: Markham.

Blumer, H. (1969). *Symbolic interactionism: Perspective and method.* Englewood Cliffs, NJ: Prentice-Hall.

Bogdan, R. (1972). *Participant observation in organizational settings.* Syracuse, NY: Syracuse University Press.

Daly, K. J. (1988). Reshaped parenthood identity: The transition to adoptive parenthood. *Journal of Contemporary Ethnography, 17,* 40-66.

Daly, K. J. (1989a). Anger among prospective adoptive parents: Structural determinants and management strategies. *Clinical Sociology Review, 7,* 80-96.

Daly, K. J. (1989b). Preparation needs of infertile couples who seek to adopt. *Canadian Journal of Community Mental Health, 8,* 111-123.

Daly, K. J. (1990). Infertility resolution and adoption readiness. *Families in Society: The Journal of Contemporary Human Services, 71,* 483-492.

Davis, F. (1959). The cabdriver and his fare. *American Journal of Sociology, 63,* 158-165.

Denzin, N. K. (1978). *The research act: A theoretical introduction to sociological methods* (2nd ed.). New York: McGraw-Hill.

Douglas, J. D. (1985). *Creative interviewing.* Beverly Hills, CA: Sage.

Friedrichs, D. O. (1981). The problem of reconciling divergent perspectives on urban crime: Personal experience, social ideology and scholarly research. *Qualitative Sociology, 4,* 217.

Gans, H. (1962). *The urban villagers.* New York: Free Press.

Gecas, V. 1981. Contexts of socialization. In M. Rosenberg and R. H. Turner (Eds.), *Social psychology: Sociological perspectives* (pp. 165-199). New York: Basic Books.

Glaser, B., & Strauss, A. L. (1967). Awareness contexts and social interaction. *American Sociological Review, 29,* 669-679.

Glick, P. C. (1977). Updating the life cycle of the family. *Journal of Marriage and the Family, 39,* 5-13.

Goffman, E. (1959). *The presentation of self in everyday life.* New York: Doubleday.

Gold, R. L. (1957). Roles in sociological field observations. *Social Forces, 36,* 217-223.

Hammersley, M., & Atkinson, P. (1983). *Ethnography: Principles in practice.* London: Tavistock.

LaRossa, R., Bennett, L. A., & Gelles, R. (1985). Ethical dilemmas in qualitative family research. In G. Handel (Ed.), *The psychosocial interior of the family* (pp. 95-111). New York: Aldine.

Lincoln, Y. S., & Guba, E. G. (1985). *Naturalistic inquiry.* Beverly Hills, CA: Sage.

Lofland, J., & Lofland, L. (1984). *Analyzing social settings: A guide to qualitative observation and analysis.* Belmont, CA: Wadsworth.

Lopata, H. Z. (1980). Interviewing American widows. In W. B. Shaffir, R. A. Stebbins, & A. Turowetz (Eds.), *Fieldwork experience: Qualitative approaches to social research* (pp. 69-81). New York: St. Martin's.

Matthews, R., & Martin-Matthews, A. (1986). Infertility and involuntary childlessness: The transition to non-parenthood. *Journal of Marriage and the Family, 48,* 641-650.

McCracken, Grant. (1988). *The long interview.* Newbury Park, CA: Sage.

Miall, C. (1985). Perceptions of informal sanctioning and the stigma of involuntary childlessness. *Deviant Behaviour, 6,* 383.

Miller, S. M. (1952). The participant observer and "over-rapport." *American Sociological Review, 17,* 97-99.

Oakley, A. (1981). Interviewing women: A contradiction in terms. In H. Roberts (Ed.), *Doing feminist research* (pp. 30-61). London: Routledge & Kegan Paul.

Polsky, N. (1967). *Hustlers, beats and others.* Chicago: Aldine.

Rossi, A. S. (1968). Transition to parenthood. *Journal of Marriage and the Family, 30,* 26-39.

Schutz, A. (1971). *Collected papers I: The problem of social reality.* The Hague: Martinus Nijhoff.

Scott, M. B., & Lyman, S. M. (1981). Accounts. In G. P. Stone & H. A. Farberman (Eds.), *Social psychology through symbolic interactionism* (2nd ed., pp. 343-362). New York: John Wiley.

Simmel, G. (1950). *The sociology of Georg Simmel* (Ed. K. H. Wolff). New York: Free Press.

Strauss, A. L. (1959). *Mirrors and masks: The search for identity.* Glencoe, IL: Free Press.

Strauss, A. L. & Corbin, J. (1990). *Basics of qualitative research: Grounded theory procedures and techniques.* Newbury Park, CA: Sage.

Stryker, S. (1980). *Symbolic interactionism: A social structural version.* Menlo Park, CA: Benjamin/Cummings.

Vidich, A. J. (1955). Participant observation and the collection and interpretation of data. *American Journal of Sociology, 60,* 354-360.

Wax, R. (1971). *Doing fieldwork: Warnings and advice.* Chicago: University of Chicago Press.

Whyte, W. F. (1955). *Street corner society.* Chicago: University of Chicago Press.

Wolff, K. H. (1964). Surrender and community study: The study of Loma. In A. J. Vidich, J. Bensman, and M. R. Stein (Eds.), *Reflections on community studies* (pp. 233-264). New York: John Wiley.

An In-Depth Interview With the Parents of Missing Children

DEBORAH LEWIS FRAVEL and PAULINE G. BOSS
University of Minnesota

On November 12, 1989, a small notice appeared in the Personals section of the want ads in the *Star Tribune,* a Minneapolis-St. Paul newspaper. It read: "KEN, DAVID, & DAN KLEIN. MISSING since Nov. 10, 1951. We are still waiting to hear from you." The notice ended with two telephone numbers and was signed "Mom and Dad." Following the appearance of the notice, a newspaper article reported that the children's parents, Kenneth and Betty Klein, still held hope for the boys' return (Grow, 1989).

The story of the Klein family attracted our attention because it presented a compelling example of a family's ambiguous loss, an area in which we have research interests. The family's experience was remarkable on two counts: It involved the disappearance of three children at once, and the parents maintained hope for the children's return almost 40 years later. This chapter presents our findings from a 3-hour unstructured interview we jointly conducted with those parents.

AUTHORS' NOTE: We are grateful to Betty and Kenneth Klein for sharing their experience and wisdom with us. We also wish to thank Carol Elde and Nancy Heitzeg for their comments on an earlier draft of this chapter, Bobbi Goess for secretarial assistance, and Donna Tebben for providing the 1951 newspaper that contained an article about the Kleins.

Our primary purpose in conducting this single-case study was to gather information that might broaden our understanding of families' experiences of ambiguous loss. We wondered how the Kleins would describe their experience and whether they could speculate about behaviors, attitudes, or other resources that had been helpful to them. We wondered, too, whether their account would reveal how their experiences with the loss had changed in the 38 years that had passed since their sons disappeared.

THEORETICAL BACKGROUND

The premise behind this study is the following: The ambiguity of a loss creates dynamics that complicate resolution of the loss. Not knowing where the missing person is, not knowing if he or she is dead or alive, family members cannot grieve and resolve the loss in the same way they might under other circumstances. Instead, families may become preoccupied with the missing person, who is psychologically present yet physically absent. Families may operate in states of uncertainty about whether the missing person is in or out of the family system. The family's reorganization may become blocked. If this occurs, a perceptual shift can help the family to change and move on. (For more on ambiguous loss, see Boss 1977, 1980, 1987, 1988, 1991; Boss, Greenberg, & Pearce-McCall, 1990.)

In this paper, we examine the Kleins' loss experiences from a symbolic interactionist perspective. Symbolic interactionism is useful for understanding ambiguous loss, in that it helps in focusing on how the family shapes its perceptions of the ambiguity by connecting meaning and symbols (LaRossa & Reitzes, in press). A family dealing with ambiguous loss would be expected to create a symbolic understanding, or reality—a reality shaped by the shared meanings from within the family, by the larger context of the world outside the family, and by the interactions that occur both within and between the internal and external contexts.

Literature on Missing Children

Scholarly literature related to families of missing children is scarce. We therefore selected, as a point of reference, a popular press article that presented brief case studies of families with missing children. We used examples from this article, along with related scholarly literature, to help us interpret the accounts of the Klein family.

Some commonalities exist across families and situations in issues of loss, grief, and mourning. At least two factors, however, are different here. First, the loss of a child is extraordinary. Parents simply do not expect their children to disappear. Losing a child may be experienced differently by parents of different children, or even by two parents of the same child. These differences in perception are critical in shaping the way a family handles loss (Rando, 1986). Second, the loss is ambiguous, and the ambiguity surrounds virtually every aspect of a child's disappearance. For example, in the United States, language practices have usurped the most appropriate descriptor for missing children: they are literally *lost*. Because "lost" has become a euphemism for "dead" in greater society (e.g., "I lost my mother 2 years ago"), however, families of missing children experience ambiguity even communicating about their missing child.

An obvious source of ambiguity is not knowing whether the child is dead or alive. Families, therefore, deal with a second layer of ambiguity: Should they mourn, be optimistic, or be brave but resigned (Teichman, 1975)? Although the parents may feel heart-wrenching grief, they may also feel that to mourn the child is to deny hope and therefore to deny the child's possible existence (Lloyd & Zogg, 1986). Those choices are complicated by yet another layer of ambiguity at the social level: Because the facts surrounding their loss are not clear, family members cannot grieve and mourn or receive support through conventional social responses and rituals (Boss & Greenberg, 1984; Doka, 1989; Rando, 1986). An official from a missing children's center commented that "Like in suffering a death, [the families] go through denial, anger, grief—but there is no funeral, no funeral director to take care of their needs" (Gelman et al., 1984, p. 85).

The effects of disappearances infiltrate families. Siblings may develop symptoms such as developmental regression and phobias (Greaves, Currie, & Carter, 1982; Lloyd & Zogg, 1986). Couples may be overwhelmed with the loss and experience difficulty supporting one another. Parents may find themselves overprotecting the remaining children or becoming hypervigilant. At the same time, parents may feel overwhelmed with guilt and shame, wondering whether they were irresponsible and in some way contributed to the disappearance (Lloyd & Zogg, 1986).

Significance of the Study

The theory of ambiguous loss is a relatively recent one. Although the theory has been tested deductively with military families in which the husband-father was missing in action (Boss, 1977, 1980) and then with a large sample of mid-life families facing the normative situation of an adolescent leaving home (Boss, Pearce-McCall, & Greenberg, 1987), this study is the first to examine the construct with reference to families of missing children. Using qualitative research methods to enhance an already existing construct offers another approach to the examination of ambiguous loss: Do findings from this case confirm or contradict conclusions drawn from previous studies? Does this case yield additional insights that enhance the theory of ambiguous loss? Examining similar constructs across substantive areas yields formal theory (Gilgun, Chapter 3, this volume; Glaser & Strauss, 1967).

The conclusions from this qualitative study also will contribute to the small body of literature related to missing children and the effects of that trauma on remaining family members. In addition, the observations may serve to generate hypotheses for further research, not only with regard to families of missing children, but also about family strengths, family resiliency, and family stress management, especially as these constructs relate to ambiguous loss. Finally, the findings may be useful as hypotheses for practitioners who are engaged in therapy with families whose children have disappeared or who are experiencing other forms of ambiguous loss.

Limitations and Acknowledgments

Two interviewers and the length of the interview may offset some of the limitations of the single interview we conducted for this study. Our conclusions are tentative, subject to correction by other research. The data were retrospective and subject to errors of memory, which traditionally is seen as a limitation. We took the perspective of Cohler (1982), who noted, "A personal narrative which is recounted at any point in the course of life represents the most internally consistent interpretation of presently understood past" (p. 207). The current interpretation can take a form that is sensible and coherent and incorporates a beginning, a middle, and an end. The narrative has a personal and a social component in that it must not only be coherent to the narrator, but it must be *heard* as coherent and sensible. Thus we acknowledge that the narrative the Kleins shared with us represents their present construction of events surrounding the disappearance of their three sons and their lives since that time.

PROCEDURES

Ethical Considerations

Under ordinary circumstances, interviewing a couple whose children had disappeared might raise serious ethical questions. For example, many scholars (including us) would consider it exploitative to seek an interview with a family still in the throes of the loss of one or more of its children. We discussed at great length whether our research would cause the family to feel compelled to talk of issues they did not wish to share, or whether the study might in some way bring them undesired publicity and thus violate their privacy. At the same time, the Kleins had already shared their story with several newspaper reporters, and in the most recent story, they said they were seeking additional exposure on the television show "Unsolved Mysteries" (Grow, 1989). Given these facts, we concluded that interviewing the Kleins would be ethically acceptable once they consented.

Though their situation was public, we implemented several layers of precaution on the Kleins' behalf. First, the Human Subjects Committee of the University of Minnesota reviewed our proposal. In its approval, the committee suggested that because of the Kleins' expressed desire to make their story well known, they be given a choice of whether or not they would like to remain anonymous. We incorporated that choice into the informed consent form. To be certain that we had explained the study and outlined their rights, we read the informed consent form to the Kleins at the beginning of the interview. We offered them an opportunity to ask questions before they signed the form and received a copy.

Another ethical issue we considered before the interview was the possibility that the interview might bring out emotions the family was not prepared or able to address. Pauline Boss is a therapist with many years' experience dealing with families under stress, and we thought her expertise would enable her to detect and deal with any such occurrences. We decided, therefore, she would initiate and guide the interview. This decision was implemented as an added layer of protection for the Kleins.

Research Design

Under the assumption that a telephone call from two university researchers might be intimidating, initial contact was made with a letter in which we said it would help us and others to hear how they had managed their not knowing where their boys were. Mostly, we said, we just wanted to listen to their story. We told the Kleins we would phone later that week. When we called, the Kleins agreed to participate. We conducted the interview in their home.

We used an in-depth, unstructured interview because we believed the greatest depth and breadth of information could be obtained by allowing the Kleins to tell the story in their own words. When appropriate, we planned to probe for additional information. The combination of open-endedness and probes provided a balance between respecting their perspective and allowing us to pursue theoretically relevant topics. We were satisfied with the quality of the data obtained from this interview. The Kleins agreed to a subsequent interview should one be necessary. In addition, we made plans to interview the one child who remained to them after the three boys disappeared and those subsequently born, all now adults. The children agreed to participate, and these interviews are presently in progress.

Data Analysis

The interview was audiotaped using a small recorder placed on a coffee table in the Kleins' living room. Transcription of the tapes was challenging. Early on, it became apparent that although our transcriptionist, a secretary and an "outsider," could capture the main statements and ideas, much of the detail would be lost. When the interview became lively and two or even three people were speaking at once, it was impossible for the secretary to sort out these comments. Additionally, she had difficulty differentiating voices on the tape. As a result, we assumed the transcription task, starting at the beginning of the tapes. We did a literal transcription, including false starts, asides, stutters, repetitions, chuckles, laughs, and other utterances. Doing the transcription ourselves led to increased understanding of the data.

Each of us independently reviewed the tape and transcript, making written notes of themes that emerged. We shared our impressions and observations with each other. No formal process was used to eliminate observations and impressions from the final account. Rather, we attempted to sort compatible observations and impressions into categories. This became an exercise in moderation as we sought balance between over-synthesizing and including all relevant and apparent observations. This process occurred over the course of several months through multiple readings of the transcript, individual pondering, innumerable discussions, and many drafts of the manuscript. Our close readings and intense discussion of these literal transcripts yielded insights into the Kleins that we had missed during the interview. For example, during the interviews, we focused intently on the Kleins and their comments relating to the loss of their children. In reviewing the tapes and transcripts, we noticed they often spoke conversationally to their animals, several times inviting the dogs to come closer into the circle where we were sitting. Only in the written transcript did we notice these multiple references and asides, which led us to conclude that the Kleins cherish their dogs and birds. Thus what had been unwittingly designated as background noise during the interview became a noteworthy observation after examination of the transcript.

FINDINGS

Several themes relevant to the purpose of the research emerged through the interview and our analysis of it. These included the development of a personal theory that appeared to have facilitated the Kleins' management of their loss and resolution of loss through a balance between hope and realistic assessment. Other themes were the Kleins' worldview, their team approach, their religious faith, and the sense that their experience had some social value. In this section, we present a general description of the Kleins and their setting, followed by separate discussion of each of the themes.

Participants and the Setting

At the time of the interview, Betty Klein was 65 and Kenny was 72. Both looked healthy and younger than we expected. The windows in their living room were undraped, allowing sunshine to stream into the room. Numerous well-cared-for house plants hung from the ceiling and rested on window ledges. A cage of singing birds hung in their living room, and several dogs roamed freely in and out of the room, at times sitting in the chairs with the Kleins, at times lying at their feet.

The Kleins appeared to be at ease, chatting comfortably even in the initial awkwardness. They were eager to cooperate. When asked about using their real names or a pseudonym, Kenny's immediate response was "Which way would be most helpful to the research?" We said we wanted them to make that decision. The Kleins decided they would like to have their real names used. They did not appear jaded from their experience. To the contrary, they were enthusiastic and upbeat.

History

The story behind this study began in an everyday manner: On a warm November day, Ken, David, and Daniel Klein, aged 8, 6, and 4, obtained their mother's permission to go to Farview Park, a public park located near their Minneapolis home. Pulling on caps and red jackets, the boys left for the park. They planned to meet their eldest brother Gordy, aged 9, later. When Gordy went to Farview Park a short time later, he was unable to find his brothers. The search that began shortly after Gordy returned home quickly escalated from one conducted by his parents and relatives to a full-scale search by police and volunteer groups, eventually including tracking dogs, air searches, and dragging of a portion of the Mississippi River. Two of the boys' caps were later found floating in the river, but the tracking dogs had lost the boys' trail at a street corner, not at the river bank. No bodies or other evidence were ever found.

After their three sons disappeared, Betty and Kenny had four more sons. They moved to a nearby small town where they raised their five remaining sons. Kenny continued to work at the same Minneapolis dairy until the business closed. Betty worked outside the home briefly, once as a housekeeper in a hospital and once in an office supply store. They now have three grandchildren, all girls.

Healing Theory

The way a family manages stress is determined to a large extent by the meaning the family attaches to the event (Boss, 1988). Figley (1989) described the creation of a system of meaning as the family's *healing theory*. In developing its healing theory, the family members, both individually and jointly, form a perception of the situation that incorporates their understanding, to the extent possible, of the situation, as well as acceptance and affirmation of their responses and the reasons behind them. A successful healing theory thus functions as the family's self-administered prescription for managing stress.

If family members are unable to develop a successful healing theory after experiencing an extreme stressor event, posttraumatic stress disorder (PTSD) may occur. The disorder may manifest itself in various ways: reexperiencing the event (flashbacks, nightmares), symptoms of persistent arousal (hypervigilance, insomnia), or avoidance of situations similar to the experienced trauma (Figley, 1989).

The Kleins seemed remarkably free of PTSD symptoms. Betty recounted what might have been symptoms of heightened arousal in the time immediately following the boys' disappearance:

> Every time a car went by slow, or we heard a door slam in the night . . . we thought it was our boys coming home. And it was pulling. It was very hard.

Although an exaggerated startle response may be typical of posttraumatic stress, it does not seem sufficient evidence for classifying the Kleins' response as a disorder. In fact, the Kleins realized they could not live indefinitely with that kind of arousal. With a thoroughness that appears to be characteristic of them, they had legal records flagged so that police would be notified if anyone requested copies of the boys' birth certificates. They notified their Minneapolis neighbors of a forwarding address, receiving assurances that the neighbors would contact them if they heard any information at all about the missing boys. The Kleins then moved back to their hometown, where kin and friends were numerous. The Kleins did not see the move as an attempt to run away from their grief. In fact, they were quick to acknowledge that they moved their grief with them. Betty continued:

> And like I, I've told different ones, I said you, you don't know how many tears were shed, you know. . . . I used to set out there on that back step and cry like my heart was breaking. . . . And I often said, uh, if you ever had a broken heart, I had it.

Hope and Loss

Generally, hope can be viewed as a desire accompanied by some degree of optimism that the desire will be fulfilled. When children are missing, however, hope takes on a different character. Kenny referred to the positive side of maintaining hope when we asked him what advice he would give to the parents of another Minnesota boy who had been kidnapped just prior to the time of our interview: "As long as they have never found the body . . . nobody can say he is dead." Betty alluded to the other side of hope, the painful lack of closure, in a segment of the interview in which we discussed a then-current news story of the finding of the dismembered body of a young boy:

Interviewer: When that little boy was found in the [Mississippi] river last week, and when you read about things like that in the paper, does that sort of stir it all up for you again?

Betty: Well, it does, but it makes us feel better. Because they found that boy. He was in the river and they found him. And they didn't find ours. . . . Because [the boy's parents] can, they can finalize their, you know. They were waiting out there, too, for something . . . for them to come home, or for them to be found, or something. And, and I think, well at least now they're, they're finalized. Yeah. I mean, they, they know. They're content, too. There's no more looking.

Indeed, the dark side of Betty's hope surfaced in that comment as she unconsciously switched from the single-person referents "he" and "him," referring to the boy in the recent news story, to "them," as if she were referring to her own multiple loss. (A comment supporting our earlier observation about immersion in the data is appropriate here: We did not notice this subtle switch in referent until about the 20th reading of the transcript.)

The newspaper article that originally attracted our attention was headed "Parents still hope they'll be reunited with three sons missing since 1951" (Grow, 1989). It is difficult for even the most compassionate scholar to avoid assessing that kind of hope as dysfunctional. In the interest of acknowledging our bias, we admit we approached the study expecting to observe some dysfunction. This expectation was tempered by our knowledge that it is hard for families *not* to keep hoping when there is ambiguity in the loss. We took seriously the observations of Lloyd and Zogg (1986):

For the family of a missing child, there is no final acceptance. To accept that the child will never be found—whether dead or alive—is to deny the very existence of the child; it also signifies the loss of hope. As a result of

the lack of acceptance, however, family members spend the rest of their
lives in hope and disarray within the family structure. (p. 271)

Our interview with the Kleins led us to challenge our own pathologizing
perspective that extended hope after ambiguous loss is dysfunctional.
Perhaps because the Kleins have spent the ensuing years in hope and
not in disarray, as mentioned earlier, their management of loss is more
functional.

Another insight that may be helpful in understanding the Kleins'
responses is the lack of social or legal conventions constraining parents
from maintaining hope for lost children, as there may be with missing
spouses. For example, if a woman wishes to remarry after her husband
has been missing for an extended length of time, she must make some
cognitive decision that her husband will not return. She then takes steps
to divorce him or have him declared legally dead before she remarries.
Parents of missing children, however, may choose to have other children without a comparable decision or declaration.

The Kleins appeared to take comfort in the speculation that their boys
might have been picked up by adults who wanted children and could
not have their own. A 1984 *Newsweek* article reported a case in which
the mother of a missing child "fantasize[d] that her son . . . miracu-
lously landed with loving foster parents" (Gelman et al., p. 86). In the
Kleins' case, such a notion is at least partially supported by the fact that
bloodhounds tracked the boys' scent to a street corner, but no further.
This evidence left open the possibility that the boys might have gotten
into a car at that point. These beliefs served as another example of the
search for meaning brought on by the lack of closure inherent in such
events. The Kleins, however, appeared to have a reasonably realistic
approach toward the return of their sons; they knew the odds of their
sons' returning were small. Betty said:

> I don't know if I would be ready for *them* [the boys], though. [laughs] You
> know what I mean. I, I, if you walked in a room and they said, "Well, this
> is your son," I wouldn't be ready for it. . . . Because in my mind I guess I
> think it could happen, but it's a very slim chance, it happening, you know,
> so it would have to be this little slim chance, and [laughs] I would probably
> say, uh, "Well, I have to have a little proof," you know. . . . The one that I
> think the safest way to get the proof is have a blood test . . . I think that'd
> be the best way to do it, because that's pretty, pretty foolproof. Although
> it isn't *completely* foolproof, but it's pretty close to it.

That Betty wanted proof is similar to requests made by families of men missing in action in Southeast Asia when remains are found and sent home decades after the loss. They often ask for second opinions from nonmilitary experts to prove that these are indeed the remains of their loved ones. Perhaps this request for proof serves as a buffer created by the family to protect itself from further disappointment. It may also be that these families, although feeling compelled to maintain a degree of hope, also feel an inner need to cut their own psychic losses by making a more realistic appraisal of the possibility that their loved one will not return. Thus the Kleins' expression of a need for proof may represent a degree of acceptance of their loss.

Although the Kleins did not define their management strategies in the language of process, analysis of the interviews provides some evidence that the family's strategies for dealing with the loss have changed over time. For example, Betty said the family received an unsigned Christmas card each year for 6 years following the boys' disappearance. Speaking in the past tense, she noted how their freedom to assign meaning to events helped them for a period of time:

> It was like somebody was sending us a card, one of our kids was sending us a card or something but didn't dare say where he was, you know. And, uh, it kinda helped you. Because you didn't know for sure, and so you could build this up in your mind to believe whatever you wanted to believe about it.

Other indicators provide evidence that the Kleins have accepted, to some degree, the loss of their sons. For example, when asked how many children they have, the Kleins usually answered "five," without including the three missing boys. Betty says she gave birth to eight children only when she is asked for her medical history. Together, these observations lead to the conclusion that the Kleins have accepted their loss more than they have denied it.

Worldview

Worldview and value systems influence how families manage stress. Family members may perceive the world as just, life as fair, and themselves in control of outcomes. Carried to an extreme, the just-world and mastery orientation may inhibit successful stress management (Boss, 1988). For example, clinicians occasionally meet parents who shift from doctor to doctor, refusing to accept the fact that their child is dying of an incurable illness.

It is not possible to determine how the Kleins' present worldview differs from their perceptions at the time of the boys' disappearance. At the present time, however, the Kleins seem to have achieved a balance between a mastery orientation and fatalistic resignation, as illustrated by this interchange that followed Betty's account of how she discouraged her granddaughter from baby-sitting for strangers:

> **Betty:** Really, I don't trust anybody. You know what I mean.
>
> **Interviewer:** It sounds like you now know there are, there is some, some unfairness in the world.
>
> **Kenny:** There are lots of dangers lurking out there. People just don't realize it. That's just all there is to it.

The Kleins' level of trust could be situational. Betty's words in the preceding passage stand in curious contrast to her earlier statement, when considering the informed consent form: "Well, we trust you." Perhaps the Kleins' hesitance to trust surfaces in situations involving the general and the unknown. The Kleins may trust themselves and their abilities to make accurate assessments in interpersonal encounters. In addition, what they called "trust" in this passage might better be described as caution. Their caution, however, seems to have been balanced by a desire not to overprotect. Betty said:

> I know that's one thing we were, we wanted to be careful with, though, was our kids, was our other boys. . . .You always wanted to say "Well, don't go, because I want to keep you close," you know, "I want to see you." . . . That was my temptation. But you can't do that if you want a healthy, normal child.

Sometimes what the Kleins expressed as a lack of trust appeared to be an expression of disappointment and anger. When we asked if they ever experienced anger over their loss, Betty replied that what irritated them most was the manner in which the police conducted their investigation. Betty and Kenny related that Betty's sister had flyers printed by the police in her hometown, Stockton, California, because the Minneapolis police would not do so. Kenny was emphatic:

See, we had a lot of reason to be disgusted with the Minneapolis Police Department because there was a lot of things they could've done but they wouldn't do for us. . . . To this very day I don't trust 'em.

Lloyd and Zogg (1986) stated that families of missing children often blame the police for what the families perceive to be inadequate service. The *Newsweek* article (Gelman et al., 1984), too, suggested that anger may be "displaced" on law enforcement officers: "The frantic families of victims understandably want an all-out effort, but what they encounter are the routine, sometimes enigmatic, processes of the law" (p. 85). The most exhaustive investigation may seem inadequate to families experiencing situations that are anything but routine to them.

A Team

In this interview, Betty and Kenny appeared to have a close personal relationship. Their communication with one another was thoughtful, considerate, and helpful. They supplied words for one another when one perceived the partner groping for a word, and they sometimes finished each other's sentences. They lovingly related the details of their courtship, he teasing that someone put a gate in the fence between their childhood homes and the "son of a gun got left open so I went over there to see her." Betty remarked, "I couldn't have gone around the world and found a man as good as I had right across the fence."

They were quite adamant, too, that their relationship helped take them through the rough times of losing the three boys. They felt strongly that couples in similar situations should "just stick together" because they need each other more than ever at such times. Betty and Kenny were vehement that spouses not blame each other when difficulties occur. Again, the Kleins' approach may be atypical; families of missing children often turn their frustration on each other (Greaves et al., 1982; Lloyd & Zogg, 1986).

Betty and Kenny acknowledged "down" times over the years. We asked them what helped pull them out of those slumps. Without hesitation, Kenny said it was their other children, Gordy and the four who were born after the disappearance. He said:

You just can't run around with a long face, because that wouldn't be fair to the boys that you've got, you know.

Later, elaborating on their intent to move forward in spite of their pain, Betty struggled for words to express their determination:

> I guess this is probably what helped us, too, was the, we, we always knew we were needed for Gordy. . . . And I was pregnant with the baby, and the baby needed us. And so, you know, it just, uh, you, you can't put your hurts up front. You have to put them in the back and live on. And it doesn't mean you're gonna forget [the missing boys] . . . .It just means you're, uh, you're taking care of today.

Religious Faith

The Kleins were open about their religious beliefs. They believed God was at work in their lives as another major force that has helped them get through the ordeal. Reflecting on his own childhood, Kenny said his widowed mother, left with eight small children, managed to raise those children by herself:

> It was really tough going for her. So I always figured it always had to do with her—she was religious. Everybody, I think, is religious in their own right. Maybe you don't go to church, but you say your prayers. I know I do. And I know she [Betty] does. So. You know what I mean. We're all religious, and I think that has a lot to do with the way we have handled this situation.

Betty differentiated between their being Catholic and their believing God had helped them:

> Because we're not that strict a Catholic. But it's because, just because we believe in God, and that He is there to help us.

The Kleins seemed at peace with what they perceive as God's part in the disappearance. Betty admitted that she did, at first, reflect about whether their boys' disappearance might be punishment from God. She concluded that they had not done anything to deserve such a punishment and decided that was not the case. She viewed their having the subsequent children as a symbol of affirmation that they were good parents:

> He was giving us children back, not ever to replace the three that were gone, because you can't, but proving to us, in a way, I thought, that we were good parents anyway.

For the Kleins, the disappearances were not punishment God inflicted, but they were of the ups and downs of life. God was there to help them through it. Betty said simply:

> I coped with it by saying, well, it was God's will, you know, and there was nothing I could do about it.

A Sense of Social Value

As discussed earlier, families who experience the disappearance of a child often deal with an added layer of ambiguity at the social level. There are no socially institutionalized responses to the disappearance of a child, no rituals that have meaning in society (cf. Boss & Greenberg, 1984). Feeling overwhelmed themselves by the ambiguity and not knowing how to respond to it, friends and neighbors often simply stay away. Other families in the immediate community may become self-absorbed, dealing with the fear that their child, too, might disappear (Greaves et al., 1982; Lloyd & Zogg, 1986; Teichman, 1975).

Another contrasting view is that a flurry of activity inevitably occurs after the disappearance of a child, hindering the family's internal reorganization. For example, Lloyd and Zogg (1986) contend that the numbers of "other people external to the immediate family . . . contribut[e] to its disorganization and dismemberment" (p. 270). In contrast to both these contentions, the Kleins felt strengthened by a tremendous outpouring of social support from family, friends, clergy, and the community at large at the time of their loss. That support has continued through the ensuing years.

At the same time, the belief that their experience has been valuable for other people has been a source of strength for the Kleins. Betty stated:

> I thought, well, maybe other mothers will look at their children and hold them a little bit closer, you know, because of it. I'm sure there was a lot of parents that took their children in their arms, you know, when that happened to our children. I'm sure there was.

Following this statement, the Kleins shared a letter from a local man who had experienced the birth of his first child about the same time the Grow (1989) article appeared in the newspaper. In part, the letter read:

The thought of losing my little boy is about the worst thing that could ever happen. I couldn't imagine going through the rest of my life without being bitter and cynical. To lose three children like that seems unendurable. I was tremendously impressed by how you adjusted to life without them and made your life successful. I am grateful there are people like you to make a fine example to the rest of us.

Other letters, along with similar telephone calls, have been a source of both comfort and purpose to the Kleins for the entire 38 years.

The Kleins' experience stands in contrast, however, to the isolation described in the literature about other cases. Betty noted that the family did not have financial resources adequate to conduct endless searches. Their strategy was to publicize the situation periodically through the media. This served to elicit publicity, but it also had the serendipitous effect of perpetuating and enlarging the Kleins' social support as well as serving as a very real example of resourcefulness, resilience, and strength to others suffering ambiguous losses.

DISCUSSION

The purpose of this study was to seek information to broaden our understanding of ambiguous loss. Betty and Kenny Klein successfully had managed the loss of their three sons by working as a team and by not blaming each other or anyone else for their loss. They developed a healing theory that provided a sense of what happened and how those events wove into the fabric of their lives. In general, their healing theory revolved around their commitment to each other, to their remaining children, and to the world around them, with their belief in God's will serving as an overarching source of strength, comfort, and meaning.

Study of the Klein family yielded evidence supporting previous contentions about families of missing children, particularly with regard to the ambiguity of their loss. The Kleins did not know whether their boys were dead or alive; they could grieve for their loss but not with the closure available to those who grieve over a death. In addition, they have had to attain what closure they could without benefit of socially institutionalized responses or rituals to help them. They have questioned themselves, and they have questioned the behavior of law enforcement officers. In all these ways, the Kleins' experience seems similar to that of many other families experiencing the loss of a child.

Earlier in this chapter, we stated we expected to observe dysfunction. Before the interview ended, however, we reassessed that perspective. We began to understand that, for these parents, giving up hope when there was no conclusive evidence that the boys were dead was unthinkable. The Kleins appeared to have accepted their loss as much as possible, given the ambiguity surrounding their sons' disappearance. They appeared to have a realistic assessment both of their loss and of the likelihood that their sons would reappear. We concluded we had observed minimal or no dysfunction.

In many ways, however, our reassessment brought us full circle: The sons were still physically absent, and they were still psychologically present. Our task at that point became one of determining how our observations of the Kleins appeared to be different from observations from the literature and from the second author's clinical experiences. When we compared our conclusions about the Kleins with those conclusions available from other sources, some differences emerged. The most notable of these is that the Kleins were a team. They worked together to manage their loss, supporting one another, and not blaming one another. Their teaming existed in nested circles, first between Betty and Kenny, then the two of them teaming with their remaining child and subsequent children, and all of them teaming with their extended family. Besides teaming as a family, however, the Kleins teamed with people who became available in an ever-widening circle of social support. Betty and Kenny Klein were active both in accepting this team support and in creating it for themselves.

The other way that the Kleins' management of their loss might differ from that of other families experiencing the loss of a child is in the strength they feel they received from their religious beliefs. Although this issue is not addressed in literature related to families of missing children, it has been observed in clinical experience with families facing other types of ambiguous loss. We offer it here, then, as a characteristic that emerged in this study as an important part of the Kleins' healing theory.

Having noted the similarities and differences between the Kleins and other families experiencing the loss of a child, our task became a bit more difficult as we sought answers to our final question: What additional insights did this case yield to enhance the theory of ambiguous loss? Our answers to this question led us along three tentative paths.

First, it is notable that, in their minds, the Kleins had allowed their sons to grow up. When they think of their missing sons, they think of them as adults who were raised by other parents. In fact, they think of their sons as adults who probably have children of their own now. Keeping others psychologically present may not be dysfunctional if the images mature and change over time. For the Kleins, time did not stop; they allowed their image of the lost boys to mature. Although the Kleins could not "forget" their sons, in some ways they relinquished them to what they imagine as their new lives. In doing so, they have symbolically placed the sons in a realm that makes sense to them. This may have helped to reduce some of the ambiguity of the loss.

The second path of conjecture relates to the Kleins' strategy of publicizing their situation and then receiving the unexpected benefit of additional social support. Earlier, we noted Cohler's (1982) contention that, for a personal narrative to be acceptable, it must be sensible and coherent to both narrators and listeners, and it must incorporate a beginning, a middle, and an end. Over the years, the Kleins have told their story many times to different persons. Each time, they attempted to make sense of their experience as they saw it at that point, to create an "ending," however temporary, to the story. The Kleins' strategy may have had yet another serendipitous benefit, that of helping them make the most sense possible out of their experience at successive points across their life span.

Clinical theory tells us that we need to learn to live with ambiguity, to develop a tolerance for the uncertainties that life delivers. The third path we considered, then, is that perhaps the Kleins, more than most people, have developed a dialectical balance between maintaining and giving up hope. They have done this with their eyes open to realistic probabilities and therefore demonstrate little of the deleterious effects seen in families where this kind of balance has not yet been achieved. Because this balance is usually observed only in clinical situations, seeing it in the Kleins gives credence to the generation of the hypothesis that managing long-term ambiguous loss may require achieving balance between hope and acceptance. Observation and validation of this phenomenon may be elicited more clearly in clinical observations and qualitative research than in deductive research methods.

REFERENCES

Boss, P. (1977). A clarification of the concept of psychological father presence in families experiencing ambiguity of boundary. *Journal of Marriage and the Family, 39,* 141-151.

Boss, P. (1980). The relationship of wife's sex role perceptions, psychological father presence, and functioning in the ambiguous father-absent MIA family. *Journal of Marriage and the Family, 42,* 541-549.

Boss, P. (1987). Family stress: Perception and context. In M. Sussman & S. Steinmetz (Eds.), *Handbook of marriage and the family* (pp. 695-723). New York: Plenum.

Boss, P. (1988). *Family stress management.* Newbury Park, CA: Sage.

Boss, P. (1991). Ambiguous loss. In F. Walsh & M. McGoldrick (Eds.), *Living beyond loss: Death and the family.* New York: Norton.

Boss, P., & Greenberg, J. (1984). Family boundary ambiguity: A new variable in family stress theory. *Family Process, 23,* 535-546.

Boss, P., Greenberg, J., & Pearce-McCall (1990). *Measurement of boundary ambiguity in families* (Station Bulletin 593-1990, Item No. AD-SB-3763). St. Paul: University of Minnesota, Minnesota Agricultural Experiment Station.

Boss, P., Pearce-McCall, D., & Greenberg, J. (1987). Normative loss in mid-life families: Rural, urban, and gender differences. Rural families [special issue], *Family Relations, 36,* 437-443.

Cohler, B. (1982). Personal narrative and life course. In P. B. Baltes & O. G. Brim (Eds.), *Life-span development and behavior* (Vol. 4, pp. 205-241). New York: Academic Press.

Doka, K. F. (1989). *Disenfranchised grief.* Lexington, MA: D. C. Heath.

Figley, C. (1989). *Helping traumatized families.* San Francisco: Jossey-Bass.

Gelman, D., Agrest, S., McCormick, J., Abramson, P., Greenberg, N. F., Zabarsky, M., Morris, H., & Namuth, T. (1984, March 19). Stolen children. *Newsweek,* pp. 78-86.

Glaser, B. G., & Strauss, A. L. (1967). *The discovery of grounded theory.* New York: Aldine.

Greaves, G., Currie, J., & Carter, A. (1982). Atlanta, psychology, and the second siege. *American Psychologist, 37,* 559-568.

Grow, Doug. (1989, November 14). 38-year vigil continues: Parents still hope they'll be reunited with three sons missing since 1951. *Star Tribune* (Minneapolis-St. Paul), pp. 1, 10, 11.

LaRossa, R., & Reitzes, D. (in press). Symbolic interactionism and family studies. In P. Boss, W. Doherty, R. LaRossa, W. Schumm, & S. Steinmetz (Eds.), *Sourcebook of family theories and methods: A contextual approach.* New York: Plenum.

Lloyd, G. M., & Zogg, C. (1986). Missing children. In T. A. Rando (Ed.), *Parental loss of a child* (pp. 269-275). Champaign, IL: Research Press.

Rando, T. A. (Ed.). (1986). *Parental loss of a child.* Champaign, IL: Research Press.

Teichman, Y. (1975). The stress of coping with the unknown regarding a significant family member. In I. Sarason & C. Spielberger (Eds.), *Stress and anxiety* (Vol. 2, pp. 243-255). New York: John Wiley.

Using Multiple Forms of Family Data
Identifying Pattern and Meaning in Sibling-Infant Relationships

SUSAN O. MURPHY
San Jose State University

The purpose of this chapter is to demonstrate the use of qualitative research methods to study sibling relationships in families with a new baby. I will describe how this longitudinal, qualitative family study evolved from research questions to findings, and I will identify some of the unique concepts concerning early sibling relationships in families that resulted from the use of qualitative research strategies.

Qualitative researchers sometimes talk about "entering the field blind." By that they mean looking at the phenomenon with fresh eyes, without the influence of other previous explanations of the phenomenon. The justification for this strategy is that it enhances the researcher's ability to be objective and to avoid personal bias. However, if one approaches a research area naively, one may also overlook more subtle factors that are operating in the situation. In addition, one might tend to describe the

AUTHOR'S NOTE: This research was supported in part by National Research Service Award No. 5 F31 NU05805-03 from the Division of Nursing and by Faculty Post-Baccalaureate Fellowship No. 1 A23 NU00025-01 from the Bureau of Health Professions. My current research is funded by Academic Research Enhancement Award No. 1 R15 NR02120-01 from the National Center for Nursing Research.

situation so much from an outsider's perspective that one fails to convey the situation as it is experienced by the individuals or families themselves.

I did not enter this research area naively. My interest in siblings and newborns emerged from my clinical practice with childbearing families. Parents often wondered what to expect from their older child following the birth of a baby and how to prepare the child for the changes that would occur. To address these concerns of parents, I conducted an extensive review of the literature on siblings and infants, including both the scholarly literature and popular writings for children and parents. Completing this extensive literature review on siblings and infants not only gave me an appreciation of the variety of perspectives on this subject, but also clarified the gaps in previous research and informed the development of a specific research plan.

PREVIOUS RESEARCH

Sibling relationships have often been viewed from a Freudian perspective emphasizing the concepts of sibling rivalry and displacement of the older child (Bank & Kahn, 1980; Griffin & De La Torre, 1985; Neubauer, 1982; Pietropinto, 1985). Bank and Kahn (1982) in their discussion of sibling loyalties, and Handel (1986), in his research that looked beyond the concept of sibling rivalry, have demonstrated some of the theoretical limitations of the Freudian perspective by addressing sibling friendship and loyalty, as well as other salient issues that arise among older siblings.

When conducting research focusing on siblings and newborns, assuming that sibling rivalry is the norm can be misleading in that it tends to bias the nature of the data collected, the instruments used, and the explanations made for sibling behavior. This theoretical perspective has led researchers to focus on the negative aspects of sibling response to the newborn and to use instruments that only measure regressive or negative behaviors (Fortier, Carson, Will, & Shubkagel, 1991; Kayiatos, Adams, & Gilman, 1984; Legg, Sherick, & Wadland, 1974; Taylor & Kogan, 1973), thereby failing to recognize the wide variation in sibling response that might occur following the arrival of a new baby.

Research on siblings and infants conducted from a broader and longitudinal perspective supports the view that sibling relationships are not based primarily on rivalry (Abramovitch, Corter, & Lando, 1979; Abramovitch, Pepler, & Corter, 1982; Stewart, 1983a, 1983b, 1990; Stewart, Mobley, Van Tuyl, & Salvador, 1987). Studies that have specifically addressed sibling response to newborns indicate that maturation as well as regression may occur when a new baby enters a family (Dunn, 1983, 1984; Dunn & Kendrick, 1982a; Nadelman & Begun, 1982), and that individual attributes of the older child as well as the developmental capabilities of the infant contribute to the ongoing evolution of the sibling relationship (Dunn & Kendrick, 1982b; Dunn & Munn, 1985; Kreppner, Paulsen, & Schutze, 1982a, 1982b; Stewart, 1990). Research also suggests that family interaction, particularly parental support and communication, may play an important role in a sibling's response to a new baby (Dunn & Kendrick, 1982b; Gottlieb, 1985; Gottlieb & Mendelson, 1986; 1987; Kreppner, 1987, 1990).

These recent studies have made significant contributions to our understanding of siblings in families. However, most have focused exclusively on firstborn toddlers' or preschoolers' responses to a newborn. The research discussed in this chapter is unique because it includes school-aged siblings and newborns and attempts to address the experience from the school-aged child's perspective.

METHODOLOGY

Sibling relationships develop within families, over time. To understand what happens when a new baby enters a family with older children, we need to study sibling relationships within their family context and to gather data from children themselves. Based on these assumptions, decisions were made to conduct a longitudinal study, to observe families in their natural settings performing everyday activities, and to gather data directly from the school-aged children as well as the parents.

At the time this research was being formulated, only one qualitative study had been conducted in which the researchers attempted to address developmental and interactional changes in families over time following the birth of a second-born child (Kreppner et al., 1982a). I am indebted to Dr. Kurt Kreppner for his consultation to me in the early phases of the development of this research and for his continued interest and collaboration. I am also grateful to Dr. Laurie Gottlieb for her ongoing collegial support and consultation on siblings and research strategies.

The research discussed in this chapter is part of a larger research program that includes two longitudinal studies. The first study gathered data from nine families for 2 years. The second study, still in progress, includes eight families, which have been followed for more than a year. To explain how the qualitative work was handled from the beginning, I am basing this discussion on the initial study, although data from the second study continues to inform these findings.

Grounded Theory Methodology

A researcher's selection of methodologies evolves not only from the research questions. The questions themselves are also influenced by the cognitive style and the research training of the investigator. I had had the opportunity to study *grounded theory methodology* with Anselm Strauss and Juliet Corbin. This training influenced both the form and the process of my research.

Grounded theory methodology (GTM) is a style of qualitative analysis developed by sociologists Glaser and Strauss (1967) in the 1960s at the University of California in San Francisco, and most recently explicated by Strauss (1987) and Corbin (1986; Strauss & Corbin, 1990). GTM has been most widely applied in research having to do with the sociology of health and illness and has also been used by researchers in anthropology, education, nursing, public health, and social work, as well as in sociology. However, grounded theory methodology has had only limited use by researchers studying families (Benoliel, 1970; Handel, 1986; Stern, 1982). Nevertheless, grounded theory methodology is well suited to studies of groups and ideally suited to questions where differing family meanings and interactions need to be addressed conceptually.

GTM is a style of systematic qualitative analysis designed to derive substantive and formal theory from data. It differs from other forms of qualitative analysis not only in the strategies used to reduce the data but also in the goal of analysis. For example, the goal of some qualitative work is to *describe* faithfully the area of interest. In phenomenological research, the goal is to understand the *experience* of the person, using exemplars from that experience. Although grounded theory analysis may result in the *description* of a process and may also lead to a better *understanding* of the meanings an experience has for an individual, the goal of analysis is the development of conceptually dense theory.

Although Strauss (1987) states that grounded theory analysis can be used with any form of data collection, it is used most commonly in field research with qualitative data from interviews, participant observations, biographies, documents, and other situational or historical sources. My study included several additional forms of data not previously used in grounded studies, including videotapes and children's drawings.

The primary reason for selecting GTM for this study was the fit between the method and the requirements of the research questions. To move from descriptions of family interaction to an understanding of sibling relationships in context, the selected method of analysis needed to forge a link between interpersonal processes and subjective experience (Murphy, 1989).

Theoretical Perspective

In grounded studies, theoretical concepts and hypotheses are derived from the data and verified in the data; that is, a theoretical framework is not used to derive hypotheses a priori. However, this does not preclude the investigator from entering the research setting with a sensitizing perspective about the nature of the research phenomenon. Researchers using GTM most frequently have assumed a symbolic interactionist perspective, but it is equally appropriate for investigators to come to a grounded study from a variety of other conceptual perspectives, based on the fit with their research question.

My own theoretical perspective came from a life-span developmental view of families (Belsky, Lerner, & Spanier, 1984; Lamb, 1982b; Lerner & Spanier, 1978). This perspective provided an appropriate "fit" for the contextual, interactive, and developmental aspects of this research. Furthermore, the life-span developmental perspective is consistent with the use of GTM, which specifically addresses interaction, context, process, and pattern in research phenomena. This theoretical perspective helped to guide the development of initial sensitizing questions and to maintain my awareness of the highly varied context within which sibling relationships develop.

Purpose of the Research and Research Questions

This longitudinal qualitative family study focused on the process through which sibling relationships develop when a new baby enters a family with a school-aged child. The purpose of the study was to derive from the data substantive theory to explain the development of early sibling relationships. The primary research question was: How do sibling relationships develop between school-aged siblings and a new baby, and what are the conditions that influence that process? Initial sensitizing questions included: What does the relationship look like over time? What meanings does the sibling relationship have for a school-aged child? and What conditions within the family underlie the development of this relationship?

SAMPLE, SETTINGS, AND DATA COLLECTION

To be eligible for this study, families had to be experiencing a normal, healthy pregnancy, have both parents in the home, and have a school-aged child over 5 years of age. Expectant families were recruited from the community through childbirth classes, obstetrical care providers, and advertisements at local birth centers. Initially, five families were accepted into the study based on the anticipated limitations of the researcher's time. Later, four more families were taken into the study, based on theoretical sampling and revised resources, thereby increasing the heterogeneity of the sample. The school-aged children in the sample ranged from 5 to 11 years of age. Five families were expecting their second child; two were expecting their third; and two families were expecting their fourth child.

The Families

Families were in the lower-middle to upper-middle income range. All nine families in the original study were Caucasian, and one family also had Hispanic cultural ties. Three of the nine families were blended families. The sample included Catholic, Protestant, Jewish, and Mormon families as well as families with no stated religious ties. It was not the purpose of this research to conduct either a cross-cultural study or a comparison of families across socioeconomic status, although those goals would be natural extensions of this research.

Data Collection Intervals

Data were gathered from the 9th month of pregnancy through the 24th month postpartum in settings where family interaction normally occurred (primarily in the home). In grounded studies, the data collection plan is partially determined ahead of time and partially determined by the ongoing process of analysis. In this study, decisions about frequency of visits and length of the study were based on theoretical considerations (concerning child growth and development and postnatal family changes) as well as realistic researcher limitations (time and resources). Therefore, I chose to specify data collection intervals at the beginning of the study.

Grounded theory methodology neither requires nor prohibits such preselection of time points; however, the nature of the research questions indicated the value of such an organizing plan. First, the research questions were developmental in nature and required frequent, repeated contacts with families in order to obtain empirical data as continuously as possible. Gathering data at the specified intervals permitted observation of stability and change in family interaction over time and also maintained sufficiently frequent family contact to minimize a sense of strangeness during researcher visits. In addition, data collection at regular intervals facilitated organization of the large quantities of data. Finally, because visits were made when all family members were at home, visits were more likely to be scheduled during evenings and weekends. Identifying certain intervals for data collection helped to respect the realistic limits on the researcher's time and energy.

Multiple Sources of Data

To understand the sibling relationship from the child's perspective as well as the parents', I collected multiple forms of family data, including both individual and whole family data. (See Daly, Chapter 1, and Handel, Chapter 2, this volume.) The following discussion explains the different forms and sources of data and the frequency with which these were collected.

1. Interviews with parents. Parents were interviewed once before the birth and then approximately every 2 to 4 months over the 2 years. Initial interviews were done in depth and included questions about the parents' families of origin and their own sibling relationships. Questions also included: When and how did the parents tell the children about the pregnancy? How much and in what way was the child involved in preparing for the baby? What had they told the child to expect of family life and infant capabilities? and How did they think the child would respond after the baby's arrival? In postpartum interviews, parents were asked about changes they saw in the sibling relationship over time and to what they attributed these changes. Other postnatal questions included: How would they characterize the relationship between the school-aged child and the infant? What limits, privileges, and responsibilities did the child have concerning the infant? What advice would they give to other families about fostering sibling relationships? and What did they think determined how sibling relationships turned out?

2. Interviews with school-aged children. Children were interviewed once before the birth and *at least* every 2 to 4 months over the 2 years. Initially they were asked: What are babies like? What do they do? If a friend of yours found out she or he was going to have a new baby in her/his family, what advice would you give her/him? What do you think she/he would need to know? Do you think she/he might be worried about anything? They were asked what they thought it would be like after the baby arrived, where the baby would sleep, who named the baby, and what activities they had done to get ready for the infant. After the birth, they were asked: What is the best thing about having a baby in the family? What is the worst thing? What does the baby do? What do you do with the baby? What helps older brothers and sisters get acquainted with a new baby? Later, they were asked about baby-sitting responsibilities, sibling conflict and how they handled it, and how they saw their role as big sister or big brother.

3. Videotaped observation of the school-aged child's first meeting with the infant. The first meeting of the infant usually took place in the hospital in the mother's postpartum room or in an alternative birth room. First meetings provided especially rich data since all family members were present and interaction focused on the infant. These were excellent opportunities to observe parent strategies pertaining to sibling-infant interaction, and to see the natural interest (or lack of it) the children had in the infant.

4. Videotaped observations of everyday family interaction in the home. These observations occurred once a month for the first 4 months, and then approximately every 2 to 3 months through the 2nd year. Home visit times were varied to include dinnertime, breakfast and before-school activities, bath and bed routines, and other common, everyday activities. Home visits were scheduled at times convenient to the fam-ily, when all children were home and the baby was awake. No restric-tions were placed on television, radio, or outside guests visiting. The videotaped observations varied in length (approximately 15 to 45 min-utes) depending on the activities of the family during the visit. (At the end of the study, each family received a complete set of the videotapes of their own family.)

5. Children's drawings. Each family was given an 8-1/2-by-11-inch blank book for family anecdotal notes and children's drawings. As entries were made in the book, they were photocopied and the book returned to the family. At the end of the study, the book remained the permanent property of the family, like a scrapbook about the sibling relationship. Drawings were treated as field data and were not analyzed according to any particular projective technique.

Initially, I expected that the blank book would help me to stay in touch with family events that might happen between data collection visits, to compensate for the monthly intervals. The book was seen as a means by which families could record ideas and anecdotes to assist them in recalling relevant events. A secondary reason for including the book came from an assumption that some children might be more comfortable *drawing* their ideas about the baby, rather than talking about them. However, neither of these expectations proved to be the most important factor in determining the contributions made by the book.

Although I expected variations in using the book, it was a serendip-itous discovery to realize that the way in which each family used the book was a reflection of family context and style. Some families did not use the book at all. Even some who intended to use it found that parenting allowed little time or energy for incorporating the book into their family life. Another family used the book extensively, filling up two books over the 2-year period. The older children in this family were very involved with the baby, sharing responsibility for raising the infant. The book was full of spontaneous, expansive drawings by both of the school-aged children. These drawings documented milestones in the baby's development, experiences in the baby's life, and the older children's perspectives on those events.

In another family, in which the parents were concerned about obeying rules and doing things right, the mother wrote her anecdotal notes on scratch paper first and then rewrote them into the book in neat handwriting. After the first few months, the book was no longer used. In a third family, issues related to control came up frequently. The mother was the gatekeeper of the book as well as of the baby. She reported that she and her son had gotten into an argument about whom the book belonged to. She had finally "given up" by letting him keep the book in his room and no longer making entries in the book herself. These patterns in family context and parenting strategies are related to the conditions for sibling-infant interaction discussed later in this chapter.

THE PROCESS OF DATA ANALYSIS

As is typical in qualitative research, analysis proceeded concurrently with data collection. Analytic work began with line-by-line analysis of the transcribed interviews of both parents and children, which included open coding and identifying conceptual categories. Open coding (Strauss & Corbin, 1990) of children's interviews led to the identification of several categories, from the data, pertaining to the children's experience of the newborn and their sibling role. (Examples of these categories included: meanings related to gender, sibling role, caretaking, reciprocity, infant characteristics, "advice," and likes and dislikes about babies.)

Analysis then moved to the videotapes. Visual data were analyzed like observational field notes, without predetermining the codes and categories. In grounded theory methodology, analytic questions based on a "coding paradigm" assist the researcher in identifying relationships among the concepts. The coding paradigm directs the researcher to look for interactions, strategies, conditions, and consequences.

The Relationship Between Data and Theory Development

The ongoing process of analysis in this study involved working back and forth between the various forms of data (videotapes, interviews, and drawings) and the developing theory. Concepts and theoretical relationships were derived from both the verbal and visual data. As the theoretical constructs took shape, I compared data within and across families. By making comparisons across families, one can see differences and similarities more clearly, gaining insight into meanings and experiences that may be common to several families or unique to one family. The analysis of each new family's data illuminates the previous family's data and helps to refine the theoretical concepts. To facilitate comparisons of the visual data across families, similar events from all families were transcribed onto one tape and viewed together. For example, all baby baths were placed on one tape, and all "first meetings of the infant" were put on another tape.

Contributions of Multiple Forms of Data

Different forms of data informed the theory development process in unique ways. For example, parent interviews provided the most valuable source of data on family values and beliefs and the rationale for parental strategies. Children's interviews provided for an understanding of the meanings that the infant had for the children and their views of the sibling role. The videotapes provided the most valuable data on parent-child communication and sibling interaction patterns and helped to identify the conditions under which various sibling interactions occurred. While the interviews and videotapes provided empirical data from which the theoretical concepts were identified and developed, the drawings were used in a more deductive way, to serve as visual examples of the concepts.

The multiple forms of data also provided important validity checks as each form of data informed the others. Relying only on one form of data would have given a less valid picture. The extended longitudinal relationship with families also made it possible to explore and verify theoretical concepts with the participants. For example, as it became clear that certain patterns of sibling-infant relationships were being identified in the data (caretaker, playful buddy, etc.), I came back to parents and asked them how they perceived the sibling relationship. I could search for the conditions and consequences of certain parental strategies related to those roles. Which child was asked to baby-sit? When and why? How did the parents interpret the rough play that was typical of very close, playful sibling relationships?

Comments on the Process of Analysis

Talking about how one conducts one's own qualitative research is like doing qualitative analysis of one's own process. For me, analytic work goes in fits and starts. There are periods of furious activity and immersion in the data with theoretical concepts being identified and connections being made. Then there are dry periods, especially while I am busy with other activities and feeling very distant from the data, when analytic results seem to be sparse.

Although I've been trained in the analytic style called grounded theory methodology, it feels presumptuous for me to say that what I do is an exemplar of GTM. I am still learning to apply the various strategies of that methodology. There are many times when I am especially conscious of using my training in GTM and there are other times when I suspect that what I am doing may be another kind of process, perhaps a search for phenomenological meanings. My analytic process is primarily driven by the questions that come up in the analysis—which I see as the essence of GTM. But there are some definite strategies that are very specific to GTM. GTM involves conscious theory building based on specific coding strategies. I encourage readers to study Strauss and Corbin's most recent book (1990), in which they provide clear explications of these strategies.

I suspect that qualitative researchers, even with common backgrounds, each bring to the analytic process their unique way of making connections. (See Gilgun, Chapter 3, this volume.) There is a sense in which the process is different simply because there is a different person conducting the analysis. Although there are some things we have in common as qualitative researchers—viewing the world spatially, perhaps—there are also unique ways in which each of us "puts it all together." Because the process remains open to the individual researcher, a space is provided in which the researcher can function; that is, the specific method does not necessarily eliminate the individual variations in style.

I want to elaborate on an ongoing dialectical tension that I feel during the process of analysis. For me, there is a constant ongoing search for the interface between *meaning* and *interaction*. I am not simply looking at interpersonal processes. I am also looking for the meanings those processes have for the family members and how meanings interface with interactions. (See Daly, Chapter 1, this volume.) The multiple forms of data provide valuable opportunities to look at that interface. The videotaped observations reveal certain interactions between an infant and the older child, whereas interviews with the older child allow me to gain a better understanding of what the relationship means from that child's point of view. In addition, I am trying to identify how these relate to the context within which the relationship is developing. For example: Under what conditions do these interactions occur? or What meaning does the interaction have for the parents and how do they respond to it?

To demonstrate my attempts at integrating *meaning, interaction,* and *context* in a conceptual way, I will discuss one of the patterns of early sibling infant relationships, its dimensions, and the individual and family conditions that appear to foster or inhibit that pattern. These findings do not constitute a completed, self-contained theory of sibling relationships; they are simply a portion of the ongoing conceptual work of developing theory about early sibling relationships in families.

FINDINGS

A Pattern of Sibling Mutuality

Seeing through the eyes and minds of children has been one of the delightfully rewarding aspects of this qualitative study. In the early months of analyzing the children's interviews, I noticed that some children talked about the baby primarily as an interacting and sentient person. For example, when asked what the baby did, instead of simply reporting crying, smiling, or other infant behaviors, these children gave answers that indicated *interaction* and *infant intent*: "She tries to grab my finger," or "He likes it when I talk to him." The meanings the baby had for these children were explained in terms of reciprocal interaction between themselves and the baby. These same children were especially sensitive in reading infant cues and responding contingently and empathic-ally to the infant—a quality I later identified as a central concept and labeled *sibling mutuality.* Analysis of the children's interview data, parental reports, and the actual videotaped observations, led to the identification of eight specific behavioral and affective dimensions of this pattern of mutuality. At least three of these dimensions appear to be manifestations of perspective taking or empathy. The eight dimen-sions are listed in Table 9.1, with definitions and specific examples of each dimension. The drawings included in this chapter further illustrate several of the dimensions (Figures 9.1, 9.2., and 9.3).

Each dimension represents a range of sibling behaviors or qualities of affective relationship. Although space does not allow an elaboration of every dimension listed on the table, data from one family may serve as an example of how these dimensions are manifested in mutual relationships.

Table 9.1 Eight Dimensions of the Patterns of Sibling Mutuality

Dimension	Definition	Examples
Maintaining Intimate Distance	Maintaining intimate spatial proximity between self and infant. Reaching out, moving in toward infant.	Searching infant's face and establishing eye-to-eye contact. Reaching out toward infant. Bringing one's face or body close to infant.
Identifying Infant Behaviors	Identifying infant capabilities and effectively reading infant behavioral cues.	Identifying infant cues of hunger, discomfort, lack of interest, or contentment. (See Figure 9.1) "When he is full, he pushes the bottle away."
Ascribing Feelings And Intent to Infant	Speaking for the infant. Stating infant's thoughts or feelings.	"[When distressed] Are you OK? Yes, I think I am." "[In infant carrier] She thinks she is still in Mommy's tummy." "He wants milk to come out of his fingers."
Empathizing	Sharing in or feeling the infant's emotions. Expressing concern or caring for infant's feelings.	Sibling winces when infant is receiving injection in nursery. Coming over and trying to comfort infant in distress.
Embodied Awareness In Handling Infant	Handling infant with an intuitive awareness of how the other person might feel when handled that way.	Sibling smoothly alters her own body to provide support for infant. Interacting *with* the infant, rather than doing something *to* or *at* the infant.
Affective Associating	Expressing affection, pleasure, or pride in being associated with the infant.	"I get the most smiles—It's me she smiles at." "I like when other people compliment the baby 'cuz it makes me glad that I am his sister."
Personification	Treating the infant as a separate person, with needs different from one's own. Pointing out infant's rights.	"I treat her like another member of our family." "[Infant pulled hair] Maybe he's ready for a rattle." (See Figure 9.2)
Reciprocal, Synchronous Interaction	Recognizing the bidirectionality of interaction; responding contingently to infant cues. Modifying one's own behavior to remain contingent.	Rhythmic turn taking and mutual imitating. Waiting for infant to respond and then responding to that response. (See Figure 9.3) "The baby likes 'Ha who.'"

When Michael drinks
a bottle he always
pushes thepersons
hand away when he
is done.

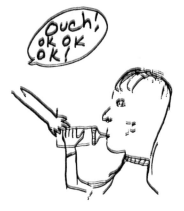

9 y o ♀
Infant 3.5 mos.

Figure 9.1. Reading Infant Behavioral Cues: In this drawing, the 9-year-old sister reveals her accurate recognition of the infant's cues of satiety.

Figure 9.2. Personification: Seeing the infant as a separate person, with needs that are separate from one's own, allows this sibling to recognize "hair pulling" as an expression of the infant's developmental readiness for grabbing objects.

Figure 9.3. Reciprocal, Synchronous Interaction: This remarkable drawing explains a sequence of sibling-infant interaction ("step 1, step 2") in which the sister responded contingently to the infant's behavior and modified her own behavior to maintain reciprocity.

The dimension of *maintaining intimate distance* has to do with spatial proximity, visually and physically positioning oneself in a way that permits closer contact with the infant. Several instances of this dimension could be seen during a baby's bath. Eric was 6 weeks old and was being bathed in a tub on the kitchen table. Elliot (6-1/2 years old) climbed onto the table and positioned himself right next to the tub. During the bath, he established eye-to-eye contact with the baby, brought his face down to the infant's face, stared intently, and reached out to stroke the baby's head. Elliot talked to the baby, asking questions, and then answered in a high-pitched voice as if he were speaking for the baby. He ascribed meaning and intent to the baby's behaviors during the bath and expressed empathic concern, both verbally and nonverbally, when the infant got water up his nose. In our interviews, Elliot often described experiences of reading infant cues and interacting reciprocally. For example, he reported that when Eric was held too tightly, he would push out against Elliot's body. He said that the baby liked to suck on things, and that Eric sucked on his fingers because "He wants milk to come out of his fingers. So I tell my mom so she will feed him."

Some children demonstrate this pattern of mutuality as early as the first month following the infant's arrival. However, it is important to realize, that sibling mutuality is just one of several patterns of sibling response. For many school-aged children, the baby simply is not a major focus of their interest or activities. Other aspects of their lives appear to be more important and more interesting than interacting with an infant.

Why do some children demonstrate sibling mutuality and others not? What fosters reciprocal relationships? What happens to these mutual relationships over time? These are some of the challenging questions that continue to drive this research program. Analysis of the data has provided some insight into the conditions that may be necessary for the development of mutual sibling relationships and the conditions under which mutual interactions are more likely to occur.

Conditions for Sibling Mutuality

In order for sibling mutuality to occur in the early months, several conditions appear to be necessary.

Condition Number 1: Child's own interest in the infant. First of all, the child needs to show an interest in being involved with the baby. In this study, most children demonstrated such interest initially. However, it is often more theoretically informing to look at those instances that provide contrasting examples. The parents of one 5-year-old boy described him as "basically oblivious" to the baby. His interviews revealed genuine caring and affection for the infant and provided stories of imaginative interaction with this newest sibling. However, during the 2 years of the study, he interacted relatively infrequently with the newborn and did not indicate any apparent desire for greater involvement with the baby. His parents understood this as a reflection of the fact that "babies are boring [to children]."

It is difficult to sort out what factors account for a sibling's early interest in the infant. The parents of this 5-year-old boy suggested gender might be the condition underlying their son's response to the baby. Certainly, Suomi's (1982) studies of nonhuman primates would support this hypothesis. He found that female siblings demonstrated great interest in the newborn, while male siblings tended to withdraw from the mother-infant pair. Gender may play a role in whether or not a child is initially interested in the infant. However, the data in this study neither support nor refute that hypothesis. Definitive examples of sibling mutuality were observed in three boys, ages 6, 7, and 11, as well as in two sisters. Many other variables in this heterogeneous group of families could be influencing the children's natural interest in the infant, including the interacting contributions of age, temperament, gender, family size, family interaction, individual differences in the older sibling, and the subtle nature of the social responsiveness of infants.

Based on my research so far, I would hypothesize that a child's interest in the baby is a matter of "fit" between the infant and the individual characteristics of the older child. A newborn may not fit the older child's natural interests or temperament. In fact, it may be more useful to think of sibling relationships longitudinally in relative and changing fit between developmental level, needs, and temperament of the older sibling and those of the infant. The 2-year data suggest that sibling closeness at any one time may be primarily a matter of such fit.

Condition Number 2: Opportunities for uncensored sibling-infant interaction. Sibling mutuality occurs when a school-aged child has generous opportunities for uninterrupted, uncensored interaction with the infant. There were some parents in this study who felt comfortable allowing even young children to handle, hold, and carry around the infant from birth. Other parents would not allow their older school-aged children to hold, carry, or interact with the infant without extensive limitations and parental control. Under these more restrictive conditions of limited access to the infant, a pattern of contingent sibling interaction was not seen.

Condition Number 3: Experience of mutuality between parents and child. In families where sibling mutuality was most visible, the parents interacted with the school-aged children with a similar kind of mutuality: They responded contingently to the child's questions, concerns, and interests. The parents communicated in a way that seemed to respect the child as a separate person, with needs and feelings that were unique. That is to say, the school-aged child had an embodied experience of being the recipient of or the participant in a relationship of mutuality. These findings suggest that the experience of mutuality between parents and the older child may be a necessary condition for the development of mutuality between the school-aged sibling and the infant.

Other conditions seem to foster the ongoing demonstration of sibling mutuality.

Condition Number 4: Strategies of inclusion and shared responsibility for the infant. Sibling mutuality is supported by parental strategies that facilitate sibling involvement with the infant and inclusion of the older child in a variety of matters pertaining to the baby. In families where sibling mutuality was observed, the parents frequently explained to the researcher that the baby belonged to the children as much as it did to them as parents, and that the children were entitled to participate in planning for, welcoming, and caring for the infant. These families' *strategies of inclusion* implied a *shared responsibility* for the infant. Before the birth, their strategies of inclusion might involve planning for the birth or naming of the infant; after the birth, their strategies might include sharing responsibility with the school-aged child for dressing, comforting, or feeding the infant. In one family the 11-year-old son took turns, along with each of the parents, caring for the crying baby while other family members ate their meals.

Condition Number 5: Strategies focused on the infant's needs or cues. Parental communications that focus the child's attention on the infant's cues or on the infant's needs or feelings—rather than on what the child is doing—are conditions that appear to foster mutuality. In several families, parents frequently remarked on the infant's response to the child, rather than focusing on the child's behavior with the infant.

These parents appeared to be teaching the older child to watch the infant's response in order to see how she/he was feeling. In one family where both school-aged children were especially mutual in their inter- action with the infant, the mother was sharing with the children a book on infant development (Brazelton, 1969), pointing out the subtleties of infant cues as the baby developed.

Condition Number 6: Strategies of relaxed facilitation of sibling- infant contact. In families where sibling mutuality was observed, parental strategies toward the sibling pair were characterized either by simply allowing sibling interaction to occur relaxed facilitation of the interaction. They did not push beyond the child's individual level of interest, and when the parents responded to sibling-infant interaction, they were permissive rather than directive or corrective in their comments.

Conditions Hindering Sibling Mutuality

The conditions that appear to *inhibit* the development of mutuality are, to some degree, inversely related to the conditions listed above that support it:

1. Apparent absence of sibling interest in the newborn
2. Parenting strategies that limit opportunities for sibling-infant interaction
3. Strategies that interrupt sibling-infant interaction with corrections
4. Strategies that encourage the older child to focus away from the infant

In families where children did not demonstrate a pattern of mutuality with the baby, opportunities for sibling-infant interaction tended to be limited and sibling-infant interaction was frequently interrupted with rules or corrections. Even comments intended to protect the infant from harm—such as, "Be careful," "Don't drop him," or "Support her head," or comments instructing the child to change his/her behavior or focus away from the baby, appeared to inhibit mutual sibling interaction.

The absence of mutuality does not necessarily mean that a child's interaction with the infant is negatively charged. There were school- aged children who had a casual, detached, but apparently affectively positive relationship with the infant. Nevertheless, an affectively negative pattern of sibling response to the infant was seen in two of the school-aged children in this study. Both of these children (a boy and a girl from different families) had expressed positive and strong interest in the infant during the prenatal and immediate postpartum period; however, the other conditions for sibling mutuality were not observed in those families.

In addition to the conditions listed above that tend to inhibit mutuality, other conditions also appeared to influence the sibling-infant relationship. In families with a lack of mutuality between the parents and older child, where parent-child communication tended to be noncontingent or controlling, older siblings tended to respond to the infant primarily in noncontingent ways, rather than responding to the infant's behavior or cues. These children also expressed a pattern of negative comments about the baby and reported receiving less attention and less affection for themselves at home. In the videotapes of family interaction, there was evidence of significant discrepant treatment of the older child and the infant.

The parents of these children believed that the siblings were emotionally close to the infant, but they also recognized behaviors and comments that indicated resentment and anger. One father said that he thought that the relationship from the beginning was a "love-hate" relationship, and that as the infant became older and more active, "the intensity of the relationship had increased, but the [love-hate] quality had not changed."

Besides the conditions discussed above, there were other conditions in these families that may have influenced these sibling responses. In both families, there was recognizable, preexisting strain in the relationship between one parent and the older child, even before the baby was born. There also were conflicts around issues of parental control and child discipline. In observing these relationships over time, the level of sibling conflict appeared to be less related to the infant's or child's developmental capabilities than to the stressful relationships already existing within the family. The findings from these two families suggest several questions for further study. Research needs to explore the relationship between sibling relationship outcomes and preexisting patterns of family stress, as well as family conditions following the arrival of an infant.

DISCUSSION

One of the primary motivations for this research was a desire to discover how families support the development of positive relationships between older children and a new baby. This interest came from my clinical background, because nurses often have contact with families precisely at the time when they are seeking assistance in dealing with sibling relationships. Although the results of this study are not yet ready for application, these findings provide hope that eventually we may be able to identify specific conditions in families that foster the development of positive sibling-infant relationships. If future research continues to support these findings, we may be able to devise interventions to help families promote more sensitive, reciprocal sibling relationships when a new baby arrives.

In weighing the significance of these research findings, it is essential *not* to view the pattern of sibling mutuality as a standard by which to evaluate early sibling relationships. To do so would be a misuse of the findings similar to the misuse that has been made of the concept of "maternal-infant bonding" (Lamb, 1982a). We do not know the long-range significance of this pattern of mutuality in school-aged siblings. Nor do we know how it might be created or nurtured in later sibling relationships when it is not present at the beginning, soon after the baby's birth.

Conducting qualitative research with families is a generative process, raising more questions and suggesting additional avenues of inquiry. This ongoing research program has led to the discovery of other patterns in school-aged children as they interact with infants (e.g., caretakers, buddies, casual siblings). It has also suggested the theoretical development of such concepts as "sibling fit" and "rough play."

Analysis of qualitative data also may lead one to explore already developed theories. Although a qualitative researcher usually does not design a study for the purpose of testing a preconceived theoretical framework, analysis of the data may suggest theoretical connections with frameworks already developed. For example, in this study, several of the dimensions of sibling mutuality appear to be manifestations of empathy or perspective taking. Based on the evidence presented in the data, a logical next step in this research program would be to explore the conceptual relationship between sibling mutuality and theories concerning the development of empathy in children.

Findings from qualitative studies may also suggest directions for quantitative research strategies. For example, in this study, the use of videotapes and the identification of specific dimensions in a behavioral pattern have laid the beginning groundwork for the development of a coding scheme for mutuality. Behavioral coding schemes lend themselves well to quantitative analysis of interactions and the sorting out of selected variables.

This chapter has provided an example of a family study using multiple sources and forms of qualitative material, including data gathered from children themselves. I have described my work as an integration of *meaning*, *interaction*, and *context* in developing substantive theory regarding siblings.

Each qualitative family researcher may describe his or her own process differently, and it is important that we maintain a pluralistic stance regarding methodologies. Qualitative strategies help us to view families holistically and to remain open to serendipitous findings. The variety of qualitative strategies will support family researchers in acquiring insight into family experiences and into the meanings those experiences have for family members.

REFERENCES

Abramovitch, R., Corter, C., & Lando, B. (1979). Sibling interaction in the home. *Child Development, 50*, 997-1003.

Abramovitch, R., Pepler, D., & Corter, C. (1982). Patterns of sibling interaction among preschool-age children. In M. E. Lamb & B. Sutton-Smith (Eds.), *Sibling relationships: Their nature and significance across the lifespan* (pp. 61-86). Hillsdale, NJ: Lawrence Erlbaum.

Bank, S., & Kahn, M. D. (1980). Freudian siblings. *Psychoanalytic Review, 67*, 493-504.

Bank, S., & Kahn, M. D. (1982). *The sibling bond.* New York: Basic Books.

Belsky, J., Lerner, R. M., & Spanier, G. B. (1984). *The child in the family.* Menlo Park, CA: Addison-Wesley.

Benoliel, J. Q. (1970). The developing diabetic identity: A study of family influence. *Communicating Nursing Research: Western Council for Higher Education in Nursing, 3*, 14-32.

Brazelton, T. B. (1969) *Infants and mothers: Differences in development.* New York: Delacorte.

Corbin, J. (1986). Qualitative data analysis for grounded theory. In W. C. Chenitz & J. M. Swanson (Eds.), *From practice to grounded theory* (pp. 91-101). Menlo Park, CA: Addison-Wesley.

Dunn, J. (1983). Sibling relationships in early childhood. *Child Development, 54*, 787-811.

Dunn, J. (1984). Sibling studies and the developmental impact of critical incidents. In P. B. Baltes & O. G. Brim, Jr. (Eds.), *Life-span development and behavior* (Vol. 6, pp. 335-353). Orlando, FL: Academic Press.

Dunn, J., & Kendrick, C. (1982a). *Siblings: Love, envy, and understanding.* Cambridge, MA: Harvard University Press.

Dunn, J., & Kendrick, C. (1982b). Siblings and their mothers: Developing relationships within the family. In M. E. Lamb & B. Sutton-Smith (Eds.), *Sibling relationships: Their nature and significance across the lifespan* (pp. 39-60). Hillsdale, NJ: Lawrence Erlbaum.

Dunn, J., & Munn, P. (1985). Becoming a family member: Family conflict and the development of social understanding in the second year. *Child Development, 56,* 480-492.

Fortier, J. C., Carson, V. B., Will, S., & Shubkagel, B. L. (1991). Adjustment to a newborn: Sibling preparation makes a difference. *Journal of Obstetric, Gynecologic, and Neonatal Nursing, 20*(1), 73-79.

Glaser, B. G., & Strauss, A. L. (1967). *The discovery of grounded theory: Strategies for qualitative research.* Chicago: Aldine.

Gottlieb, L. N. (1985). *Parental responsiveness and firstborn girls' adaptation to a new sibling. Unpublished doctoral dissertation, McGill University, Montreal.*

Gottlieb, L. N., & Mendelson, M. J. (1986, April). Adaptation and responsiveness to a new sibling in firstborn girls [Abstract]. *Infant Behavior and Development: Abstracts of Papers Presented at the Fifth International Conference on Infant Studies, 9,* 150.

Gottlieb, L. N., & Mendelson, M. J. (1987, July). *Patterns of adaptation in firstborn girls following a sibling's birth* [Abstract]. International Nursing Research Conference, Edinburgh, Scotland.

Griffin, E. W., & De La Torre, C. (1985). New baby in the house: Sibling jealousy. *Medical Aspects of Human Sexuality, 19*(3), 110-116.

Handel, G. (1986). Beyond sibling rivalry: An empirically grounded theory of sibling relationships. In P. A. Adler & P. Adler (Eds.), *Sociological Studies of Child Development* (Vol 1, pp. 105-122). London: JAI Press.

Kayiatos, R., Adams, J., & Gilman, B. (1984). The arrival of a rival: Maternal perceptions of toddlers' regressive behaviors after the birth of a sibling. *Journal of Nurse-Midwifery, 29,* 205-213.

Kreppner, K. (1987, April). *Patterns of early family socialization and the development of verbal skills: A longitudinal approach.* Paper presented at the biennial meeting of the Society for Research in Child Development, Baltimore, MD.

Kreppner, K. (1990, April). *Father participation in family socialization during the first two years after a second child's arrival.* Paper presented at the Seventh International Conference on Infant Studies, Montreal, Canada.

Kreppner, K., Paulsen, S., & Schutze, Y. (1982a). Infant and family development: From triads to tetrads. *Human Development, 25,* 373-391.

Kreppner, K., Paulsen, S., & Schutze, Y. (1982b). Kindliche Entwicklung und Familienstruktur: Zur Erforschung der frühkindlichen Sozialisation in der Familie (Child development and family structure: Studying early childhood socialization within the family). *Zeitschrift für Pädagogik, 28,* 221-244.

Lamb, M. E. (1982a). The bonding phenomenon: Misinterpretations and their implications [Editor's Column]. *Journal of Pediatrics, 101,* 555-557.

Lamb, M. E. (1982b). Sibling relationships across the lifespan: An overview and introduction. In M. E. Lamb & B. Sutton-Smith (Eds.), *Sibling relationships: Their nature
and significance across the lifespan* (pp. 1-11). Hillsdale, NJ: Lawrence Erlbaum.

Legg, C., Sherick, I., & Wadland, W. (1974). Reaction of preschool children to the birth
of a sibling. *Child Psychiatry and Human Development, 5,* 3-39.

Lerner, R. M., & Spanier, G. B. (1978). A dynamic interactional view of child and family
development. In R. M. Lerner & G. B. Spanier (Eds.), *Child influences on marital and
family interaction: A life-span perspective.* New York: Academic Press.

Murphy, S. O. (1989). *The early development of sibling relationships in childbearing
families.* Doctoral dissertation, University of California, San Francisco.

Nadelman, L., & Begun, A. (1982). The effect of the newborn on the older sibling:
Mothers' questionnaires. In M.E. Lamb & B. Sutton-Smith (Eds.), *Sibling relation-
ships: Their nature and significance across the lifespan* (pp. 13-37). Hillsdale, NJ:
Lawrence Erlbaum.

Neubauer, P. B. (1982). Rivalry, envy, and jealousy. *Psychoanalytic Study of the Child,
37,* 121-142.

Pietropinto, A. (1985). The new baby. *Medical Aspects of Human Sexuality, 19*(9),
155-163.

Stern, P. N. (1982). Affiliating in stepfather families: Teachable strategies leading to
stepfather-child friendship. *Western Journal of Nursing Research, 4,* 75-90.

Stewart, R. B. (1983a). Sibling attachment relationships: Child-infant interactions in the
strange situation. *Developmental Psychology, 19,* 192-199.

Stewart, R. B. (1983b). Sibling interaction: The role of the older child as teacher for the
younger. *Merrill-Palmer Quarterly, 29,* 47-68.

Stewart, R. B. (1990). *The second child: Family transition and adjustment.* Newbury
Park, CA: Sage.

Stewart, R. B., Mobley, L. A., Van Tuyl, S. S., & Salvador, M. A. (1987). The firstborn's
adjustment to the birth of a sibling: A longitudinal assessment. *Child Development,
58*(2), 341-355.

Strauss, A. L. (1987) *Qualitative analysis for social scientists.* Cambridge, UK: Cambridge University Press.

Strauss, A. L., & Corbin, J. M. (1990). *Basics of qualitative research: Grounded theory
procedures and techniques.* Newbury Park, CA: Sage.

Suomi, S. J. (1982). Sibling relationships in nonhuman primates. In M. E. Lamb & B.
Sutton-Smith (Eds.), *Sibling relationships: Their nature and significance across the
lifespan* (pp. 329-356). Hillsdale, NJ: Lawrence Erlbaum.

Taylor, M. K., & Kogan, K. L. (1973). Effects of birth of a sibling on mother-child
interactions. *Child Psychiatry and Human Development, 4,* 53-58.

A Family Case Study
An Examination of the Underclass Debate

ROBIN L. JARRETT
Loyola University of Chicago

In this chapter, I argue that qualitative methods constitute an important approach for capturing the complexity of low-income African-American family life. I base my argument on a two-step qualitative study that began with focus group interviews and moved to in-depth case studies based on participant observation and in-depth interviews of multiple family members. I used this two-step approach to explore hypotheses from William J. Wilson's (1987), *The Truly Disadvantaged.* Wilson and others currently involved in the "underclass" debate, though citing different causes (e.g., Auletta, 1982; Lemann, 1986; Murray, 1984), derive many of their insights on African-American family life from aggregate data and statistical analyses of family structure and dynamics. What often emerges from such approaches is a generalized profile of

AUTHOR'S NOTE: This research was funded by grants from the Spencer Foundation and a Rockefeller Foundation Minority-Group Post-Doctoral award. Support from Professor Richard P. Taub and the Chicago Department of Human Services staff also made the research possible.. Margaret Breslau and Carol Gagliano skillfully transcribed and coded the intensive interviews. Saadia Adell, Deanne Orput, Chris Schiller, and Pat Summers did similar work with the focus group interviews. Jane Gilgun, Kirsten Gronbjerg, Helena Z. Lopata, and Rebecca Blank offered helpful comments on an earlier draft of this paper. Any inaccuracies are those of the author. Ann Barret provided useful editorial comments. The participation of the Moore family is sincerely appreciated.

dysfunctional families. In a few instances, my qualitatively derived findings overlapped with Wilson's analysis, but in general I found inner-city African-American family life to be far more complex and heterogeneous than the more quantitatively based research suggests (Burton & Jarrett, 1991; Jarrett, 1991). This chapter is based upon data from the Moore family (not their real name), a multigeneration African-American family. My detailed research with the Moores sheds light on three components of Wilson's discussion: the economic vulnerability of households headed by women, geographic concentration and social isolation of impoverished families, and negative neighborhood effects on individual and family life-styles.

My findings in the present study are consistent with findings on family life from existing ethnographies, many done 20 or more years ago. These studies move beyond one-dimensional profiles and provide descriptions of well-functioning families within impoverished neighborhoods (Aschenbrenner, 1975; Clark, 1983; Hannerz, 1969; Jeffers, 1967; Ladner, 1971; Stack, 1974; Sullivan, 1985; Valentine, 1978; Williams & Kornblum, 1985). My research suggests that well-functioning families continue to reside in impoverished areas despite the tremendous odds that Wilson articulates so well.

To make my argument, I first outline key issues from the current "underclass" debate on family life and poverty and describe the quantitative data used. Next, I discuss the general use of the qualitative case study and its applications to low-income, African-American families. Then, I examine hypotheses from the underclass debate using in-depth data from the case study of the Moore family. Finally, I summarize the strengths and limitations of the qualitative case study and its value in portraying low-income family life.

THE UNDERCLASS DEBATE

The rise in female-headed households and nonmarital childbearing among low-income African-Americans has spurred researchers to reexamine the relationship between family life and poverty. Not since the 1970s has this issue been so intensely argued (Katz, 1989). Under the rubric "the underclass debate," a number of hypotheses have been advanced to explain changes in household and family formation patterns (Auletta, 1982; Bane & Ellwood, 1984a, 1984b; Lemann, 1986; McLanahan, Garfinkel, & Watson, 1988; Murray, 1984; Vinovski, 1988;

Wilson, 1987). For a broader overview, see Cook and Curtin (1987), Jencks (1988); Jencks and Mayer (1989), Jencks and Peterson (1991), McGeary and Lynn (1988), Massey and Eggers (1990), and Ricketts and Sawhill (1988).

Wilson's book *The Truly Disadvantaged* (1987) offers an important scholarly statement on the plight of African-American poor and provides the conceptual framework for the present discussion. Using a comprehensive approach based on macro- and micro-levels of analysis, Wilson examines the impact of economic change on inner-city neighborhoods, families, individuals, and social mobility.

Wilson (1987) depicts inner-city communities, particularly those with rates of concentrated poverty at or above 40%, as chaotic and disorganized. According to Wilson, such neighborhoods lack functional social institutions and house the most socially and economically disadvantaged individuals and groups. Due to the loss of middle- and working-class families, present-day residents have few positive examples to emulate. Socially isolated from mainstream institutions and economically secure relatives and neighbors, inner-city dwellers are exposed to role models whose ghetto-specific behaviors limit social mobility.

Defining the underclass as a heterogeneous collection of extremely disadvantaged groups and individuals who live outside of mainstream society, Wilson (1987) includes households headed by women in this category. He characterizes them as examples of the most economically insecure families and, in the absence of a stable male provider, at risk for long-term poverty and welfare dependency. Moreover, he sees children in such families as especially at risk. On the basis of their living arrangements, Wilson implies that children who spend a significant portion of time in mother-only households are not only economically vulnerable but susceptible to the negative effects of neighborhood impoverishment.

Wilson (1987) bases his arguments on national and local data, including statistics on community poverty levels, female headship, family dissolution, family poverty rates, out-of-wedlock births, welfare dependency, unemployment, crime, and school dropout, as well as secondary references to other quantitative studies. He relies on aggregate statistical data to make inferences about individual behaviors and neighborhood processes. While explicitly noting the heterogeneity of individuals within the group he labels underclass, Wilson pays little attention to the issue of heterogeneity between families within the larger neighborhood. Clearly, quantitative data are important in documenting broad demographic changes in family and neighborhood patterns and establishing relationships between variables. Such data, however, often do not extensively explore the processes associated with these changes, nor their meaning.

Ethnographic Research Challenges Generalized Findings

A review of the existing ethnographic literature (Jarrett, 1990) indicates that family processes and dynamics, such as strong parental supervision of youth, isolation from street-oriented life-styles, network coalitions with conventionally oriented families, pooled family resources, household interdependence, and flexible living arrangements, are critical in ameliorating the detrimental effects of neighborhood impoverishment. Despite limited neighborhood resources for family maintenance, youth in families with these characteristics are more likely to exhibit mainstream social mobility outcomes, such as school completion, economic independence, and postponement of early parenthood. In contrast, youth in families lacking these vital dimensions are less likely to exhibit conventional social mobility outcomes.

QUALITATIVE APPROACHES TO AFRICAN-AMERICAN FAMILY LIFE AND POVERTY

This project began with exploratory focus group interviews, followed by in-depth interviews and participant observation. The project's goal was to gain a broader view of poor families than is available in contemporary discussions. Key themes were first explored in group interviews and later examined in more detail in intensive interviews.

Focus Group Interviews

A method for gathering qualitative data through group interaction, focus group interviews are primarily concerned with subjective perceptions, opinions, attitudes, values, and feelings. An interviewer or moderator convenes a homogeneous group of respondents to discuss a particular topic or issue. Focus group interviews are particularly useful for exploring the range and patterns of subjective perspectives in a relatively short period of time (Bellenger, Bernhardt, & Goldstucker, 1976; Calder, 1977; Downs, Smeyak, & Martin, 1980; Hedges, 1985;

Merton, Fiske, & Kendall, 1956; Morgan, 1988; Morgan & Spanish, 1984; Smith, 1972).

Ten focus groups were conducted between January and July 1988 with a total of 82 low-income African-American women. The sample was purposive and drawn from Chicago-wide Head Start programs. Based on profiles of women hypothesized to be at risk for long-term poverty, I established criteria for selection to include: (a) never-married mothers; (b) recipients of AFDC at the time of the interviews; and (c) residents of low-income or economically transitional neighborhoods in the city of Chicago. Most of the women began their childbearing careers as adolescents. The focus group sample differed from the usual research emphasis on adolescents in concentrating instead on older, never-married mothers in their early to middle twenties. In choosing research respondents past adolescence, the study traced young women in the early stages of the family life cycle when decisions concerning household formation, family maintenance, and active parenting are most salient.

Interviewing and Observations

In-depth interviewing and limited participant observation began in the fall of 1988 and continued for 9 months. Although many of the women who participated in the focus group interviews also agreed to participate in this phase of the study, due to time constraints only nine families were targeted. A key consideration in the selection process was the willingness of other family members to participate.

The Case Study

The case study is a detailed and in-depth investigation of a single unit (Becker, 1970; Yin, 1989). Units of analysis include individuals, families, organizations, and communities. Frequently used in medical and psychological investigations, the case study in social science research generates a comprehensive and holistic understanding of social events within a single setting (Aschenbrenner, 1975; Bulmer, 1986; Cohler & Grunebaum, 1981; Gilgun, 1991; Handel, 1991). Case studies that rely upon qualitative methods are desirable when researchers seek firsthand knowledge of real-life situations and processes within naturalistic settings (Burgess, 1982, 1984; Bulmer, 1986; Emerson, 1981, 1983) and an understanding of the subjective meanings that actors give to the behaviors and events being observed and discussed (Burgess, 1984; Emerson, 1981; Jorgensen, 1989).

The Moore Family

Diane Moore, who participated in the focus group interviews, became a key informant for this case study. (All names, including names of neighborhoods, are pseudonyms.) She provided access to the family. She and her sisters generally fit the current demographic profiles of unmarried mothers discussed in the underclass debate. Diane relies on AFDC income and bore a child outside of marriage when she was 20 years old, slightly older than women typified in current discussions. Three of her siblings, Belinda, Marlene, and Sandra, all bore children when they were adolescents. Although the key informants were Diane and later her mother, Ella, informal conversations with Diane's three sisters provided additional data. Weekly or biweekly for 4 months, I visited the home Diane and her two children shared with her parents and other family members. I tape-recorded interviews, usually 1-1/2 hours in length. I supplemented the interviews with half-day observational periods and informal discussion.

Topically Guided, Informal Interviews

Guided by issues in the underclass debate, particularly those concerning household and family formation patterns and their dynamics, I chose topics for exploration in the focus groups and more detailed examination in the intensive interviews. Topics included individual life histories and genealogies, residence life histories, child care and socialization, intergenerational relations, female-male relationships, and welfare, work, and social opportunities.

I set up the interviews to be topically guided, yet informal in tone and style, and in some respects, conversational and free flowing. I encouraged informants to discuss what they perceived as the important dimensions of these issues and to do so in the language and categories they deemed meaningful. I wanted to approximate as much as possible a chat between friends (Burgess, 1984; di Leonardo, 1984; Spradley, 1979; Yancey & Rainwater, 1970). Due to the instrumental task at hand, however, most visible through the embeddedness of questions (Fetterman, 1989), the interviews were different from pure conversations; they were "conversations with a purpose" (Burgess, 1984, p. 102). The flexibility of the interviews facilitated the emergence of new and unanticipated data (Fetterman, 1989; Taylor & Bogdan 1984). Overall, a diverse range of information was collected.

I conducted most of the taped interviews with Ella and Diane separately. Some privacy was assured by interviewing mother and daughter on separate days, when one or the other was absent, or in separate parts of the house. Sometimes, however, this was impossible. Children were almost always present and some interviews were interrupted by resident or visiting kin. On such occasions, we ended our taped individual interviews, but I became involved in informal group discussions. Sometimes I taped the group sessions. Together, the collective interviews furnished multiple perspectives on issues. On other occasions, informal discussions and participant observation were the primary activities. These periods provided an opportunity to observe family dynamics and to compare the relationship between verbal accounts and actual behavior.

Data Analysis

The interviews were transcribed, and the transcriptions were coded using The Ethnograph (Seidel, Kjolseth, and Seymour, 1988), a computer program for managing qualitative data. Although the categories of the research provided broad topics for initial coding, the interview data elaborated on the general codes, adding greater specificity to them. New codes were developed as unanticipated topics emerged from the interview data. Once the data were coded, comparisons were made between interviews. Because Diane Moore alone participated in the focus group discussions, comparisons between the individual and group interviews were done only in her case. I gave attention to similarities and differences among key topics, as well as interpretations of particular events. Observations from the field notes provided a contextual background for interpreting the interview data.

FINDINGS

As discussed earlier, I used the data from the Moore family to examine three components of Wilson's (1987) discussion: the economic vulnerability of households headed by women, the geographic concentration and social isolation of impoverished families, and neighborhood effects on family life-styles.

Household Composition and Female Headship

The economic vulnerability of households headed by women figures prominently in Wilson's (1987) discussion of the underclass. As he explicitly documents numerical increases in female headship among poor African-American women, he implicitly suggests that such families are handicapped because of the absence of a male provider. By concentrating on the living arrangements of single mothers and their children, it is easy to conclude that female-headed households receive little or no support for day-to-day functioning. When female-headed households are viewed independently, their connection to larger familial units and, perhaps most important, access to domestic support are obscured (Stack, 1974). Although one-shot surveys may be correct in documenting who lives within a particular household at a given time and longitudinal panel surveys may document change over time, most have not focused on between-household interactions nor interactions within larger family units. Intensive interviews and observations, in contrast, can more effectively discern the nature and content of familial relationships as well as the organizational principles undergirding them.

Flexible Household Arrangements

In this section, I illustrate how flexible household arrangements provide support to single mothers and children, irrespective of marital status or living arrangements. The Moore family fits Martin and Martin's (1978) definition of an extended family. It is

> a multigenerational, interdependent kinship system which is welded together by a sense of obligation to relatives; is organized around a "family base" household; is generally guided by a "dominant family figure"; extends across geographical boundaries to connect family units to an extended family network; and has a built-in mutual aid system for the welfare of its members and the maintenance of the family as a whole. (p. 1)

The base household consists of Pervis and Ella Moore, members of the grandparent generation. Ella is the instrumental and affective core around which family life revolves. Ella and Pervis have 5 children and 14 grandchildren. Figure 10.1 identifies key members of this extended family.

The Moore Family

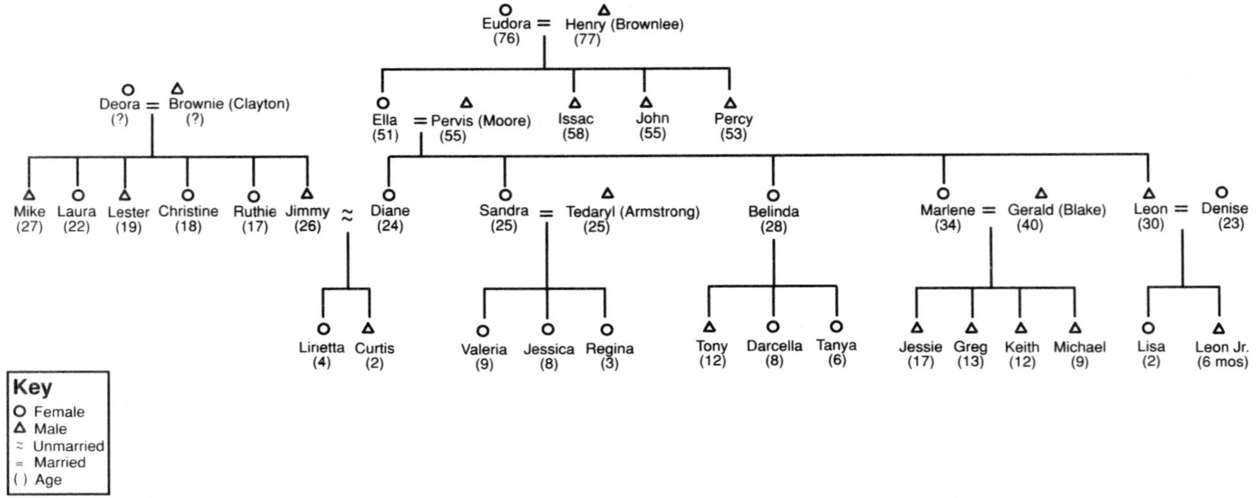

Figure 10.1. The Moore Family

Key
O Female
△ Male
≈ Unmarried
= Married
( ) Age

Sub Extended Households

Family members, though bound together by a sense of communal responsibility, may or may not live coresidentially. Several separate but interdependent, sub extended households cluster around the base household of Pervis and Ella. When the Moore family living arrangements are examined over time, the significance of the distinction between family membership and household composition is highlighted. Precipitated by domestic, economic, and personal crises, households expand and con- tract to accommodate family members. Although living arrangements are extremely fluid, the core of interdependent kin remains stable. Figure 10.2, constructed from interview data, shows the changes in living arrangements for a 4-year period, 1986-1989.

In 1986, the base household of Pervis and Ella consisted of the grandparent couple, three daughters (Diane and her sisters Belinda and Marlene), Marlene's husband (Gerald), and the nine children of the three daughters. Diane and her two children resided consistently in the base household. A single, unemployed parent, Diane never lived inde- pendently. Economic and medical crises led to the incorporation of the families of the other two daughters. Gerald, for example, was ill, and Belinda was unemployed. The families of the other two Moore adult children (Sandra and Leon) were economically secure and lived in separate, but related, households.

In 1987, the base household consisted of Pervis and Ella, Diane and her two children, and Marlene, her husband Gerald, and their four children. Belinda had secured a job and moved to an independent household with her three children. The other two Moore adult children and their families continued to live independently.

In 1988, the household composition shifted once again. Although Pervis and Ella, along with Diane and her children, formed the consis- tent household core, the life circumstances of other family members changed. Gerald's health improved and he, Marlene (a Moore daugh- ter), and their children moved out of the base household. Sandra, her husband Tedaryl, and their three children moved into the household. Belinda's two daughters moved back into the household of Pervis and Ella although Belinda kept her oldest child with her in her separate residence. Tedaryl's loss of his job and Belinda's child care problems motivated these household realignments. Sub extended units not living in the base house- hold then included the families of three of the Moore adult children (two-parent households of Marlene and Gerald and Leon and Denise and

182

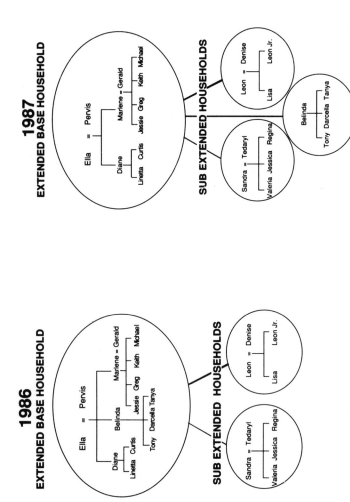

Figure 10.2. The Moore Family Households, 1986-1989

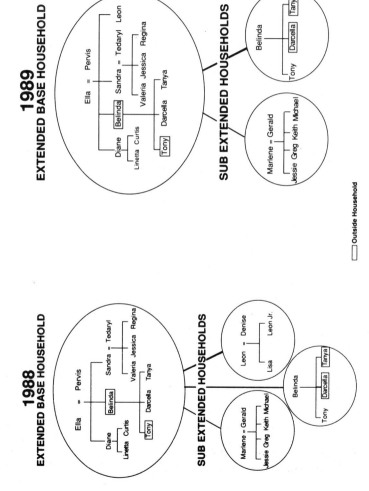

Figure 10.2. (continued)

183

the female-headed household of Belinda and her son Tony). In 1989, the composition of the base household remained unchanged except for one addition: Leon, then separated from his wife, moved in.

Internal Dynamics of Households

A closer look at the internal dynamics of households illustrates the nature of family relationships and the types of support various members receive. For the Moores, domestic tasks and kinship roles extend beyond the residential boundaries of individual households. Belinda (who at that time lived in a separate residence) and Sandra, describing the family's daily and weekly routine, underscore household interdependence:

> *Sandra:* I got up, washed clothes. . . . I washed all day . . . .12 o'clock came, I was still washing. . . . I kept getting interrupted. Marlene came over to wash in between mine. I went on and let her do it . . . helped her washing over a little bit, so she helped mine over a little bit. I let her go and wash 'cause I knew she had to go back home.

> *Belinda:* I'm getting ready to help Mama with her bathroom. I told Diane if you go half with me we can get the bathroom a vanity set.

The distinction between family membership and household composition points out the limitations some surveys and census data have in helping us to understand the degrees of support independent heads of households may receive from kin and close family friends. Consider the case of Belinda. A standardized survey asking for household composition in 1987 would elicit the response that Belinda and her three children were the sole occupants of their household. Based on official census codes, Belinda would be considered a female head of household. Consequently, some quantitative researchers might assume that Belinda, an unmarried single mother living alone with her children, had little or no social or economic support.

Participant observation and interviewing would reveal otherwise. Even when Belinda lived independently, as she did at the time of the interviews, she remained interactionally linked to the base household. Belinda's daily routine typically included visits to the parental household of Pervis and Ella, where in 1988 two of her three children were being fostered by Diane. Tony, Belinda's oldest child, remained in the household with her. She felt that the younger girls, Tanya and Darcella, unlike their older brother, required more supervision. As an example of household linkages, Diane and Belinda discuss their child care arrangements:

> *Diane:* I was at home anyway. I had to run by and pick up Tanya and Darcella anyway because Belinda was at work. Anyway, I don't have nobody to keep Linetta and Curtis, so I started keeping Tanya and Darcella. . . . After they got out of school . . . I told Belinda they gonna go to school over here. It save us gas money running back to your house and missing them sometimes and they be sitting out there . . . trying to wait.

> *Belinda:* I tell Tanya and Darcella, when I'm not here, Diane's in charge. She's responsible for them. They go to her for everything. And she will come to me to know what's going on, or if they bring something to me, I will let her know. That's the way we do it. Whatever she say is just fine 'cause I know she's not going to mistreat them. I couldn't work like I'm doing [without Diane's help]. . . . I just don't have a choice. I have to work in order to keep a roof over my head. It's hard trying to do it on your own and raise kids. You got to run a whole household and all the bills that's on you. If you don't get out here and work, where you going to live? Can't live off of aid. You get tired of aid.

Fosterage, or the practice of maintaining children in a household in which the parent does not reside (Stack, 1974), further solidifies personal and household interdependence. But most important, it provides support to single mothers and their children.

Diane, who lives coresidentially with her parents, as discussed earlier, has strong support from Jimmy Clayton, the father of her children, and his family, and when Jimmy is not able to help, Diane's mother does:

> I got help from my mother and the kids' father. . . . Jimmy helped. He buy Pampers. . . . If I didn't have the money, he didn't have the money right then, [my mother] would loan it to us. . . . Sometime she would say: "Naw, you don't have to pay this back." Or she would just go out and buy [it]. So, I got help [in] different situations. So, I never really was in a bind.

Genealogical information further documents strong kinship links to Jimmy and his family. When I asked Diane to list people she considered relatives, she included Jimmy and gave a detailed account of his maternal kin:

[My kids'] grandmother, Deora, [lives] on Hale. And [the kids] have
auntie[s], Christine and Laura . . . and [they] got two uncles, Lester and
Mike . . . and another aunt, Ruthie. . . . Curtis and Linetta got some cous-
ins. . . . That's Mike's son and daughter. . . . And Laura has . . . what's her
name?. . . . I got her picture upstairs. . . . Maybe I'll run upstairs and get
[her] picture. [Diane goes upstairs and returns.] Angie is the girl's name.

The genealogical information suggests extensive knowledge and contact
with Jimmy's family. In our conversations, she also showed a working
knowledge of paternal and more distant kin.

Data from a short questionnaire I administered after the focus group
interview provided additional information on the bonds between Diane
and Jimmy's family. In response to the question, "When you have a
problem, or when you are feeling sad or depressed, who do you go to
talk over that problem?" Diane listed her mother, sisters, and Deora
Clayton, her children's paternal grandmother. Also as part of the locating information, when asked to "Give the name, address, and telephone
number of people with whom you keep in touch," Diane again listed
Deora Clayton.

Recent census surveys can potentially identify mother-child subunits
within individual households, but they are often unable to link accurately these subunits to other interdependent households (see Bane &
Ellwood, 1984a). Consequently, a survey researcher might conclude
that Diane, an unmarried mother, is rearing her children, Curtis and
Linetta, without a father and possibly in isolation from the father's
family. This inference would be incorrect. The interdependence of
Belinda and Marlene and their families with the base household also
would not be apparent.

Distinctions Between Family Membership
and Household Composition

The in-depth data illustrate a major point. *Family membership* refers
to a set of socially defined kinship relationships, but *household composition* refers to residence or living arrangements. Depending on the time
frame, the two may or may not overlap (Yanagisako, 1979). As illustrated by the Moores, family members who are in daily and weekly
interaction with one another do not always live coresidentially. When
family and associated domestic functions are largely defined by

coresidence—an implicit assumption in the Wilson thesis and one drawn from an idealized model of the nuclear family (Reed, 1988)— extraresidential relationships are overlooked. Among the Moores, when a broader definition of family is used, one that transcends narrowly defined coresidential arrangements, household composition becomes less significant as an indicator of family dynamics. Thus, single mothers and children may live independently but receive social, economic, and child care support from other households. Similarly, parental roles can be fulfilled in the absence of a legal, coresidential marital union.

Geographic Concentration and Social Isolation of Impoverished Families

The second dimension of Wilson's (1987) argument I address in this chapter is his view, based on demographic data, that contemporary, inner-city neighborhoods are increasingly made up of the most impoverished families. Wilson argues that these families, geographically concentrated in decaying neighborhoods, lack sustained interaction with more economically secure relatives.

Previous ethnographic literature on low-income neighborhoods and families, however, indicates that, depending on the composition of kinship networks, family and individual interactions may transcend local geographic boundaries (Aschenbrenner, 1975; Clark, 1983; Hannerz, 1969; Jeffers, 1967; Martin & Martin, 1978; Zollar, 1985). Within heterogeneous family networks including a variety of persons at differing socioeconomic levels, poor family members were found to be in contact with working- and middle-class relatives. Recent in-depth data from the Moores allow us to track neighborhood locations and interaction patterns of key family members and explore Wilson's thesis.

At the time of the intensive interviews, the base household and three of the sub extended households were located primarily within the almost exclusively African-American Thorndale community. Data from 1980 census indicated that although it was not among the most impoverished communities in Chicago (less than 20% of the population was below the poverty level), Thorndale nevertheless experienced social and economic problems. Unemployment, business failures, mortgage defaults, and gang-related problems increased between 1970 and 1980 (Chicago Fact Book Consortium, 1984). Indeed these are strong indicators that the 1990 census data will reveal worsening conditions that more accurately describe the conditions under which the Moore family currently live. For example, during this 10-year period, unemployment rates rose from 4.2 to 8.3%, and in a community of approximately 64,500, single-parent families increased from 2,700 to 5,600 (City of Chicago, Department of Human Services, 1990). Moreover, many of Thorndale's impoverished families were concentrated on particular blocks or within "pockets of poverty," thereby approximating the ecology of neighborhoods with higher overall rates of poverty.

When the adult children of Pervis and Ella lived outside of Thorndale, a largely working-class neighborhood, they all resided in economically comparable or economically improved neighborhoods. Leon, who returned to the parental household in 1989, lived in Avon Park, a working-class neighborhood. Prior to Sandra's return in 1988, she and her family lived in Gulf Stream, a middle-class suburb. In 1985, preceding Marlene's return to Thorndale, she and her family lived in Eastern Ridge, a neighborhood with a combined working- and middle-class population.

Although none of Pervis and Ella's adult offspring live in deteriorated, impoverished neighborhoods, the Moore family has links to two households located in such areas: the Brownlees and the Claytons. The household of Ella's parents, Deora and Henry Brownlee, is located some 20 miles away in Highpoint, an extreme poverty area. According to census data, at least 40% of the households were below the poverty line in 1980. The household of Jimmy Clayton, the father of Diane's children, is located in the even more impoverished neighborhood of Chesterfield, nearly 10 miles away from the Moore base household. Census data documented that at least 50% of the households in Chesterfield were below the poverty line in 1980. Both neighborhoods are expected to show greater impoverishment in the 1990 census.

To some extent, the geographic location of households in Thorndale parallels the socioeconomic status of different family members. Mirroring the working-class status of Thorndale, the grandparent generation is stably employed in working-class occupations: Ella works as a lunchroom manager in a high school, and Pervis is employed at Vistar, a plastic casing factory. Some of the adult offspring duplicate their parent's socioeconomic status: Marlene works for the telephone company; Leon works for a local bus company; and Belinda, assisted by her mother, recently became employed as a teacher's aide. They, too, live in working-class neighborhoods.

A Refinement of the Geographic Concentration and Social Isolation Thesis

The case study materials underscore why some poor individuals do not live in neighborhoods with high concentrations of povery and why some economically secure individuals do. Morever, they highlight the nature of the interactions between family members in neighborhoods with varying socioeconomic statuses. Diane currently receives welfare, as other family members have on occasion. Recently, Sandra made the transition from work to welfare, and Belinda made the transition from welfare to work. Yet none of the Moore siblings have ever lived in neighborhoods of high poverty concentration as adults. Now retired, Ella's parents, Henry and Eudora, had consistent employment histories: Henry worked most of his adult life at Vistar (along with his son-in-law, Pervis), and Eudora worked at several factory jobs. Yet they continue to live in a neighborhood of high poverty concentration.

As single parents and potentially economically vulnerable, Diane and Belinda are unlikely to reside in impoverished neighborhoods as long as they are buffered by the larger extended family. Due to age and existing social ties, it is equally unlikely that Eudora and Henry will move to a more economically secure neighborhood. As Ella points out: "My mother [Eudora] never, never lived anywhere else, and I think it is her favorite part of town."

Despite the geographic dispersal of households in neighborhoods of differing socioeconomic levels, family members continue to interact with one another. Ella describes contact with her parents' household:

> I spend time with my mother. . . . My father and three of my brothers live there. I'm the only one out of the house. . . . I like to go over there at least once a week, or if I'm over there in that area, I just drop in to see how they doing. . . . When I first started working, I was more or less sleeping and eating over there and dressing out of a suitcase, because I couldn't really come all the way home, get some rest, and then go back to work. . . . I spend quite a bit of time with [my mother]. Sometimes I have to take her to different appointments. . . . We be talking about some of the relatives, . . . how they doing, . . . or what they did at church. . . . My father [sits] in the living room and he'll look at TV and let the women have the kitchen.

Similarly, Diane provided a great deal of information on the extent of the contact her children have with their father and his family, who live in an impoverished area in a household largely reliant on income from ADFC; the children have daily contact with their father and frequently visit him in his home. The data offer an addendum to Wilson's hypotheses concerning geographic concentration and social isolation.

Although it is true that some poor, as exemplified by members of the Clayton household (Jimmy's family), live in impoverished neighborhoods, working-class individuals, as exemplified by members of the Brownlee household, may also live there. Conversely, poor individuals, as represented by Diane and, depending on the availability of work, Belinda Moore, may live in working-class neighborhoods. These data highlight–a point that remains implicit in the concentration thesis–that residence in a particular neighborhood is not in all cases directly related to individual socioeconomic status, but influenced by the presence or absence of external sources of support as well as stages in the family life cycle.

When family is defined largely as a nuclear, coresidential arrangement and neighborhood is conceived exclusively as a geographic entity, as they are in the Wilson (1987) book, social relations that transcend household and neighborhood boundaries are obscured. Examples from the Moore family indicate that some families more accurately function as a network of interacting individuals. Linked by affective and instrumental ties, these relationships exist across household and neighborhood boundaries (Olson, 1984; Wireman, 1984).

Neighborhoods' Effects on Family Life-Styles

Based on profiles derived from census data, Wilson (1987) focuses almost exclusively on families overwhelmed by negative neighborhood forces. He provides little information on functional families within poor neighborhoods. Yet, ethnographic research documents heterogeneous family life-styles and coping strategies within low-income neighborhoods (Aschenbrenner, 1975; Clark, 1983; Hannerz, 1969; Ladner, 1971; Valentine, 1978; Williams, 1981; Williams & Kornblum, 1985). Moreover, Wilson fails to address the strategies that some families employ to ameliorate the potentially debilitating effects of poverty. Firsthand accounts from the Moore family illustrate the issue of life-style heterogeneity and provide examples of family dynamics that obviate the adverse consequences of neighborhood impoverishment.

Members of the Moore family recognize and cope with the neighborhood conditions Wilson outlines. Ella notes:

The jobs are folding up. . . . We wouldn't have so much crime as when they was with jobs. . . . Now you got gang banging, you got stealing automobiles, and dope and stuff like this. You got a lot of people now that's out of jobs. So you got a lot of people on relief.

Ella corroborates that some of the problematic social conditions Wilson (1987) ascribes to the most impoverished neighborhoods also exist in Thorndale. However, in contrast to the universally negative neighborhood effects Wilson depicts, her description indicates positive coping strategies:

The neighbors across the street, they watch out for us. And if any of us go on vacation, we'll tell them to keep an eye on the house. . . . So we're pretty close. This block itself is pretty nice so far. We don't have too many gang bangers. . . . I always pull my car up in the drive and I always come through the back. So they actually don't know whether I'm in here. . . . They don't know when somebody's here or not.

Far from being victims of their environment, Ella further discusses how as parents she and Pervis coped with the environmental risks of the housing projects, where they lived before they moved to their present single-family home:

I usually kept them restricted until I came home or until their daddy came home. Then, if he let them go out and play, fine. Or if I came home, I would let them play on the ramp until I got ready to feed them. It worked out real nice 'cause that way my husband was home at night and I was home during the day. So they always had an adult at home or someone there with them while they was young. . . . I didn't bother about youngsters running in and out of the house and all that stuff or them staying out, not going to school and running the streets somewhere. I kept a hand on them. I didn't have to run up to the school with them, because both of us would always tell them that more than us was watching them. . . . Our children was pretty good. . . . I was fortunate enough that they wasn't having babies at 10 and 11, 13 years old. They did try to finish high school. . . . Diane is doing pretty much like I did. She participate quite a bit with her kids' activities. She spend a lot of time with them.

Similar socialization and management strategies are currently employed with the grandchildren within the Thorndale neighborhod.

Although less stable individual and family patterns exist in the Thorndale neighborhood—the result of economic factors—the Moores lead a stable, home-centered life, in which they perform routine, domestic tasks. An excerpt from Diane's description of a typical day, much of which was confirmed through observation, illustrates this point:

> On a Monday I do all my house chores for the whole week. . . . Like now, I'm washing. . . . [After the children are in school] I may be washing my clothes and cleaning up the house. . . . Then I pick the kids up. I may still be washing. Then, when they come in from school, I make them change their clothes . . . . I clean up go out and mop, iron . . . . I iron every day. I don't iron all my clothes up 'cause they'd be right back wrinkled. . . . I clean up the living room, dining room, . . . clean the fish bowl out. . . . I set the garbage out for the garbage man to come. . . . Tuesday, until three o'clock, it's the same as Monday. . . . Sometimes I do volunteer work at the school. . . . The only day I tell them "no" is on the day I wash and that's mostly on Monday. But any other day of the week, I volunteer anytime. . . . Wednesday's the day that I have free where all day I can come home. . . . Thursday from three to six I'm across the street [baby-sitting]. . . . Fridays, I do anything that I have to do that I ain't done in the beginning of the week. Sundays, I get up, get the kids ready for church. . . . We get out of bed, get washed up, get our clothes on, get ready for church. . . . I'm in the choir, the kids in the choir. . . . We at church, singing in the choir, praising the Lord.

Sandra describes a similar routine, which includes daily cooking, going to church, watching television, and visiting relatives.

A Variety of Life-Styles

The qualitative data document the presence of various individual and family life-styles within African-American neighborhoods. In response to neighborhood conditions, home-oriented patterns coexist with street-oriented life-styles in the working-class and low-income neighborhoods where the Moores have lived. (See, for example, Gans, 1982; Hannerz, 1969; Howell, 1973.) Although family members are exposed to street-oriented patterns—stealing, drug dealing, gang banging—such exposure does not encourage them to adapt this alternative life-style.

In the home, much of the family routine, quite mundane in nature, centers around the fulfillment of domestic and child care responsibilities. Despite early childbearing, nonmarital childbearing, or both, and in some cases, reliance on AFDC income, women in the Moore family are considered competent, if not exemplary, mothers. The children of the mothers' generation (Ella and Pervis's grandchildren) are performing well in school and have been sheltered from the potential pitfalls of the neighborhood. To a large extent, the stability of the Moores derives from their sense of communal obligation to one another. By pooling resources, various households are stabilized during crises. Overall, they represent a well-functioning family.

DISCUSSION

Critics maintain that methodological biases limit the reliability and validity of qualitative data (Denzin, 1970; Emerson, 1981). Their concerns have some basis. Retrospective life history interviews may be compromised by memory lapses, informants' need to present a coherent narrative, or their developmentally changing interpretive schemes (Becker, 1970; Denzin, 1970; Plummer, 1983). In general, interviews can elicit idealized accounts that depart from actual behavior (Becker & Geer, 1969). Participant observation may be hampered by over-rapport and biased reports (Miller, 1969; Schwartz & Schwartz, 1969). Further, focus group dynamics potentially inhibit individual disclosures (Hedges, 1985; Morgan, 1988). More fundamentally, researcher characteristics—race, social class, age, and gender—can have an impact on each of these methodological strategies (di Leonardo, 1984; Sawyer, 1973; Warren, 1988; Warren & Rasmussen, 1977; Wax, 1979; Yancey & Rainwater, 1970).

All research methods, both qualitative and quantitative, are inherently limited, but researchers employ a variety of strategies to reduce sources of bias. This study's use of multiple methods, including focus group interviews, individual interviews, and limited participant observation, as well as multiple sources of information and multiple interviews, provided checks on potential threats to reliability and validity.

Often viewed as exclusively descriptive, case studies are assumed to be of little or no value for theory development. Further, the ability to provide generalizable propositions from a single example is questioned. In both instances the criticisms are ill-founded (Becker, 1970; Bulmer, 1986; Gilgun, 1991; Yin, 1989). Although true experiments focusing on individual behavior are powerful tests of theory, qualitative data have theory-generating capabilities. (See Gilgun, Chapter 3, this volume.) Qualitative data can inductively generate new theories or inform existing theories. Embedded in the experiences of real people and situations, such theories more closely approximate social reality (Bulmer, 1986; Emerson, 1983). Observations from the Moore family provide an example of how the qualitative case study can offer theoretical direction to the underclass debate.

Although focusing on one family, the case study materials here are interpreted within a larger body of research findings. As discussed earlier, in-depth data from the Moore family are consistent with past ethnographies with respect to family life-styles, family-neighborhood interactions, and family composition and dynamics. Thus, when the single case study is examined in light of existing research, it approximates a comparative research design. It does not stand alone. Moreover, as part of a larger research focus, the single case study adds to the larger cumulative knowledge base (Suttles, 1986).

Some poor African-American families are adversely effected by the conditions of poverty. Others manage to cope, despite economic obstacles. In light of the interconnectedness of their lives, often within the same neighborhoods, a well-rounded research agenda seeks to explain both outcomes. As illustrated by the case study materials, family process dimensions that explain these differences can be fully explored using qualitative approaches.

Research does not exist in a vacuum, but is effected by the larger social and political content in which it is conducted (Rainwater & Pittman, 1967; Suttles, 1976). The types of information sought on some poor African-American families contradict idealized norms and values, encouraging stereotypical depictions of their lives and neighborhoods. Yet if the goals of research are to provide accurate portrayals of the poor and to generate effective and humane public policies, then these efforts must be informed by the firsthand accounts of those whose lives are directly touched by poverty. Qualitative methods provide an avenue for their voices.

REFERENCES

Aschenbrenner, J. (1975). *Lifelines: Black families in Chicago.* New York: Holt, Rinehart & Winston.

Auletta, K. (1982). *The underclass.* New York: Random House.

Bane, M. J., & Ellwood, D. T. (1984a). *The dynamics of children's living arrangements* (Working Paper Contract No. HHS-100-82-0038). Washington, DC: U. S. Department of Health and Human Services.

Bane, M. J., & Ellwood, D. T. (1984b). *Single mothers and their living arrangements* (Working Paper Contract No. HHS-100-82-0038). Washington, DC: U. S. Department of Health and Human Services.

Becker, H. S. (1970). *Sociological work: Method and substance.* Chicago: Aldine.

Becker, H. S., & Geer, B. (1969). Participant observation and interviewing: A comparison. In G. J. McCall & J. L. Simmons (Eds.), *Issues in participant observation: A text and reader* (pp. 322-331). Reading, MA: Addison-Wesley.

Bellenger, D., Bernhardt, K. L., & Goldstucker, J. L. (1976). *Qualitative research in marketing.* Chicago: American Marketing Association.

Bulmer, M. (1986). The value of qualitative methods. In M. Bulmer, with K. G. Banting, S. S. Blume, M. Carley, & C. Weiss (Eds.), *Social science and social policy* (pp. 180-204). Boston: Allen & Unwin.

Burgess, R. G. (1982). *Field research: A sourcebook and field manual.* London: Allen & Unwin.

Burgess, R. G. (1984). *In the field: An introduction to field research.* Boston: Allen & Unwin.

Burton, L. M., & Jarrett, R. L. (1991). *Studying African-American family structure and process in underclass neighborhoods: Conceptual considerations.* Paper presented at the annual meeting of the American Sociological Association, Cincinnati, OH.

Calder, B. J. (1977, August). Focus groups and the nature of qualitative marketing research. *Journal of Marketing Research, 14,* 353-364.

Chicago Fact Book Consortium. (1984). *Local community fact book of Chicago metropolitan area: Based on the 1970-1980 census.* Chicago: Chicago Review.

City of Chicago, Department of Human Services. (1990). *1990 Community needs assessment: Head Start.* Chicago: Department of Planning, Research and Development.

Clark, R. M. (1983). *Family life and school achievement: Why poor Black children succeed or fail.* Chicago: University of Chicago Press.

Cohler, B. J., & Grunebaum, H. U. (1981). *Mothers, grandmothers, and daughters: Personality and child care in three-generational families.* New York: John Wiley.

Cook, T., & Curtin, T. (1987). The mainstream and the underclass: Why are the differences so salient and the similarities so unobtrusive? In J. C.. Masters & W. P. Smith (Eds.), *Social comparison, social justice, and relative deprivation: Theoretical, empirical, and policy perspectives* (pp. 218-264). Hillsdale, NJ: Lawrence Erlbaum.

Denzin, N. K. (1970). *The research act: A theoretical introduction to sociological methods.* Chicago: Aldine.

Downs, C., Smeyak, G. P., & Martin, E. (1980). *Professional interviewing.* New York: Harper & Row.

Emerson, R. M. (1981). Observational field work. *Annual Review of Sociology, 7,* 351-378.

Emerson, R. M. (1983). *Contemporary field research: A collection of readings.* Prospect Heights, IL: Waveland.

Fetterman, D. M. (1989). *Ethnography: Step by step.* Newbury Park, CA: Sage.

Gans, H. J. (1982). *The urban villagers: Group and class in the life of Italian-Americans* (expd. and upd. ed.). New York: Free Press.

Gilgun, J. F. (1991). *A case for case studies in social work research.* Manuscript submitted for publication.

Handel, G. (1991). Case study in family research. In J. R. Feagin, A. M. Orum, & G. Sjoberg (Eds.), *A case for the case study* (pp. 244-268). Chapel Hill: University of North Carolina Press.

Hannerz, U. (1969). *Soulside: Inquiries into ghetto culture and community.* New York: Columbia University Press.

Hedges, S. (1985). Group interviewing. In R. Walker (Ed.), *Applied qualitative research* (pp. 239-269). Brookfield, VT: Gower.

Howell, J. (1973). *Hard living on Clay Street: Portraits of blue collar families.* New York: Anchor.

Jarrett, R. L. (1990). *A comparative examination of socialization patterns among low-income African-Americans, Chicanos, Puerto Ricans, and Whites: A review of the ethnographic literature.* New York: Social Science Research Council.

Jarrett, R. L. (1991). *Ethnographic contributions to the study of African-American families and children: Past and future directions.* Paper presented at preconference meeting of the Society for Research on Child Development, Seattle, August 16-17.

Jeffers, C. (1967). *Living poor: A participant observer study of priorities and choices.* Ann Arbor, MI: Ann Arbor Press.

Jencks, C. (1988). Deadly neighborhoods. *The New Republic, 198,* 23-32.

Jencks, C., & Mayer, S. E. (1989). *The social consequences of growing up in a poor neighborhood: A review.* Evanston, IL: Northwestern University, Center for Urban Affairs and Policy Research.

Jencks, C., & Peterson, P. E. (Eds.). (1991). *The urban underclass.* Washington, DC: Brookings Institution.

Jorgensen, D. L. (1989). *Participant observation: A methodology for human studies.* Newbury Park, CA: Sage.

Katz, M. B. (1989). *The undeserving poor: From the war on poverty to the war on welfare.* New York: Pantheon.

Ladner, J. A. (1971). *Tomorrow's tomorrow: The black woman.* New York: Anchor.

Lemann, N. (1986, June). The origins of the underclass. *Atlantic Monthly, 258,* 31-55.

di Leonardo, M. (1984). *The varieties of ethnic experience: Kinship, class, and gender among California Italian-Americans.* Ithaca, NY: Cornell University Press.

McGeary, M. G., & Lynn, L. E. (Eds.). (1988). *Urban change and poverty.* Washington, DC: National Academy Press.

McLanahan, S., Garfinkel, I., & Watson, D. (1988). Family structure, poverty, and the underclass. In M. G. McGeary & L. E. Lynn (Eds.), *Urban change and poverty* (pp. 102-147). Washington, DC: National Academy Press.

Martin, E., & Martin, J. M. (1978). *The black extended family.* Chicago: University of Chicago Press.

Massey, D., & Eggers, M. (1990). The ecology of inequality: Minorities and the concentration of poverty, 1970-1980. *American Journal of Sociology, 95,* 1153-1188.

Merton, R. K., Fiske, M., & Kendall, P. (1956). *The focused interview: A manual of problems and procedures.* Glencoe, IL: Free Press.

Miller, S. M. (1969). The participant observer and "over-rapport." In G. J. McCall & J. L. Simmons (Eds.), *Issues in participant observation: A text and reader* (pp. 87-89). Reading, MA: Addison-Wesley.

Morgan, D. L. (1988). *Focus groups as qualitative research.* Beverly Hills, CA: Sage.

Morgan, D. L., & Spanish, M. T. (1984). Focus groups: A new tool for qualitative research. *Qualitative Sociology, 7,* 253-270.

Murray, C. (1984). *Loosing Ground: American social policy, 1950-1980.* New York: Basic Books.

Olson, P. (1982). Urban neighborhood research: Its development and current focus. *Urban Affairs Quarterly, 17,* 491-518.

Plummer, K. (1983). *Documents of life: An introduction to the problems and literature of a humanistic method*. Boston: Allen & Unwin.

Rainwater, L, & Pittman, D. J. (1967). Ethical problems in studying a politically sensitive and deviant community. *Social Problems, 14,* 357-366.

Reed, A., Jr. (1988, February 6). The liberal technocrat. *The Nation, 246,* 167-170.

Ricketts, E. R., & Sawhill, I. V. (1988). Defining and measuring the underclass. *Journal of Policy Analysis and Management, 7,* 316-25.

Sawyer, E. (1973). Methodological problems in studying so-called "deviant" communities. In J. Ladner (Ed.), *The death of white sociology* (pp. 361-379). New York: Random House.

Schwartz, M. S., & Schwartz, C. G. (1969). Problems in participant observation. In G. J. McCall & J. L. Simmons (Eds.), *Issues in participant observations: A text and a reader* (pp. 89-105). Reading, MA: Addison-Wesley.

Seidel, J.V., Kjolseth, R., & Seymour, E. (1988). The Ethnograph. Qualis Research Associates, PO Box 3219, Littleton, CO 80161.

Smith, J. M. (1972). *Interviewing in market and social research*. Boston: Routledge & Kegan Paul.

Spradley, J. P. (1979). *The ethnographic interview*. New York: Holt, Rinehart & Winston.

Stack, C. B. (1974). *All our kin: Strategies for survival in a Black community*. New York: Harper & Row.

Sullivan, M. (1985). *Teen fathers in the inner city*. New York: Ford Foundation.

Suttles, G. D. (1986). School desegregation and the "national community." In J. Praeger, D. Longshore, & M. Seeman (Eds.), *School desegregation research: New directions in situational analysis* (pp. 47-78). New York: Plenum.

Taylor, S. J., & Bogdan, R. (1984). *Introduction to qualitative methods: The search for meanings* (2nd ed.). New York: John Wiley.

Valentine, B. L. (1978). *Hustling and other hard work: Life styles in the ghetto*. New York: Free Press.

Vinovski, M. (1988). Teenage pregnancy and the underclass. *Public Interest, 93,* 87-96.

Warren, C.A.B. (1988). *Gender issues in field research*. Beverly Hills, CA: Sage.

Warren, C.A.B., & Rasmussen, P. K. (1977). Sex and gender in field research. *Urban Life, 6,* 349-369.

Wax, R. H. (1979). Gender and age in fieldwork and fieldwork education: No good thing is done by any man alone. *Social Problems, 26,* 509-522.

Williams, M. (1981). *On the street where I lived*. New York: Holt, Rinehart & Winston.

Williams, T., & Kornblum, W. (1985). *Growing up poor*. Lexington, MA: Lexington.

Wilson, W. J. (1987). *The truly disadvantaged: The inner city, the underclass, and public policy*. Chicago: University of Chicago Press.

Wireman, P. (1984). *Urban neighborhoods, networks, and families: New forms for old values*. Lexington, MA: Lexington.

Yanagisako, S. J. (1979). Family and household: The analysis of domestic groups. *Annual Review of Anthropology, 8,* 161-205.

Yancey, W. L., & Rainwater, L. (1970). Problems in the ethnography of the urban underclass. In R. Habenstein (Ed.), *Pathways to data: Field methods for studying ongoing social organizations* (pp. 245-269). Chicago: Aldine.

Yin, R. K. (1989). *Case study research: Designs and methods* (rev. ed.). Newbury Park, CA: Sage.

Zollar, A. C. (1985). *A member of the family: Strategies for Black family continuity*. Chicago: Nelson-Hall.

A Feminist Analysis of Interviews With Elderly Mothers and Their Daughters

KATHERINE R. ALLEN
Virginia Polytechnic Institute

ALEXIS J. WALKER
Oregon State University

Our purpose is to address empirically two underlying assumptions in the intergenerational caregiving literature: That elderly family members are passive, dependent recipients of care (Stueve, 1982) and that the outcomes of caregiving for the caregiver are overwhelmingly negative (Motenko, 1989; Mutran & Reitzes, 1984). We do so with a sample of adult, caregiving daughters and elderly, physically impaired mothers pairs. A feminist perspective and methodology facilitate the achievement of our goals.

Research on family caregiving emphasizes the perspectives of caregivers with little attention to the experiences of care receivers (Rakowski & Clark, 1985). The result is an emphasis on the burdens or

AUTHORS' NOTE: Work on this project was supported by Grant No. AG06766 from the National Institute on Aging and by a grant from the Virginia Tech Women's Research Institute. We thank Debra Murphy, Melanie Place, and Hwa-Yong Shin for data management and project organization.

198

strains of caregiving and a limited view of the contributions of elderly family members in their intergenerational relationships (Barer & Johnson, 1990; Matthews, 1985; Stueve, 1982).

Feminist research offers a corrective to the restrictive nature of family caregiving scholarship. Feminists attempt to set the record straight by incorporating voices previously unheard (Westkott, 1979). In this chapter, we work toward highlighting a relationship between two women from the point of view of each. Published research about the relationship between a dependent elderly mother and her caregiving daughter has tended to distort the reciprocity and uniqueness in their relationship. In our culture, the relationship between mother and daughter is either problematized or sentimentalized. Women are elected to play out the dissension in families; they become the repositories of conflict (McGoldrick, Anderson, & Walsh, 1989). As feminists, our goal is to see what women in an intergenerational relationship value about each other.

INTERGENERATIONAL CAREGIVING

Our feminist, qualitative approach facilitates a focus on the meanings of caregiving experiences to those involved (Fischer, 1986; Hasselkus, 1988). This approach differs from the dominant paradigm in intergenerational caregiving, which emphasizes caregiving burdens. Researchers, for example, have identified a multitude of emotional strains experienced by caregivers, such as frustration, impatience, and tension (e.g., Abel, 1986; Archbold, 1983; Fischer, 1986; Robinson, 1983; Zarit, Riever, & Bach-Peterson, 1980). Care receivers, too, have been described as experiencing declines in morale, restrictions in their outlook for the future, and increases in depression (Dunkle, 1985; Rakowski & Clark, 1985; Stoller, 1984). In addition, adult children who are caregivers have been described as making major, deleterious changes in their lives, such as abandoning plans to move or quitting a job (e.g., Archbold, 1983; Cantor, 1983; Montgomery, Gonyea, & Hooyman, 1985). The financial burdens of caregiving to the adult-child caregiver also have been emphasized (e.g., Archbold, 1983). Finally, it has been suggested that relationships with aging parents suffer as a result of caregiving (e.g., Jarrett, 1985; Johnson & Catalano, 1983; Poulshock & Deimling, 1984). There have been few attempts to identify positive caregiving outcomes (e.g., Archbold, 1983; Miller, 1988; Sheehan & Nuttall, 1988; Walker & Allen, 1991; Walker, Shin, & Bird, 1990).

A feminist view enables us to see a range of caregiving outcomes, both negative and positive. As feminists, we offer an alternative view—that there are potential benefits that arise from caregiving and that aging mothers have something intrinsically important to offer to their caregiving daughters. We incorporate the previously unheard voices of care receivers themselves (Westkott, 1979). We avoid problematizing or sentimentalizing the mother-daughter relationship. As feminists, our goal is to see what women in an intergenerational relationship value about each other, and, in the process, we discover these women's version of the reality of mother-daughter ties. Their absence from the literature demonstrates that exploration of potential positive caregiving outcomes is warranted. In addition, greater attention must be paid to the potentially active role of the care receiver.

We restricted our study in a number of ways. First, we focused on caregiving relationships in which care receivers exhibited physical but not cognitive impairments. Such a restriction was necessitated by the considerable evidence that caregiving outcomes differ for care receivers suffering from dementia rather than physical decline (Birkel, 1987; Burdz, Eaton, & Bond, 1988). Second, we focused exclusively on women: caregiving daughters and their elderly, unmarried mothers. Most elderly are widowed women. When widows need help, they usually receive it from an adult child, typically a daughter (e.g., Horowitz, 1985). In addition, there is reason to believe that there is a high likelihood of positive outcomes in mother-daughter relationships. Such ties are generally warm and particularly close (Boyd, 1989). The mother-daughter bond is central to the lives of women (Abel, 1986). Troll (1987) argued that women emphasize vertical or intergenerational ties, i.e., with parents and children, whereas men emphasize horizontal or intragenerational ties. Positive outcomes also are likely in female intergenerational relationships because women are socialized to nurture. That is, women may be more likely than men to consider the potential outcomes of caregiving or care receiving to their intergenerational partner. Even daughters-in-law demonstrate this concern (Beck, 1988). The search for positive outcomes and the focus on the active role of care receivers signify a neglected aspect of women's caring labor.

In this study, we examined the statements made by caregiving daughters and care-receiving mothers for evidence of positive outcomes. Such evidence could be of unique importance given the need to identify positive caregiving outcomes and the perspectives of care receivers. Our method was designed to incorporate what others have neglected: the reciprocal experience of caring between mothers and daughters.

FEMINIST METHODOLOGY

Feminist research is distinguished from other types of research by worldview rather than method (Nielsen, 1990). There is nothing uniquely feminist about any particular method. Feminist researchers use the same kinds of methods as other researchers: Feminists interview and observe people and examine documents (Harding, 1987). Feminist methods are primarily, but not exclusively, qualitative (Allen & Baber, 1992; Harding, 1987; Peplau & Conrad, 1989; Stanley, 1990). In this project, both qualitative and quantitative methods were employed.

What is unique to feminist scholarship and methodology is that women and their concerns are at the center of investigation pursuant to an explicit intention of conducting research that is *useful for* women, not just about them (Harding, 1987; Smith, 1987; Westkott, 1979). Feminist researchers critique both the positivist and the naturalistic traditions in social science as well as both quantitative and qualitative methods (Stanley & Wise, 1979). Conducting feminist research is an experience of resistance: Feminists resist efforts to package methods so that they look like standard research products. As Stanley and Wise (1979) argued, scientific products in the positivist and naturalistic traditions are rendered "hygienic" by the exclusion of the researcher's role and experience of change during the research process. Traditionally, the process of knowledge generation is filtered through standards designed to objectify the ways in which data are obtained, leaving much of what happens to those involved unsaid and unanalyzed (Stanley & Wise, 1979). We join other feminist scholars (e.g., Fonow & Cook, 1991; Nielsen, 1990; Stacey, 1988, 1990; Stanley, 1990; Stanley & Wise, 1979) in documenting explicitly our research process and addressing the emancipatory product of our work.

Feminism is a perspective (a way of seeing), an epistemology (a way of knowing), and an ontology (a way of being in the world) (Stanley, 1990). Feminist scholarship is closer to phenomenology than to positivism, but it does not completely embrace or reject either paradigm

(Nielsen, 1990). Feminism joins the chorus of phenomenological voices in critiquing the claim of "objectivism" within positivism (Nielsen, 1990) and scientism (Stanley & Wise, 1979), and yet, in its postempirical modification, it still has room for modest claims of empirical evidence. It would be archaic for feminist scholars "to endorse a return to nonempirical inquiry" (Nielsen, 1990, p. 31), despite the fact that some postmodern feminists have called for a rejection of empiricism (see Nicholson, 1990). Phenomenology is not an acceptable substitute for feminist methods because it does not go far enough in incorporating women's voices. A feminist construction of reality as applied to social science research is grounded in the willingness to name oneself "feminist" and to perceive the social construction of women as oppressive. As Stanley (1990) said, "It is the experience of and acting against perceived oppression that gives rise to a distinctive feminist epistemology" (p. 14).

As feminist social scientists and practitioners, we are concerned with family arrangements as sources of both oppression and support for women. The subject matter we address here is the relationship between aging mothers and caregiving daughters. The positive aspects of this relationship are devalued in the caregiving literature: As discussed earlier, elderly mothers are characterized as burdensome to their overworked daughters. As feminists, we offer an alternative view—that caregiving also has positive consequences for the caregiver and that aging mothers have something intrinsically important to offer. Further, we allow our knowledge claims to be informed by our own experiences as mothers and daughters, in the ways we uniquely and jointly define our experiences. Finally, our own relationship as feminists, collaborators, and friends influences the research we conduct; that is, in the process of discovering this reality of mother-daughter relationships, we do not ignore ways in which we value each other. Our commitment to social change translates into "a search for research techniques which take account of and record everyday processes, and which reduce the isolation between research participants" (Fonow & Cook, 1991, p.6).

Feminist research is consciously reflexive (Stanley, 1990), or "excruciatingly self-conscious" (Stacey, 1988, p. 25). Reflexivity is defined as a source of insight and critical examination of the research process (Fonow & Cook, 1991). We acknowledge that the process of conducting this research changes us. Our relationship is altered and reorganized as we work. We live 3,000 miles apart. The physical distance is a metaphor for the dialectical relationship, one of experiential distance, between collaborators, between researcher and subject, between one human being and another. We make as explicit as we can the processes we follow. We are aware of the personal and professional vulnerability associated with doing feminist research (Fonow & Cook, 1991; Stanley, 1990; Stanley & Wise, 1979). To relinquish the subject-object distance can lead to charges of essentialism, or not being scientific. Being at all personal can be construed as being too personal (Allen & Baber, 1992).

Feminism has many meanings. Feminist methods and feminist consciousness are not final products, but negotiable realities. We do not share a static, congruent definition of feminism as we work. There is fertile conflict and tension in the ways we negotiate the products of our feminist process (Du Bois, 1983). Yet, at the risk of oversimplification of feminist ideas and practices, we agreed that women have been devalued, oppressed, and exploited, and that scholarship is androcentric. And we are committed to change—personally, intellectually, and politically (Acker, Barry, & Esseveld, 1983). As we will discuss below, aside from certain similarities—we are white women in our late 30s, trained in family studies and life-span human development—our differences are vast. One of us is more experienced in quantitative methodologies, the other in qualitative. By choice, one of us is a mother; the other is child free. We each have intense histories with our mothers, a reality of most U.S. women (e.g., Chodorow & Contratto, 1982; Rich, 1976). Perhaps most reflective of the negotiation process in our work is that one of us is intensely self-disclosing, the other intensely private. We provide this information because this is what is unique about feminist scholarship and practice: Who the researchers are as people is relevant to the research process, yet hardly ever discussed in most positivist and naturalistic research reports (Stanley & Wise, 1979).

METHOD

Sample

We interviewed 29 white mother-daughter pairs who were a subset of 222 pairs who volunteered for a study on mother-daughter relationships in adulthood, responding to newspaper articles describing our interest in female intergenerational relationships, particularly those in which the daughters were providing assistance to their mothers. The mothers and daughters of each pair were interviewed separately in 1988. A wide array of quantitative measures was administered and extensive field notes compiled during the interviews with the 58 women included in this study. Thus, the subsample was comprised of the women from whom we had the most extensive data.

The daughters, who defined themselves as the primary caregivers, provided at least one service (housekeeping, transportation, meal preparation, laundry, personal care, or financial support) for their mothers. The mothers were aged 65 or older, lived within 45 miles of their daughters, showed no evidence of cognitive impairment as indicated by the daughters, and were unmarried. In the typical pair, the daughter provided help with transportation, housekeeping, and meal preparation but not with personal care.

The mean age of daughters in the study was 55 years, although there was a range from 33 to 72. More than half (52%) were married, although 21% were widowed and 14% were divorced. They averaged two children, 1.4 below the age of 18. The mean education level was 13 years. The average annual household income for daughters was $24,000, although one daughter reported no income and another's income was $67,500. Daughters reported that they had been giving care to their mothers for an average of 12 years.

The mean age of mothers in the study was 80, although there was a range from 64 to 93. Most (76%) were widowed, and 24% were divorced or separated. The mean education level was 11 years. Mothers' average annual income was $8,836, with a range from $0 to $18,000. Mothers reported that they had been receiving care from their daughters for an average of 10 years.

Procedures

All interviews took place in respondents' homes. The women responded to questions about the health of the mothers, activities daughters performed with or for their mothers, the caregiving situation, and their relationship with their intergenerational partners. Demographic items were assessed as well. The interviews were semistructured, and the women were encouraged to elaborate on their responses and to provide additional information. They also had the opportunity to raise any additional issues they wished to discuss. Both mothers and daughters had much to say beyond the range of questions they were asked, and each sought to characterize her caregiving experiences. Their comments were captured in extensive, verbatim field notes taken throughout the interview. Except for demographic information, all data reported in this chapter are from these field notes.

Our collaborative work began after the interviews had been completed. We joined our respective expertise in qualitative and quantitative methodologies as well as our willingness to be "taught" by the data. We met regularly to analyze the empirical data, to create and adapt various methods for our project, and to incorporate feminism with our interest in intergenerational caregiving.

Data Analysis

In our practice as feminist researchers, we were at once student, teacher, and peer to the other. We brought a gendered understanding to our work that reflected our feminist practice (Walker, Martin, & Thompson, 1988) and a belief that the knower cannot be separated from the known (Du Bois, 1983). That is, as women, feminists, and daughters, we brought to our work certain prejudgments that helped to construct the way in which we analyzed the data (Nielsen, 1990). We pooled our expertise in conducting and analyzing subjective life histories, in-depth interview techniques, and content analysis with survey design, questionnaire construction, and statistical procedures, thus assisting each other in translating qualitative field notes into a meaningful dialogue that reflected and sought to explain the experiences of the women in the study. Our collaborative procedures were isomorphic to the feminist values underlying our practice in working with the data. Our process as peers and practitioners was based on our commitment to feminism and social change.

The physical proximity and distance of our relationship to each other was an important component in our work (Mascia-Lees, Sharpe, & Cohen, 1989; Nielsen, 1990; Oakley, 1981; Smith, 1987; Stacey, 1988). Because of the multiple layers of distance between us, in miles, personal experience, and training, our collaboration involved frequent visits, telephone calls, and mailings. The labor of the data analysis was intensive and interactive. We often clashed in ideas and personality.

The data analyzed for this chapter consisted of field notes and in-depth responses to semistructured questions. A thematic analysis was conducted by reading the field notes, discussing the case histories of the mother-daughter pairs, and developing a coding scheme. Coding categories were developed, revised initially through five thorough, joint examinations of the data, and then applied to the transcriptions of the field notes. A qualitative content analysis of the field notes was conducted with the purpose of identifying themes (Taylor & Bogdan, 1984) suggesting positive outcomes in the caregiving situation as perceived by mothers and daughters. Data were read repeatedly and screened for statements that reflected positive comments and anecdotes about caregivers or care receivers and the experience of providing or receiving care. We also coded for positive statements about the intergenerational partner or the relationship with that partner. We compiled, read, and reread the mother and daughter comments to generate themes reflective of the content. The three positive themes that emerged from the collaborative process of coding the data were companionship, concern and caring, and appreciation and gratitude.

Here, we report only positive outcomes in order to address the overfocus on negative outcomes in the caregiving literature. Elsewhere, we report on an analysis of the data based on relationship patterns, in which, using a social exchange perspective, we found evidence of rewards, costs, conflict, and concern in all of these relationships (Walker & Allen, 1991). Among the 29 mother-daughter pairs, three distinct relationship types were found: intrinsic (13 pairs), ambivalent (10 pairs), and conflicted (6 pairs). Intrinsic partnerships were experienced as mutually rewarding, with few costs or conflicts and much positive, reciprocal concern for each partner. Ambivalent relationships lacked this mutuality; rewards were experienced in the context of pronounced costs and recurrent conflicts. Concern did not appear to be reciprocal, especially by daughters. Conflicted pairs experienced few rewards or positive outcomes, many costs, and frequent conflicts. These women appeared to be more concerned for themselves than for their intergenerational partners. Thus, although positive outcomes were evident in all the pairs, the typology suggests a continuum of relationship outcomes ranging from rewarding to unbalanced to unrewarding (Walker & Allen, 1991).

POSITIVE OUTCOMES OF CAREGIVING

Companionship

Both mothers and daughters revealed that their intergenerational partner was a companion to them. The pairs participated in activities defined as mutually beneficial. For example, one daughter reported on the extent of her activities with her mother, who suffers from debilitating allergies and is financially dependent:

> We go once a month to the theater; we have lunch two to three times a week; we go out to dinner at least once a month; we take long drives.

These two women, despite the mother's poor health, are more than companions; they appeared to be friends.

The perception that their relationship was composed of affection, honesty, and respect for the individuality of each partner was part of companionship. Another mother and daughter play Scrabble daily. In contemplating the future, the daughter revealed the benefits companionship brings to her as she asked:

> What will I do if something happens to my mother? I realize how much she does for me.

Her mother said:

> Being honest is the secret of the whole relationship.

Another daughter, whose mother depended on her for transportation, reported:

> I've learned a lot about her . . . things that she would tell her friend. She's not just my mom; she's a person.

Concern and Caring

These mothers and daughters were also concerned for each other. They worried about each other. They were watchful about potentially problematic situations that might arise and sought to express their care through positive and reciprocal concern. For example, one daughter, in addition to help with transportation and errands, gave her mother money each month. The mother gave her daughter money, too:

> She finally consented to let me give her $10 a month for gasoline. I know she could care less but I feel better about it, and she accepts that.

The daughter also mentioned this $10 in the interview, but neither suggested that the money came from that contributed to the mother by the daughter. By acknowledging her mother's contribution, the daughter revealed her own concern for preserving her mother's perception of herself. Similarly, a mother with osteoporosis said of her only child:

> I hate to have her do so much—If I'd had two kids, maybe they could have divided the work she does for me.

A daughter whose mother was unable to walk without assistance and spent most of her time in bed reported:

> I keep her socks pulled up; Mother really likes that.

A different daughter, whose mother's arthritis severely limited her ability to get around, said:

> I tell her, "You're coming down to dinner"; it's good for her to see the dogs.

The following example reveals the process of watchful care and concern between mothers and daughters. A daughter's husband liked to spend weekends at the couple's mobile home on the coast. They did so whenever the daughter felt the mother would be able to make it through the weekend alone without a flare-up of her arthritis. The mother did not like it at the coast. We talked about what she thinks when she knows her daughter will be leaving for another of these trips. She said:

> I know I'll miss my daughter when she goes away, but I won't say anything to her; I want her to enjoy herself. Once a year, I go to the coast to please her.

Thus, the care and concern these intergenerational partners expressed for each other were not burdensome or sacrificial, but reflective of mutual respect for the wishes of the other.

Attention to the well-being and pleasure of the other was also characteristic of concern and care. An 89-year-old mother who needed help with transportation and household tasks summed up this position:

> My daughter and I are very happy to see each other happy.

Appreciation and Gratitude

Both mothers and daughters indicated appreciation for each other. A daughter whose mother is dependent for household tasks, food preparation, and financial support said:

[My family and I] never do anything for her but what she's very grateful.

Another daughter, whose mother has Parkinson's disease, said:

She's always bright and chipper, and when you're down she picks you up.

A financially dependent mother said:

My daughter is the most wonderful mother.

Another mother reported:

My daughter thinks we have the best relationship. I admire her so much. She seldom comes to see me without bringing something for me.

This appreciation was particularly evident when it was unexpected. One mother, who gets help from her daughter financially and with household tasks and meal preparation, said:

My daughter does so many things for me that sometimes I don't even need. The things my daughter does overwhelm me sometimes.

Daughters reported the satisfaction they felt when they pleased their mothers. A daughter whose mother depended on her for transportation described the history of appreciation in their current relationship:

After my father died, my brother came up with a way for us to spend time with my mother. On Wednesday nights, she would make dinner for him. On Thursdays, I would take her out to dinner. Now, she takes me out to dinner every Thursday night. Usually, she makes me pick [the restaurant].

A mother dependent for transportation and household tasks said:

Just knowing I have my daughter makes me feel better.

A different mother, dependent financially and for transportation, household tasks, and meal preparation, reported:

> You can't beat a daughter for a lot of things. I don't know what I'd do without her. She's always getting me something. How are you going to stop her? She'll think of things to do for me all the time.

A mother recovering from a fall in which several bones were shattered said:

> I wanted to do this study because my daughter deserves to get credit for what she's done for me. She never plans [anything] without including me.

DISCUSSION

In this sample of mothers and daughters, we found considerable evidence for both positive caregiving outcomes and the active role of mothers in intergenerational dyads. Our findings raise questions about the focus of the family caregiving literature on the difficulties or burdens of caregiving (Matthews, 1985; Motenko, 1989; Stueve, 1982). The findings also clarify that aging care receivers experience their own set of rewards from receiving care and contribute to the rewards of their caregivers.

First, there was ample evidence of companionship among these mothers and daughters. Companionship involves mutually beneficial activities in which intergenerational partners participate. In addition to friendship, it includes affection, honesty, and respect for each partner's individuality. Mothers and daughters in this sample enjoyed spending time with each other. Second, feelings of concern and worry elicited the watchfulness with which mothers and daughters approached their caregiving relationship. Concern and caring were evident in the mutual respect and esteem with which partners were held, as opposed to the burden and sacrifice typically assumed in the caregiving literature. Third, mothers and daughters appreciated and valued each other, particularly when their partner contributed to them in unexpected ways. Appreciation was also evident in a woman's obvious satisfaction at having pleased her intergenerational partner. The importance of appreciation and gratitude signaled a recognition of the costs inherent in caregiving. For care receivers especially, expressing appreciation was a meaningful reward they could offer their daughters.

The examination of caregiving from a feminist perspective increases our understanding of intergenerational caregiving. Caregiving to a physically impaired elder occurs in a relational context. This relationship can produce positive outcomes for both the caregiver and the care receiver. It is also clear that although aging care receivers may prefer to be independent, they can still find ways to maintain or develop their relationships with their adult-child caregiver.

We emphasize caution in generalizing from these findings. First, the results are not generalizable to situations in which care receivers suffer cognitive disabilities (Birkel, 1987; Burdz et al., 1988). Second, because we interviewed women only, the particular outcomes of caregiving and care receiving may differ when the caregiver is a son or the care receiver is a father. Third, the women we interviewed volunteered to participate in this study. It is possible that volunteers have "better" relationships; thus, we may have overestimated the positive aspects of the caregiving situation. Finally, we would not want readers to have the impression that caregiving and care receiving yield only positive outcomes. We report only positive outcomes, but as we have described elsewhere (Walker & Allen, 1991), several respondents mentioned negative outcomes, and some did not comment on outcomes at all. Our exclusive attention to positive outcomes reflects our concern over the disinclination in the caregiving literature to consider rewards or the good things that come from caregiving relationships. Nonetheless, the findings of this study provide working hypotheses about the possibility of reciprocal positive aspects of caregiving relationships. (See Gilgun, 1991, and Chapter 3, this volume, for a discussion of applications of findings to other settings.)

CONCLUSION

In this qualitative, feminist study, respondents spoke enthusiastically about the rewards that accrue from giving and receiving care across two generations. Positive outcomes should be added to the concepts measured in intergenerational caregiving research. If not deliberately incorporated into research designs, this aspect of caregiving will continue to be rendered invisible, with an overfocus on burden to the exclusion of rewards and affection, many of which may be experienced within the same intergenerational dyad.

Our collaborative work serves as a reminder of the importance of incorporating the experiences of both partners in a relationship into an investigation. Our feminist beliefs and practices allowed us to be sensitive to the perceptions of a neglected group of research subjects: elderly female care receivers. Rather than reinforcing the standard conceptualization of older women as dependent, passive recipients of their daughters' time and energy (Stueve, 1982), this study reveals how elderly mothers reciprocate through companionship, concern, and appreciation as well as offering care themselves. Our feminist approach allowed us to place these women in the center of study so that we could understand how they incorporate changes in their lives.

Based on these findings, we recommend that positive outcomes be considered as essential a component of the caregiving relationship as role strain and burden. We propose that our findings be tested and refined in caregiving situations reflecting both a diversity of care needs and various caregivers and care receivers. We suggest that the feminist practice of addressing the process and the product of the research endeavor be made as explicit as possible, thereby valuing all the participants of a study.

REFERENCES

Abel, E. K. (1986). Adult daughters and care for the elderly. *Feminist Studies, 12,* 479-497.

Acker, J., Barry, K., & Esseveld, J. (1983). Objectivity and truth: Problems in doing feminist research. *Women's Studies International Forum, 6,* 423-435.

Allen, K. R., & Baber, K. M. (1992). Ethical and epistemological tensions in applying a postmodern perspective to feminist research. *Psychology of Women Quarterly, 16,* 1-15.

Archbold, P. G. (1983). Impact of parent-caring on women. *Family Relations, 32,* 39-45.

Barer, B. M., & Johnson, C. L. (1990). A critique of the caregiving literature. *Gerontologist, 30,* 26-29.

Beck, K. (1988). Full circle. In J. Norris (Ed.), *Daughters of the elderly* (pp. 125-131). Bloomington: Indiana University Press.

Birkel, R. C. (1987). Toward a social ecology of the home-care household. *Psychology and Aging, 2,* 294-301.

Boyd, C. J. (1989). Mothers and daughters: A discussion of theory and research. *Journal of Marriage and the Family, 51,* 291-301.

Burdz, M. P., Eaton, W. O., & Bond, J. B., Jr. (1988). Effect of respite care on dementia and nondementia patients and their caregivers. *Psychology and Aging, 3,* 38-42.

Cantor, M. H. (1983). Strain among caregivers: A study of experience in the United States. *Gerontologist, 23,* 597-604.

Chodorow, N., & Contratto, S. (1982). The fantasy of the perfect mother. In B. Thorne & M. Yalom (Eds.), *Rethinking the family: Some feminist questions* (pp. 54-75). New York: Longman.

Du Bois, B. (1983). Passionate scholarship: Notes on values, knowing and method in feminist social science. In G. Bowles & R. D. Klein (Eds.), *Theories of women's studies* (pp. 105-116). London: Routledge.

Dunkle, R. E. (1985). Comparing the depression of elders in two types of caregiving arrangements. *Family Relations, 34,* 235-240.

Fischer, L. R. (1986). *Linked lives: Adult daughters and their mothers.* New York: Harper & Row.

Fonow, M. M., & Cook, J. A. (1991). Back to the future: A look at the second wave of feminist epistemology and methodology. In M. M. Fonow & J. A. Cook (Eds.), *Beyond methodology: Feminist scholarship as lived research* (pp. 1-15). Bloomington: Indiana University Press.

Gilgun, J. F. (1991). *A case for case studies in social work research.* Manuscript submitted for publication.

Harding, S. (1987). Introduction: Is there a feminist method? In S. Harding (Ed.), *Feminism & methodology* (pp. 1-14). Bloomington: Indiana University Press.

Hasselkus, B. R. (1988). Meaning in family caregiving: Perspectives on caregiver/professional relationships. *Gerontologist, 28,* 685-691.

Horowitz, A. (1985). Sons and daughters as caregivers to older parents: Differences in role performance and consequences. *Gerontologist, 25,* 612-617.

Jarrett, W. H. (1985). Caregiving within kinship systems: Is affection really necessary? *Gerontologist, 25,* 5-10.

Johnson, C. L., & Catalano, D. J. (1983). A longitudinal study of family supports to impaired elderly. *Gerontologist, 23,* 612-618.

Mascia-Lees, F. E., Sharpe, P., & Cohen, C. B. (1989). The postmodernist turn in anthropology: Cautions from a feminist perspective. *Signs, 15,* 7-33.

Matthews, S. H. (1985). The burdens of parent care: A critical evaluation of recent findings. *Journal of Aging Studies, 2,* 157-165.

McGoldrick, M., Anderson, C. M., & Walsh, R. (Eds.). (1989). *Women in families: A framework for family therapy.* New York: Norton.

Miller, B. (1988, November). *Adult children's perceptions of caregiving stress and satisfaction.* Paper presented at the meeting of the Gerontological Society of America, San Francisco.

Montgomery, R.J.V., Gonyea, J. G., & Hooyman, N. R. (1985). Caregiving and the experience of subjective and objective burden. *Family Relations, 34,* 19-26.

Motenko, A. K. (1989). The frustrations, gratifications, and well-being of dementia caregivers. *Gerontologist, 29,* 166-172.

Mutran, E., & Reitzes, D. C. (1984). Intergenerational support activities and well-being among the elderly: A convergence of exchange and symbolic interaction perspectives. *American Sociological Review, 49,* 117-130.

Nicholson, L. J. (Ed.). (1990). *Feminism/postmodernism.* New York: Routledge.

Nielsen, J. M. (1990). Introduction. In J. M. Nielsen (Ed.), *Feminist research methods* (pp. 1-37). Boulder, CO: Westview.

Oakley, A. (1981). Interviewing women: A contradiction in terms. In H. Roberts (Ed.), *Doing feminist research* (pp. 30-61). London: Routledge & Kegan Paul.

Peplau, L. A., & Conrad, E. (1989). Beyond nonsexist research: The perils of feminist methods in psychology. *Psychology of Women Quarterly, 13,* 379-400.

Poulshock, S. W., & Deimling, G. (1984). Families caring for elders in residence: Issues in the measurement of burden. *Journal of Gerontology, 39,* 230-239.

Rakowski, W., & Clark, N. M. (1985). Future outlook, caregiving, and care-receiving in the family context. *Gerontologist, 19,* 618-623.

Rich, A. (1976). *Of woman born.* New York: Bantam.

Robinson, B. (1983). Validation of a caregiver strain index. *Journal of Gerontology, 38,* 344-348.

Sheehan, N. W., & Nuttall, P. (1988). Conflict, emotion, and personal strain among family caregivers. *Family Relations, 37,* 92-98.

Smith, D. E. (1987). *The everyday world as problematic: A feminist sociology.* Boston: Northeastern University Press.

Stacey, J. (1988). Can there be a feminist ethnography? *Women's Studies International Forum, 11,* 21-27.

Stacey, J. (1990). *Brave new families.* New York: Basic Books.

Stanley, L. (1990). Feminist praxis and the academic mode of production. In L. Stanley (Ed.), *Feminist praxis* (pp. 3-19). London: Routledge.

Stanley, L., & Wise, S. (1979). Feminist research, feminist consciousness and experiences of sexism. *Women's Studies International Quarterly, 2,* 359-374.

Stoller, E. P. (1984). Self-assessments of health by the elderly: The impact of informal assistance. *Journal of Health and Social Behavior, 25,* 260-270.

Stueve, A. (1982). The elderly as network members. *Marriage and Family Review, 5,* 59-87.

Taylor, S. J., & Bogdan, R. (1984). *Introduction to qualitative research methods* (2nd ed.). New York: John Wiley.

Troll, L. E. (1987). Mother-daughter relationships through the life span. In S. Oskamp (Ed.), *Applied social psychology annual: Vol. 7. Family processes and problems: Social psychological aspects* (pp. 284-305). Newbury Park, CA: Sage.

Walker, A. J., & Allen, K. R. (1991). Relationships between caregiving daughters and their elderly mothers. *Gerontologist, 31,* 389-396.

Walker, A. J., Martin, S.S.K., & Thompson, L. (1988). Feminist programs for families. *Family Relations, 37,* 17-22.

Walker, A. J., Shin, H., & Bird, D. L. (1990). Perceptions of relationship change and caregiver satisfaction. *Family Relations, 39,* 147-152.

Westkott, M. (1979). Feminist criticism of the social sciences. *Harvard Educational Review, 49,* 422-430.

Zarit, S. H., Riever, K. E., & Bach-Peterson, J. (1980). Relatives of the impaired elderly: Correlates of feelings of burden. *Gerontologist, 20,* 649-655.

Part 3

Observation

Participant observation is the classic qualitative technique for coming to an understanding of everyday meanings and experiences. Anita Lightburn immerses herself in the secret world of both adoption and family life by choosing to live for several days with three special needs adoptive families. From peeling potatoes to driving to the hospital, she crosses the difficult boundaries of family privacy. In addition to her participant observer role, she also conducted interviews with family members. Rather than focusing on a person or a relationship as the unit of analysis, Lightburn examines "incidents of mediation." She uses discourse analysis in order to capture the dynamic elements of mediation. Jane Gilgun uses a combination of participant observation, open-ended interviewing and a grounded theory approach in the study of decision-making processes in family incest treatment. For Gilgun, qualitative methods are a good fit with family therapy research. Observation, interviews, and procedures of grounded theory are similar to processes skilled clinicians use in their everyday practice. Not only will findings from qualitative, grounded theory research fit experiences of clinicians, but the methods used to generate findings can easily be adapted by clinicians who want to do research on their own practices.

Participant Observation in Special Needs Adoptive Families
The Mediation of Chronic Illness and Handicap

ANITA LIGHTBURN
Columbia University

In one of the earliest familiar stories of adoption, a birth mother who saved her child's life by placing him for adoption became both a participant and an observer in his adoptive home. Moses' mother placed him in the bulrushes so Pharaoh's daughter would find him, but the mother herself became his wet nurse. She was privy to and participated in the care given him in his royal family. Her situation undoubtedly was fraught with tension as she concealed her identity lest she jeopardize her son's adoption and his life. Her qualitative grasp of life in Pharaoh's house could not be publicized, even though her story would have enlightened and entertained. To be a participant observer in an adoptive family is unusual, as the typical adoption excludes observers to protect the adoption. The secrets that are stored can include more than the identity of biological parents, for parents sometimes do not want their growing children to know they were adopted.

These concerns remain even though the culture of adoption has been changing since the 1970s, lifting the veil on processes of adoption. In light of this closed tradition in adoption, coupled with attitudes about privacy in families (see Daly, Chapter 1, this volume), my participant observation of three families who adopted special needs children is unique. The present chapter is a report on this research, in which I studied the ways parents shelter, shield, and provide for their adopted children with special needs. The research was initiated by an adoption agency concerned with how special needs adoptive families cope. Recognition, but little understanding, of the difficulties of adopting special needs children comes from other family members, friends, and professionals who often call them crazy or saints. Saintliness or craziness explains to outsiders how families can deal with challenging and enduring situations: The use of these descriptions removes these people from the company of ordinary parents, and their ability to cope is often attributed to an unusual nature or special living conditions.

Describing what families do to protect and care for children with multiple handicaps, developmental disorders stemming from chromosomal abnormalities such as Down syndrome, emotional problems, and chronic illness can enhance our understanding of special needs adoption. These adoptive parents are part of the deinstitutionalization and normalization movement. They have adopted children who previously were hidden from the public. On behalf of their children, they are challenged to cope with their children's continual requirements for services and care. Little is known about how these families manage, although data are accumulating that describe family characteristics and satisfaction with their choices (Gath, 1983; Glidden, 1986; Nelson, 1985). To build on this developing picture, personnel from the adoption agency and I chose three families to work with me as a participant observer in their homes, with the hope that we would learn more about how families care for and cope with their adopted special needs children.

Concepts of Mediation

Although the term *mediation* is associated with conflict resolution (Chandler, 1985), previous research on family adaptation and coping used the term to describe transactional processes between family members and systems outside of families. These processes include socialization, interpretation, education, provision of support, and procurement of resources (Antonovsky, 1979, 1987; Olson et al., 1983; Rabkin & Struening, 1976; Reiss, 1981). The process of mediation has been described as central to the family's social construction of reality (Berger & Luckmann, 1967). Leichter (1974, 1979) defined mediation as ways families negotiate and create meaning in the educational experiences of their members. Leichter's research on families as educators was guided by Berger and Luckmann's (1967) notion of the centrality of families' roles in learning about the social world. Yet another view of mediation was developed by Schwartz (1969, 1976) in his reciprocal model of group work. Shulman (1984) applied this model of mediation to family functioning: The "mediating" model emphasizes reciprocal processes as central in the establishment and maintenance of mutual aid. Negotiation for or by the group with the larger system also is part of mediation (Lightburn, 1989).

Many of these studies found that the transactional processes of mediation were not well understood. In addition, previous research had measured coping in families quantitatively. In personal communication with me and in his writing, Antonovsky (1979, 1987) recommended that qualitative methods be used to explore what families actually do to cope.

There are numerous examples of how these definitions of mediation assist in guiding research that describes what families do to cope. The life situations of these adoptive families present such considerable challenges in living that they logically would require several strategies, such as political mediation in gaining essential medical and educational resources, caretaking, and provision of supportive resources from their families and communities (Fewell & Vadasy, 1986; Goldstein, Strickland, Turnbull, & Curry, 1980; Patterson & McCubbin, 1983; Wikler, 1986). In a similar way, mediating constructions of the children dilutes prejudice and stigma and reframes perceptions of the children to emphasize their beauty, humor, and normality to kin and those outside families who find them hard to accept (Argent, 1984; Birenbaum, 1970; Jones, Farina, & Hastorf, 1984). Likewise, mediating processes that establish and maintain mutual aid would be providing the staple of family life that is indispensable to the process of coping with handicap and illness (Murphy, 1982; Pilisuk & Parks, 1986; Reiss, 1986). From all of these perspectives, processes of mediation stand out as transactions central in considering how special needs adoptive families cope with their children's needs.

The refinement of the main question: How do families cope with chronic illness and handicap? then became: How do families mediate chronic illness and handicap? To answer this question meant using qualitative methods to "catch the details of actual occurrences" of families living together, in the belief that the detailed study of phenomena would lead to a more complex understanding of what people do (Sacks, 1984, p. 24). The following elaboration of these methods describes the specific traditions that supported this approach and why they were chosen for this study.

METHOD

Comparative Case Studies

The first three families that we asked agreed to be part of the study. Personnel from the special needs adoption agency and I selected them purposefully, on the basis of their differences from each other: They differed in household composition, number of parents, marital status, socioeconomic status, cultural backgrounds, religion, education, location, kinship affiliations, community involvement, and their children's handicaps and illnesses. Three contrasting contexts, then, provided opportunities to study the same phenomena under a range of conditions under which coping with chronic illness and handicap existed. This would enable as many properties and categories as possible to be developed in describing how families coped (Glaser & Strauss, 1967; Varenne & McDermott, 1986).

Working With the Families

The agency's support for this study undoubtedly influenced the families' willingness to participate. The families reported positive experiences with the agency. Furthermore, the families readily identified with the purpose of the research. They understood that the agency and researcher were interested in how they coped. All of the families felt that they struggled in caring for their children. Caretaking demands were high, and financial resources limited. Although willing to participate in the study, they were unsure of what the process of talking to me and allowing me to observe them in action would accomplish. Without prior experience in this type of research, they gingerly went forward with me into the process.

I made arrangements for my visits weeks in advance, negotiating to spend three 8- to 12-hour days with each family, scheduled at their convenience. Such long days meant I sometimes accompanied family members on tasks done outside of the home. Initially, I did structured interviews to obtain historical data and to construct time utilization and activity charts. I also asked questions about how the families experienced using various services. This period purposefully was used for us to get to know each other, with photo albums shared and stories told of the family's experience with adoption. My interest in these stories enabled a gestalt to develop, a gestalt that was a construction of each family's history and beliefs, representing one version of the family's life. I spent more time asking for clarification and elaboration of the stories than responding with comments.

I audiotaped all conversations, whether in homes or cars. I did not tape in a hospital room, where it was inappropriate. I acted as a participant and not just a recorder. This I believe was the basis for the relationships that unfolded as family members shared intimate details of their lives. I helped make meals and care for the children. There were times, however, when the family did not include me in their meals. This was the case in homes where mealtimes were staggered to accommodate complex work and school schedules. In retrospect, I wish I had discussed mealtimes with the families so that they would have had opportunities to consider my joining them. In two families, they assumed I would eat with them. In the other family, it was awkward on the first day, as they made no mention of dinner. They went ahead and ate without inviting me to join them. I left soon after dinner, which made a long day for me.

My presence with the families was an imposition because of the extended period I spent with them each time. Although they had agreed to this period of time, they were not used to this type of relationship. We had to discuss what to do when unexpected circumstances arose. For example, one family hesitated over an unexpected business call from the tax accountant. Should I be included, or could business be conducted in the background while I observed other family activities? (I was excluded.) Because activities can happen in many rooms of the house at one time, working out where I would be and where audiotaping would occur was continually but casually discussed as family events emerged. We agreed on the principle of focusing first on issues related to the children.

I did not attempt to catch everything going on in the family. This would have taken a number of researchers and additional technical equipment. I did not venture into rooms until I was taken there or invited. We also agreed I was not to be entertained, so they could do their work, attend to unanticipated situations, and conduct life as closely as possible to the usual. Teenagers ran in and out with a brief hello and a report to Mom that they were off to the mall; they did not stay in the house during the day to "perform" for me. Getting up and going to bed were not determined by my presence. People appeared to do what they wanted, when they wanted. They seemed to accept my explanation that the purpose of the research was to observe how they lived each day. In all of these ways, their voices could be heard as we hear each other in public and in semiprivate conversation.

This type of exposure limited my data, but the limitations enabled me to allow the family to control the degree of access, and this I felt influenced their willingness to open up their homes and lives for observation. Although each family and I spent only 3 days together, we all felt as though we had known each other for considerably longer. We knew that I could not understand their whole story or describe all the ways they coped, but this was to be a beginning that other research in other families could build on. This limitation was helpful, in that such a boundary was perceived as protective of their privacy; for the purpose of the research was not to know everything about their coping, but to describe how they did cope with the events, demands, and needs that occurred over 3 particular days.

The Participant Families

The Nolan Family

A small apartment in a rural area was home for Mrs. Nolan and her three young children. Their limited space was crammed with medical equipment and toys of every description. An old station wagon stood parked at the front door ready with three car seats and specialized strollers to make trips to school, pharmacy, clinic, or hospital. The Nolan family includes three special needs children, two of whom were adopted and one who was fostered, awaiting adoption. Two daughters, Lara, 8, and Kelly, 4, are both profoundly challenged. Lissa, 10, was seriously handicapped both mentally and physically from a rare chromosome disorder. She has lived 7 years beyond doctors' predictions; she walked when she was 7 and has continued to gain in functioning. Mrs. Nolan divorced her husband after he sexually abused Lissa when she was 3. Mrs. Nolan's own parents, who were frail and elderly, lived 40 minutes away and required her attention. Adoption subsidies provided her only income. Before marriage, Mrs. Nolan was a dancer and teacher. Now she was a full-time mom who enjoyed needlepoint for relaxation.

The Succi Family

A modern two-story home in a pleasant residential area, part of an old suburban industrial town 40 minutes from a large city, provided tight living quarters when all eight members of the Succi family were home. They were part of a family neighborhood where neighbors were friends and where their children had grown up together. This community was so important to the Succis that they had recently decided not to sell their present house and move to a larger house in the next town. The Succi family had three adolescent daughters on the way to or in college or graduate school and three younger adopted children between 4 and 13 years of age, all with Down syndrome. Harry, 13 and in need of constant supervision, had come to live with them when he was 3. Their 4-year-old daughter was totally dependent, with severely delayed development. Only 8-year-old Tony could talk and participate fully in family and community activities. A self-described homebody who said he would love to have more children, Mr. Succi was in the catering business. Mrs. Succi enjoyed managing her home and volunteered for community organizations.

The Cabot Family

A few years earlier, when Mr. Cabot had secure employment in a factory, he and his wife had struggled to buy their 100-year-old, three-story home for their large family. Now he was between jobs, training as a plumber and working as a custodian at their church. Finances were a continual worry. They could not even think of repairing the rundown house to sell it. Located in an old industrial town in decline, this once handsome home now was in the poor section of town. The vacant lot next to the house was a parking spot for their old van. It was cluttered with old tires and refuse. In contrast to this discouraging physical environment, the Cabots' extended family and friends were a constant part of the home environment, adding rich textures of interactions. Of the eight Cabot children, one son was from their marriage, and a teenaged boy and girl from Mrs. Cabot's first marriage were adopted by Mr. Cabot. The rest of their children were adopted or fostered and awaiting release for adoption. Each child had different special needs stemming from complex medical and emotional problems, including a teenaged girl with Down syndrome, a brother and sister in their early teens, and a 4- and 5-year-old boy and girl. The youngest boy was hydrocephalic at birth, did not talk until he was 3, had 11 placements in foster homes before the Cabots, and arrived at the Cabots as a place of last resort before institutional care. He had no words when he was placed with them, but he expressed himself in house-shaking tantrums. He could not settle down to sleep at night and would not allow anyone to touch him. Mrs. Cabot worked long days, and in a quiet, gentle way, managed the continuous flux of her complex family's needs.

Ethnographic Methods: An Overview

An ethnographic approach was used to provide contextual data with specific use of discourse analysis of incidents of mediation (Labov & Fanshel, 1977; Varenne, 1990). As discussed earlier, I drew conceptualizations of mediation from the theoretical and practice literature (Lightburn, 1989). I brought these to the data as possible ways of categorizing findings. Further development of categories of mediation followed the tradition used in grounded theory (Glaser & Strauss, 1967). The multiple levels of data collection and analysis enabled me to develop complex descriptions of mediation in their various forms with specific strategies and phases.

Methods of data collection included a combination of open and closed structured interviews, participant observation resulting in data collection through field notes, audiotapes of all time spent with the family, and diagrams of the families' use of space and time (Spradley, 1979, 1980). All members of the family were included, as they were observed in their homes and wherever we went together by car to hospitals, shopping, or to school. Friends, professionals, and business acquaintances also were a part of the research, as they naturally interacted with family members during the day. I spent some time interviewing each family member; the remainder of the time I observed or interacted with the natural groupings of the families in the course of a day's activities. This meant that mothers figured predominantly, although fathers and children also were involved actively in family life. With some exceptions noted earlier, whatever the family was doing I also did, from driving to the hospital to helping peel potatoes for dinner. A full range of daily living occurred during our time together, from friends visiting for cups of coffee and cake to intense arguments, mundane cleaning, talking on the telephone, and doing the grocery shopping.

How mediation contributed to coping provided the focus for the analysis. Transcriptions were made from the audiotapes so that all narrative and discourse could be examined. Paralinguistic cues were not included in the transcriptions. Utilizing the method demonstrated in Labov and Fanshel's (1977) study of therapeutic discourse, I constructed propositions from the narrative that described basic rules, norms, and apparent constructs. (See Lightburn, 1989, for details on the application of this method in the study of family discourse.) From the transcripts, I studied families' constructions of incidents of mediation and my direct observation of events of mediation. This approach also provided the contextual data for analysis and extended my understanding beyond the internal transactions of the family to their acting (mediating) in their culture.

Identification and Analysis of Incidents of Mediation

Following Bryce (1980) and Leonard (1986), I identified incidents of mediation from taped conversations and consideration of temporal organization. I did not specify incidents of mediation by a unit of time, such as 10 minutes of conversation, but by words and actions that comprised activities I identified as mediating for the children. Units of mediation ranged from 5-minute exchanges to hours of progressive interactions that also included activities over days and months.

Active mediations were incidents I observed between family members, neighbors, and others. As noted earlier, I also became a focus of mediations, as I was a participant in the family's life. I was like any other individual outside the family who could not easily understand how the children tried to communicate or how they acted. Nor could the parents assume I understood how they managed the children's behavior and symptoms; hence, the parents had to cope with me just as they coped with neighbors and professionals. I recorded active incidents both in field notes and in tape recordings. I did the same with family members' accounts of past incidents of mediation. The stories family members told were a natural part of family interaction and were recorded as such.

A Grounded Theory Approach

I chose the approach used in the development of grounded theory to continue data gathering until I established a number of categories of mediation. For instance, the families' management of a child's unusual behavior and utterances is described as symptom management. I expect that more extensive experience with these families over a longer period would have enabled me to identify more forms and strategies of mediation, but I chose to limit this exploration because of the richness of data initially collected. I was interested in studying the identified incidents through structured discourse analysis. What did the family do to mediate? How were the acts connected to each other? What were the ways that competence was part of the pattern of these interactions? Was there a definable process, as has been suggested in the research describing mediators who work to bring about conflict resolution (Chandler, 1985)?

How context influenced mediations was another focus in the analysis. Both specific contexts for acts of mediation as well as the broader context were considered. The work of Varenne and McDermott (1986) provided an essential methodological perspective, as it demonstrated an approach to data analysis that could show how coherence emerges in conversation and how it finally relates to culture. This line of analysis, from the coherence evident in familial talk to the social order, demonstrated the efficacy of detailed analysis of texts and incidents for the study of how families cope with chronic illness and handicap. Patterns of familial interaction and their relationship to culture were both important to this study. Stigma, deinstitutionalization, normalization, and the medicalization of health concerns are examples of cultural patterns that have been shown to influence coping (Birenbaum, 1970; Bogdan & Taylor, 1987; Fagerhaugh & Strauss, 1977; Goffman, 1963; Leonard, 1986). Contexts were important to identify, for their influence on both the form and outcome of interactional patterns (mediations).

MAJOR FINDINGS

Mediating activities were observed in three arenas: mediation of medical care, mediation of educational resources, and mediation in relationships. Mediation proved to be a useful way of identifying a range of coping strategies. Parents' efforts to cope with their special needs children directed my choices of incidents of mediation to analyze; these choices were not based on forms of mediation identified in the research and theoretical literature. As mediators, families acted as educators, as negotiators, and as agents who established mutual aid in

the families. The families generally were aggressive and skillful mediators, with some striking similarities and differences in the different
families mediating strategies. Families' mediating activities created
bridges in communication and contained and resolved conflict as well
as securing essential services so that special needs could be met.

Definitions of these major forms of mediation follow, but only
negotiation will be elaborated upon in this chapter. As the findings from
this study are extensive, it will only be possible to present a brief
overview of major categories of mediation. As *educators* families
mediated by interpreting to family members, friends, and the community the meaning of handicap, particularly unusual multiple handicaps.
They also fostered their children's learning by influencing cognitive
and behavioral achievements and social development.

Keeping the families working together to meet the demands of care,
and at the same time balancing everyone's needs was managed by the
skillful *mediation of mutual aid.* Mediating mutual aid was interactional
work that established and maintained boundaries and role flexibility. It
demanded work from the children, work that the parents believed
enabled the children to develop and mature with respect and dignity.

Families' skills in *negotiating services* included dealing with conflicted perspectives between themselves and professionals, friends,
family members, and the community about who was entitled to resources and how they should receive them. Advocacy and establishing
authority were central to successful negotiations. These negotiations
saved the children's lives, gained educational resources that made significant differences to their development, and provided opportunities to
participate in sports and other activities most children take for granted. The
full report of this study elaborates these in detail (Lightburn, 1989).

Families as Negotiators

Families negotiated with doctors, nurses, medicaid administrators, a
health care supplier, teachers, school administrators, social workers,
and Little League personnel. The active negotiations I observed were
consistent with the stories I was told about gaining services. Present in
all three families' narratives about negotiations conducted in the past
were constructions that defined what the family believed. These beliefs
were enacted in observed incidents. Negotiation involved a complex
range of strategies, including investigation and research that went as far
as, in effect, spying; interpretation of rights, laws, and policies; building

a case; cognitive and emotional functioning; presenting the case in the language of the medical or educational system; using the parents' own experience as parents of special needs children as the basis for their authority in medical and educational settings; developing plans and options based on careful assessment of realities and alternatives; developing written contracts; and monitoring services. Parents constructed their cases with family members, friends, professionals, and strangers, using rehearsal to test their premises and the soundness of their case. Often feeling angry and frustrated, they also were anxious over the possibility their cases would be discounted in meetings with professionals, who outnumbered them and whom they perceived as having power over them and their children. They learned to contain anger and worked hard to function more competently on professionals' turf.

They sought and obtained advice from many quarters. They developed systems of information exchange among parents they met through weekend retreats sponsored by the adoption agency. Parents spent hours talking to each other by phone and developed close relationships. They called upon sympathetic social workers and public health nurses who helped to substantiate their views of what was happening in classrooms and who also advocated for parents' viewpoints in working out conflicts with school personnel. Parents often advocated for each other. Public Law 41-142 supported their requests and "rights" for appropriate services. I believe their negotiations on behalf of their children would have failed without this law.

Negotiation as Mediation: Strategies and Outcomes

Processes of mediating in the form of negotiation that maintained important medical, educational, and recreational resources for children required complex strategies, stamina, and occasionally bending of rules. The story of the Succi family illustrates these processes. Mr. and Mrs. Succi were concerned because they felt the individual educational plan (IEP) the school developed for Harry, who was then 8, was just a "show." IEPs are vital documents the Succis learned to read, understand, and even write. These documents were contracts that specified what a school was to provide. The Succis surreptitiously checked out their suspicions, and Mr. Succi reported:

> In a sneak visit, my wife distracted the receptionist while I walked to Harry's room. As I watched from the door, I could see him lying on a mat

unattended while teachers read magazines. No program was observed over
the next half hour.

The Succis then had evidence they could use in a court of law if necessary.
Other parents also caught public schools responding to their children in
ways characteristic of the most deficient institutional programs. Their
children were entitled to appropriate programs, and they knew it.

The Succis spent the next several months working to obtain appropriate education for Harry. Their investment cost them emotional energy and time as well as straining their limited financial resources. Mr.
Succi was between jobs, their car had burned, and their youngest
daughter was recovering from meningitis. They had few reserves. Their
extended family did not understand why they had adopted Harry, and
support from kin was limited. Negotiating from this position, with
depleted resources and added stressors, was possible partly because the
Succis had time to negotiate with personnel of the school—negotiations in
which they discovered what they valued, believed in, and would fight for.

The Succis identified the personal and institutional investments of
key personnel in order to prepare persuasive arguments that might be
understood and heard. They sought independent evaluations to document the type of program their son Harry needed. In their negotiations,
they used the evidence of the evaluations as a "voice of authority" that
school officials recognized.

The prolonged process provided ample opportunity to examine their
situation and build Harry's case. Determination was forged through
tough examination of everyone's position and the facts. They remembered a turning point after 6 months of hard effort:

> We almost gave in and accepted the school's minimal offer. Harry would
> have been back on the mat. His schooling would amount to little more than
> baby-sitting. At the next meeting, school officials walked out on us,
> throwing their pencils on the table. From this point, we held firmly to our
> demands that Harry have reasonable educational opportunities.

When agreements were finally reached, the Succis asked that these be
documented in writing. Advocates were used at the final stages to support
their case. This work had been done 5 years before my observations,
and it extended over 1 year. The Succis presented it in narrative as they
reflected on how they helped Harry. As a result of changes in Harry's
educational plan, he made significant educational gains. He also walked

within the year, progress the Succis said resulted from improvements in Harry's program.

General Negotiating Strategies

As the Succi case suggests, negotiating for services was not easy. In their first approach to service providers, parents said that they purposely got to know school administrators, doctors in charge of pediatric and outpatient services, floor nurses, social workers, medical suppliers, and even medicaid officers. They spoke positively about individuals they described as "well-intended helpers," even if they as parents were not treated like "partners or coworkers." The parents acknowledged help and praised helpers for their skills and expertise. Months of adjustment time was accorded to new teachers to learn how best to work with their children. Inexperienced teachers were excused when they had difficulties relating to and developing successful approaches to a child. Glowing reports were given of the few teachers who had been supportive. The parents described working hard at communicating with teachers. They sent notes daily to the school with information, special needs, and questions. Except for unannounced school visits, they generally waited to use review meetings to bring up their most serious concerns, because the school preferred to use a formal structure.

Parents often perceived teachers as not reciprocating their efforts to communicate about the children. For instance, teachers rarely phoned parents except to ask parents to pick up an ill child. Parents felt teachers acknowledged them minimally in learning processes; teachers did not encouragement or help parents to reinforce significant school learning at home. It took a month for Mrs. Nolan to learn that Lissa had mastered a new sign in sign language. She previously had known only four, and learning a new one was a major achievement. Mrs. Nolan commented, "Some coordination between school and Mom!" Parents hoped for coordination and made significant efforts to promote it. I observed parents cautiously choosing the way they communicated so that teachers would understand their concerns and be able to join them in working with a child's special problems. Mrs. Nolan rehearsed a note she was writing to Lissa's teacher with me:

I am worried that I won't get her attention about Lissa's broken glasses. [The glasses had been taped together after Lissa broke them in a fall.] A new pair will come in a week, but until then, Lissa [who was legally blind] needs her glasses. Lissa can easily trip and fall. She's so unstable on her feet. The broken glasses could injure her eyes or face. How can I make sure she will give her extra attention? Maybe she'll end up keeping her in her seat all day. I found her once in a wooden pen. You wouldn't believe what they do to these kids. I know it's hard, but I don't want another accident.

Mrs. Nolan took extreme care in analyzing the teacher's needs and in communicating information so that the child's needs would be met; she did not want to be misread or her concerns dismissed. Even the smallest services had to be negotiated. Investments had to be known and worked with; information had to be marshaled and communicated in a strategic way so that it would be accepted; a case had to be made and a commitment won. These untrained adoptive parents—the Succis and Mrs. Nolan—used skills and strategies similar to those identified by Chandler in his study of court-appointed mediators (Chandler, 1985).

Results of "Going Along"

The alternative was to do what the Cabots had done for years: Expect school personnel to do their job. In fact, 15-year-old Jennie Cabot experienced humiliation and lost opportunity because the Cabots never questioned her 2-year assignment to a special class for emotional problems. The class was comprised of 14 acting-out, behavior-disordered boys and Jennie, who has Down syndrome. Jennie's needs were poorly met and she often complained, but neither her parents nor the school took up her concerns. Mediations did not occur until a new school administrator evaluated the program and replaced Jennie in the mainstream, commenting in the process that she should not have been placed in this particular class. Mrs. Cabot was glad for the change, but she did not express concern that she might have acted on Jennie's behalf. She and Mr. Cabot expected professionals to know what they were doing and were accepting of what they did.

Legal Battles

To achieve their goals, some parents escalated their negotiations to legal battles to deal with pronounced conflicts. Parents were not accustomed to fighting for health care and educational resources, or for that matter, recreational opportunities. Their behavior and the words they used to describe their actions presented a picture of a "them against us" mentality. When the Succi family joined other parents of handicapped children to confront the National Little League for prejudicial treatment, lawyers were hired, spokespersons were selected, newspapers were used to influence, and politicians were approached and pressured. The parents pressed their case until negotiations resulted in handicapped children being permitted to play in Little League. Successful mediation was determined in part by the parents' collective action, which took individual commitment and initiatives.

Parents Use of Authority in Medical Settings

Parents used personal authority to strengthen their cases in medical settings. They saw this use of authority as highly significant. For example, Mrs. Nolan believed two of her children would not be alive had she not negotiated for needed portable medical equipment. In less dramatic but no less important ways, the parents saw their negotiations working to enhance the emotional lives of the families through the nurturing of hospitalized special needs children. Parents' use of their authority often led to helping to provide medical care in hospitals, interpreting and monitoring the children's physical conditions, evaluating prescribed treatments, and monitoring ongoing care. While their children were in hospital with life-threatening illnesses, mothers demonstrated two different types of authority that they believed resulted in restored health when there had been little hope for recovery. Two examples from the Nolan and Succi families make this point.

Mrs. Succi negotiated with the medical team to provide in-hospital primary care to her 2-month-old, 8-pound daughter with Down syndrome, who had meningitis. In supplementing for one month the daily medical care usually given by nurses, Mrs. Succi's authority as mother was enacted as prime care giver and nurturer for her adopted daughter. She also was providing essential nurturing for bonding and attachment that she deemed equally important to the healing process. The family's support of her actions enabled her to manage at home and at the hospital. Her authority was based in the family's mutual aid system.

In the second situation, Mrs. Nolan saw herself as a coworker with doctors. She often negotiated from this self-ascribed position. She said, "Mothers are head doctors," a designation doctors largely did not recognize. Nonetheless, such self-designated status was a powerful construction that influenced the many tactics she used to interpret her knowledge to the doctors. Her effectiveness as a mediator depended upon her conviction of her authority to mediate her children's care. She had expert knowledge from her years of experience as their mother. She saw this knowledge as vital to diagnosis and treatment. She communicated this knowledge using scientific terminology and in the detached manner characteristic of medical talk.

In both of these situations, authority born of experience and supported by families' systems of mutual aid meant mothers could become involved in the medical care process. They challenged medical authority and used a repertoire of tactics. For instance, they solicited support from medical personnel, whose "voices of authority" doctors appeared to recognize. These voices of authority came from friendly doctors, nurses, and the use of medical records. These parents did not invest ultimate responsibility and power for their children's care with the medical profession as some parents in faith willingly do.

DISCUSSION

This study has shown how three families responded to their children's special needs through acting as educators, negotiators, and agents of mutual aid in their homes. The examples of negotiation elaborated upon here have shown how their efforts were influenced by their beliefs, experience, and the contexts in which they acted. Families' use of authority was central to their effective negotiations. The Cabot family did not negotiate as Mrs. Nolan and the Succis did, but believed professionals would act in their children's best interests. In contrast, Mrs. Nolan and the Succis actively mediated mutual aid and acted as educators in their home and community where they believed they had authority.

Adoptions for these families were symbolic acts of mediation that bridged two worlds, one of isolation and abnormality and the other of community and normality. These parents demonstrated that adoption was their first act of mediation. Just as adoption was a firm commitment, so was the parents' holding firmly to their children's rights when they believed they had the authority to do so. The children challenged both the norms of development and functioning. On behalf of the children, the parents in turn challenged the community to respond to the children's special needs. Mediation indeed was central to their coping efforts and success.

Participant observation and interviewing made it possible to describe how these families coped with chronic illness and handicap. From this work with three families, I developed a complex picture of coping based on the happenings of everyday life.

REFERENCES

Antonovsky, A. (1979). *Health, stress and coping.* San Francisco: Jossey-Bass.

Antonovsky, A. (1987). *Unraveling the mystery of health.* San Francisco: Jossey-Bass.

Argent, H. (1984). *Find me a family.* London, UK: Souvenir (E&A).

Berger, P., & Luckmann, T. (1967). *The social construction of reality.* New York: Doubleday.

Birenbaum, A. (1970). On managing courtesy stigma. *Journal of Health and Social Behavior, 11,* 196-206.

Bogdan, R., & Taylor, S. (1987). Toward a sociology of acceptance: The other side of the study of deviance. *Social Policy, 18,* 34-39.

Bryce, J. (1980). *Families and television: An ethnographic approach.* Dissertation, Columbia University Teachers College, Dissertation Abstracts International, Ann Arbor: University of Michigan Press.

Chandler, S. (1985). Mediation: Conjoint problem solving. *Social Work, 30,* 346-350.

Fagerhaugh, S., & Strauss, A. (1977). *Politics of pain management: Staff-patient interaction.* Menlo Park, CA: Addison-Wesley.

Fewell, R., & Vadasy, P. (1986). *Families of handicapped children.* Austin, TX: Pro-Ed.

Gath, A. (1983). Mentally retarded children in substitute and natural families. *Adoption and Fostering, 7,* 35-40.

Glaser, B., & Strauss, A. (1967). *The discovery of grounded theory.* Chicago, IL: Aldine.

Glidden, L. M. (1986). Families who adopt retarded children: Who, why and what happens. In J. Gallagher & P. M. Vietze (Eds.), *Families of handicapped persons* (pp. 129-142). Baltimore, MD: Brookes.

Goffman, E. (1963). *Stigma.* Englewood Cliffs, NJ: Prentice-Hall.

Goldstein, S., Strickland, B., Turnbull, A., & Curry, L. (1980). An observational analysis of the IEP conference. *Exceptional Children, 46,* 278-286.

Jones, E., Farina, A., & Hasterof, A. (1984). *Social stigma: The psychology of marked relationships.* New York: Freeman.

Labov, W., & Fanshel, D. (1977). *Therapeutic discourse.* New York: Academic Press.

Leonard, D. H., Jr. (1986). *Families and autism: An ethnographic approach.* Doctoral dissertation, Columbia University Teachers College.

Leichter, H. J. (Ed.). (1974). *The family as educator.* New York: Teachers College Press.

Leichter, H. J. (Ed.). (1979). *Family and community as educator.* New York: Teachers College Press.

Lightburn, A. (1989). A study of the mediation of chronic illness and handicap by special needs adoptive families. Doctoral dissertation, Columbia University Teachers College.

Murphy, L. (1982) *Home hospital.* New York: Gardner.

Nelson, K. (1985). *On the frontier of adoption: A study of special needs adoption families.* Washington, DC: Child Welfare League of America.

Olson, D. H., McCubbin, H. I., Barnes, H. L., Larsen, A. S., Muxen, M. J., & Wilson, M. A. (1983). *Families: What makes them work.* Beverly Hills, CA: Sage.

Patterson, J., & McCubbin, H. (1983). Chronic illness: Family stress and coping. In C. Figley & H. McCubbin (Eds.), *Stress and the family: Vol. 11. Coping with catastrophe and traumatic transition* (pp. 21-36). New York: Brunner/Mazel.

Pilisuk, M., & Parks, S. H. (1986). *The healing web: Social networks and human survival.* Hanover, NH: The University Press of New England.

Rabkin, J., & Struening, E. (1976). Life events, stress and illness. *Science, 194,* 1013-1020.

Reiss, D. (1981). *The family's construction of reality.* Cambridge, MA: Harvard University Press.

Reiss, D. (1986). Family systems: Understanding the family through its response to chronic illness. In M. Yogman & B. Brazelton (Eds.), *In support of families* (pp 13-28). Cambridge, MA: Harvard University Press.

Sacks, H. (1984). Notes on methodology. In J. M. Atkinson and J. Heritage (Eds.), *Structures of social action* (pp. 21-27). Cambridge, UK: Cambridge University Press.

Schwartz, W. (1969). Private trouble and public issues: One social work job or two? *The Social Welfare Forum.* New York: Columbia University Press.

Schwartz, W. (1976). Between client and system: The mediating function. In R. W. Roberts & H. Northern (Eds.), *Theories of social work with groups* (pp. 171-197). New York: Columbia University Press.

Shulman, L. (1984). *The skills of helping individuals and groups* (2nd ed.). Itasca, IL: Peacock.

Spradley, J. (1979). *The ethnographic interview.* New York: Holt, Rinehart & Winston.

Spradley, J. (1980). *Participant observations.* New York: Holt, Rinehart & Winston.

Varenne, H. (1990). Parents and their children talk. In B. Dorval (Ed.), *Conversational organization and its development* (pp. 239-275). Norwood, NJ: Ablex.

Varenne, H., & McDermott, R. (1986). "Why" Sheila can't read: Structural indeterminacy in the reproduction of familial literacy. In B. Schefflen & P. Gilmore (Eds.), *The acquisition of literacy: Ethnographic perspectives* (pp. 129-151). Norwood, NJ: Ablex.

Wikler, L. (1986). Family stress theory and research on families of children with mental retardation. In J. Gallagher & P. Vietze (Eds.), *Families of handicapped persons* (pp. 167-196). Baltimore, MD: Brookes.

Observations in a Clinical Setting
Team Decision-Making in Family Incest Treatment

JANE F. GILGUN
University of Minnesota, Twin Cities

Participant observation and open-ended interviewing are ideally suited for research on family processes in general and on family therapy in particular. Kantor and Lehr's (1975) classic study of family interaction was based almost exclusively on these two methods. The unacknowledged methodological underpinnings of foundation knowledge in family therapy were participant observation and open-ended interviewing (Gilgun, 1990c). Pioneering therapists developed their theories through direct interaction with clients and postsession reflection and analysis, although the kinds of observations, the nature of the interviews, and data collection and analysis were not explicitly stated in the writings of foundation family therapists (e.g., Ackerman, 1958; Haley, 1987; Minuchin, 1974; Minuchin & Fishman, 1981; Satir, 1967) or their more contemporary colleagues, such as Real (1990), Thomm (1987a, 1987b, 1988), and the Milan group (Cecchin, 1987; Selvini-Palazzoli, Boscolo, Cecchin, & Prata, 1978, 1980).

AUTHOR'S NOTE: This research was sponsored by funding from the Minnesota Agricultural Experiment Station, Project No. 55-018.

In the past, information on method might not have been of interest to major segments of family therapy audiences, but such information is central to the development of knowledge. Making explicit the details of research procedures demystifies knowledge development, provides guidance for others on how to conduct research, and as Mishler (1990) pointed out, helps in the interpretation of findings. Individuals who have made contributions to knowledge have done so not so much because they have special brilliance, but because they know how to develop their knowledge and how to put what they have learned on paper (R. Bogdan, personal communication, August 1991).

The purpose of this chapter is to demonstrate the use of participant observation and open-ended interviewing in research on family incest treatment. The approach in the present study was based on grounded theory procedures (Charmaz, 1990; Glaser & Strauss, 1967; Murphy, Chapter 9, this volume; Snyder, Chapter 4, this volume; Strauss & Corbin, 1990). Processes of data collection and analysis are specific. An assumption of this chapter is that family therapists and other individuals who work in therapeutic relationships with others already possess the fundamental skills needed to conduct qualitative research. They have finely honed interviewing and observational skills, and they work in the inductive-deductive mode characteristic of grounded theory. In addition, the processes and products of participant observation and open-ended interviewing are congruent with the processes and substance of clinical work (Gilgun, 1989b, 1991a, 1991c; Moon, Dillon, & Sprenkle, 1990). Research findings developed from these methods, therefore, are more accessible to clinicians and more applicable to clinical settings than findings developed from methods incongruent with clinical practice. Qualitative methods and clinical practice fit like a "hand into well-made glove" (Gilgun, 1991c, p. 3).

Whatever impulses clinicians might have in conducting research may be thwarted by their training in research methods, however. The training in research that clinicians receive usually is based on probability theory and group designs, and there often is a lack of fit between research training and clinical realities. Group designs average out individual differences and vitiate context, and they look at only a few variables. This type of research is nomothetic (Gilgun, 1991a), and clinical experience is much different from the model implicit in such training.

Case study methods, as opposed to group methods, fit clinical experiences. Clinicians deal with one case at a time, are well aware of how context influences families, and confront multiple interacting variables in their work with families. They want to understand change processes on the individualized, contextualized case level before moving to more general principles of client change. Research operating within this model is idiographic. In short, the training clinicians normatively receive is nomothetic, but they work in idiographic settings (Gilgun, 1991a, 1991c).

Case study research has a long and respected history in social and behavioral sciences (Feagin, Orum, & Sjoberg, 1991; Yin, 1989), although in recent years case studies may have been regarded as "an inadequate leftover from an earlier time" (G. Handel, personal communication, December 1991). Contemporary clinicians and social scientists have begun to recognize and affirm case studies as viable forms of research (Gilgun, 1991a; Handel, 1991; Jarrett, Chapter 10, this volume; Moon, 1991; Yin, 1989). As case studies once more gain favor and clinicians recognize they have basic skills to do research, we are likely to see an explosion of clinician-conducted research. Before this can happen, clinicians need to be educated about case study research methods. This chapter provides guidelines on how to do qualitative case study research in therapy settings.

The Present Research

The focus of the present research was to understand how a multidisciplinary incest treatment team made decisions about family members' progress in treatment. I negotiated this focus with the director of the treatment program and the treatment team, who wanted detailed feedback about how they were evaluating clients' movement through therapy. The team members were concerned about these processes because their decision-making had enormous implications for public safety and safety of family members. If they were mistaken in their evaluation that an incest perpetrator was no longer a danger to others and was ready to graduate from the program, the consequences could be extremely serious. They also were motivated to provide the best possible treatment for all members of families. They recognized the potential of incest to result in long-term negative consequences for victims and all other family members.

"Black Box" Research

Team treatment of multiple families may be the ultimate in "black box" research, a term often used to characterize process research. The term connotes how rarely research is conducted on the processes of change in human interactional systems and how little we know about these processes. A major challenge in process research is the number of interacting variables—e.g., the "busyness" of clinical interaction. In the relatively simple triad of marital therapy, there are many points of view and many possible interactional patterns. To name a few: wife to therapist, husband to therapist, wife to husband, husband to wife, therapist to wife, therapist to husband, therapist to husband and wife, and husband and wife to therapist. Add one more person to the triad, and the number of interactional patterns increases exponentially. In family incest treatment programs, several families typically are in treatment at one time. Over the course of treatment, they interact with multiple therapists. Relationships with persons outside of the therapy setting often become part of treatment. Research on team treatment of multiple families, therefore, presents unique challenges.

The interactional patterns in these programs are highly complex and may number in the hundreds or even thousands. Such complexity is difficult to track. Yet, an understanding of process is necessary if we are to understand families and how they change in therapy settings. Unidimensional quantitative instruments, based on linear, not interactional models, cannot represent these patterns. A more naturalistic, open-ended approach is appropriate for process studies and evaluations (Patton, 1990; Sandelowski, Holditch-Davis, & Harris, Chapter 16, this volume). Standardized and nonstandardized instruments do have a place in clinical research, but more for punctuating therapy processes than for uncovering change processes.

Participant observation and open-ended interviewing provide a window through which to view interactional processes. The data collection methods of videotaping, audiotaping, and field notes fit these approaches. (See Murphy, Chapter 9, this volume.) Data analysis through content analysis, coding, constant comparison, and linkages to related research and theory can help manage and interpret data and transform them into research findings accessible to others. The interactional nature of family treatment, then, fits well with the data collection and data analysis procedures of participant observation and open-ended interviewing.

Qualitative methods only recently have been identified as a good fit with family therapy research (Gilgun, 1990c; Moon et al., 1990). Earlier, family therapy research was in search of appropriate methods. Without methods, there can be no research, and therefore few examples of qualitative family therapy research yet exist. Here I both discuss methods and provide an example of research using clinically appropriate methods. As Mischler (1990) pointed out, exemplars are important in discussions of research methods. Learning how to do research is acquired through firsthand experience, or learning in context. Knowledge of abstract rules alone is not sufficient; not examining the "craft and tacit knowledge" (p. 422) of research processes contributes to the reaffirmation of science as "objective" and promotes ideas that "normal science" involves a set of procedures that do not involve and perhaps do not require the engagement of the mind and emotions of the researcher. In this chapter, I examine both the "craft and tacit knowledge" of clinical research processes.

Types of Qualitative Family Therapy Research

This chapter illustrates one type of qualitative research in family therapy in attempting to discover the major themes in a particular type of clinical practice. I pulled these general themes together from observations and interviews focused on microlevel interactions between family members and between members of the treatment team and family members. There are many other possible forms of qualitative family therapy research. Most are in discussion phases and have not been carried out. A growing field is in the analysis of therapeutic discourse. Gale and Newfield's (in press) use of conversation analysis in marital therapy and Gale's (1990) book-length discussion of conversation analysis provide examples of completed studies of discourse. Another emerging style of qualitative family therapy research is Keeney's (1987) recursive frame analysis, which has been applied in various treatment settings, such as for domestic violence (Keeney & Bobele, 1989; Stewart & Valentine, 1991) and parents' interpretations of referrals for their children to cardiologists (Chenail et al., 1990). Specimen analysis (Honeycutt, 1987) is well suited to the study of interactions in family therapy.

Other possible ways of doing research on family therapy can be adapted from discussions of methods and from examples taken from other types of therapy. Scheela (1991), a nurse-clinician, used participant observation and open-ended interviewing with perpetrators in incest treatment to develop a grounded theory of perpetrators' change processes from both "insiders'" and "outsiders'" points of view. Scheela also was a cotherapist for a therapy group with these perpetrators and thus did research on her own practice setting. Berlin, Mann, & Grossman (1991) used task analysis in their study of depressed women. Task analysis, which is similar to analytic induction (see Bogdan & Biklen, 1982; and Gilgun, Chapter 3, this volume, for a discussion of analytic induction), begins with a conceptual model, which is tested against and modified by emerging clinical data. Greenberg & Johnson (1988) and Safran, Greenberg, and Rice (1988) have written extensively on task analysis. Others who have discussed qualitative methods adaptable to family therapy research are Hill (1990) on exploratory process research; Greenberg (1986), Pinsof (1989), and Reid (1990) on change process research; Mahrer and Nadler (1986) on the discovery of "good moments" in therapy; Gilgun on event analysis (1990c); and Gurman, Kniskern, and Pinsof (1986) on outcome research.

Family therapists throughout the country are developing other innovative qualitative approaches to family therapy research. (See Blaisure, 1990; and Chenail, 1990-1991.) Qualitative methods also are useful in developing clinical rating scales, which I did using the same data set on which I drew for this present report. (See Gilgun, 1991c.) Imle and Atwood (1988) also developed scales using qualitative methods for scale development. Scales developed from data on clinical sessions fit clinical realities and therefore promise to be useful in evaluation of both process and outcome.

Another form of much-needed clinical research is research on the situations into which clinicians intervene, apart from change processes in clinical sessions. Clinicians could become effective researchers on the issues clients bring to therapy. Both Wright (1990) and Gilgun (Gilgun, 1990a, 1990b; Gilgun & Connor, 1989; Gilgun & Reiser, 1990) did research on child maltreatment, adapting their interviewing procedures from procedures they learned in their clinical work. Neither of them was looking at the change process: Wright was interested in the effects of incest perpetrator removal on family functioning, and Gilgun sought to identify risk and resiliency factors in the lives of adults maltreated as children. Clinicians are on the front line and often see significant issues far sooner than nonclinical researchers. They, therefore, are well positioned to do research on emerging social problems. The research they develop would be highly useful to other clinicians, program planners, and public policy makers.

Common and Differentiating Elements
in Qualitative Clinical Research

What these qualitative approaches to clinical research share are:

- Data collection methods, which are various combinations of observation, interviewing, and document analysis, in the forms of clinical case notes, videotapes, and transcripts of clinical sessions;
- A unit of analysis, which is the case;
- A primary focus on the microlevel of clinical interaction.

The approaches differ in the levels of analysis they develop from the microlevel data and in the scope of their analysis. The present study, for example, has a wide scope and sought a general level of findings in addition to the specific, microlevel findings. The scope is the overall decision-making processes of the treatment team. In addition, I hoped that the general findings not only would apply to this particular incest treatment team, but to other incest teams, and even to group decision-making in general. I make a case for the generality of application of findings through the related research and theory that support my argument for wider applicability.

Other styles of clinical research may aim for other types of generalizability. Discourse analysis has a more delimited scope. Results of research on parts of sessions could move to other levels of generality and abstraction through incorporation of related research and theory. A major criticism of discourse analysis is an overfocus on the details of the analysis and an underemphasis on the development of more general principles that could be helpful in other clinical settings.

This chapter also exemplifies ecological family research, which is research that investigates the interface between families and external environments (Bubolz & Sontag, in press). The external environment in this study is the incest treatment team. Bronfenbrenner (1979, 1986) consistently has pointed out the importance of understanding the influence of external environments on families. Understanding these influences adds to knowledge of the processes of family interaction and human development.

Research Question

The research question I negotiated with the treatment team was: What procedures does the incest treatment team use to make decisions about clients' progress in treatment? When I began this research, I was unfamiliar with the processes of multidisciplinary incest treatment teams, despite 11 years of social work practice with families. I read what little there was on multifamily sexual abuse treatment teams (e.g., Bander, Fein, & Bishop, 1982; Giaretto, 1982; Sandall, Bell, & Cady, 1982; Sgroi, 1982a) and on multidisciplinary teams for the evaluation of child sexual abuse (Sgroi, 1982b). The body of work barely touched upon decision-making and provided me with little on which to base hypotheses. I wanted to be responsive to the team's request and I, therefore, choose to use the open-ended, more discovery-oriented approach of grounded theory.

METHOD

The treatment team and the client families of an incest treatment program were the subjects of this study. The program was located in a small city about 70 miles west of a major metropolitan area in the upper Midwest. The program site was a regional mental health center that served a predominantly rural, four-county area. Practitioners from the mental health center and from social service agencies in all four counties staffed the incest treatment program. At the time of data collection, the team consisted of 14 members: a mix of bachelor and master's level social workers, master's and Ph.D.-level psychologists, practitioners in general counseling, two Ph.D. psychology interns, and three volunteer foster grandmothers. The general therapeutic orientation of the program was structural-strategic family therapy (Minuchin, 1974; Minuchin & Fishman, 1981; Papp, 1983; Selvini-Palazzoli et al., 1978) in combination with an emphasis on linking families to community resources.

Clients

During the period of data collection, the number of clients ranged from 35 to 55. The number of families ranged from 9 to 14. When data collection began, 55 clients who were members of 14 families were in treatment. Eight of these families were nuclear; three others were mothers with children. Two perpetrators attended without their families, and one victim-survivor attended without her family. Victim-survivors ranged in age from 12 to 18. Nonvictimized siblings also were in treatment. They ranged in age from 5 to 18. All clients were white. The parents' work was primarily blue collar or farming.

Program Structure

The program used three different types of group treatment: peer groups, multifamily groups, and a didactic group called family lab. Peer groups met weekly, and there were six: two each for victim-survivors and siblings and one each for perpetrators and nonoffending partners. The number of multifamily groups varied, depending upon the numbers and sizes of families in treatment at any one time. Multifamily group and family lab met on alternate weeks. Family labs were classes on topics such as sexuality, the dynamics of incest, family communication, and parenting. Each group had two facilitators, usually a woman and a man, from the professional staff. A foster grandmother participated in the nonoffending spouse group, and one foster grandmother was in each of the two sibling groups. Each family also was "staffed" once a quarter. At the staffings, family members met with team members and professionals involved with families, such as child protection workers and probation and parole officers who supervised perpetrators. They negotiated individualized treatment goals and evaluated progress on both individual and programmatic goals.

Programmatic Goals

Besides meeting individualized goals, clients worked with each other and with practitioners to meet programmatic goals. Some of these goals were similar for each family member, such as establishing the perpetrator as responsible for the incest, expressing and managing the emotions engendered by the incest, and reestablishing functional family roles. A common task was writing and sharing an autobiography. Goals specific to each family member were also part of the program. Perpetrators, for example, were expected to apologize for their incestuous behavior and to develop a plan for avoiding the sexual abuse of children. Victim-survivors were helped to develop equitable relationships with peers and to develop strategies for dealing with unwanted sexual advances.

Families entered the program in January or August each year; they graduated when they had completed both programmatic and individual goals. Length of treatment varied from 9 months to 2 years, with an average of 15 months.

Treatment Day

The treatment day was about 5-1/2 hours long, from 3 p.m. to 8:30 p.m. The day began with a 2-hour staff meeting and was followed by peer groups, dinner break, multifamily groups or family lab, and then wrap-up and writing in clients' charts. The families ate dinner together in one large room, and the staff ate in a separate, smaller room. The team, therefore, had three opportunities to discuss treatment strategies and clients' progress in treatment: at the staff meeting, over dinner, and at the wrap-up.

Data Collection and Analysis

I negotiated with the treatment team to observe them during team meetings and to interview them after I developed some understanding of their process. Although I had wanted to observe therapy sessions and interview clients, the team saw these as intrusive and possibly harmful to families. They did not allow direct contact between me and clients, but I did observe family labs and the families at dinner, settings that the team saw as safeguarding the confidentiality of clients. I observed the treatment team 10 times between February and July 1985. I interviewed each professional team member (11 members) during June, July, and August 1985. I did three additional observations in January, April, and May 1986. I conducted a group interview of the team in May 1986. I also attended one all-day planning meeting held in July 1986. Total observation period was 18 months.

Participant observation and open-ended interviewing worked well together in this research. I was able to observe the interactions, points of view, and reasoning of team members over an extended period of time. I followed the team's evaluations of the progress of family members over the time of the observations. The interviews were opportunities to explore team members' reasoning and viewpoints in detail. The use of two methods resulted in a much fuller picture of the program than one method alone would have done. Other researchers have reported the fit between observation and interviewing (Lofland & Lofland, 1984; Marshall & Rossman, 1989; Rubin & Babbie, 1989; Spradley, 1979, 1980).

Following Bogdan and Biklen (1982), I did not take notes, nor did I mechanically record team meetings, a mutual decision between myself and the team to reduce my intrusiveness. While the team was involved in treatment sessions, I dictated field notes into my tape recorder. During the ride home after the final session of the day, I continued to tape-record my observations. I included in these field notes both observer comments and memos, reserving observer comments for my subjective reactions to my observations, and the memos for final comments on emerging patterns (cf. Gilgun, Chapter 3, this volume; Bogdan & Biklen, 1982). I took notes for the individual and group interviews and in addition, tape-recorded four of the interviews. All tapes were transcribed; the written notes were expanded into narrative form within 24 hours. I content analyzed the transcripts and field notes during and after data collection. I thus had the opportunity to test hypotheses and clarify my understanding of emerging concepts and patterns during the observation period. During data collection and as part of data analysis, as is standard procedure in grounded theory research, I reviewed bodies of literature that the emerging hypotheses suggested to me.

My Status as Observer

The team was ambivalent about me. For the most part, team members were friendly and cooperative. Yet, in their eyes I probably had an outsider status; their shielding clients from direct contact with me was one indicator of this. I understood this stance, but regretted the missed research opportunities. Another indicator was a comment by an otherwise friendly practitioner about how I was "always watching." I laughed when she said this to me and took it as an expectable and acceptable response. A third indicator occurred when the team asked me not to speak during the all-day planning meeting. That hurt. I like to feel part of situations in which I participate. Such experiences, however, are common in participant observation studies (Bogdan & Biklen, 1982; Wax, 1971). In addition, although the team requested my services, I was a volunteer researcher for the program. Funding for the research was provided to me, not to the treatment program, by the Minnesota Agricultural Experiment Station, which has a special interest in rural families. I was unsure about whether this funding from a source external to the program affected the team's perceptions of me. Finally, I was a university professor with several years' experience doing research on incest. I also had a clinical background. My status could have been a barrier for some of the clinicians.

RESULTS

The major finding of this study was the following: The decision-making processes of the incest treatment team were analogous to procedures used in social research to establish validity and reliability.

Team members observed family members and whole families multiple times in multiple settings over time and under a variety of conditions. Behaviors of each client and the quality of their interactions with others were continually noted and later discussed in team meetings. In this section, I present data supporting these statements. Two bodies of literature were used to help interpret data: research on group decision-making and the social science concepts of reliability and validity.

I did not immediately turn to the research methodology literature to help me interpret the findings as they were emerging. Rather, I first consulted the literature on group decision-making. There I made two significant discoveries: (a) laboratory studies have shown that decisions made by groups whose members have the opportunity to interact and discuss their perspectives are more accurate than judgments made by individuals and (b) why this is so is not clear. This research also identified "group think," in which members of a group may agree, but their decisions are not accurate. I also learned that procedures by which groups come to decisions have not been delineated, nor have criteria for judging the quality of group decision making been developed (Hart, 1986). There I was, in the midst of a study, and after consulting what I thought would be appropriate literature, I was left high and dry, a researcher in search of a theory to help me interpret findings.

I did get some reassurance from the literature: Research on group decision making suggested that the team's process was probably accurate, but it could not tell me how to judge its accuracy or what procedures might lead to accuracy. Since that time, I often have wondered why researchers in this field did not do observations and interviews of group processes in decision-making. These approaches made the most sense to me. Finally, the group decision-making literature suggested that I possibly was about to delineate processes that until then were obscure.

Finding little help in this literature, I had to pay attention to my only other clue about how to interpret findings. I realized quite soon in this research that the team was using replication logic and multiple sources of data. These, of course, are principles relating to reliability and validity. I resisted linking my findings to principles of research methodology. I had assumed findings of the grounded theory approach would relate to substantive social science theory and research. I had to let go of this preconception and also think about whether I was bringing positivistic assumptions into a qualitative study. I have decided that certain processes may underlie many forms of research, and the terms used to label these processes, such as reliability and validity, may be associated with certain methodologies and philosophies of science, such as positivism. This does not mean, however, that the terms and the processes they describe only are operative under some philosophies of science and not others. In the end, my choice was pragmatic—I had no other body of literature on which to draw to help me interpret my findings.

Multiple Observations and Sources of Data

According to research methodologists, reliability has to do with consistency and repeatability of findings (Kerlinger, 1973; Rubin & Babbie, 1989). Findings are judged reliable when they are consistent across subjects, observers, and settings. In the incest treatment setting, therapists judged that family members were making progress in treatment when they were consistent in meeting their treatment goals in peer groups, multifamily groups, family lab, quarterly staffings, and in reports from persons in the community, such as teachers, social workers, and probation and parole officers. The professional staff also looked for evidence that clients' behaviors were consistent over time. One "breakthrough" in one setting followed by no evidence of this new behavior in other settings over time was not an indicator of progress. Some inconsistencies, of course, were expected, because different settings and persons in those settings may evoke different behaviors, but inconsistencies on behaviors related to treatment goals led to the judgment that the client needed further work and were not ready to graduate from the program. In meetings that took place three times in the treatment day, week after week, team members shared their observations. Over time, a detailed longitudinal picture of individual and family interaction emerged. These processes meet the consistency and repeatability consistency criteria for the establishment of reliability.

Reliability takes on meaning when coupled with validity. The concept of validity arises from the difficulty of actually measuring what we think we are measuring. There are several types of validity, including face, content, construct, predictive, and concurrent. The validity on which I focused was construct validity (Cook & Campbell, 1979; Kerlinger, 1973). In estimating construct validity, data that converge are judged to be related, whereas conversely, those that do not converge are thought not to be related. Triangulation of data sources leads to the confidence in the validity of research findings (Cook & Campbell, 1979; Denzin, 1978; Rubin & Babbie, 1989). In the incest treatment setting, there were multiple sources of data, including 11 professional staff, three volunteer foster grandparents, reports from professionals in the community, reports of family members on their own and others' behaviors, and team observations of family interaction in several different settings.

This large array of data and data sources, based on direct observations and interactions with families as well as many collateral sources, provided the team with rich, in-depth information on family functioning and status over time. In social research, findings emerging from multiple sources are judged more valid than findings from a single source (Cook & Campbell, 1979; Denzin, 1978; Rubin & Babbie, 1989). The incest treatment team's processes of obtaining information on clients' progress fit descriptions of what constitutes construct validity in social research, although the members of the team did not structure their decision-making processes on an explicit understanding of the logic of reliability and validity. Rather, how they made decisions evolved from the structure of the team and of the program day. That the team followed these procedures is supported by the data.

The team evaluated clients as having made progress in meeting treatment goals under three conditions: (a) when clients' behavior was consistent across treatment settings, (b) when client self-reports converged with reports of other family members, and (c) when clinical observations of progress converged with evaluations of other professionals involved with the families. Inconsistency of behavior across settings, divergence of client self-reports and self-reports of other family members, and indicators of lack of progress in reports of outside professionals were markers that clients had more work to do. Below are findings supporting these statements.

Consistency as Indicator of Progress

The team judged clients to be making progress when clients' behaviors were consistent across settings and over time. The following descriptions of behavior of two different perpetrators illustrate these points. One perpetrator graduated from the program. The other did not. The team evaluated the man who did not graduate for 10 months before asking him to leave the program.

The man who did not graduate was inconsistent in meeting his treatment goals. At the time of my observations, he had recently and while in treatment fondled his daughter's breasts, an indicator of lack of treatment progress. In multifamily group, peer group, and staffings, professional staff worked to help him understand the implications of his behavior. He consistently minimized the impact of his behavior on his daughter. He also refused to apologize to her. Then in peer group, he heard a man new to the group minimize his own incestuous behaviors. He told this man, "You may have hurt your daughter a great deal." He went on to explain how and why. Later that day, in multifamily group, he apologized to his daughter by saying:

> I'm really sorry I did this to you. I'm really sorry I touched your breasts. I will do all in my power to make sure it doesn't happen again. I'm sorry I hurt you.

As the team discussed this man's behaviors during team meetings, they agreed these consistencies might be indicators of progress. Some therapists thought these new behaviors might represent a breakthrough. Because these two events occurred on one day, however, the team took a wait-and-see attitude. During the following weeks, this client's behavior, self-reports, and reports of other family members indicated that once again he was minimizing the impact of his behaviors. The team became skeptical whether he was capable of taking responsibility for his behaviors and understanding their impact.

The victim of the man who graduated did not participate in the program. The team assessed his ability to take responsibility for his incestuous behaviors through self-reports and observations in multi-family group, peer group, family labs, and reports of his probation officer, where he consistently showed he was fulfilling treatment goals, including taking responsibility for his behavior and understanding its impact. In multifamily group, he said to another man's daughter:

> I hope you are not blaming yourself for the abuse. I knew a lot more than my own daughter, and I took advantage of her. It is very important for you to understand that. I took advantage of her.

This clear statement, in combination with many other observations, became part of a picture of man capable of dealing with incest, a picture that emerged over time and in several different settings and was observed by multiple practitioners.

Need for More Work: Consistency Within Settings But Not Across Settings

Some clients showed consistencies in their behavior within treatment settings, but across treatment settings they were inconsistent. In an interview, a sibling group facilitator told a story that illustrates these processes:

> The client, an adolescent boy, the brother of an incest victim, operated in two such different ways. The boy was definitely one of the most active members of the peer group and was extremely insightful and could be very responsive to others' feelings. I would, in that group, describe him as a very caring person. Then we would go into family group, and not always, but on occasion, he would be a pure snot, typically to his mother. He would find it very difficult to verbalize his own feelings. I'm not sure if he could even get in touch with his feelings, he was so upset, but I know for sure that he had trouble verbalizing what was happening to him in multifamily group.

Two other therapists had seen this client in treatment on many occasions: one in peer group and one in multifamily group. Each of them validated her observations in both settings. Had the information come from one setting only, the team's judgment of the boy's ability to deal with his feelings would have been inaccurate. Furthermore, team members might not have realized that their knowledge was limited.

Need for More Work: Inconsistency of Self-Reports

In peer groups, clients reported on the status of their marriage and family lives. The accuracy of their reports could be evaluated through reports from other family members or through therapists' observations of interactions of family members. The following is an example of this process. At a team meeting, a therapist reported that a man in the perpetrator peer group said he had been having great sex with his wife. The cofacilitator of the nonoffending spouse group responded:

His wife said she hasn't had sex with him for 6 months, and she's divorcing him.

The wife may or may not have been truthful, but her report placed her husband's report in doubt. Her plans for divorce supported her statement. Over time, observations and self-reports helped to clarify the status of the marriage and the veracity of the clients' self-reports.

Another example of divergence in self-reports occurred in a team discussion of the relationship of a father and his sons. A perpetrator group cofacilitator reported that the father said things were going much better with his sons. The cofacilitator of the sons' group said:

That's funny. The boys said they're ready to kill their father.

The structure of the treatment program created conditions that maximized the opportunities to increase reliability and validity of the team's judgments.

Under varying conditions, consistency, divergence, and convergence of client behaviors and self-reports were evaluated both through self-reports of other family members and through observation of clients' interactions with members of their own family and members of other families. The rich mix of client configuration, therapist configuration, setting, and sources of data supported the incest treatment team's decision-making process.

DISCUSSION

Participant observation and open-ended interviews, in combination with a grounded theory approach, led to the finding that the incest treatment team used decision-making procedures similar to those used in social research for establishing reliability and validity. The structure of the treatment program created opportunities for multiple therapists to observe clients in different settings and different family configurations over time and to discuss their observations three times each treatment day.

Treatment programs with similar structures can be hypothesized to provide similar opportunities for observation and decision-making. The findings of the present research, then, may have implications for the quality of decision-making in other multiple-family treatment programs. The findings of this research also may contribute to the development of procedures for evaluating the quality of group decisions in other, nonclinical settings. The need for such procedures was established through a literature review.

Treatment teams provide clear advantages over practitioners operating alone. Most practitioners, however, work alone, although they commonly seek to expand their perspectives through individual and peer supervision and case conferences. Observations through one-way mirrors provide multiple perspectives and opportunities to test convergence, divergence, and consistency over time. This research supports many common practices in the conduct of family therapy and other forms of therapeutic work, such as individual therapy and case management.

Participant observation and open-ended interviewing, in conjunction with a grounded theory approach, was ideally suited for this research. These methods provided a means to view, collect, organize, and interpret the complex interactions among family members and treatment professionals. The methods, then, fit the phenomena of interest.

Using these methods as a researcher in these complex settings was challenging. It took me a long time to understand and interpret the interactions. I continually had to interact with team members, which was not always comfortable. I came away from this experience with a deep respect for team treatment of multiple families and a sense that this type of treatment used procedures in which we can have confidence. The interactive methods of open-ended interviewing and participant observation provided me with perspectives I otherwise could not have obtained.

In clinical research, partnerships of outside researchers and clinicians may be the ideal, given the findings of the present research. In this research, I was not part of the treatment team and had an outsider status. Despite my discomforts, such a role has much to recommend it. I, for example, had little vested interest in what I might find. I might have been much less tempted to find positives about the team processes than members of the team. I also brought an additional perspective to the team and helped them to see processes deeply embedded in their work but outside of their awareness.

There are times, however, when clinicians themselves appropriately can take the roles of researchers. Scheela's (1991) work, cited earlier, is clinician-conducted research on her own clients, and it is valuable research in its own right. The analysis of significant therapeutic events (Gilgun, 1990c) also can be done without outside researchers. In this style of research, clinicians and sometimes clients share their thoughts and feelings as they review transcripts or tapes of clinical sessions. Sharing of inner processes can provide important information about clinical processes. Adding outsiders to the clinical process to the research team, however, does provide an additional layer of validity to the research.

Both analytic induction and grounded theory are well suited to clinician-conducted research because the processes of these approaches parallel those of clinical work. Field notes, content analysis, coding, constant comparison, moving between the clinical work and the more conceptual world of theory and previous experience are basic processes in qualitative research. They are analogous to clinical processes.

Clinical training hones both interviewing and observation skills. Clinicians, therefore, have great potential as researchers on client issues such as child maltreatment, blended families, and sibling relationships. These are issues that appear in clinical practice and are also of interest to more general audiences of family scholars and educators. Lightburn, Matocha, and Snyder, authors of chapters in this volume; Gilgun (Gilgun, 1990a, 1990b; Gilgun & Connor, 1989; Gilgun & Reiser, 1990); and Wright (1990) are examples of clinicians who have done research on client issues and not on change processes themselves. Like research on therapeutic change processes and outcomes, this type of research is applied; that is, it is conducted to be used in practice, programs, and policy. It is done because it is theoretically interesting, as is basic research, but it also is done for immediate use.

When clinicians undertake this type of research, however, they may experience role ambiguity and role conflict. In the course of conducting research, informants (subjects) may reveal issues that to clinician-researchers are in obvious need of clinical intervention. Sometimes informants directly ask for interventions; sometimes they may be less direct or even ambivalent about asking for direction. In addition, clinicians may feel exploitive by focusing on data collection instead of working toward client change.

There are many possible ways to handle these situations. Much of the foundational work can be done before the research begins. The informed consent form that the client signs should make clear that the purpose of the research is to develop knowledge and not to do therapy. In the first meeting between clinician-researchers and potential informants, the clinician could point out the potential for therapeutic outcomes for informants, although not the purpose of the research. Often in my research, informants state that they have two purposes in participating in the research—to provide information and to learn something about themselves. I say, that is fine with me, and I will be glad if you do learn something about yourself, but my purpose is research.

In the conduct of the research, informants frequently disclose intense pain and suffering. When this happens, I call upon my clinical skills— which to me actually are human responses—and acknowledge the suffering. Depending on the nature of my relationships with informants, I may blend my roles at this point. Minimally, I ask if they would like to work on changing how they are feeling, and if they do, I ask if they would like referrals for some clinical intervention. Under no conditions would I become the therapist for persons with whom I have done research interviewing. This is a boundary issue and an ethical stance. Self-disclosure is something I use when I want to create a safe environment for subjects so they can tell me more about themselves. Sometimes I explicitly use it as a therapeutic tool in the hope that informants will feel less isolated with their issues.

I rarely blend my roles, but sometimes it seems appropriate from a humanitarian point of view. I attempt to be self-critical and self-aware at these moments, and I move back to a clear research stance as quickly as feasible. A general principle that helps me in these intense moments is the reality that my contract with informants is for research and not therapy, and for me to change that contract would be unethical, even if informants requested the change. In all cases of open-ended interviewing, researchers should be ready with a list of referrals that informants might want. See Daly (Chapters 1 and 7, this volume) for a complementary perspective.

Participant observation and interviewing in combination with the procedures of grounded theory fit well with clinical practice. These research methods and clinical work have processes in common. Doing therapy and doing research, however, are not the same thing. Yet knowing how to do therapy provides clinicians with basic skills for becoming effective researchers.

REFERENCES

Ackerman, N. (1958). *The psychodynamics of family life*. New York: Basic Books.
Bander, K. W., Fein, E. & Bishop, G. (1982). Evaluation of child-sexual-abuse programs. In S. M. Sgroi (Ed.), *Handbook of clinical intervention in child sexual abuse* (pp. 345-376). Lexington, MA: Lexington.

Berlin, S. B., Mann, K. B., & Grossman, S. F. (1991). Task analysis of cognitive therapy for depression. *Social Work Research & Abstracts, 27*(2), 3-11.

Blaisure, K. (1990). Qualitative research and family therapy. *Qualitative Family Research, 4*(2), 5-6, 18-20. (Available from Jane Gilgun, School of Social Work, University of Minnesota, 224 Church Street, S.E., Minneapolis, MN 55455)

Bogdan, R., & Biklen, S. K. (1982). *Qualitative research for education.* Boston: Allyn & Bacon.

Bronfenbrenner, U. (1979). *The ecology of human development: Experiments by nature and design.* Cambridge, MA: Harvard University Press.

Bronfenbrenner, U. (1986). Ecology of the family as a context for human development: Research perspectives. *Developmental Psychology, 22,* 723-742.

Bubolz, M. M., & Sontag, M. S. (in press). Human ecology theory. In P. Boss, W. Doherty, R. LaRossa, W. Schumm, & S. Steinmetz (Eds.), *Sourcebook of family theories and methods: A contextual approach.* New York: Plenum.

Cecchin, G. (1987). Hypothesizing, circularity, and neutrality revisited: An invitation to curiosity. *Family Process, 26,* 405-413.

Charmaz, K. (1990). "Discovering" chronic illness: Using grounded theory. *Social Science in Medicine, 30,* 1161-1172.

Chenail, R. J. (1990-1991). Before you give up on research, or please re-search this. *The Qualitative Report, 1*(2/3), 1, 3-7. (Available from Ron Chenail, Nova University, School of Social and Systemic Studies, 3301 College Avenue, Fort Lauderdale, FL 33314)

Chenail, R. J., Douthit, P. E., Gale, J. E., Stormberg, J. L., Morris, G. H., Park, J. M., Sridaromont, S., & Schmer, V. (1990). "It's probably nothing serious, but . . . ": Parents' interpretation of referral to pediatric cardiologists. *Health Communication, 2,* 165-167.

Cook, T. D., & Campbell, D. T. (1979). *Quasi-experimentation: Design and analysis for field settings.* Boston: Houghton Mifflin.

Denzin, N. K. (1978). *The research act: A theoretical introduction to sociological methods.* New York: McGraw-Hill.

Feagin, J. R., Orum, A. M., & Sjoberg, G. (Eds.). (1991). *A case for the case study* (pp. 244-268). Chapel Hill: University of North Carolina Press.

Gale, J. E. (1990). *Conversation analysis of therapeutic discourse.* Norwood, NJ: Ablex.

Gale, J. E., & Newfield, N. (in press). A conversation analysis of a solution-focused marital therapy session. *Journal of Marital and Family Therapy.*

Giaretto, H. (1982). *Integrated treatment of child sexual abuse.* Palo Alto, CA: Science and Behavior Books.

Gilgun, J. F. (1989a). Freedom of choice and research interviewing in child sexual abuse. In B. R. Compton & B. Galaway (Eds.), *Social work processes* (4th ed., pp. 358-368). Belmont, CA: Wadsworth.

Gilgun, J. F. (1989b, March). *Starting where the practitioner is: Toward a conceptual framework for social work research.* Paper presented at the annual program meeting of the Council on Social Work Education Symposium on Philosophical Issues in Social Work, Chicago, March 4-7.

Gilgun, J. F. (1990a). Resilience and the intergenerational transmission of child sexual abuse. In M. Q. Patton (Ed.), *Family sexual abuse: Frontline research and evaluation* (pp. 93-105). Newbury Park, CA: Sage.

Gilgun, J. F. (1990b). The sexual development of men sexually abused as children. In M. Hunter (Ed.), *The sexually abused male: Prevalence, impact, and treatment* (pp. 177-190). Lexington, MA: Lexington.

Gilgun, J. F. (1990c, November). *The place of qualitative methods in the study of the family.* Paper presented at the Theory Construction and Research Methodology preconference workshop, National Council on Family Relations, Seattle, November 9-15.

Gilgun, J. F. (1991a). *A case for case studies in social work research.* Manuscript submitted for publication.

Gilgun, J. F. (1991b). Discovery-oriented qualitative methods relevant to longitudinal research on child abuse and neglect. In R. Starr & D. A. Wolfe (Eds.), *The effects of child abuse and neglect: Issues and research* (pp. 144-163). New York: Guilford.

Gilgun, J. F. (1991c, August). *Hand into glove: Grounded theory and social work practice research.* Paper presented to a conference on Qualitative Methods in Social Work Practice Research, Nelson A. Rockefeller Institute of Government, State University of New York at Albany, Albany, August 23-25.

Gilgun, J. F., & Connor, T. M. (1989). How perpetrators view child sexual abuse. *Social Work, 34,* 249-251.

Gilgun, J. F., & Reiser, E. (1990). The development of sexual identity among men sexually abused as children. *Families in Society, 71,* 515-523.

Glaser, B., & Strauss, A. L. (1967). *The discovery of grounded theory.* New York: Aldine.

Greenberg, L. S. (1986). Change process research. *Journal of Consulting and Clinical Psychology, 54,* 4-9.

Greenberg, L. S., & Johnson, S. M. (1988). *Emotionally focused therapy for couples.* New York: Guilford.

Gurman, A., Kniskern, D., & Pinsof, W. (1986). Research on the process and outcome of marital and family therapy. In S. Bergin & A. Garfield (Eds.), *Handbook of psychotherapy and behavior change* (3rd ed., pp. 565-624). New York: John Wiley.

Haley, J. (1987). *Family problem solving* (2nd ed.). San Francisco: Jossey-Bass.

Handel, G. (1991). Case study in family research. In J. R. Feagin, A. M. Orum, & G. Sjoberg (Eds.), *A case for the case study* (pp. 244-268). Chapel Hill: University of North Carolina Press.

Hart, S. L. (1986). Toward quality criteria for collective judgments. *Organizational Behavior and Decision Processes, 36,* 209-228.

Hill, C. E. (1990). Exploratory in-session process research in individual psychotherapy: A review. *Journal of Consulting and Clinical Psychology, 58,* 288-294.

Honeycutt, J. M. (1987). Recent improvements in portraying acts in symbolic interaction behavioral specimens. *Symbolic Interaction, 10,* 279-293.

Imle, M. A., & Atwood, J. R. (1988). Retaining qualitative validity while gaining quantitative reliability and validity: Development of the Transition to Parenthood Concerns Scale. *Advances in Nursing Science, 11,* 61-75.

Kantor, D., & Lehr, W. (1975). *Inside the family: Toward a theory of family process.* New York: Harper & Row.

Keeney, B. P. (1987). *Recursive frame analysis: A method for organizing therapeutic discourse.* Unpublished manuscript, Texas Tech University, Department of Human Development and Family Studies, Lubbock.

Keeney, B. P., & Bobele, M. (1989). A brief note on family violence. *Australian and New Zealand Journal of Family Therapy, 10,* 93-95.

Kerlinger, F. N. (1973). *The foundations of behavioral research.* New York: Holt, Rinehart & Winston.

Lofland, J., & Lofland, L. H. (1984). *Analyzing social settings: A guide to qualitative observation and analysis* (2nd ed.). Belmont, CA: Wadsworth.

Mahrer, A. R., & Nadler, W. P. (1986). Good moments in psychotherapy: A preliminary review, a list, and some promising research avenues. *Journal of Consulting and Clinical Psychology, 54,* 10-15.

Marshall, C., & Rossman, G. B. (1989). *Designing qualitative research.* Newbury Park, CA: Sage.

Minuchin, S. (1974). *Families and family therapy.* Cambridge, MA: Harvard University Press.

Minuchin, S., & Fishman, H. C. (1981). *Family therapy techniques.* Cambridge, MA: Harvard University Press.

Mishler, E. G. (1990). Validation in inquiry-guided research: The role of exemplars in narrative studies. *Harvard Educational Review, 60,* 415-442.

Moon, S. M. (1991). Case study research in gifted education. In N. K. Buchanan & J. F. Feldhusen (Eds.), *Conducting research and evaluation in gifted education: A handbook of methods and applications* (pp. 157-178). New York: Teachers College Press.

Moon, S. M., Dillon, D. R., & Sprenkle, D. H. (1990). Family therapy and qualitative research. *Journal of Marital and Family Therapy, 16,* 357-373.

Papp, P. (1983). *The process of change.* New York: Guilford.

Patton, M. Q. (1990). *Qualitative evaluation and research methods* (2nd ed). Newbury Park, CA: Sage.

Pinsof, W. M. (1989). A conceptual framework and methodological criteria for family therapy process research. *Journal of Consulting and Clinical Psychology, 15,* 53-59.

Real, T. (1990). The therapeutic use of self in constructionist/systemic therapy. *Family Process, 29,* 255-272.

Reid, W. J. (1990). Change-process research: A new paradigm? In L. Videka-Sherman & W. J. Reid (Eds.), *Advances in clinical social work research* (pp. 130-148). Silver Spring, MD: National Association of Social Workers.

Rubin, A., & Babbie, E. (1989). *Research methods for social work.* Belmont, CA: Wadsworth.

Safran, J. D., Greenberg, L. S., & Rice, L. N. (1988). Integrating psychotherapy research and practice: Modeling the change process. *Psychotherapy, 25,* 1-17.

Sandall, H., Bell, C. M., & Cady, K. (1982). *Treating incest in rural families: A guideline to a set of principles and procedures for the treatment of sexual abuse in rural families.* St. Paul: Minnesota Department of Public Welfare.

Satir, V. (1967). *Conjoint family therapy.* Palo Alto, CA: Science and Behavior Books.

Scheela, R. A. (1991). *The remodeling process: A grounded theory study of adult male incest offenders' perceptions of the treatment process.* Unpublished doctoral dissertation, University of Texas at Austin.

Selvini-Palazzoli, M., Boscolo, L., Cecchin, G., & Prata, G. (1978). *Paradox and counterparadox.* New York: Aronson.

Selvini-Palazzoli, M., Boscolo, L., Cecchin, G., & Prata, G. (1980). Hypothesizing-circularity-neutrality: Three guidelines for the conductor of the session. *Family Process, 19,* 3-12.

Sgroi, S. M. (1982a). How to start a child sexual-abuse intervention program. In S. M. Sgroi (Ed.), *Handbook of clinical intervention in child sexual abuse* (pp. 377-384). Lexington, MA: Lexington.

Sgroi, S. M. (1982b). Multidisciplinary team review of child-sexual-abuse cases. In S. M. Sgroi (Ed.), *Handbook of clinical intervention in child sexual abuse* (pp. 335-343). Lexington, MA: Lexington.

Spradley, J. P. (1979). *The ethnographic interview.* New York: Holt, Rinehart & Winston.

Spradley, J. P. (1980). *Participant observation.* New York: Holt, Rinehart & Winston.

Stewart, K., & Valentine, L. N. (1991). Metaphors in domestic violence. In B. P. Keenye, W. L. Madsen, & F. F. Nolan (Eds.), *The systemic therapist* (Vol. 2, pp. 60-77). St. Paul, MN: Systemic Therapy Press.

Strauss, A., & Corbin, J. (1990). *Basics of qualitative research: Grounded theory procedures and techniques.* Newbury Park, CA: Sage.

Thomm, K. (1987a). Interventive interviewing: Part II. Reflexive questioning as a means to enable self-healing. *Family Process, 26,* 167-183.

Thomm, K. (1987b). Interventive interviewing: Part III. Intending to ask lineal, circular, strategic, or reflexive questions? *Family Process, 27,* 1-15.

Thomm, K. (1988). Interventive interviewing: Part I. Strategizing as a fourth guideline for the therapist. *Family Process, 26,* 3-13.

Wax, R. (1971). *Doing fieldwork: Warnings and advice.* Chicago: University of Chicago Press.

Wright, S. (1990). Family effects of offender removal from the home. In M. Q. Patton (Ed.), *Family sexual abuse: Frontline research and evaluation* (pp. 135-146). Newbury Park, CA: Sage.

Yin, R. K. (1989). *Case study research: Design and methods* (2nd ed.). Newbury Park: CA: Sage.

Part 4

Document Analysis

Although qualitative researchers typically rely on the firsthand accounts of their participants for data, a wealth of meaningful data lies dormant in diaries, letters, books, and magazines. Researchers who do document analysis examine historical records and contemporary texts to trace the cultural meanings embedded within them. In the chapter by Ellen Harbert, Barbara Vinick, and David Ekerdt, the implications of retirement for marriage are examined in popular magazines and self-help books published between 1960 and 1987. The identification of key themes in the popular literature over this time period allows the authors to meet several important goals: First, by identifying "nonacademic" themes, they are able to compare and contrast popular and scientific conceptions of retirement; second, they provide an account of historical changes in the meaning of retirement; and third, they are able to bring into sharper focus a set of cultural norms with respect to marriage and retirement.

Analyzing Popular Literature
Emergent Themes on Marriage and Retirement

ELLEN M. HARBERT
Framingham, MA

BARBARA H. VINICK
Veterans Administration Hospital, Boston

DAVID J. EKERDT
University of Kansas Medical Center

Retirement commonly is assumed to be a difficult transition for marital relationships. To explore the mystique surrounding marriage in retirement, we did a content analysis of popular books and articles published between 1960 and 1987 that offered information about this important period in couples' lives. We developed five themes related to issues discussed and advice offered. Generally, popular literature stressed problems couples might encounter in retirement—although most authors expressed optimism for positive adjustments— but we also discovered changes from earlier to later publications. We then compared

---

AUTHORS' NOTE: Research for this paper was supported in part by the Medical Research Service of the Veterans Administration and by a grant from the National Institute on Aging, No. AGO5661.

these findings to themes in academic literature, finding overlap between academic literature and popular books and articles, the most salient being that retirement in both sets of literature has meant *husbands'* retirement. These findings demonstrate a need for more recognition of women's retirement in both academic and popular publications.

Content analysis is well suited to research probing widespread cultural notions or stereotypes. As a method, it can be utilized with a minimum of high-tech equipment at low cost, it can be taught to and practiced by persons with a minimum of special background knowledge, and it can yield valuable insights. Reliability of data and validity of results are essential elements that can be fostered by careful attention to data extraction and categorization criteria.

For Better or Worse, But Not For Lunch?

During a separate study of marital quality before and after husbands' retirement, time and again we heard sentiments from our respondents like, "I'm very happy in retirement, but my wife and I are exceptions," or "I know that most wives are driven crazy by their husbands after they retire, but not me." Comments like these, as well as discussions with colleagues and friends, convinced us that people of all ages commonly believe that the transition from the end of working life to the beginning of retirement is a traumatic one for the male retiree and an equally difficult adjustment for his wife. Even interviewees who were themselves satisfied in retirement, and whose peers were likewise content, harbored such conceptions.

What is the basis for such negative lore about marriage in retirement? We reasoned that one source of common perceptions might be found in the popular press, specifically books and magazine articles of the self-help variety. We wanted to discover the "slant" of authors who discussed marriage in retirement. These sources might provide a better understanding of the mystique surrounding this topic. Furthermore, analysis of these materials could be useful on several levels: as a significant source of information consumed by individuals prior to retirement, as a window on current understanding of retirement from a nonacademic point of view, and as a reflection of societal norms concerning marriage and retirement.

METHOD

Originally, we organized the research around three questions we viewed as important and illuminating and that generated reasonable expectations for the provision of answers by the research data: (a) What issues and concerns are expressed concerning the effects of retirement on marital relationships? (b) What advice is dispensed to couples regarding their relationship? (c) How does the information presented in the popular literature compare with the results of studies reported in academic literature? As the research progressed, we added a fourth question, suggested by initial data collected: (d) How has the nature of the discussion and the advice proffered changed with the passage of time?

As sources of data, mass-market books and periodical articles dealing with retirement and marriage were determined to be the quarry. Newspapers are another source of knowledge, but we decided to tackle less ephemeral documents targeted to a wider audience. Publication dates between 1960 and 1987 were deemed appropriate: By 1960 retirement had been institutionalized, and the period 1960-1987 encompassed an explosion in the publication of how-to and advice books and included the most recent publications up to the time the analysis began.

We located articles through the *Guide to Periodical Literature,* using the key words "couples," "marriage," and "retirement." Books were found through the card catalogues of the main branch of the Boston Public Library and two smaller suburban libraries. Although not exhaustive, these sources seemed representative of the resources available to the average person. In all, 19 magazine articles and 13 books that discussed retirement marriage exclusively or in part were included in the present study.

Guided by the research questions, we proceeded with data collection. Limited funds mandated a low-tech approach throughout, although various software applications could perhaps have speeded operations. (Tesch [1990] is helpful in selecting computer software for qualitative data analysis.) To determine whether the content was appropriate, we first skimmed the entire book or magazine article. If any part or all of the document discussed an aspect of marriage in retirement, we wrote extracts on cards. These cards included summaries of the content according to our first two questions above—the issues discussed and the substance of the advice offered. We recorded verbatim quotes and paraphrased some specific points.

Because the bulk of material published on retirement concerned finances and housing options rather than retirement satisfaction or the marital relationship, the choice of materials to extract was not large. Nevertheless, at the beginning of the project when the text classification scheme was still relatively vague, some subjective assessment played a role. As the project progressed, we continually reviewed the extract cards and delineated categories for classifying texts and identifying broader themes. From around 10, we reduced major categories to 5, each encompassing specified subcategories. For example, we subsumed the issue of newly-retired husbands being "underfoot" under the major topic of togetherness versus autonomy, and we included discussions of health under retirement as a prelude to late life. We drafted a brief document describing materials to be recorded under the five designated categories and subcategories as discussed further below.

This set of encoding instructions was appropriate for the study's goal of describing content under rather broad rubrics as objectively as possible. More detailed coding specifications would probably be necessary for other ends, such as determining associations between units of material or testing specific hypotheses. In those circumstances, issues of reliability (consistency of judgments concerning categorization) would come to the fore; they could be dealt with by, for example, comparing results of data extractors working independently on the same materials (Krippendorf, 1980) or having the same coder assess the material at different times to determine if the same results are obtained (Weber, 1985).

After selecting the "recording units" (Krippendorf, 1980, p. 58), we reviewed the data cards with an eye toward overarching conclusions regarding changes in presentation of advice from the 1960s to the late 1980s. We compared these findings with themes from the academic literature. What follows are discussions of the five primary topical areas we found through our content analysis and then a discussion of the changing nature of issues and advice both in the popular and the academic literatures.

ISSUES DISCUSSED IN THE POPULAR LITERATURE

Advice presented to couples could be classified according to five major topical categories: togetherness versus autonomy, communication between spouses, sexual intimacy, level of activity, and retirement as a prelude to late life and death. Much of the content was age specific, but many items of advice could be appropriately targeted to couples of any age.

Togetherness Versus Autonomy

One of the most prevalent topics in the literature concerned the task of newly retired couples to work out satisfactory compromises between togetherness and autonomy. "We are better companions if part of our life is directed toward fulfillment of our own uniqueness" (Staley & Singleton, 1976, p. 126) was a common sentiment. During the early years of retirement, stated one author (Willing, 1981), couples usually are caught in conflicts, which then give way to a new balance between dependency and autonomy. Too much togetherness can be stifling, but too much autonomy can lead to a breakdown in the relationship. Generally, couples were advised to retain separate interests, as contributing to the vibrancy of the relationship (e.g., Butler, 1979; Dickinson, 1981; Finkelhor, 1978). One book (Staley & Singleton, 1976) suggested that each partner make a list of interests and then compare them. Spouses were encouraged to assess areas of shared enthusiasm and to pursue both individual and mutual experiences.

Communication

Closely related to issues of mutuality and autonomy is communication. In general, advice stressed the importance of openness and honesty as keys to achievement of a positive relationship (Finkelhor, 1978; Rice, 1969; Weitzman, 1978). Full discussion of each partner's expectations and desires was viewed as important.

Another skein of advice, such as that Ott (1971) gave, cautioned against too much disclosure:

> This is the crummiest, most unfair time to become expert in stoical endurance. In self-pitying sufferance ... [but] why not simply write out a mutual moratorium on all picky, petty, pouty fiddle faddle. Then everyone can relax. (p. 101)

Similarly, others, such as Legler (1967), counseled moderation of criticism and avoidance of being overly demanding.

No matter how bruised or battered a marriage has become, it can be repaired and refurbished, repainted and polished and oiled until it runs like new with this three-word formula—SAY SOMETHING NICE. (p. 287)

In sum, open communication was seen as important in marital relationships for airing resentments or grievances that could fester and undermine the relationship. Some authors decried too much openness, however, as leading to petty quarrels, overemphasis on minor annoyances, and failure to express appreciation of the spouse's better qualities.

Sexual Intimacy

Sexuality was not widely discussed in any of the literature reviewed, especially works published before the mid-1970s. Although it was seldom overtly dismissed, the implication of the relative absence of discourse relating to sexuality was that the sexual aspect of the marital relationship in later life was considered unimportant, or even inappropriate. Although rebutted by considerable scientific evidence to the contrary, the stereotype of the asexual older person was given at least tacit support by this reticence.

Still not a prominent topic, in later works, sexual intimacies, especially "cuddling" and touching, were seen as important aspects of the marital relationship (e.g., Finkelhor, 1978; Staley & Singleton, 1976). Retirement was designated as a time when couples can derive special pleasure, with sexual activity enhancing the quality of emotional life together. Asexuality of older people was denounced as a myth, perhaps fostered by the young. In a particularly frank statement, Staley and Singleton advised:

To preserve such treasures of life . . . requires imagination, inventiveness, variety, and appreciation. . . . Now is the time for husband and wife to stop being coy or inhibited and to talk about, read about, discuss openly, and experiment with sex. (p. 144)

Activity in Retirement

Involvement in activities emerged as another much discussed issue. Willing (1981) noted the fear of inactivity prevalent among retired men as something they and their wives should recognize:

At some level of awareness, the new retiree realizes that a source of his vitality has been cut off and that he must exert himself from falling into a deadly lassitude. . . . Most men laugh at the idea and speak of being "busier than ever." And most men are very concerned with the level of the busy-ness, go to extraordinary lengths to make busy work for themselves, and thus reveal a great anxiety about it. (p. 112)

It was commonly acknowledged that the sudden release from a structured day can be bewildering. An individual who has previously invested a great deal of energy in work must suddenly find new ways with which to be occupied (Bromberg, 1981; Caraher, 1981; Collins, 1970; Lindeman, 1986; Perlmutter, 1981; White, 1982; Willing, 1981; Zinsser, 1986). According to one husband and wife who chronicled their own transition to the husband's retirement, "Removing [structured time] can be like sneaking the foundation out from under the house" (Hershey & Hershey, 1969, p. 24). In general, however, the opportunities for new options in retirement were emphasized. Retirement was observed to provide time for exploration and expansion of interests. Freedom from the 9-to-5 schedule was considered a boon, with daily agendas set according to individual desires (Alpert, 1974; Hershey & Hershey, 1969; White, 1982).

Several authors suggested that in the transition period at the beginning of her husband's retirement, the wife should help him to develop new interests and activities to take the place of work, to keep him busy and prevent him from becoming bored and depressed ("When your husband retires," 1968; Collins, 1970; Lord, 1970; Ware, 1960).

Prelude to Late Life

Retirement as prologue to late life and death was discussed directly by only a few authors, although others alluded to such themes. Butcher (1978), the only author who explicitly cited retirement of men as a cause of morbidity and mortality, quoted an American Medical Association opinion linking the "cessation of work and earning power . . . caused by compulsory retirement" among men to "physical and emotional deterioration and premature death" (p. 69). Ware (1960) suggested that chief among a wife's concerns should be to keep her husband healthy and alive, because without him she would lose companionship and social status; this patently sexist position is discussed further below.

Others urged recognition of the inevitability of death. Collins (1970), for example, characterized retirement as "a dramatic milestone in your life and . . . probably . . . your last one," and advised action on "certain death-connected issues" (p. 76) such as drawing up a will and deciding on burial plots. He urged couples to make younger friends as a way to avoid the loneliness of isolation as older friends die. Similarly, Finkelhor (1978) advised acceptance of the inevitability of death as an emotionally mature retirement attitude, one that can help each individual to acknowledge the value of time. Release from the fear of death could be achieved through religious beliefs or from reading scientific discussions of near-death experiences (White, 1982).

The Changing Nature of Advice

Review of our extracts from articles and books according to year of publication suggested trends in the ways authors have written about retirement issues. Although not clearly delineated, there appeared to be differences when comparing materials published before and after the mid-1970s.

Authors discussing communication in books published before the mid-1970s endorsed frankness and openness, but for the most part, they did not suggest looking at underlying emotional issues at the root of communication problems. In general, their advice was to forgive and forget, and then to establish improved patterns of communication (e.g., Legler, 1967; Ott, 1971).

Later authors no longer advised couples to "say something nice." Rather, emotional issues tended to be perceived as causes of ineffective communication. Weitzman (1978), for example, wrote that retirement may trigger tension and anger in the marital relationship that can lead to withdrawal from mutual activities:

> Rejection is a form of aggression, as are dominance and manipulation, all of which can be avoided with direct communication. (pp. 198-199)

Similarly, Fromme (1980) warned against scapegoating the spouse in response to the stress of retirement. Finkelhor (1978) advised each partner to become aware of his or her own positive and negative steps in reaching emotional maturity—a necessity for good communication. Only mature partners can pool personal resources to strengthen their relationship.

Only after the mid-1970s did sexuality emerge as an significant aspect of the marital relationship between retired spouses. Previously, as noted earlier, few authors referred to sex, and little advice was given. In one of the few early references to sexuality, Collins (1973), in an advice column for *Retirement Living,* answered a husband whose wife wanted to "retire" from sex by supporting the wife's position, suggesting that sexual expression is inappropriate for aging women:

> You're not bragging are you? Some wives put sex on the shelf by age 35 or in their 40's. While nobody knows for sure what goes on in bedrooms, it would seem not unnatural for a wife to choose knitting at 65. (p. 9)

In contrast to the previous comment, later authors recognized the desirability and capability of maintaining an active sexual relationship until very old age. As noted, several authors extolled the warmth and emotional closeness engendered by caressing and touching (Finkelhor, 1978; Lord, 1970; Staley & Singleton, 1976).

In a more global vein, popular literature published before the mid-1970s tended to view retirement solely as the husband's concern. His plans should, of course, be communicated to his wife and should be "blessed" by her. Collins (1970), for example, advised husbands to inform their wives about the details of retirement as a way of educating them and including them in the process. He suggested that the husband take his wife to the Social Security office to have her checks made out in her own name, even though "she is probably going to endorse them and turn them over to you anyway" (p. 75). In all, retirement was considered a masculine turning point. Buckley (1974) wrote:

> Though her life will be changed, it will not be as changed as his. He will need understanding and sympathy because his whole way of life is changed. (p. 13)

To today's readers, the tenor of such advice demonstrates more than a modicum of sexist prejudice. Women seem to be regarded as childlike innocents who have to be "educated" by husbands, whose social status wholly determines their own standing in the community. Yet, it was the women who were admonished to support husbands through the initial phases of retirement adjustments, presumably subordinating their own needs to their husbands'.

Authors writing after the mid-1970s tended to treat retirement (albeit still the husbands' retirement) as a major adjustment for wives as well as husbands. Husbands' reactions to retirement were seen as raising important issues for wives, who have personal issues with which to contend. Consistent with the sensibilities of the women's movement that emerged in the 1970s, wives were counseled to become accountable for their own adjustment and for fulfilling their own needs within retirement relationships. In a book specifically targeted to women, Friedman and Nussbaum (1986) advocated self-expression and development of autonomy for women, as part of taking responsibility for personal happiness.

Academic and Popular Literature

Since the early 1960s, a small but expanding body of academic literature has investigated the marital relationship in retirement. The focus of research studies has varied, with task sharing in the household a primary concern, as is marital quality in the wake of retirement and retirement satisfaction and attitudes.

The hypothesis underlying many of these studies is that retirement causes marital strain as spouses realign their roles. As a whole, however, the research literature has not found that retirement often prompts dramatic changes in relationships or in role behavior. For example, findings concerning household tasks have confirmed that retired husbands generally increase their share of domestic activities, but that couples tend to maintain a traditional division of responsibility, with the wife's burden remaining substantially the same (Brubaker & Hennon, 1982; Dorfman, 1992; Keith, Dobson, Goudy, & Powers, 1981; Szinovacz, 1980). One study found that the majority of couples increased participation in leisure activities together, but that the level of participation in social activities and in personal without-spouse leisure pursuits most often remained at the same level pre- to postretirement (Vinick & Ekerdt, in press).

Almost without exception, interviews with husbands and wives and results of various measurement techniques have not revealed decreased marital satisfaction following husbands' retirement (e.g., Atchley, 1992; Dressler, 1973; Ekerdt & Vinick, 1991; Keating & Cole, 1980; Szinovacz, 1980). Some small-sample studies have found substantial proportions of wives who regret their husbands' retirement (Fengler, 1975; Heyman & Jeffers, 1968), but a consensus has emerged that the prevalence of marital discord as the direct result of retirement is relatively minor. In the course of almost 200 interviews with retired husbands and their wives, we encountered only a few couples for whom retirement provoked serious marital problems that were not there before the husband's retirement (Vinick & Ekerdt, 1991a). At the same time, some couples had long-standing issues in their relationships that prevented them from experiencing retirement as a satisfying time in their lives.

The factors shown to contribute to conjugal satisfaction in retirement are those well known to predict retirement adaptation of individuals—sufficient health and income and a supportive social network. Some studies (Dorfman & Hill, 1986; Hill & Dorfman, 1982; Keating & Cole, 1980; Vinick & Ekerdt, 1991b) have qualitatively described the advantages and difficulties couples have encountered in retirement. For example, it was not unusual for women to feel "hemmed in" by their husbands' increased presence in the home when husbands first retire. Such feelings were not considered by respondents to be greatly consequential in terms of marital quality, however, and generally were short lived (Vinick and Ekerdt, 1991b). In all, current academic findings have converged on the conclusion that retirement generally entails continuity and gratification.

The popular literature, however, presents a different picture. Nearly all of the sources that we reviewed emphasized not the possible gratifications of retirement, but its potential stressfulness. Advice books and articles tended to focus on the problems of daily life, the things that can go wrong, and the potential risks of certain actions. The overall message was upbeat as far as the prospect for positive adjustment by couples, but the genre abounds with warnings and examples of situations to recognize and avoid, which become the occasions for authors' advice.

As portrayed in the popular literature, retirement brings dramatic changes as the man ends his working life and turns to other pursuits. He has spent much of his adult life dedicating himself to a career that has provided him with an identity as well as security. Popularly, this change is described as a demotion, a time of confusing reorientation, when a man loses the status and identity afforded him by his career (e.g., Butcher, 1978). In a portrayal closer to academic findings, Willing (1981) noted wives' disorientation at husbands' intrusion.

> It's like having your husband crawl into bed after you have long since gotten comfortably settled down. All at once there is a pushing and tugging at the blankets, such turnings and poundings on the pillow, that you can never get back into the original position that felt so good. (p. 91)

At the very least, the husband's retirement is viewed as a time of major adjustment, one in which the relationship will change and arrive at a new point of stabilization.

DISCUSSION

Content analysis of popular books and articles on the subject of marriage and retirement has revealed that retirement—with few exceptions—has meant *husbands'* retirement. The research literature, too, has generally confined itself to the marital impact of husbands' retirement. As more women retire from the labor force, there is a need for more recognition of women's retirement in both academic and popular publications.

Academic research found that retirement entails adjustment by couples, but that it often does not represent a crisis. By contrast, the advice given to couples in the popular literature presumes considerable marital stress at the time of retirement. For the most part, however, recommendations focusing on togetherness and autonomy, communication, sexual intimacy, level of activity, and the onset of late life were (especially in more recent publications) worthwhile and clinically appropriate. The possibility of growth and positive change, even in unsatisfactory relationships of long duration, was a notable feature of much of the advice. The disparity found in the content of academic and popular publications was related not so much to the accuracy of information presented as to the overall emphasis of the material. The impression conveyed to the popular reader is that although the transition to retirement can be successful for everyone, it almost inevitably involves pain.

Our study of couples in retirement, cited earlier, included a panel of couples in which husbands were at or approaching retirement age, but still working. We frequently heard concerns about impending retirement similar to issues raised in the popular press. Couples worried about their financial future, whether they both would be healthy, whether the husband would have enough to do, and whether he would be "underfoot" (Vinick & Ekerdt, 1989). A few near-retirees indicated concerns about growing old and dying. One man, for example, stated that "the end of the tunnel [was] getting closer," and he was frightened.

Overall, it is difficult to say whether images of retirement raised in the popular press create or mirror couples' preconceptions. That correspondence exists, however, is less open to question. Moreover, it seemed quite obvious that advice reflects societal norms, as evidenced by the change over time from the perception of women as nurturers of husbands' adaptation to individuals responsible for their own well-being and the change in the view of sexuality from being less appropriate than knitting to being a wellspring of marital happiness in later life.

Based on couples' reports of concerns and apprehensions prior to retirement, topics presented in the popular press address relevant issues and are, therefore, appropriate in that sense. To the extent that potential problems are overemphasized and images of retirement difficulties overdrawn, the main drawback is that apprehensions may be confirmed unnecessarily.

The major benefit of the popular literature may be in stimulating discussion and thought as part of the process of preparing for retirement. Similarly, although less valuable to the majority of couples in which husbands have already retired, some of the information and advice contained in popular books and articles could no doubt be useful to couples experiencing difficulties in retirement.

Clinicians and counselors should be aware that the popular emphasis on the stress of couples' transition into retirement may be more hyperbole than reality. Although retirement requires some adaptive behavior on the part of spouses in most cases, the distress commonly portrayed as the accompaniment to retirement may be far less typical than usually depicted. As the body of knowledge continues to grow, authors whose advice is consumed by the public should be aware of balancing views of retirement as a time of marital crisis with those who conceive of retirement in terms of continuation of the long-term marital relationship.

Endnote

This chapter is an example of document analysis, which has a long and hallowed tradition in qualitative family research. Thomas and Znaniecki (1927), in *The Polish Peasant in Europe and America,* used a wide range of documents on which to base their landmark work, the first widely recognized piece of qualitative family research. (See Handel, Chapter 2, this volume.) Contemporary examples of work based on document analysis are Rosenblatt (1983) and LaRossa, Gordon, Wilson, Bairan, and Jaret (1991). Other significant writings on document analysis include Blumer (1939), Denzin (1978), Gottschalk, Kluckhohn, and Angell (1951), Mariampolski and Hughes (1978), Plummer (1983), and Thernstrom (1965).

REFERENCES

Alpert, H. (1974). Readers point best way to successful retirement. *Retirement Living, 14*, 27-29.

Atchley, R. (1992). Retirement and marital satisfaction. In M. Szinovacz, D. J. Ekerdt, & B. H. Vinick (Eds.), *Families and retirement* (pp. 145-158). Newbury Park, CA: Sage.

Blumer, H. (1939). *An appraisal of Thomas and Znaniecki's "The Polish Peasant in Europe and America."* New York: Social Science Research Council.

Bromberg, J. (1981). Retirement: Boredom or bliss? *Aging, 317*, 17-21.

Brubaker, T. H., & Hennon, C. B. (1982). Responsibility for household tasks: Comparing dual-earner and dual-retired marriages. In M. Szinovacz (Ed.), *Women's retirement: Policy implications of recent research.* Beverly Hills, CA: Sage.

Buckley, J. C. (1974). *The retirement handbook.* New York: Harper & Row.

Butcher, L. (1978). *Retirement without fear.* Princeton, NJ: Dow Jones Books.

Butler, R. (1979). Choosing a lifestyle—a look at five ways. *U.S. News and World Report, 86*, 59-62.

Caraher, J. (1981). Ramblings of a successful failure in retirement. *Aging, 317*, 12-16.

Collins, T. (1970). *The complete guide to retirement.* Englewood Cliffs, NJ: Prentice-Hall.

Collins, T. (1973). Inquiring about retirement. *Retirement Living, 13*(6), 9.

Denzin, N. K. (1978). *The research act.* New York: McGraw-Hill.

Dickinson, P. A. (1981). Practical answers to personal questions about retirement planning. *Aging, 317*, 4-11.

Dorfman, L. T. (1992). Couples in retirement: Division of household work. In M. Szinovacz, D. J. Ekerdt, & B. H. Vinick (Eds.), *Families and retirement* (pp. 159-173). Newbury Park, CA: Sage.

Dorfman, L. T., & Hill, E. A. (1986). Rural housewives and retirement: Joint decision-making matters. *Family Relations, 35*, 507-514.

Dressler, D. M. (1973). Life adjustment of retired couples. *International Journal of Aging and Human Development, 4*, 335-348.

Ekerdt, D. J., & Vinick, B. H. (1991). Marital complaints in husband-working and husband-retired couples. *Research on Aging, 13*, 356-382.

Fengler, A. P. (1975). Attitudinal orientation of wives toward their husbands' retirement. *International Journal of Aging and Human Development, 6*(2), 139-152.

Finkelhor, D. C. (1978). *The triumph of age: How to feel young and happy in retirement.* Chicago: Follette.

Friedman, R., & Nussbaum, A. (1986). *Coping with your husband's retirement.* New York: Simon & Schuster.

Fromme, A. (1980, September). Don't make your spouse a scapegoat. *Fifty Plus*, pp. 60-61.

Gottschalk, L. C., Kluckhohn, C., & Angell R. (1951). *The use of personal documents in history, anthropology, and sociology.* New York: Social Science Research Council.

Hershey, J., & Hershey, R. (1969). *These rich years: A journal of retirement.* New York: Scribner.

Heyman, D. K., & Jeffers, F. C. (1968). Wives and retirement: A pilot study. *Journal of Gerontology, 23*(4), 488-496.

Hill, E. , & Dorfman, L. T. (1982). Reactions of housewives to the retirement of their husbands. *Family Relations, 31,* 195-200.

Keating, N., & Cole, P. (1980). What do I do with him 24 hours a day? Changes in the housewife role after retirement. *Gerontologist, 20,* 84-89.

Keith, P. M., Dobson, C. D., Goudy, W. J., & Powers, E. A. (1981). Older men: Occupation, employment status, household involvement, and well-being. *Journal of Family Issues, 2, 336-349.*

Krippendorf, K. (1980). *Content analysis: An introduction to its methodology.* Newbury Park, CA: Sage.

LaRossa, R., Gordon, B.A., Wilson, R.J., Bairan, A., & Jaret, C. (1991). The fluctuating image of the 20th century American father. *Journal of Marriage and the Family, 53,* 987-997.

Legler, H. (1967). *How to make the rest of your life the best of your life.* New York: Simon & Schuster.

Lindeman, B. (1986, April). Retirement: You've got to work at it. *Fifty Plus,* pp. 6-7.

Lord, S. (1970, June). How to live with your husband when he retires. *Harpers Bazaar,* pp. 104-105.

Mariampolski, H., & Hughes, D. C. (1978). The use of personal documents in historical sociology. *American Sociologist, 13,* 104-113.

Ott, E. (1971). *Retirement rehearsal guidebook.* Indianapolis, IN: Pictoral.

Perlmutter, E. R. (1981). Retirement blues. *Aging, 317,* 22-25.

Plummer, K. (1983). *Documents of life: An introduction to the problems and literature of a humanistic method.* London: George Allen & Unwin.

Rice, C. (1969, May). Retirement: Dangerous time for marriages? *Harvest Years,* pp. 46-48.

Rosenblatt, P. (1983). *Bitter, bitter tears.* Minneapolis: University of Minnesota Press.

Staley, M., & Singleton, R. (1976). *How to retire and love it.* Cleveland, OH: Uniline.

Szinovacz, M. (1980). Female retirement: Effects on spousal roles and marital adjustment. *Journal of Family Issues, 3,* 423-438.

Tesch, R. (1990). *Qualitative research: Analysis types and software tools.* Philadelphia: Taylor & Francis.

Thernstrom, S. (1965). Yankee City revisited: The perils of historical naivete. *American Sociological Review, 39,* 234-242.

Thomas, W. I., & Znaniecki, F. (1927). *The Polish peasant in Europe and America.* New York: Knopf.

Vinick, B. H., & Ekerdt, D. J. (1989). Reports of couples in the first year of retirement: Pleasures and peeves. *Retirement Planning, 15,* 13-17.

Vinick, B. H., & Ekerdt, D. J. (1991a). Retirement: What happens to husband-wife relationships? *Journal of Geriatric Psychiatry, 24*(1), 23-40.

Vinick, B. H., & Ekerdt, D. J. (1991b). The transition to retirement: Responses of husbands and wives. In B. Hess & E. Markson (Eds.), *Aging in America* (4th ed., pp. 305-317). New Brunswick, NJ: Transaction Books.

Vinick, B. H., & Ekerdt, D. J. (in press). The transition to retirement among married couples: Satisfaction and changes in activities. In M. Featherstone (Ed.), *Proceedings of the Future of Adult Life 2nd International Conference.* Middlesbrough, UK: Teeside Polytechnic.

Ware, G. (1960). *The new guide to happy retirement.* New York: Appleton-Century-Crofts.

Weber, R. P. (1985). *Basic content analysis.* Beverly Hills, CA: Sage.

Weitzman, H. (1978). *The retirement day book.* Radnor, PA: Chilton.

When your husband retires. (1968, July). *Changing Times,* pp. 39-40.

White, F. J. (1982, February). Ready for the role changes of retirement? *Christianity Today,* pp. 34-36.

Willing, J. Z. (1981). *The reality of retirement: The inner experience of being retired.* New York: William Morrow.

Zinsser, J. (1986, September). Retirement in focus: Getting the most out of your challenge. *Fifty Plus,* pp. 74-75.

Part 5

Combined Qualitative and Quantitative Approaches

Given the multifaceted nature of what we need to know in the social scientific study of families, the combined use of qualitative and quantitative methods is often an appropriate means by which to capture this complexity. In Chapter 15, Mark Rank presents compelling arguments for combining both quantitative and qualitative methods. He successively used participant observation, a quantitative analysis of prospective, longitudinal case record data, and semistructured interviews to understand the dynamics of childbearing among welfare recipients. Qualitative data are used to provide a number of possible explanations for the quantitative results that indicate a low rate of fertility for women on welfare. The chapter by Margarete Sandelowski, Diane Holditch-Davis, and Betty Glenn Harris blends a variety of methods to capture the complexity of transitions to parenthood for infertile couples. They use both selective and theoretical sampling, observation with parent-child triads and interviewing with couples, symptom inventories, longitudinal assessments, and the quantification of the verbal, observational, and self-report data. They also are attentive to the myriad uses of theory and methodological principles in research—as orienting frameworks for the inquiry and for viewing subjects, as a point of reference for comparison of findings, and as a product of analysis.

The Blending of Qualitative and Quantitative Methods in Understanding Childbearing Among Welfare Recipients

MARK R. RANK
Washington University, St. Louis

Perhaps the place to begin is with a personal story. Some time ago I was revising a manuscript on families receiving welfare. The article combined qualitative and quantitative data. One reviewer had been positive about the blending of methods. The other suggested eliminating the qualitative material altogether. While I was attempting to resolve these differences, a colleague of mine stopped by, and I quickly sought his advice to the problem. His solution was simple—write two different papers. One paper could present the qualitative data, the other the quantitative data. I tried to explain how one of the main contributions of my work, as I saw it, was bringing several methods to bear in the same analysis. I argued for the insights to be gained, the greater validity of the findings, and so on. My arguments were to no avail. With a shrug, he wished me good luck and said I would need it for the reviewers who lay ahead.

AUTHOR'S NOTE: I would like to express my appreciation to the editors of this volume for their helpful suggestions. In addition, I would like to thank Peter Adler, Alan Bryman, Greer Fox, Kathleen Gilbert, and David Gillespie for their insightful comments on earlier drafts.

This chapter expands upon the arguments presented to my colleague that summer afternoon. The purpose is to demonstrate the use of a multiple-method approach to address family research questions—specifically the blending of qualitative with quantitative data. My research on families receiving welfare is used to demonstrate the processes and types of analysis that can result from applying this technique to family research questions. The arguments and examples in this chapter are an extension and illustration of more general work advocating triangulation in constructing research designs (e.g., Brewer & Hunter, 1989; Bryman 1988a; Denzin, 1978). The arguments are applied here, however, to family researchers interested in combining qualitative and quantitative approaches.

A scanning of family journals and books reveals an exceedingly low number of studies relying on both qualitative and quantitative data. Yet, such an approach has the potential for improvements in the construction, execution, and analysis of family research designs. Interestingly, a number of early studies dealing with family issues combined qualitative and quantitative data in their research designs and analyses. As Cavan (1983) and LaRossa and Wolf (1985) noted, much of the family research that came out of the University of Chicago during the 1920s and 1930s employed both quantitative and qualitative data analyses. The work of Burgess, Cavan, Frazier, and others were reflective of this. There was a concern with "how qualitative methods and quantitative methods could complement each other" (LaRossa & Wolf, 1985, p. 534). Likewise, the Lynds' (1929, 1937) Middletown studies were characterized by a blending of methodologies: Surveys, interviews, and ethnographic data were used in conjunction with each other to portray a picture of life in Middletown and its families.

Beginning in the later 1930s, family researchers increasingly turned to the survey as their method of choice (e.g., Burgess & Cottrell, 1939; Terman, 1938). Although survey research had been used prior to this time, it quickly became the dominant and sole method for many family researchers. This trend characterized not only family research, but the social sciences as a whole (Kalton, 1983). With a greater use of survey methods, data analysis began to rely heavily upon quantitative and statistical techniques. Reviews of family research methods note that the past 30 years have seen a trend toward greater quantification and more elaborate statistical methods (Galligan, 1982; Hodgson & Lewis, 1979; Miller, 1986; Nye, 1988). Both LaRossa and Wolfe (1985) and Nye (1988) documented that most articles published by family researchers became exclusively quantitative. Certainly, qualitative family studies were conducted during this time as well (e.g., Komarovsky, 1962; LeMasters, 1975; Ostrander, 1984; Stack, 1974). Yet these studies constituted a small percentage of the total research output. Research projects employing both qualitative and quantitative data were rarer still.

What might account for the avoidance of combining qualitative and quantitative data in family research over the past 30 years? First, some, like Filstead (1979) and Rist (1977), argue that quantitative and qualitative research are based upon fundamentally incompatible epistemological positions. Thus, many researchers view them as mutually exclusive research models (Bryman 1988a). Second, the tendency to follow the natural scientific paradigm often precludes the use of qualitative methods for anything other than exploratory research (Miller, 1986). Third, cost may be an obstacle. Bringing several methods to bear upon a specific issue can be expensive (Bryman 1988b). A fourth potential obstacle is the perceived difficulty in publishing such research. Researchers may feel they are leaving themselves open to unnecessary criticisms from reviewers who take either a quantitative or qualitative approach. Finally, the training of family researchers has been heavily weighted towards quantitative methods. Such training may result in a reluctance to combine various methodologies (Reiss, 1968).

Although these obstacles are real, there are significant advantages for family researchers in integrating qualitative and quantitative methods into their research designs. To illustrate this, I first will describe a research project blending qualitative and quantitative data. Next, I will discuss several specific findings of this study to illustrate the types of analysis possible from blending qualitative and quantitative data. Finally, I will examine at length the advantages of executing such a design and analysis.

STUDY DESIGN

Various research designs could be constructed for integrating qualitative and quantitative data. Elsewhere I have discussed the techniques of embedding in-depth interviews within random sample surveys, adding survey research to fieldwork, and using targeted small-scale research with available records (Rank 1988a). In this chapter, I describe a study of families receiving public assistance in which both qualitative and quantitative data were gathered. I used three separate yet complementary sources of data in this project. All three sources deal with a similar population. The emphases in each data set, however, clearly differ. The quantitative analysis of case record data was longitudinal and designed for statistical modeling of various events, with in-depth interviews and fieldwork providing greater insight into these and other events. Each is described below.

Data Gathering From Case Records

In 1980, administration of the Aid to Families With Dependent Children (AFDC), Food Stamp, and Medicaid programs in the state of Wisconsin was computerized. Those applying for one or more of the three programs are required to fill out a combined application form. The information is entered into a mainframe computer, stored, and updated with periodic reviews.

As the universe of welfare recipients is contained in this data base, it was relatively easy and inexpensive to draw a large, random sample of households on public assistance. I drew a 2% random sample of all cases that were participating in one or more of these three welfare programs as of September 1980. This resulted in a sample of 2,796 households. There was no refusal rate, as case records rather than actual individuals were sampled.

The cases were then followed at 6-month intervals for 3 years, through September 1983. The variables available in these files were primarily economic and demographic, including information on heads of household as well as all other household members. In addition, as family, economic, and welfare status changes occurred, such information was updated in the case records, allowing for a detailed analysis of specific events occurring to families while on welfare. Such events included length of welfare recipiency, changes in household structure, and shifts in employment status.

In-Depth Qualitative Interviews

During June and July 1986, I gathered qualitative data through in-depth interviews of welfare recipients. In drawing this sample, I used procedures similar to those used in drawing the longitudinal case record sample. The sample was stratified by household type and welfare eligibility status. Of interest were families both on and recently off welfare. Because the interviews were face to face, it was impractical to take a random sample of the entire state, given the cost and time constraints involved. I chose a representative county with characteristics reflecting the overall state population on such factors as urban and rural areas, occupational diversity, race, and socioeconomics.

The response rate was 76%. This represents the number of interviews conducted, divided by all households we attempted to locate, whether contact was made or not. For those we were able to contact, the refusal rate was 5%. Individuals without telephones were tracked down. We conducted several interviews in Spanish with the aid of an interpreter. In short, I used a variety of ways to contact potential subjects. Participating respondents were paid $15.

A research assistant and I interviewed 50 families along with five families in the pretest. By design, the demographic composition of the sample approximately mirrored that of the longitudinal data set. We conducted the interviews in respondents' homes. Length of interviews was between 1-1/2 and 3 hours. All interviews were tape-recorded. For female-headed families and single welfare recipients, the heads of households were interviewed. For married couples, we attempted to interview both the husband and wife together. In several cases, however, we were only able to interview the wife.

At the outset of each interview, we informed respondents there were no right or wrong answers to the questions being asked. Our concern was in understanding their honest appraisals of their feelings, experiences, and behaviors. In addition, we stated that our affiliation was university based, and that we were not a part of the welfare system or administration. We also stated verbally and in writing that all responses would be confidential.

Most respondents appeared open and frank about their feelings and behaviors. For example, respondents would often volunteer information about sensitive subjects (e.g., incest, violence in the family, painful childhoods). They often expressed genuine emotion. Overall, rapport between interviewers and interviewees was excellent. This was assessed in two ways. First, after each interview, my assistant and I recorded our evaluations of the rapport during the interview. Second, I also assessed rapport by listening to each interview several times.

The interviews were open ended and semistructured around such major topics as attitudes regarding welfare, family dynamics (such as marriage, divorce, pregnancy, and raising children), employment, and the experience of getting on and off public assistance. Based on my prior research and knowledge of the field, the interview schedule was constructed to cover what I felt were the most critical areas in under- standing a family's situation of being on public assistance. As a reli- ability check on the answers given during the interviews, information from respondents' case records, which the state had made available to me, was compared to information given during the interviews. The match was high, thus lending confidence in the interview data.

In addition to the interviews, I kept notes describing the settings in which the interviews took place, the recipient's dwelling, the surround- ing neighborhoods, the rapport during the interview, the physical ap- pearance of the recipient, and any other information that might provide greater understanding of respondents' situations. Photographs were taken of recipients who gave their consent. The interviews were tran- scribed verbatim into files on a mainframe computing system. Each transcript was triple checked with the original tape for accuracy.

Fieldwork

A third source of data was through fieldwork in which I explored observable aspects of welfare systems. The fieldwork took place be- tween 1986 and 1988. It occurred almost entirely in the same county as the in-depth qualitative interviews. I took extensive field notes, which served as a third source of data. I observed several aspects of the welfare system, beginning with visiting various social service offices and sitting in on the process of applying for public assistance. Offices were located in both urban and rural locations and served a wide range of individuals and families. I then attended several job-training programs that were manda- tory for welfare recipients. The programs were designed to increase the likelihood of locating and landing employment. I also observed the daily routines and activities in low-income housing projects and neighborhoods and a wide variety of food pantries. Toward the end of the month, welfare recipients often rely on emergency food from food pantries.

I relied on other sources of data as well. Throughout the fieldwork, I spoke with dozens of individuals associated with the welfare system. These included both welfare recipients and those dealing directly with welfare recipients, such as case workers, state employees, and volun- teers. To keep a visual record of various aspects of welfare systems, I also took photographs.

CHILDBEARING DYNAMICS AMONG
WELFARE RECIPIENTS

The issue of family dynamics among welfare recipients has been debated long and hard among policymakers. Within these debates is an underlying fear that welfare contributes to the breakdown of families and, more specifically, encourages families to become dependent upon public assistance, women to have more children, and marriages to dissolve (Gilder, 1981; Murray, 1984; Working Group on the Family, 1986). I have addressed these issues in a number of studies, examining patterns of welfare recipiency by household structure (Rank, 1985, 1986), probabilities of marriage and dissolution (Rank, 1987), and differences in exiting from welfare for black and white female-headed families (Rank, 1988b).

The Fertility of Women on Welfare

The fertility among women on welfare has been the subject of controversy for many years. How often do women receiving welfare give birth? Is their fertility rate higher or lower than that of the general population? What factors are related to childbearing for women on welfare? Although such questions have been frequently asked, no single study has provided a satisfactory answer. As a result, I became interested in exploring these issues. (See Rank, 1989.) The analysis described here illustrates how qualitative and quantitative data can be brought to bear upon such questions. The analysis also demonstrates how the research process moves between qualitative and quantitative data. As described below, I began with qualitative insights from the fieldwork, shifted to a quantitative analysis of the caseload sample, and then returned to qualitative interviews for further investigation.

Preliminary Insights Through Fieldwork

Fieldwork began the research process. The interviews I conducted with persons working in the welfare system provided opportunities to begin an examination of fertility and welfare. Through informal discussions, I was able to explore the perceptions of those in daily contact with welfare recipients as well as with recipients themselves. During these discussions, I began to view critically the stereotype of women on welfare bearing more children to get larger public assistance payments. That is, although caseworkers and recipients could point to individual examples fitting such a stereotype, they believed most women on welfare did not wish to have more children but rather wanted to get off public assistance. These observations provided me with preliminary insights that pushed me to delve further. I wondered whether these perceptions reflected the reality of the situation or perhaps something else. If they were correct assessments, why did the stereotype not hold up?

Incidence and Rates

As a result of the fieldwork, I decided to address several questions using the longitudinal quantitative data. Among these questions were, first: What was the likelihood of childbearing among women on welfare? And, second: How did these rates compare with those of the general population?

The Likelihood of Childbearing

Table 15.1 presents a life table analysis of childbearing among women on welfare aged 18 to 44. The life table allows us to calculate the proportion of women giving birth during a specified period of time.[1] The table lists the six observed half-year intervals during which women could enter into the analysis. The 0-6 month interval represents September 1980 to March 1981, the 6-12 month interval represents March 1981 to September 1981, and so on. Column 1 shows the number of women of childbearing age. I allowed women who had not been on welfare for 9 months prior to September 1980 to enter the analysis during the 6-12 or 12-18 month intervals. Column 2 presents the number of births occurring during intervals. Column 3 shows the proportion of births among women (Column 2 divided by Column 1), and Column 4 represents the cumulative proportion of births that occur across intervals.

During the first observed 6-month interval, 1.89% of women on welfare gave birth (Column 3). During the 6- to 12-month interval, 2.74% gave birth. The percentage giving birth during any 6-month interval is relatively stable at approximately 2%. In Column 4, it is estimated that 4.58% of women will give birth during a 1-year interval. The overall fertility rate for women on welfare, therefore, is 45.8 per 1,000 women on welfare. In addition, 11.49% of women will bear children during a 3-year period on welfare.[2]

Table 15.1   Life Table Analysis of Births Among Women Aged 18-44 on Welfare

Monthly Interval	Number at Risk	Number of Births	Proportion of Births	Cumulative Proportion of Births
0-6	795	15	.0189	.0189
6-12	950	26	.0274	.0458
12-18	910	22	.0242	.0689
18-24	717	12	.0167	.0844
24-30	624	13	.0208	.1035
30-36	553	7	.0127	.1149

Comparisons With the General Population

How do these estimates compare with the overall population? One-year fertility rates among women on welfare occurred from 1980 to 1981. Based on data from the Wisconsin Department of Health and Social Services (1981) and the U.S. Bureau of the Census (1981), the fertility rates in Wisconsin and the national population in 1980 per 1,000 women aged 18-44 were 75.3 (Wisconsin) and 71.1 (national population). These rates are considerably higher than the 1-year fertility rate of 45.8 for women on welfare. Consequently, women on welfare have a substantially lower fertility rate than women in the general population.

Yet, to what extent are these differences the result of differences across populations? For example, perhaps the demographic structure of the welfare population lends itself to a lower overall fertility rate. The key demographic differences between women on welfare and women in the general population (which can be controlled for) are race, marital status, parity, education, and age. Women on welfare are more likely to be black, unmarried, have at least one child, possess less education, and be in their 20s compared to women in the general population.

To account for these population differences, I standardized welfare fertility rates for the national and Wisconsin populations on the above characteristics.[3] In other words, if the welfare population had the same demographic makeup as the general population (in age, race, parity, marital status, and education), what would the fertility rate for women on welfare be? Table 15.2 indicates that when I standardized for age, children, marital status, race, or education, the fertility rates of women on welfare were still considerably below those of the national and Wisconsin populations. The lower overall fertility rate among women receiving public assistance programs is therefore not an artifact of a more favorable demographic structure. Rather, it clearly is lower even when major demographic factors are taken into account.

Finding Reasons Through In-Depth Interviews

The two tables indicate welfare recipients have a relatively low fertility rate, a rate considerably below that of women in the general population, and is not an artifact of a more favorable demographic structure. I then asked: Why is the rate of fertility among women on welfare relatively low? What accounts for these findings? At this point, I turned to the in-depth interviews, which were well suited for exploring the potential reasons behind the overall demographic patterns found in Tables 15.1 and 15.2. The interviews enabled women on welfare to construct their experiences and attitudes regarding pregnancy and childbirth. These experiences and attitudes shed considerable light on why fertility behavior appears to be suppressed. Twenty-nine of the 50 interviews were with female household heads or wives aged 18-44. Ages ranged from 18 to 43, with most women in their 20s or 30s. Two women were pregnant at the time of the interview. Most of the women had one or two children.

None of the 27 nonpregnant women wanted a child in the near future, and only a handful were considering having more children in the long term. Consistent with findings from the quantitative analysis and the fieldwork, women clearly wished to avoid childbearing. Several examples illustrate these attitudes and, more important, the reasons behind the attitudes. A 25-year-old separated woman was asked: "Do you think you'll ever want to have any more children?"

> No. No. I don't think that I ever [with emphasis] want to have another child. I think that will stop me from doing things that I want to do. And it won't be fair to me. It won't be fair for the new child. And it won't be fair at all for the two that I have.

A never-married woman in her early 30s with one child commented:

Table 15.2 Welfare Fertility Rates Standardized for Population Characteristics

Characteristics	Standardized for National Population Characteristics	Percentage Difference From National Rate	Standardized for Wisconsin Population Characteristics	Percentage Difference From Wisconsin Rate
Age	45.8	−35.6	48.3	−35.9
Children	50.2	−29.4	50.6	−32.8
Marital Status	53.1	−25.3	53.3	−29.2
Race	37.1	−47.8	34.3	−54.4
Education	37.7	−47.0	36.3	−51.8
	71.1—National Rate		75.3 —Wisconsin Rate	

Try to avoid the accidents now. I figure, well, it's bad enough . . . it's not bad enough . . . it's hardest to get by with one, let alone have another one just me by myself, you know. Trying to raise two.

Another example of not wanting more children was the following exchange that took place with a married couple aged 29 and 31:

Interviewer: Have you thought about having any more children?

Wife: [answers very quickly] No!

Husband: No! Not at all. . . . Never crossed our minds.

Interviewer: Could you say why?

Husband: Why? Nowadays you can't afford it. And three of them are enough. Yeah. Three of them. It's just right. Just the way it is.

When a 19-year-old woman with one child was asked if she had considered having any more children, she said:

Not quite yet. [laughs] I kinda thought about, you know, the age difference. I don't want it to be real far, but I'm not quite ready for another kid, financially or mentally. I don't think I could handle two kids. [laughs]

These examples illustrate several of the predominant feelings and attitudes of families who were interviewed. They provide a potential explanation for why the fertility rate of women on public assistance is relatively low. That is, the economic, social, and psychological situations in which women on welfare find themselves simply are not conducive to wanting more children. The women and their families perceived becoming pregnant and having a child as making the situation worse, not better.

Virtually all of the interviewed women also expressed the desire to get off public assistance. They saw another child as severely limiting the likelihood of escaping welfare dependence. A married woman in her late 20s was asked why she was planning not to have a third child. She said:

> I suppose mostly, it has to do with me. Depression is a factor. I just don't know that I can handle more than this. And also, I want to get on preparing for my own career. And I don't want to have to go back to square one and raise a child, and stay home with it again.

In the interviews, we directly addressed the issue of whether having additional children was motivated by wanting more money from welfare. The question was: "Did knowing that the welfare payments were there have anything to do with having another child?" Recipients overwhelming rejected this as an option. As one woman put it:

> Well, for one thing, with aid you don't get enough money to live on. I don't see how someone can do it. I know they keep having babies so they get more money. But then you got to take care of those babies. There's just no way for that to happen. Even if there was, I don't think I could do that. I'd have to be doing something.

A female head of household with two children said:

> I know a person says you get more money the more children you have, but then again they backfire because it doesn't work like that. You had more money, but you need more than what you got, because you're going to spend it.

Finally, a woman in her 30s responded quickly to the question of how much the additional money from welfare was a factor in her having children:

> Nothing. I've read a lot of studies about that, and they're not true. No. It had nothing to do with it. You know . . . having a child is very traumatic.

It's a very beautiful experience, but it's also very traumatic. And I suppose there are some women that just might have additional children to get an increase in money, but I would say that that's less than a very small percentage. Because you're committing yourself to anywhere from 15 to 20 years of your life to that individual. You're taking 9 months from the very beginning and doing all kinds of traumatic things to your body. So, no. That [more money from welfare] was not a consideration in having additional children.

A question about qualitative findings is the representativeness of quotes. In this study, 26 of the 27 nonpregnant women responded in a manner consistent with the attitudes reported here. The one exception was a married woman who stated that although she was not planning on having any more children (she was in her 40s), when she was in her early 20s and on welfare, she had had several children in order to collect greater welfare benefits.

Women often described their pregnancies as accidental. Several examples are typical of this pattern. A never-married woman in her mid-20s was questioned about her previous three pregnancies, all of which ended in abortion, and whether she had wanted to have a child.

Never. After that first time [her first pregnancy], my mom kept drilling into me about school and the importance of education and all. So that stuck with me all those years. And I always got pregnant through carelessness, you know. I kept saying, Well, when I get married one day and settle down and make sure my life is secure, then I'll have the children.

Another woman who had recently had a child was asked:

Interviewer: Was she planned? I mean, did you plan to get pregnant, or was it pretty much an accident?

Woman: It was an accident, because Tom and I had been only going out for like 3 months. And then I got pregnant.

A never-married women, aged 33, was asked about her only child:

Interviewer: Can you say, is there a reason why you got pregnant?

Woman: It was an accident [small laugh]. Put it that way [more laughter]. That was the only thing that happened. It was just one accident that happened. But, I don't regret it.

The two women who were pregnant at the time of the interviews stated that their pregnancies were accidental. When asked about becoming a parent, a 19-year-old, pregnant, never-married woman replied:

> I was a little nervous, and kind of scared because we didn't have the funds. We don't really have the money for it but. . . . We have a lot of people supporting us, like his family and his aunts and uncles and everybody. And my parents are kind of supportive about it.

She was then asked about her boyfriend's reaction to the pregnancy. She answered:

> Well, he's pretty scared because he doesn't have a job. And he's . . . he's been looking for quite awhile now, and he can't seem to find a job.

To summarize, the in-depth interviews suggested that the financial and social situations in which women on public assistance find themselves are not conducive to having additional children. These women appeared to be motivated by cost-benefit considerations. But it was the costs that outweighed the benefits, not vice versa. The economic, social, and psychological costs of becoming pregnant and having a child on public assistance are perceived as clearly outweighing the benefits. The economic and psychological stress that virtually all welfare recipients experienced exerted a powerful effect on women's fertility behavior. That effect was to lower the overall fertility rate.

From the point of view of public policy, these findings are significant. They indicate that receiving public assistance suppresses the likelihood of childbearing. Yet, policy analysts often implicitly accept the assumption that public assistance encourages women to have more children. For example, President Reagan's Working Group on the Family (1986) noted,

> Does the welfare system, particularly AFDC, give some women incentives to bear children? Statistical evidence does not prove those suppositions; and yet, even the most casual observer of public assistance programs understands that there is indeed some relationship between the availability of welfare and the inclination of many young women to bear fatherless children. (p. 35)

For women on public assistance, such beliefs simply are not supported by the analyses presented here.

DISCUSSION: ADVANTAGES OF
COMBINING METHODS

Complementary Nature

The term *complementary* is defined by Webster as "mutually support-ing each other's lack." The integration of qualitative and quantitative data fits such a description in that their strengths and weaknesses are largely opposite of each other. Methodologically speaking, a strong argument can be made for such an integration.

The strength of qualitative data lies in its richness and depth, as the chapters in this volume demonstrate. Field notes, verbatim transcripts from in-depth interviews, document analysis, and other qualitative data can provide a wealth of information. Furthermore, these approaches allow participants to structure the world as they see it, rather than as the analyst sees it. As a result, researchers are able to come to a deep understanding of a particular research topic.

However, if research goals include generalizing to a population with a probable estimated error, quantitative data derived from large random sampling is the more appropriate approach. Qualitative approaches do not lend themselves to studies of incidence and prevalence. (See Daly, Chapter 1, this volume.) Data gathered through random sampling of large populations obviously can describe the characteristics of a popu-lation as well as model statistically events and processes occurring within the population. When questionnaires and instruments are stan-dardized, researchers can argue for reliability.

Nevertheless, quantitative data from such studies reduce social or family processes to numbers. The results of these studies may suffer from superficiality to explain complex issues. Second, quantitative analyses seldom capture the overall context and underlying mecha-nisms behind predicted events—for example, why women on welfare have a relatively low fertility rate. Again, such outcomes often result from the reduction of social patterns into quantifiable categories. (See Jarrett, Chapter 10, this volume, for an extended discussion of these issues.) Third, biases may exist in how individuals respond to standard-ized questions as well as how they behave in an experimental situation, which consequently affects the quality of the data. Again, the issue is one of validity. In short, quantitative data tend to be strong in relation to reliability and generalizability. Yet, the validity surrounding such data may be questionable.

Depending upon the research question, therefore, qualitative and quantitative analyses can be complementary. In my study, by combining quantitative data from a large longitudinal sample with qualitative data from in-depth interviews and fieldwork, I was able to answer my research questions in ways that built upon the strengths of both approaches.

Additional Insights

A second advantage of blending qualitative and quantitative data in research design and analysis are the additional insights attained as result of such an integration. Like theoretical perspectives, specific methodological approaches are various ways of viewing and interpreting the world. They are not necessarily correct or incorrect, but rather they often grasp at different aspects of reality. Family researchers should be interested in understanding such multiple dimensions of reality. By bringing together both qualitative and quantitative data in an analysis, insights are gained that may have been unattainable without such an integration. As Denzin (1978) stated:

> Each method implies a different line of action toward reality—and hence each will reveal different aspects of it, much as a kaleidoscope, depending on how they are approached, held, and acted toward, different observations will be revealed. This is not to imply that reality has the shifting qualities of the colored prism, but that it too is an object that moves and that will not permit one interpretation to be stamped upon it. (pp. 292-293)

Bryman (1988a) discussed how combinations of methods can work together: "Quantitative research can establish regularities in social life while qualitative evidence can allow the processes which link the variables identified to be revealed" (p. 142). This is precisely the type of analysis I utilized in my own research study. The longitudinal quantitative data were ideal for describing and modeling specific events occurring to families on welfare (here, fertility rates). At the same time, the qualitative data acquired from in-depth interviews then provided insight and understanding into the mechanisms driving these events. By bringing together these disparate analyses, I was left with a richer understanding and insight into my research topic.

Increased Validity

A third advantage of combining quantitative and qualitative data is the potential increment in the validity of the study's findings. Assuming researchers discover consistent results across the qualitative and quantitative methods, such findings acquire a greater validity. As Webb, Campbell, Schwartz, and Sechrest (1966) stated, "When a hypothesis can survive the confrontation of a series of complementary methods of testing, it contains a degree of validity unattainable by one tested within the more constricted framework of a single method" (p. 174). Consistent findings across methods increase our confidence in the results. Assuming that the findings are consistent, the validity of the results acquired from integrating qualitative and quantitative data is enhanced.

In the analysis here, fieldwork generated serious doubts about the idea of women on welfare bearing large numbers of children. In the analysis of case records, I found women on welfare to have a relatively low fertility rate in comparison to other women. In the interviews, women emphasized they did not want to have more children. The data from these three approaches reinforced each other and enhanced the validity of the findings.

Pushing the Research Further

Surely, though, qualitative and quantitative results will not always be consistent with each other. Rather than a disadvantage, this can be seen as a fourth advantage or reason to combine such data. Researchers are faced with a dilemma when the qualitative and quantitative results appear at odds with each other. Which is the correct interpretation? Some may choose one over the other. Analysts who confront discrepancies head on, however, are likely to push their research one step further. By probing into the reasons behind such discrepancies, they may redirect the research process. Thus, as Bryman (1988a) stated, researchers could:

> Use the incongruent findings as a springboard for the investigation of the reasons for such contrasting findings. After all, since quantitative and qualitative research undertaken in the same investigation may provide mutually reinforcing results . . . the possibility of discrepant findings also exists. When there is evidence of a clash, further exploration of the issue would seem warranted. (p. 133)

Such exploration furthers research processes by redirecting both the hypotheses and the research design intended to test those hypotheses.

These, then, are several of the major advantages of gathering and integrating qualitative and quantitative methods. They include a strengthening of the research design and analysis through their complementary nature, greater acquired insight, enhanced validity, and the potential for redirecting the inquiry in positive and fruitful directions. When brought together, the blending of qualitative and quantitative methods provide a powerful tool for understanding the processes and dynamics behind family life.

NOTES

1. Analysis is confined to women aged 18 to 44, which is one of the two standard age brackets used for estimating fertility rates. This age bracket is used rather than 15 to 44 because there are very few women aged 15 to 17 who are heading households on welfare. Using either age bracket allows for a comparison of welfare fertility rates with the overall national and state rates.

The analysis pools married and unmarried women. This is standard procedure for calculating and reporting overall fertility rates of women. Marital status is taken into account in the aggregate comparisons, however.

The event being modeled in the life table analyses is the first observed spell of childbearing. Once a birth has occurred, women are no longer included in later time intervals. The numbers of women experiencing a birth are extremely small, which prevents a detailed analysis of the occurrence and determinants of a second observed birth.

Once women exit from the welfare rolls they are no longer included in the analysis even if they subsequently reenter the welfare system. Including such women distorts the representativeness of the sample. Separate analyses were also conducted including such women, however. No significant differences were found from the results presented here.

Finally, I included in the analysis all women who have been on welfare for at least 9 months. The reason for this is obvious. Some women may have entered the welfare system as the result of an upcoming birth. In these cases, cause and effect are reversed—a forthcoming birth leading to welfare use, rather than welfare use leading to birth. By including only women who have been receiving welfare for at least 9 months, this bias is eliminated.

2. Thus the average fertility rate over this period was 38.3. The 1-year rate of 45.8 is used for comparison purposes instead, however. To use a 3-year average distorts the representativeness of the sampled welfare population (e.g., longer-term cases are overrepresented).

3. These characteristics were categorized as follows: age (18-24, 25-29, 30-34, 35-39, 40-44); children (no children, one or more children); marital status (married-spouse present, not married); race (white, black); and education (less than 12 years, 12 or more years). The fertility rates for each of these categories were calculated for women on welfare. The rates were then multiplied by the proportion of women in each category for the

Wisconsin and national populations. This technique results in a direct standardization using the general population as the standard. (See Shyrock & Siegel, 1976.) The population proportions for the nation were based upon information from the U.S. Bureau of the Census (1981); the Wisconsin proportions were derived from the Wisconsin Department of Health and Human Services (1981) and the U.S. Bureau of the Census.

REFERENCES

Brewer, J., & Hunter, A. (1989). *Multimethod research.* Newbury Park, CA: Sage.

Bryman, A. (1988a). *Quantity and quality in social research.* London: Unwin Hyman.

Bryman, A. (1988b). Introduction: "Inside accounts" and social research in organizations. In A. Bryman (Ed.), *Doing research in organizations* (pp. 1-20). London: Routledge & Kegan Paul.

Burgess, E. W., & Cottrell, L.S., (1939). *Predicting success or failure in marriage.* Englewood Cliffs, NJ: Prentice-Hall.

Cavan, R. S. (1983). The Chicago school of sociology, 1918-1937. *Urban Life, 11,* 407-420.

Denzin, N. K. (1978). *The research act.* New York: Aldine.

Filstead, W. J. (1979). Qualitative methods: A needed perspective in evaluation research. In T. D. Cook & C. S. Reichardt (Eds.), *Qualitative and quantitative methods in evaluation research* (pp. 33-48). Beverly Hills, CA: Sage.

Galligan, R. J. (1982). Innovative techniques: Siren or rose. *Journal of Marriage and the Family, 44,* 875-886.

Gilder, G. (1981). *Wealth and poverty.* New York: Basic Books.

Hodgson, J. W., & Lewis, R. A. (1979). Pilgrim's progress III: A trend analysis of family theory and methodology. *Family Process, 18,* 163-173.

Kalton, G. (1983). *Introduction to survey sampling.* Beverly Hills, CA: Sage.

Komarovsky, M. (1962). *Blue-collar marriage.* New York: Random House.

LaRossa, R., & Wolf, J. H. (1985). On qualitative family research. *Journal of Marriage and the Family, 47,* 531-542.

LeMasters, E. E. (1975). *Blue-collar aristocrats.* Madison: University of Wisconsin Press.

Lynd, R. S., & Lynd, H. M. (1929). *Middletown: A study in American culture.* New York: Harcourt & Brace.

Lynd, R. S., & Lynd, H. M. (1937). *Middletown in transition: A study in cultural conflicts.* New York: Harcourt & Brace.

Miller, B. C. 1986. *Family research methods.* Beverly Hills, CA: Sage.

Murray, C. (1984). *Losing ground.* New York: Basic Books.

Nye, F. I. (1988). Fifty years of family research, 1937-1987. *Journal of Marriage and the Family, 50,* 569-584.

Ostrander, S. A. (1984). *Women of the upper class.* Philadelphia: Temple University Press.

Rank, M. R. (1985). Exiting from welfare: A life table analysis. *Social Service Review, 59,* 358-376.

Rank, M. R. (1986). Family structure and the process of exiting from welfare. *Journal of Marriage and the Family, 48,* 607-618.

Rank, M. R. (1987) The formation and dissolution of marriages in the welfare population. *Journal of Marriage and the Family, 49,* 15-20.

Rank, M. R. (1988a, November). *The blending of quantitative and qualitative data in family research.* Paper presented at the preconference workshop on Theory Construction and Research Methodology, National Council on Family Relations, Philadelphia, November 11-13.

Rank, M. R. (1988b). Racial differences in length of welfare use. *Social Forces, 66,* 1080-1101.

Rank, M. R. (1989). Fertility among women on welfare: Incidence and determinants. *American Sociological Review, 54,* 296-304.

Reiss, A. J. (1968). Stuff and nonsense about social surveys and participant observation. In H. S. Becker, B. Geer, D. Reisman, & R. S. Weiss (Eds.), *Institutions and the Person: Papers presented to Everett C. Hughes* (pp. 351-367). Chicago: Aldine.

Rist, R. C. (1977). On the relations among educational research paradigms: From disdain to detente. *Anthropology and Education Quarterly, 8,* 42-49.

Shyrock, H. S., & Siegel, J. S. (1976). *The methods and materials of demography.* New York: Academic Press.

Stack, C. B. (1974). *All our kin.* New York: Harper & Row.

Terman, L. M. (1938). *Psychological factors in marital happiness.* New York: McGraw-Hill.

U.S. Bureau of the Census. (1981). *Fertility of American women: June 1980* (Current Population Reports, Series P-20, No. 364). Washington, DC: U.S. Government Printing Office.

Webb, E., Campbell, D.T., Schwartz, R.D., & Sechrest, L. (1966). *Unobtrusive measures: Nonreactive research in the social sciences.* Chicago: Rand McNally.

Wisconsin Department of Health and Social Services. (1981). *Public health statistics: 1980.* Division of Health, Bureau of Health Statistics, Madison, WI.

Working Group on the Family. (1986). *The family: Preserving America's future.* Washington, DC: United States Department of Education, Office of the Under Secretary.

Using Qualitative and Quantitative Methods

The Transition to Parenthood of Infertile Couples

MARGARETE SANDELOWSKI
DIANE HOLDITCH-DAVIS
BETTY GLENN HARRIS
University of North Carolina at Chapel Hill

In 1987, we began a research program to study the transition to parenthood of infertile couples. The immediate purpose of the TTP Project was to describe the pregnancy, adoption waiting, and early parenting experiences of couples with fertility impairments. The long-term objective was to provide nurses and other health professionals with a theoretical basis for practice that was grounded in the lived experiences of infertility, biomedical conception, and adoption. Although infertility is currently a focus of family research, no studies have yet comprehensively investigated the experiences of infertility and biomedical conception over time. Moreover, historical developments since the 1970s,

AUTHORS' NOTE: The study was initially (1987-1988) funded by a Research Council Award from the University of North Carolina at Chapel Hill and was subsequently (1988-1993) funded by a grant from the National Center for Nursing Research, National Institutes of Health. We thank our research assistants, Beth Perry Black and Debra Miller; the project secretary, Geneva Knight; and, of course, the couples who participated in this study.

such as the declining availability of infants to adopt, delayed childbearing, and advancements in reproductive technology, have foregrounded new issues in adoption. Accordingly, we chose a naturalistic research design, as being well suited to exploring complex and sensitive phenomena about which little is known or that require fresh reexamination. In this chapter, we describe this project, using our results to date to foreground its distinctive methodological features.

RESEARCH DESIGN

The focal groups of study in the TTP Project were infertile couples who were expecting a child conceived spontaneously or through biotechnical means (including fertility drugs, artificial insemination, in vitro fertilization, and corrective surgery) or waiting to adopt a U.S. or foreign child. The comparison group used were couples with no histories of fertility impairments who were also expecting a child. Couples were recruited primarily through intermediaries in private physician practices, infertility treatment centers, adoption agencies, and infertility and adoption support groups; and also through advertising and personal referral.

Sampling

Sampling for the TTP Project was both selective (Schatzman & Strauss, 1973) and theoretical (Strauss, 1987). Selective sampling refers to a decision made prior to beginning a study to sample subjects according to a preconceived, but reasonable initial set of criteria. Theoretical sampling refers to a sampling decision made on analytic grounds developed in the course of a study. Within any one research project, selective sampling typically precedes theoretical sampling for several reasons. First, neither human subject committees nor funding agencies are likely to approve a research proposal without a clear specification of the kinds of subjects desired for a study. Second, investigators never begin any inquiry with no idea of the kind of subject most likely to provide information about the phenomenon being studied. Although naturalistic inquiry typically mandates that investigators suspend their commitments to a priori views of this phenomenon, it also requires that they be explicit about what those views are at the outset of a study. Projecting a sampling framework at the beginning of a study is one way in which investigators clarify their assumptions and orientations early in the inquiry process. Finally, selective sampling permits the researcher to develop the hunches and conceptual lines that will ultimately drive theoretical sampling (Charmaz, 1990). We illustrate a theoretical sampling decision later in the chapter.

In the TTP Project, where lists of potential subjects' names were not available and for ethical reasons direct contact with subjects in agencies and private practices was not possible, we initially outlined for the intermediaries assisting us the kinds of couples we required and provided them with "Dear Couple" letters of introduction. As couples responded, they were included in the study. Given the varying availability of subjects and the long-term commitment required of them by a study like the TTP Project, it was not always possible to recruit particular subjects at the time and analytic place in the study when they were most needed. We could not simply decide where to turn to next in sampling and then expect to do so, as implied in texts on theoretical sampling. We had to wait for the subjects we wanted to respond to the letters of introduction.

We selected recruitment sites that were most likely to have the subjects we were initially seeking. We made an a priori decision to recruit subjects from sites providing a variety of medical and adoption services. Because couples using these services tend to be white, married, and in a middle- to upper-income group, we decided to maintain this homogeneity in race, class, and marital status and for the purposes of comparison sought expectant couples with these same background characteristics, but with no fertility impairments. Although infertility affects individuals of all races and income levels, we decided to maintain homogeneity in these background characteristics to limit the numbers of couples we would have to recruit for both theoretical and statistical purposes. The feasibility and meaningfulness of any one research project are dependent on setting reasonable (although admittedly always arbitrary) limits on who and what will be studied.

Maximizing Variability

In contrast, we sought to maximize the variability in fertility status by recruiting couples with a wide range of fertility and parenting experiences. This selective sampling strategy was modified by theoretical sampling as the project proceeded. We started with an a priori view of variability in fertility that was largely based on conventional classification systems (including diagnostic and treatment categories). As a consequence of the analytic work we completed, we found a different way to group couples that was based on their own (as opposed to medical) explanations of infertility. Couples used two referents—the *presence* or *absence* of a desired pregnancy or child and the *timing* of these events in relation to their infertility—to explain their current fertility situations (Sandelowski, Holditch-Davis, & Harris, 1990). We discerned five patterns of explanation: (a) *once fertile always fertile,* (b) *once infertile always infertile,* (c) *fertile but infertile by prescription,* (d) *pregnancy as cure for infertility,* and (e) *infertile enough but not proven infertile.* For example, couples who had once achieved pregnancies (even if lost) or who had biological children tended to see themselves as essentially fertile, despite their current difficulty in conceiving or carrying a child to term—once fertile always fertile. In contrast, there were couples who spontaneously conceived and successfully delivered a baby after an encounter with infertility diagnosis or treatment who continued to categorize themselves as infertile—once infertile always infertile.

Using an a priori system of classification, fertile and infertile, and childbearing and adopting, couples fall into different groups. Yet, when we used the theoretical categories derived from the interview data, certain fertile and infertile, and certain childbearing and adopting couples fell into the same groups. We initially sought by selective sampling to include couples who fell into preconceived groups, but once we began to recognize, as a direct consequence of our analysis of the data, that couples could be compared on other than conventional medical and social criteria, we adopted a theoretical sampling strategy: looking with new eyes at all of the interview data we had already collected, eliciting more information from couples already in the study the next time we saw them, and seeking other couples to be included in the study to obtain the information we needed to "fill out" or "saturate" the new categories we had invented (Charmaz, 1983). This sampling strategy is the basis for constant comparison, the analytic strategy in which elements of data are compared with each other to develop and refine reductions of that data.

DATA COLLECTION TECHNIQUES AND PROCEDURES

In the TTP Project, we contacted respondents at comparable points in time in childbearing and adopting couples' transition to parenthood.

Childbearing (fertile and infertile) couples who entered the study in the first trimester of pregnancy were interviewed together in their homes three times during the pregnancy (by 12 weeks, and around 22 and 37 weeks) and twice after delivery (within 1 week of the mother, and usually the baby, coming home from the hospital and 3 months following the baby's arrival home). Adopting couples were interviewed together in their homes every 4 months until placement and then within 1 week and 3 months of the child's arrival in the home. As we anticipated that adopting couples would typically not get infants younger than 1 month old, and that childbearing couples could have premature infants requiring longer hospital stays, we selected as the point of comparison time in parenting as opposed to age of the child. Consistent with the emergent nature of naturalistic research designs (Lincoln & Guba, 1985), the protocol was flexible, allowing for variations in the numbers of interviews per couple to occur in cases where couples entered the study later than 12 weeks of pregnancy, had a preterm delivery, or had a child placed with them very soon after obtaining approval to adopt.

Conjoint Interviews

The interviews were conjoint, intensive, and intended to create an atmosphere conducive to free expression. They were audiotaped and transcribed verbatim, with brief notes about the interview situation itself added at the end. Two of us (MS, BH) conducted the interviews, and each couple had the same interviewer throughout the course of the study. In the first interview, couples were asked to tell the story of their infertility or impending parenthood. In subsequent interviews, couples were asked to talk about what happened since the last interview. We allowed couples to reach a natural end in their talk. We then sought further clarification or elaboration of topics they had raised. In addition, we decided in regular meetings of the research team and on analytic grounds what topics needed to be pursued in the future.

Although there are advantages to individual interviews, we selected conjoint interviewing as the best approach for this study for ethical and pragmatic reasons. First, infertility is typically viewed in this country as a couple problem, so it seemed appropriate to treat the couple as a unit of study during the interviews. Second, we knew that men were underrepresented in infertility studies, in part because of their reluctance to participate in such projects. We correctly surmised that through their wives we would be able to reach men who would otherwise not participate in such a study. (See Daly, Chapter 7, this volume.) Third, we knew that infertility is itself a factor that can disrupt a partnership and did not wish to contribute in any way to furthering such disruptions by asking to interview partners separately. Conjoint interviews can foster the climate of openness and trust essential to a family study (LaRossa & LaRossa, 1981).

Fourth, conjoint interviews permit a fuller presentation of information (Allan, 1980). As individual partners describe their experiences, they often generate responses from their spouses, and spouses can clarify, confirm, amend, or refute each others' descriptions of events. In the course of the interviews we conducted, spouses often jogged each others' memories about the correct sequencing and nature of events, and they engaged each other in conversation about subjects they had not previously discussed. Although such situations can also have negative implications for a marriage, one partner having less control over what the other partner reveals (LaRossa, Bennett, & Gelles, 1981), we were not aware of any instance in which this kind of event operated against couples. Finally, the interaction of a couple in the course of a conjoint interview itself constitutes data (Allan, 1980). As couples create the accounts they provide the interviewer, they also exhibit behaviors that would ordinarily not be observable to a stranger in the privatized world of marriage and family. Conjoint interviewing permitted us to witness how partners acted together, how they sought to help or influence each other, and how they handled disagreements arising in the interview situation.

Interviews as Friendly Conversations

Again, the transformation of the interview situation into one resembling a friendly conversation can cause couples to forget the investigative parameters of the situation and reveal what they might not otherwise have revealed (LaRossa, Bennett, & Gelles, 1981). Couples expressed no detrimental effects, and in many cases, stated that the interviews were beneficial and even therapeutic to them. Both longitudinal and qualitative research on sensitive topics can have a therapeutic role, a factor that influences both the nature of knowledge developed from the research and respondents' well-being (Collins, Given, & Berry, 1989; Cowles, 1988). The knowledge we gained from this study is a product of our interaction with couples. In addition, these couples, accustomed to being scrutinized, evaluated, and putting their best foot forward to gain access to medical and adoption services, often appreciated talking to a person who was in no position to withhold any desired services.

Naturalistic Observations

We also conducted two observations of mother-father-infant interactions. The first observation occurred between 8 and 21 days after the arrival of the infant home and the second approximately 1 week later. The 1-2 week lag before the first observation allowed couples to begin their adjustment to parenting without intrusion, but still allowed us to observe parent and infant behaviors early in the relationship. The second observation served to verify the typicality of the first observation; significant changes in parent and infant behaviors are not expected to occur within 1 week.

The observations were conducted using a naturalistic technique derived from ethology and that has been demonstrated to be a reliable and valid method for observing parent-infant interactions (Holditch-Davis & Thoman, 1988; Thoman, 1990; Thoman, Acebo, Dreyer, Becker, & Freese, 1979). Two of us (DHD and our research assistant, Beth Black), who maintained high levels of interrater reliability throughout the course of the study, conducted the observations. Couples were informed that we were observing, but not evaluating, their behavior and the baby's in interaction. Both mother and father were asked to be home for the observation to give them an opportunity to interact with their baby if they desired to do so and to permit us to conduct the observation at a time when the baby would be fed. Each observation began when a parent picked up the infant and ended after 1-1/2 hours or when the baby was put to sleep. The time span for observation (determined on the basis of our experiences with the first four couples observed) was long enough to help couples adjust to being observed, but not so long that they would find it overly intrusive.

The observations involved recording on specially blocked paper every 10 seconds the occurrence of any of 21 maternal, 21 paternal, 1 couple, and 15 infant behaviors. The activities of both parents were recorded regardless of which parent was caring for the infant. An ongoing record of the behavior of each parent is thus available, making it possible to identify times when only one parent is involved with the infant, when one parent is watching the other parent care for the baby, when one parent is interacting with the baby while the other provides care to the infant, and times when parents are jointly caring for the baby. Each behavior coded is qualitatively different from all of the others. All the behaviors are value free; they represent neither "good" nor "bad" parenting. Importantly, this coding schema, or ethogram of parent-infant behaviors (derived from more than 6,000 hours of observation and 25 years of research) identifies representative parent and infant behaviors only (Thoman et al. 1979). This data collection technique is appropriate for a study like this one in which efforts are made to suspend prior conceptual commitments, because multiple analytic approaches to the data drawing from a variety of theoretical perspectives can be used to arrive at different interpretations of the parent-infant relationship.

Ecological Validity

Although no ethically conducted observations of human behavior can be completely unobtrusive, we sought to maintain ecological validity: to study behaviors in the setting in which they naturally occur with minimal observer interference (Gibbs, 1979). For example, the observer was not the person who conducted the interviews and with whom couples had already established a relationship. This design feature served to reduce couples' desire to talk to the observer during the observation period or to draw her into the scene. Moreover, by not knowing what the interviewer knew about a couple, the observer could maintain as neutral a stance as possible. In addition, the observer remained out of the limited visual field of the infant and dressed in dull, pastel, or noncontrasting colors without dangling jewelry, to avoid attracting infants' attention and thereby altering their behavior (Thoman, 1990). Both observers were female to permit couples to be comfortable during observations of breast feeding. After the observation was completed, however, the observer did offer caregiving advice to parents who indicated (by asking or by behavior) a need for it. All of our interventions were recorded as part of our data and were evaluated for their potential impact on couples' experiences.

Couples Records and Inventory

Couples recorded their infant's sleeping and feeding times during the 1 week interval between observations. They also completed a mailed Symptom Inventory every month they were in the study. This inventory was a further modification of a data collection technique, the Pregnancy

Symptom Diary, developed by Erickson (1967) and modified by Leifer (1980), to obtain frequent measures of symptoms commonly associated with childbearing. Like the observational schema, the 42-item inventory is neither related to nor derived from a particular theoretical model, but rather lists physical symptoms and emotions that women and men commonly experience in the childbearing cycle. We modified items to make them applicable to both childbearing and adopting couples and to women and men.

The TTP Project demanded a considerable amount of time and energy from couples. Yet between 1987 and 1991, only two couples terminated the study prior to having their babies because it was emotionally difficult for them to continue. (Five couples lost their pregnancies or decided to terminate the adoption process). The few couples who moved out of state prior to having their babies have maintained contact with us through letters and tapes. At this point, we anticipate that 80-85 couples will complete the protocol of regularly scheduled interviews, two observations, and monthly symptom inventories. Several couples repeated the study when they became parents for a second time. In addition, we mailed the monthly Symptom Inventories, yearly Christmas cards (mailed while couples were in the study and after they completed it), and research reports (after couples completed the study), which helped us maintain contact with respondents. Such contact is especially critical when ongoing validation of analyses or clarification of information may be required. We also expressed our appreciation by giving couples gifts when their child arrived.

METHODOLOGY

The TTP Project can be described as a longitudinal field study that operationalized the ground assumptions of two different forms of naturalism—a naturalistic paradigm and a naturalistic methodology. The naturalistic paradigm within which the TTP Project was conceived draws from such theoretical perspectives as symbolic interactionism and phenomenology, is commonly (although not wholly accurately) referred to as qualitative, and emphasizes understanding respondents' worlds (for example, their perceptions, lived experiences, intentions, meanings) (Denzin, 1989; Lincoln & Guba, 1985). The naturalistic methodology (systematic observation) used in the project draws from ethology and emphasizes recording respondents' behaviors in a natural environment in which they occur so that conclusions can be drawn about the ontogeny, causation, survival value, and evolution of behavior (Tinbergen, 1963). In both cases, investigators attempt to capture a phenomenon in its naturally occurring state, foreground the individual subject, minimize the artifice of studying a phenomenon, and suspend any a priori theoretical commitments concerning the phenomenon.

These two forms of naturalism draw from constructivist and postpositivist belief systems (Guba, 1990). We recognize that the issue of "accomodation" (Firestone, 1990; Skrtic, 1990) of different paradigms and methods continues to be debated, yet we also believe that the kind of phenomenon we chose to study demands multiple approaches. For example, infants are an integral part of a couple's transition to parenthood, but they are not capable of describing their worlds. Moreover, parenting itself often involves elements that cannot be captured in verbal descriptions. Importantly, we sought to capture, as much as was reasonable within the confines of one project, the experiences of certain couples and their babies and, by virtue of this desire, designed a project that could credibly satisfy it. In practice, if not in philosophy, such accommodations appear necessary.

A Qualitative and a Quantitative Study

The TTP Project can also be described as both qualitative and quantitative. The study is *qualitative* in that we selected data collection and analysis techniques (such as open-ended interviewing and constant comparison) to elicit couples' verbal descriptions of their experiences—or words, which we, in turn, reduced and transformed into other words, or the descriptions and theoretical explanations that comprised the findings of the study. The study is also *quantitative* in that we used a variety of descriptive and inferential statistical methods to reduce and transform the verbal, observational, and symptom self-report data we collected into numbers that could be interpreted. Both qualitative and quantitative data collection and analysis techniques may be used to operationalize naturalistic inquiry if they do not tie investigators prematurely to descriptions and explanations of a phenomenon that are not developed from or grounded in the data obtained in the course of the study. Qualitative research is not naturalistic if the researcher manipulates the conditions in which the phenomenon appears or imposes a priori units on the phenomenon (Willems, 1967). Naturalistic research is, in turn, not necessarily qualitative, as verbal data may be transformed into numbers for analytical purposes.

A Grounded Theory Study

The TTP Project can also be described as a grounded theory study, as the long-term aim of the project was to offer a theoretical basis for practice with infertile couples that was grounded in actual experience. Our interpretation of grounded theory had a phenomenological cast (Charmaz, 1990, p. 1164); as the study progressed, it also acquired a narrative cast (Polkinghorne, 1988). We began the project with a grounded theory objective—to conceptualize the psychosocial processes involved in the transition to parenthood of infertile adopting and childbearing couples—and a phenomenological objective—to describe the subjective world of couples undergoing this process. In the course of the study, we also recognized that couples often rendered their experiences in story form, embellishing and revising—(re)creating—their stories.

Conducting a grounded theory study with a phenomenological and narrative cast had implications for the way we prepared and analyzed data. For example, we sought to preserve as much of the interview situation in the transcript as possible, including such speech events as respondents' false starts, repetitions, and nonverbal expressions such as crying and laughing. There is no one method for representing speech, and investigators generally decide on the basis of some (often implicit) theory of speech what set of conventions to use in the creation of transcripts (Atkinson, 1988). We began the TTP Project thinking only of the informational content and not the narrative context of interview data (Mishler, 1986). By the 2nd year of the project, however, we became aware not only of the meaning couples made from their experiences and the strategies they used to cope with events, but also how the manner in which they conveyed those experiences itself constituted a strategy for making meaning that required interpretation.

Perspectives on Coding

In addition, we found that the line-by-line coding approach offered in instructional texts on grounded theory was neither analytically useful nor pragmatic in initially approaching the interview data, especially with the massive volume of data collected in this project. The most useful first step in attempting to understand the data was to determine the one or more story lines arising in any one interview session. Once we identified a story line, we could pursue any one of several analytic paths available within that story line and begin coding the data. An initial line-by-line coding approach without an orienting gestalt for coding is empty coding, only producing more words that have to be worked but that do not necessarily move the inquiry forward analytically. This kind of coding also has a distinctively reductionistic cast, removing items from the overall context that gives them meaning and threatening the integrity of respondents' narratives. Partitioning interview data first into the story lines they comprise still permits an open-coding approach; the same story or elements of the same story may be differently interpreted and used in pursuing different analytic paths.

For example, we recognized fairly early in the project that couples used the first interview to describe all of the options they pursued in trying to have a child. (We engendered this response in part by asking them to talk about how they got to the point in their lives where they were awaiting a child. Yet, we found that many couples also had difficulty "shifting gears" from pursuing a child to actually waiting for a specific child, and their talk reflected this impediment in their transition to parenthood.) Having identified this story line, we then decided to analyze the elements of this pursuit, employing a model grounded theory coding paradigm (Strauss & Corbin, 1990, p. 99) specifying the circumstances in which infertile couples pursue parenthood, the 4-point calculus they use to decide what path to parenthood to pursue, 6 patterns of pursuit, and the 3 outcomes of pursuit. As a consequence of following this one analytic path within the how-we-got-to-be-pregnant or how-we-got-on-an-adoption-waiting-list story line, we constructed the theory of *mazing* to contain all of the elements of the process of pursuit we could discern from couples' descriptions (Sandelowski, Harris, & Holditch-Davis, 1989). This theory is illustrated in Figure 16.1.

Previous Research and Theory

We also used theories and conceptualizations developed elsewhere to organize and frame some of the findings of the study. For example, we found Kleinman's conceptualization of illness models (1980, 1988) and Williams' conceptualization of narrative reconstruction (1984) useful in understanding and describing the continuity and change over

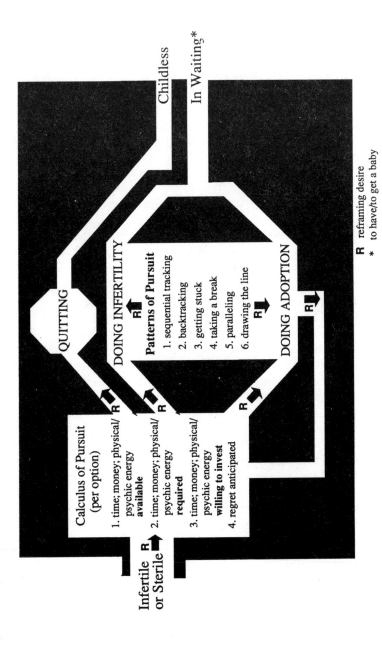

Figure 16.1. The Theory of Mazing. Originally appeared in *Image: Journal of Nursing Scholarship*, 1989, vol. 21, p. 222.

313

time in couples' explanation of their fertility status (Sandelowski, Holditch-Davis, & Harris, 1990). In summary, "theory" entered the TTP Project in several ways and at different points in time: (a) as an orienting framework for viewing inquiry; (b) as an orienting framework for viewing research subjects and the data they and investigators together produce; (c) as an original product of analysis of the data; and (d) as frameworks developed outside the study that served to organize or illuminate findings, to which findings were compared, and to which findings contributed by supporting, expanding, or refuting existing ideas about a phenomenon.

RESULTS TO DATE: ANALYTIC PATHS AND TECHNIQUES

In a study like the TTP Project, where a large volume of data is amassed over several years, many analytic paths can be pursued, but they cannot all be pursued at the same time or even within the boundaries of the one study. Our overall analytic objective for the TTP Project was to capture as much of the complexity of a life transition as possible: to describe individual, husband-wife, and mother-father-child processes over time and in time, and to make group comparisons of these processes employing both a priori and theoretically derived categories.

Accordingly, multiple triangulation (Knafl & Breitmayer, 1989) was used to achieve a multidimensional, contextualized view of infertile couples' transition to parenthood. The research design incorporated triangulation across: (a) data sources (focal and comparison groups of study achieved by selective and theoretical sampling); (b) investigators (two conducting the interviews and two conducting the observations); (c) data collection techniques tapping different domains of knowledge (perceptions, feelings, attitudes via interviews; symptoms and moods via Symptom Inventory; and behavior via observation); (d) time (multiple and comparable points of contact with couples over a 1-3 year period); (e) analytic techniques (qualitative and statistical); and (f) units of analysis (individual, and marital and parent-child dyads).

Strategies of Data Analysis

Our strategy for analyzing the large and diverse data sets we have has been first to approach the "qualitative" data (from the interviews) and the "quantitative" data (from the Symptom Inventories, observations, and sleep records) separately. Because theoretical closure can often be achieved with a smaller sample size than is required for statistical analyses and because a grounded theory approach to inquiry demands simultaneous data collection and analysis, we have completed more work using the interview data than the other data sets. We have already referred to two completed analyses concerning: (a) couples' pursuit of parenthood and (b) their explanations of infertility.

ANALYSIS

Conceptual Ambiguity and Persistence: Qualitative Analysis

Other work using qualitative approaches to analyzing interview data has also been completed. The interview data has been used to show how the "never-enough" quality of conceptive technology itself and certain cultural values contribute to couples' persistence in undergoing largely ineffective treatments (Sandelowski, 1991; Sandelowski, Harris, & Holditch-Davis, 1990). For example, most therapies for infertility are treatments that have to be repeated for at least several menstrual cycles to achieve conception. In addition, couples in the study, like many middle-class Americans, believed that persistence pays off. Moreover, they anticipated regretting not using an available "technological opportunity." We also interpreted the process of conception in infertile couples to include forcing conception to occur, resolving conceptional ambiguity, and reconciling the idea and fact of conception. The conceptional ambiguity that women conceiving with biomedical techniques experienced involved uncertainty about whether they had achieved a pregnancy-with-a-baby; some women described pregnancies without babies, babies without pregnancies, and pregnantlike bodies. In addition, they had varying notions of exactly when a woman can be said to be pregnant (Sandelowski, Harris, & Holditch-Davis, 1990).

The findings from both of these analyses have particular relevance for practice because they suggest some reasons why couples have difficulty giving up the pursuit of pregnancy and why women and couples conceiving biomedically have difficulty believing they are pregnant. In addition, because women may see their externally fertilized eggs as babies, they may grieve over a failed procedure as a baby who died. We have also described the process of parental claiming in adopting couples in the waiting period for a child. This process involved: (a) constructing an image of a child somewhere-out-there and (b) construing that child as the "right" child for them (Sandelowski, Harris, & Holditch-Davis, in press). Understanding this process may have some important implications for claiming in other situations where there is no genetic or gestational tie between parent and child.

Congruence Between Couples and Physicians: Quantitative Analysis

The previous analyses involved using qualitative analytic techniques. In contrast, our analysis of how couples encountered amniocentesis involved some quantification of verbal data (Sandelowski, Harris, & Holditch-Davis, 1991a). For example, we created a table from information drawn from interview data comparing the congruence of couples' decisions about having amniocentesis (yes versus no) with their physicians' counsel (encouraged versus neutral/discouraged). We determined that there was no statistically significant relationship between these factors. By means of another table comparing couples' decisions about having amniocentesis (yes versus no) with fertility status (fertile versus infertile) and maternal age (over versus under 35), we concluded that age was the most prominent factor determining whether couples accepted the procedure.

As we have achieved the numbers of respondents required to begin statistical analyses, we have begun to shift our focus toward the symptom and observation data. For example, our first analysis of the Symptom Inventories involved comparing infertile and fertile couples' pregnancy symptoms (Black, Holditch-Davis, Sandelowski, Harris, & Belyea, 1991). We found that fertile and infertile couples did not significantly differ in the overall numbers of symptoms reported. Emotional and physical symptoms were highly correlated in infertile couples, however, but not in the fertile couples; and symptoms were correlated in the husbands and wives in infertile but not in fertile couples.

Understanding Problematic Interactions Through Triangulation

An interesting departure from the strategy of first analyzing data sets separately is the use of the comparative case study combining interview and observation data (Holditch-Davis, Harris, & Sandelowski, 1990).

We wanted to look more closely at the situations of three couples (two adopting and one infertile childbearing) that interviewers identified as having difficulty adjusting to parenting once their babies arrived. We looked for factors that distinguished them from the rest of the couples who had also had their babies. We found that although no factor clearly differentiated these three couples from the others, two of these couples had known risk factors for parenting problems (psychiatric illness and marital discord), and two couples were the only couples in the sample involved at the time of this analysis in which body image concerns and a strong desire to maintain a pre-baby life-style were expressed. Observation data revealed that all three of the wives had less frequency of interaction with their babies than the other women observed. Two of the husbands demonstrated a similar reduced pattern of interaction, and the third man demonstrated more frequent interactions than the other men (perhaps to compensate for his wife's reduced level).

Triangulation for Convergence

This work is an illustration of triangulation for convergence, in that we drew from two information sources (interviews and observations) first to validate, via systematic observation, interviewers' impressions of problematic parent-infant interaction observable in the interview situation; then to search for factors from both data sources common to all three couples, but different from the other couples not identified as having a problem; and finally, to offer a preliminary interpretation of why these couples appeared different from the others. One of the three couples consented to repeating the study when a second child was conceived; that child has since been born and information gathered from this pregnancy will expand this case study work, as will data from an additional fertile childbearing couple we recently identified as having some early parenting difficulties.

Use of Theoretically Derived Categories

Another analytic path we are pursuing combining our different data sets involves employing theoretically derived categories (from the interview data) to analyze symptoms in the adoption waiting period. We found that adopting couples established a time line for their waiting period from adoption approval to placement by designating three periods: (a) *could-be time,* when couples hope for but do not really anticipate getting a child; (b) *anytime-now,* when couples expect their child at any moment; and (c) *past-time,* when couples perceive they are overdue for a child (Sandelowski, Harris, & Holditch-Davis, 1991b). We will examine whether this theoretical schema is more or less useful than an empirical (calendar) time frame in understanding couples' symptom reporting in the waiting period. In addition, we can use these theoretical categories to explore whether, for example, couples in past-time report more negative symptoms than they did when they were in could-be or anytime-now. Such a finding would lend further support to our interpretation from the interview data that couples experience a great deal of anguish in this period. Again, we are triangulating for convergence by using more than one information source to focus on a phenomenon.

COSTS OF THE TTP PROJECT

One of the factors most important to the successful execution of a study such as the TTP Project is a realistic assessment of the commitment of time and labor it requires. Not only is this knowledge critical to making the decision to pursue such a project, but it is the basis for calculating the considerable resources required to accomplish it. Collecting and preparing the interview data for analysis included the costs of: (a) the telephone calls to arrange meeting times; (b) automobile travel to and from couples' homes; (c) time in the home, including interview time; (d) dictating process notes at the end of tapes; (e) verbatim transcription of interviews and notes; (f) proofing transcripts against recordings; and (g) correcting and formatting transcripts. In the TTP Project, couples lived an average of 1 hour away from their interviewer, but as much as 3 hours away. Couples wanting infertility and adoption services frequently have to travel long distances to obtain those services; we, accordingly, decided that we would be willing to travel up to 6 hours round trip by car for each research contact. Interviews lasted an average of 1 hour, but as long as 2-1/2 hours; typically an additional 15-30 minutes was spent in the home. For an experienced (quick and virtually 100% accurate) transcriptionist, each hour of taped interview time requires 3-1/2 hours of transcription time. Thus far in the project, both childbearing and adopting couples have been interviewed an average of 5 times, with some adopting couples interviewed as many as 10 times. We have conducted more than 400 interviews to date.

Collecting and preparing the observation data for analysis included the costs of: (a) telephone calls to arrange meeting times; (b) automobile travel to and from couples' homes; (c) time in the home, including observation time; (d) dictating or writing process notes; (e) editing the data; (f) entering the data into the computer and printing a hard copy; (g) first and second corrections; and (h) final corrections and formatting. Each observation, typically lasting 1-1/2 hours, required an additional 6 hours to accomplish the steps following data collection. Couples were observed twice, resulting in a time expenditure per couple of 15 hours. Thus far, 76 couples have been observed. Collecting and preparing the symptom data included the costs of: (a) preparing the mailings; (b) computer entry; and (c) filing. Childbearing couples (each husband and wife) completed an average of 7 sets of inventories over their course of the study; adopting couples completed an average of 10 sets. About 12 minutes per couple per set was required to collect, prepare, and enter the data.

In addition, the TTP Project required considerable use of space. We bought an IBM PC computer with 124 megabytes of hard disk space to store all of the interview, observation, and symptom data collected. The use of the Ethnograph software alone requires that at least 3 copies of the same interview be initially stored in different formats. In addition, by the end of the 3rd year of the project, we had virtually filled a double-sized file cabinet with hard copies (averaging 25 pages each, typed and double-spaced, but up to 100 pages) of the interview data alone, and required two additional conventionally sized cabinets to store hard copies of symptom and observation data.

In addition to these material factors, the TTP Project required us to limit our time away from home in order to maintain the schedule for our research contacts and to be available for the calls informing us that a baby had arrived. Virtually all of our research contacts occurred on weekends and evenings and there were some months in which each interviewer had 12 interviews to conduct and in which observers had four to five sets of observations to complete. In addition to this project, we have all carried considerable faculty and doctoral student (our research assistant) work loads. Yet, we believe that the design we selected is the most comprehensive, the most congruent with the life events our couples were experiencing, and the most valuable for the understanding of infertility. We believe our methods can be fruitfully used to examine any key life event, whether it is an anticipated life transition or an unanticipated life crisis. We also believe that to conduct any worthwhile and sensitive study of families requires the kind of effort we have made. This kind of inquiry is also especially satisfying to those who provide care to individuals and families.

CONCLUSION

In a sense, we lived the transition to parenthood along with the couples in our study. Each of us began the project with very different experiences related to infertility. All of us had varying levels of academic or clinical knowledge of infertility; two of us had personal knowledge of the struggle to conceive a child, one of us was one of those "blissfully fertile" women our couples often mentioned, and one of us is voluntarily childless. Yet we all very quickly started seeing the world through our couples' eyes, identifying with their experiences and gaining insights about our own lives from them. Immersed in these couples' experiences, we were able to share their joy at finally reaching the goal for which they had struggled and in a few cases felt something of their sorrow when a child in sight was lost in pregnancy or through adoption failure. We are all the wiser for having done so. The TTP Project is and remains labor intensive as we continue with the collection and analysis of data. But there has never been a moment when it has not been a labor of love.

REFERENCES

Allan, G. (1980). A note on interviewing spouses together. *Journal of Marriage and the Family, 42,* 205-210.

Atkinson, P. (1988). Review of Elliott Mishler, *The discourse of medicine. Culture, Medicine, and Psychiatry, 12,* 249-256.

Black, B. P., Holditch-Davis, D., Sandelowski, M., Harris, B. G., & Belyea, M. (1991). *Fertility status and symptoms in childbearing couples.* Manuscript submitted for publication.

Charmaz, K. (1983). The grounded theory method: An explication and interpretation. In R. M. Emerson (Ed.), *Contemporary field research: A collection of readings* (pp. 109-126). Boston: Little, Brown.

Charmaz, K. (1990). "Discovering" chronic illness: Using grounded theory. *Social Science and Medicine, 30,* 1161-1172.

Collins, C., Given, B., & Berry, D. (1989). Longitudinal studies as intervention. *Nursing Research, 38,* 251-253.

Cowles, K. V. (1988). Issues in qualitative research on sensitive topics. *Western Journal of Nursing Research, 10,* 163-179.

Denzin, N. (1989). *Interpretive interactionism.* Newbury Park, CA: Sage.

Erickson, M. T. (1967). Method for frequent assessment of symptomatology during pregnancy. *Psychological Reports, 20,* 447-450.

Firestone, W. A. (1990). Accomodation: Toward a paradigm-praxis dialectic. In E. G. Guba (Ed.), *The paradigm dialog* (pp. 105-124). Newbury Park, CA: Sage.

Gibbs, J. C. (1979). The meaning of ecologically oriented inquiry in contemporary psychology. *American Psychologist, 34,* 127-140.

Guba, E. G. (1990). The alternative paradigm dialog. In E. G. Guba (Ed.), *The paradigm dialog* (pp. 17-27). Newbury Park, CA: Sage.

Holditch-Davis, D., Harris, B. G., & Sandelowski, M. (1990, March). Factors associated with problematic early parenting after infertility. Symposium on "Parenting in at-risk populations," In M. S. Miles (chair), *Conference on Human Development.* Virginia Commonwealth University, Richmond, VA.

Holditch-Davis, D., & Thoman, E. B. (1988). The early social environment of premature and fullterm infants. *Early Human Development, 17,* 221-232.

Kleinman, A. (1980). *Patients and healers in the context of culture: An exploration of the borderland between anthropology, medicine, and psychiatry.* Berkeley: University of California Press.

Kleinman, A. (1988). *The illness narratives: Suffering, healing and the human condition.* New York: Basic Books.

Knafl, K. A., & Breitmayer, B. J. (1989). Triangulation in qualitative research: Issues of conceptual clarity and purpose. In J. M. Morse (Ed.), *Qualitative nursing research: A contemporary dialogue* (pp. 209-220). Rockville, MD: Aspen.

LaRossa, R., Bennett, L. A., & Gelles, R. J. (1981). Ethical dilemmas in qualitative family research. *Journal of Marriage and the Family, 43,* 303-313.

LaRossa, R., & LaRossa, M. M. (1981). *Transition to parenthood: How infants change families.* Beverly Hills, CA: Sage.

Leifer, M. (1980). *Psychological effects of motherhood: A study of first pregnancy.* New York: Praeger.

Lincoln, Y. S., & Guba, E. G. (1985). *Naturalistic inquiry.* Beverly Hills, CA: Sage.

Mishler, E. G. (1986). *Research interviewing: Context and narrative.* Cambridge, MA: Harvard University Press.

Polkinghorne, D. E. (1988). *Narrative knowing and the human sciences.* Albany: State University of New York Press.

Sandelowski, M. (1991). Compelled to try: The never-enough quality of conceptive technology. *Medical Anthropology Quarterly, 5,* 29-47.

Sandelowski, M., Harris, B. G., & Holditch-Davis, D. (1989). Mazing: Infertile couples and the quest for a child. *Image: Journal of Nursing Scholarship, 21,* 220-226.

Sandelowski, M., Holditch-Davis, D., & Harris, B. G. (1990a). Living the life: Explanations of infertility. *Sociology of Health and Illness, 12,* 194-215.

Sandelowski, M., Harris, B. G., & Holditch-Davis, D. (1990b). Pregnant moments: The process of conception in infertile couples. *Research in Nursing and Health, 13,* 273-282.

Sandelowski, M., Harris, B. G., & Holditch-Davis, D. (1991a). Amniocentesis in the context of infertility. *Health Care for Women International, 12,* 167-178.

Sandelowski, M., Harris, B. G., & Holditch-Davis, D. (1991b). "The clock is ticking, the calendar pages are turning, and we are still waiting": Infertile couples' encounters with time in the adoption waiting period. *Qualitative Sociology, 23*, 147-173.

Sandelowski, M., Harris, B. G., & Holditch-Davis, D. (in press). Somewhere out there and somebody else's: Parental claiming in the preadoption waiting period. *Journal of Contemporary Ethnography.*

Schatzman, L., & Strauss, A. (1973). *Field research: Strategies for a natural sociology.* Englewood Cliffs, NJ: Prentice-Hall.

Skrtic, T. M. (1990). Social accomodation: Toward a dialogical discourse in educational inquiry. In E. G. Guba (Ed.), *The paradigm dialog* (pp. 125-135). Newbury Park, CA: Sage.

Strauss, A. (1987). *Qualitative analysis for social scientists.* Cambridge, MA: Cambridge University Press.

Strauss, A., & Corbin, J. (1990). *Basics of qualitative research: Grounded theory procedures and techniques.* Newbury Park, CA: Sage.

Thoman, E. B. (1990). Sleeping and waking states in infancy: A functional perspective. *Neuroscience and Biobehavioral Reviews, 14*, 93-107.

Thoman, E. B., Acebo, C., Dreyer, C. A., Becker, P. T., & Freese, M. P. (1979). Individuality in the interactive process. In E. B. Thoman (Ed.), *Origins of the infant's social responsiveness* (pp. 305-338). Hillsdale, NJ: Lawrence Erlbaum.

Tinbergen, N. (1973). On aims and methods of ethology. *Zeitschrift für Tierpsychologie, 20*, 410-433.

Willems, E. P. (1967). Toward an explicit rationale for naturalistic research methods. *Human Development, 10*, 138-154.

Williams, G. (1984). The genesis of chronic illness: Narrative re-construction. *Sociology of Health and Illness, 6*, 175-200.

Author Index

Subject Index

About the Authors

Katherine R. Allen is Associate Professor, Department of Family and Child Development, Virginia Polytechnic Institute and State University, Blacksburg. She received her master's degree and Ph.D. in child and family studies, with a certificate in gerontology, from Syracuse University. In her research and teaching, she uses a combination of feminist and qualitative methods, such as personal narratives, life histories, and in-depth interviews. She has published extensively, including books, book chapters, and journal articles, with her work appearing in the *Journal of Marriage and the Family, Family Relations, The Gerontologist, Psychology of Women Quarterly,* and other family studies, gerontological, and feminist oriented journals. A member of the steering committee of the Qualitative Family Research Network, she also is active in the Feminism and Family Studies Section of the National Council on Family Relations.

Pauline G. Boss is Professor, Department of Family Social Science, University of Minnesota, Twin Cities. She received an M.S. and a Ph.D. in child development and family studies from the University of Wisconsin-Madison. The major developer of the theory of ambiguous loss, she has published numerous book chapters as well as articles in *Journal of Marriage and the Family, Family Process, Family Relations, Journal of Home Economics,* and other major journals devoted to family studies. She has written or edited several books, including a work in progress on ambiguous loss. She also is one of five editors of the forthcoming *Sourcebook of Family Theories and Methods: A Contextual Approach.* A former president of The Groves Conference on Marriage and the Family as well as a fellow and a supervisor of the American Association of Marital and Family Therapy, she has received many awards for her contributions to research on families.

Kerry Daly is Assistant Professor, Department of Family Studies, University of Guelph, Ontario, Canada. He received his Ph.D. in sociology from McMaster University, Hamilton, Ontario. His qualitative study of how infertile couples become adoptive parents has been published in *The Journal of Contemporary Ethnography, Social Casework, Clinical Sociology Review,* and *The Canadian Journal of Community Mental Health.* In addition to these published reports, he has presented papers dealing with various aspects of doing qualitative research at conferences throughout North America, including the National Council on Family Relations, the annual Interactionist Research conference, and the Canadian Learned Society Meetings. Currently, he is doing a qualitative study of the social construction of fatherhood and national study of adoption issues in Canada.

Daniel F. Detzner is Associate Professor, Department of Family Social Science, University of Minnesota. His bachelor's and master's degrees are in political science from Georgetown University, and his Ph.D. is in American Studies from the University of Minnesota, Twin Cities. His research currently is focused on the elderly within their families, including longitudinal case studies of families caring for an Alzheimer's patient at home and life history studies of older Southeast Asian refugees. He has published his work in *Perspectives: Journal of General and Liberal Studies, Gerontology and Geriatrics Education,* and numerous book chapters.

David J. Ekerdt is Associate Director, Center on Aging, University of Kansas Medical Center and Adjunct Professor, Department of Sociology. He formerly was Research Sociologist for the Normative Aging Study, Boston Veterans Administration Hospital. He has a Ph.D. in sociology from Boston University. A fellow of the Gerontological Society of America, he has published widely in the areas of aging, health, and retirement, including in *The Gerontologist, The Journal of Gerontology,* and *The American Journal of Public Health.* He serves on numerous editorial boards. With Maximiliane Szinovacz and Barbara Vinick, he is coeditor of *Families and Retirement,* published by Sage.

Deborah Lewis Fravel is Project Manager for the Minnesota site of the Minnesota/Texas Adoption Research Project and a Ph.D. student in the Department of Family Social Science, University of Minnesota, Twin Cities. She received her bachelor's and master's degrees at the University of North Carolina, Greensboro. Her research interests are in the areas of family stress and resiliency, seeking to understand why some family members weather stress and others appear to be severely harmed by it. The chapter in this book is her first published work, developed from a project she did to fulfill a requirement for a course in qualitative research at the Department of Family Social Science, University of Minnesota.

Jane F. Gilgun is Associate Professor, School of Social Work, University of Minnesota. She received her Ph.D. in family studies from Syracuse University, her master's in social service administration from the University of Chicago, and a licentiate in family studies and human sexuality from the University of Louvain, Belgium. She also has bachelor's and master's degrees in English literature, specializing in British and American narrative poetry. Her research areas are resiliency and the developmental pathways of rape and child molesting behaviors. The author of many articles and book chapters, all based on her qualitative research on families, she has published in journals such as *Social Work, Families in Society,* and *Journal of Social Service Research.* She is a member of the steering committee of the Qualitative Family Research Network of the National Council on Family Relations and the editor of the network's newsletter, *Qualitative Family Research.*

Gerald Handel is Professor, the City College and Graduate School, City University of New York. He received his bachelor's, master's, and Ph.D. degrees in sociology from the University of Chicago. One of the pioneers in qualitative research with families, particularly in studies of whole families, he is coauthor of *Family Worlds* (University of Chicago Press, 1959) and *Workingman's Wife: Her Personality, World and Life Styles* (Oceana, 1959), which was selected by Lewis Coser and Walter W. Powell for inclusion in their series, "Perennial Works in Sociology," published by Arno Press. His paper, "Psychological Study of Whole Families" (*Psychological Bulletin,* 1965) has been reprinted in seven anthologies and translated into Japanese. Portions of his 1985 paper, "Central Issues in the Construction of Sibling Relationships," have been reprinted in two anthologies. From 1969-1975, he was an associate editor of *Journal of Marriage and the Family.* He edited an anthology, *The Psychosocial Interior of the Family,* which has gone into three editions, published by Aldine and Aldine de Gruyter between 1967 and 1985.

Ellen M. Harbert is in the private practice in psychotherapy in Framingham, MA. Her practice focuses on families of persons with chronic illnesses and those at mid-life, aging, or in retirement. She is a former research associate for the Normative Aging Project, Boston Veterans Administration Hospital. She has an M.A. in American history and a master's in social work, both from Tulane University. Her history thesis, in which she used document analysis, was on criticism in U.S. art during the 1870s. An article based on her thesis was published in the *Journal of American Art.*

Betty Glenn Harris is Clinical Associate Professor and Acting Chair, Department of Women's and Children's Health, School of Nursing, University of North Carolina at Chapel Hill. She received a master's degree in maternity nursing from the University of Alabama and a Ph.D. in sociology from North Carolina State University. She has published papers in *Journal of Obstetric, Gynecologic, and Neonatal Nursing* and *MCN: American Journal of Maternal-Child Nursing.*

Diane Holditch-Davis is Associate Professor, Department of Women's and Children's Health, School of Nursing, University of North Carolina at Chapel Hill. She received a master's degree in parent-child nursing and a Ph.D. in developmental psychobiology from the University of Connecticut. She has held clinical positions in neonatal intensive care. Her research interests include the behavioral development of infants and parent-child interactions. She uses ethological observation in her research. She has published papers in such journals as *Infant Behavior and Development, Developmental Psychobiology, Neuropediatrics, Early Human Development,* and *Research in Nursing and Health.*

Robin L. Jarrett is Assistant Professor, Department of Sociology, Loyola University of Chicago. She received her Ph.D. in sociology from the University of Chicago. Her research interests are the family and socialization, qualitative methods, and urban poverty. For the Social Science Research Council, she recently completed a review of the ethnographic literature on patterns of ethnic family socialization. The recipient of fellowships from the American Sociological Association, Rockefeller Foundation, Social Science Research Council, and the Spencer Foundation, she was on leave from Loyola University at Northwestern University as a National Science Foundation Fellow at the time of the writing of her chapter.

Anita Lightburn is Assistant Professor, Columbia University School of Social Work. She received her Ed.D. and M.Ed. from the Columbia University Teachers College in the Department of Family and Community Education and her master's in social work from Columbia University. Her research area is in the field of child and family welfare. She has published in the journal *Families and Society*. Her role as a consultant to children and family services and health facilities includes both clinical and program development.

Linda K. Matocha is Associate Professor, College of Nursing, University of Delaware. She received her Ph.D. from the University of Delaware in Family Studies and her M.S. from Texas Woman's University in maternal-child nursing. Her research interests include sexuality issues in nursing practice, use of computers in nursing education, transcultural issues in individuals and families, and the effects of infectious diseases on patients and their families. Currently she is the assistant chairperson of the State of Delaware's AIDS Advisory Task Force. She has several publications in nursing journals examining issues of caring for persons with AIDS and transcultural issues in nursing.

Susan O. Murphy is Associate Professor of Nursing, San Jose State University, California. She received her bachelor's and master's degrees in nursing and D.N.S (Doctor of Nursing Science) from the School of Nursing, University of California at San Francisco. An instructor and professor of nursing for more than 15 years, she worked for several years as a public health nurse. She recently received a grant from the National Center on Nursing Research to expand her theoretical findings related to sibling relationships in families with a new baby. She has published several articles in nursing journals, including *Image: The Journal of Nursing Scholarship*.

Mark R. Rank is Associate Professor, George Warren Brown School of Social Work, Washington University, St. Louis, MO. His M.A. and Ph.D. are in sociology, from the University of Wisconsin-Madison. His research has appeared in a number of journals, including *American Sociological Review, Social Forces, Journal of Marriage and the Family,* and *Social Service Review.* His work has focused on poverty and families on public assistance. He uses a variety of methods in his work, but is particularly interested in blending qualitative with quantitative data.

Margarete Sandelowski is Associate Professor, Department of Women's and Children's Health, School of Nursing, University of North Carolina at Chapel Hill. She received a master's degree in maternal-child nursing from Boston University and her Ph.D. in American Studies from Case Western Reserve University. The author of two books on women and health, she has published many papers in journals such as *Research in Nursing and Health, Image: The Journal of Nursing Scholarship, Signs, Feminist Studies, Sociology of Health and Illness,* and *Qualitative Sociology.* She is currently working on a book exploring the personal experience of infertility.

Susan U. Snyder is a marriage and family therapist and member of the clinical faculty at the Onondaga Pastoral Counseling Center, Syracuse, New York. She received a Ph.D. in child and family studies and her M.A. in marriage and family therapy from Syracuse University. She is a clinical member and approved supervisor of the American Association for Marriage and Family Therapy. Her primary research interests are qualitative approaches to understanding intimate relationships and couple and family dynamics. With Sol Gordon as coauthor, she published an annotated bibliography, *Parents as Sexuality Educators* (1984) and "Sex Education" in the *Handbook of Clinical Child Psychology* (1986).

Barbara H. Vinick is Research Associate at the Normative Aging Study, Boston, a longitudinal study of the aging process sponsored by the Veterans Administration that has followed a group of 2,000 men since the early 1960s. She is also Assistant Professor at the School of Public Health, Boston University. She received her M.A. and Ph.D. in sociology from Boston University and did postdoctoral work in human development at Harvard University. She currently is conducting a longitudinal study of retirement and marital quality, utilizing both quantitative and qualitative methods. She is the author of two books, including *Families and Retirement,* coedited with Maximiliane Szinovacz and David Ekerdt, published by Sage. She has published many articles in journals such as

Journal of Gerontology, Journal of Geriatric Psychiatry, and *Research on Aging.*

Alexis J. Walker is Associate Professor and Director of the Graduate Program, Department of Human Development and Family Studies, Oregon State University. She has a master's degree in child development and family life from Purdue University and a Ph.D. in human development and family studies from Pennsylvania State University. Her research interests are in family caregiving, gender and family relationships, and longitudinal methods. She has published widely, including articles in *Journal of Marriage and the Family, Family Relations, Journal of Gerontology, Psychology of Women Quarterly,* and *The Gerontologist.*

Nora Ro~~~
best~~~ ~~~ ~~~. ~~~th over 400
million copies of her books in print, she is indisputably one
of the most celebrated and popular writers in the world. She
has achieved numerous top five bestsellers in the UK,
including a number one for *Savour the Moment*, and is a
Sunday Times hardback bestseller writing as J. D. Robb.

Become a fan on Facebook at
www.facebook.com/norarobertsjdrobb
and be the first to hear all the latest from Piatkus
about Nora Roberts and J. D. Robb

www.noraroberts.com
www.nora-roberts.co.uk
www.jd-robb.co.uk

Many of Nora Roberts' other titles are now available in eBook and she is also the author of the In Death series using the pseudonym J.D. Robb. For more information about Nora's work please visit her websites at www.nora-roberts.com or www.nora-roberts.co.uk